Ethics and the Foundations of Education

Teaching Convictions in a Postmodern World

Patrick Slattery
Texas A&M University

Dana Rapp
Massachusetts College of Liberal Arts

Boston ■ New York ■ San Francisco
Mexico City ■ Montreal ■ Toronto ■ London ■ Madrid ■ Munich ■ Paris
Hong Kong ■ Singapore ■ Tokyo ■ Cape Town ■ Sydney

KH

Executive Editor and Publisher: *Stephen D. Dragin*
Editorial Assistant: *Barbara Strickland*
Marketing Manager: *Tara Whorf*
Editorial-Production Service: *Omegatype Typography, Inc.*
Manufacturing Buyer: *Andrew Turso*
Composition Buyer: *Linda Cox*
Cover Administrator: *Kristina Mose-Libon*
Electronic Composition: *Omegatype Typography, Inc.*

For related titles and support materials, visit our online catalog at www.ablongman.com.

Library of Congress Cataloging-in-Publication Data

Slattery, Patrick
    Ethics and the foundations of education : teaching convictions in a postmodern world / Patrick Slattery, Dana Rapp.
        p. cm.
    Includes bibliographical references (p.) and index.
    ISBN 0-321-05401-6
    1. Moral education.   2. Postmodernism and education.   I. Rapp, Dana.   II. Title.

LC268 .S52 2003
370.11'4—dc21

                                                                2002028213

Printed in the United States of America

10 9 8 7 6 5 4 3 2 1   07 06 05 04 03 02

8/21/05

For
Kathy and Craig

CONTENTS

ACKNOWLEDGMENTS

We are most grateful to our friends and colleagues who share our passion for teaching convictions. We thank Rebecca McElfresh for her insights on aesthetics and photography that informed our discussions in Chapter 3 (Slattery & McElfresh, 2001; Spehler-McElfresh & Slattery, 1999); Kevin Daigle for his penetrating wisdom about the novels *The Thanatos Syndrome* and *The Autobiography of Miss Jane Pittman* that framed our discussion of ecology in Chapter 4 (Slattery & Daigle, 1994); James Kirylo for his unique insights on liberation theology in Chapter 3; and John Weaver and Toby Daspit for their collaboration on the *Museums and Memory Project* that informed our thinking on memory constructions in Chapter 2 (Weaver, Slattery, & Daspit, 1998). We gratefully acknowledge Pattie C. S. Burke for allowing us to use her penetrating poetry and narratives in Chapters 1 and 2.

We appreciate and thank the authors, artists, colleagues, and students who have inspired our thinking about ethics, aesthetics, and education over the years, especially Janet Miller, Liz Ellsworth, David Purpel, Nelson Haggerson, Joe Norris, Bill Ayers, Lanny Beyer, Bill Doll, Gene Gibbs, Dennis Sumara, Brent Davis, John B. Cobb, Jr., Sue Books, Susan Edgerton, Roy and Lori Graham, Bill Pinar and Jeff Turner, John and Pattie C. S. Burke, Kevin and Lindsey Slattery and family, Donna and Bob Ferrell and family, Gillian and Jo Kinzie, Bill Foster, Martha McCarthy, Jim Sears, Richard Chachere, Jim Henderson, Peter Taubman, Yatta Kanu, Christopher Reynolds, Jane Piirto, Gregory Pappas, Mady Noble, Ellen Barber, Geri Cassone, Lisa Goldstein, Duncan and Susan Waite, Linda Gradijan Ritzer, Nel Noddings, Kris Sloan and Claire Morris, John Weaver, Maxine Greene, Paul Klhor, Ted Aoki, Kathleen Kesson, Ian MacGillivray, Carl Walley, Carolyn Clark, Jim Scheurich, Carol Stuessy, Christine Stanley, Linda Skrla, Yvonna Lincoln, Jane Conoley, Sherri Reynolds, Peter McLaren, Chris Higgins, Karen Wilson Baptist, Karen Krasny, Spenser Maxcy, Lisa Cary, Jim Koschoreck, Will Letts, Jeanne Brady, Sr. Helen Jean Novy, Dan Marshall, Marty Galloway, Jane Haggard, Hassana Alidou, Charles Chargois, Susan Finley, Patrick Diamond, Carol Mullen, Noreen Garman, Cathy and Jerry Loving, Roemer Visser, Anna Maria Perez Gabriel, Rafael Lara, Stephanie Springgay, Kent den Heyer, Gene Provenzo, Susan Lowey, Ginny Macdonald, Brandon Fitzgerald, Leslie Sadasivan, Greg Gerrick, Dawn Hogan, Deni Blum, Michelle Solberg, Jim Kilbane, Peter Applebaum, Glen Nolly, Mary Thomas, Bobbi Gideon, Collette Bloom, Nancy Langerock, Bob Slater, Patti Picard, Cathy Hackney, Bob Cullinen, Art Pomponio, Terry and Rilla Carson, David G. Smith, Mike Connolly, Mary O'Brien, Jenny Rytel, Yusef Nur, Mitch Balonek, Rev. Sterling Lands, Rev. Foster McElfresh, Karen Anijar, Deborah Yates, Tom Barone, Donald Blumenfeld-Jones, Celia Olyer, Mara Sapon-Shevin, Bill Schubert, Roni Ibrahim, Nancy Lesko, Alan Tom, Jesse Goodman, Paul Shaker, Bob Murphy, Paul Passano, José Gonzalez, Aoestra Johnson, Louise Fleming, Dan Shepard, David Orr, Mary Ann Doyle, Louise Allen, Bob Donmoyer, Craig Kridel, David Ray Griffin, Bob Bourdon, Rex Clark, Molly Quinn, Noel Gough, Ann Poutz, Rob

Linne, Paula Salvio, Doug McKnight, Tony Whitson, John St. Julien, Wen Song Hwu, Cameron McCarthy, Tonya Hueber, Vicki Hillis, David Dees, Jun Yasuda, Sam and Elizabeth Smith, Mike Mullman, Tom Pittenger, Steven Gullifer, Monique Theoret, Mary Lou Alcetta, Gail Lucy, and Greg Coleridge.

Many thanks to our children who give us so much joy: Michelle, Kayty, Joshua, Madeline, and Heron, son-in-law Gannon Lamson, and grandson Kaiser; our students and colleagues at Texas A&M University, Massachusetts College of Liberal Arts, University of Texas at Austin, Ashland University, University of Manitoba, University of Alberta, Louisiana State University, Indiana University, University of Louisiana-Lafayette, St. Mary's College of California, and Ursuline College of Cleveland; our friends at the Ruta Maya Coffee House in Austin, the Aribica Coffee House at University Circle in Cleveland, and the Muddy Waters Café in Wooster, Ohio, where much of this book was written and edited; and especially Kathy Rapp and Craig Johanns, to whom this book is dedicated.

We would also like to thank William F. Pinar, Louisiana State University, and Jennifer A. Vadeboncoeur, University of Queensland, for reviewing our manuscript.

—Patrick Slattery and Dana Rapp

The Process of Writing about Critical Ethical Issues and Education

We have been waiting for years for someone to write a critical ethical analysis of education that would not only be intellectually stimulating and philosophically sound, but also passionate about the possibilities of contemporary living, compassionate toward human diversity, respectful of the environment in all of its biodiversity, and prophetic in addressing global conflicts. (Not that past works have been unsuccessful.) John Dewey is perhaps the foremost American philosopher of education, and his *Lectures on Ethics* provides a solid theoretical foundation for all discourses on educational ethics (see Koch, 1991). In the realm of contemporary literature, Alan Tom's (1984) *Teaching as a Moral Craft* has guided students and teachers for many years. Philip Jackson's work, particularly as explicated in *Moral Life in Schools* (Jackson, Boostrom, & Hansen, 1993), contains penetrating ethical portraits. Valerie Polakow (1993, 2000) investigates single parents, poverty, and violence in schools and society, and challenges educators to work tirelessly for justice for neglected children. Edward Said (1994, 1997), scholar, political activist, and social critic, offers important ethical insights on peace, conflict, and intolerance in our contemporary global milieu. David Ray Griffin (1988) inspires with his postmodern theological sensibilities and proposal for the reenchantment of the cosmos. Zygmunt Bauman's (1993) *Postmodern Ethics* is a lucid defense of the constructive postmodern position. *The Ethics of Teaching* by Ken Strike and Jonas Soltis (1992) provides a solid rationale for the centrality of ethics in classrooms. Our friend and mentor at Louisiana State University, William Doll (1993), has proposed a postmodern vision founded on democratic justice, cosmological complexity, ecological sustainability, and social change—important components of any useful contemporary ethical system. David Purpel (1989, 1999) speaks forcefully for justice and compassion in his penetrating analysis of moral issues in his books *The Moral and Spiritual Crisis in Education* and *Moral Outrage in Education*. Any discussion of ethics and education would be incomplete without a review of the work of Nel Noddings (1984, 1992). She has continuously challenged educators to move beyond a technical position to an ethic of care. It is inspiring to us that so many contemporary authors and educational leaders are committed to justice, caring, and ethics.

In addition to these academic scholars in education, writers from various religious and philosophical traditions throughout history have inspired ethical reflection on teaching and community living. These prophetic voices continue to inspire. We think of Socrates in the fifth century B.C.E. who was accused of corrupting the youth of Athens and eventually lost his life because he raised questions about traditional religious beliefs and social practices. His style of questioning with a penetrating analysis as he walked the streets of Athens with his students is called the Socratic method. We think of Oscar Romero, the Catholic bishop of El Salvador in the early 1980s who aligned himself with the poor, and Martin Luther King, Jr., a leader of the Civil Rights movement in the United States in the 1960s who organized peaceful nonviolent boycotts on behalf of African American workers. Both of these leaders were outspoken critics of social injustice and both were assassinated.

The Lutheran pastor Dietrich Bonhoeffer also provides a noteworthy example of a prophetic voice. Bonhoeffer was born in Germany in 1906 and studied theology at Tübingen before being offered a parish post in Berlin in 1933. He refused the appointment because "non-Aryans" were denied consideration, and the following year he was a founding member of the "confessing church," a leading center of the Protestant resistance. In 1938 he was expelled from Germany and came to the United States to lecture, but he returned to Europe and became a member of the *Abwehr* military intelligence to gain support for resistance. In 1940 he worked with Operation 7 to support smuggling Jews out of Germany. Bonhoeffer was forbidden to publish or preach, yet he continued to work with the resistance. He had many influential relatives who urged him to be silent; he also had many opportunities to sit out the war in peace while lecturing in the United States. But he chose critical prophetic resistance. When it was discovered that he was involved in the failed assassination of Hitler on March 13, 1943, an involvement that he anguished over and discussed in the book *The Cost of Discipleship* (Bonhoeffer, 1966), Bonhoeffer was jailed and eventually sent to Buchenwald. He was court-martialled and hung on April 9, 1945, at Flossenburg, one week before the Allies liberated the camp. Those who choose to reflectively address difficult social, economic, religious, historical, and political issues may find their job security, popularity, and community status threatened. Maybe, like Romero, King, and Bonhoeffer, their very lives may be endangered or condemned.

We also believe it is important to remember that Buddha, Solomon, Confucius, Jesus, Francis of Assisi, Hildegard of Bingham, and Muhammed were all teachers in their own unique ways. Likewise, the Sumarian goddess Inanna, the Hindu goddess Saraswathi, and the Vedic goddess Maya-Shakti-Devi also inspire teaching and learning. Inanna is a goddess who undergoes death and resurrection and teaches ways of being that necessitate sacrifice, humility, and reunification. Saraswathi is the goddess of wisdom who is always shown with a book in one of her hands; Hindu children are taught to pray to her for the gift of education and success in school (Viruru, 1998). Devi (the Indian name for woman) is the teacher of the Vedic gods themselves concerning the ultimate ground and source of their own powers and being (Campbell, 1988). These prophets, teachers, gods, and goddesses from religious traditions inspire the ethical and moral teachings and social mythology of many global cultures.

When I (Patrick) reflected on the ideal educational ethics text, I envisioned including the insights of all of these important scholars, teachers, and religious figures, but I also wanted to expand the dialogue to include such topics as aesthetics, autobiography, ecology, politics, culture, theology, and constructivist approaches to learning. Our (Dana and Patrick) vision demands a book on educational ethics that inspires a passion for social justice, economic equity, and racial equality. Examples of this are found in Jonathan Kozol's (1991) *Savage Inequalities,* bell hooks's (1994) *Teaching to Transgress,* Paulo Freire's (1970) *Pedagogy of the Oppressed,* James Scheurich's (2002) *Anti-Racist Scholarship: An Advocacy,* and Joseph Barndt's (1991) *Dismantling Racism: The Continuing Challenge to White America.* We want the autobiographical honesty and global focus of Mary Catherine Bateson's (1994) *Peripheral Visions;* the commitment to moral development in educational reform of John Goodlad, Roger Soder, and Kenneth Sirotnik's (1990) *The Moral Dimensions of Teaching;* the focus on transformative democratic communities in James Henderson and Robert Hawthorne's (1995) *Transformative Curriculum Leadership;* the prophetic urgency and commitment to the poor in Sue Books's (1998) *Invisible Children in the Society and its Schools,* Angela Valenzuela's (1999) study *Subtractive Schooling: US-Mexican Youth and the Politics of Caring,* and Derrick Bell's (1992) *Faces at the Bottom of the Well;* and the commitment to environmental issues in the schools and in the curriculum of David Orr's (1992) *Ecological Literacy,* C. A. Bowers's (2001) *Educating for Eco-Justice,* and Carolyn Merchant's (1992) *Radical Ecology: The Search for a Liveable World.*

We are particularly inspired by David Orr's personal and practical commitment to ecological sustainability and ecojustice. Orr, chair of environmental studies at Oberlin College in Ohio, is well known for his collaboration on curriculum and ecology projects and his membership in the Greening of Higher Education project at Claremont Graduate School. David Orr not only advocates for environmental sustainability, but he has also directed the construction of a prototype green building for college campuses. His work was featured in *The Chronicle of Higher Education* (January 14, 2000). Orr's process for building community consensus and financial support, his attention to curriculum and teaching in every phase of the planning, and his orchestration of the building process as a pedagogical event in the community all combined to so impress the American Institute of Architects that he received national recognition for innovative and imaginative design solutions. He explains this project in his book *The Nature of Design: Ecology, Culture, and Human Intention* (Orr, 2002).

Our new book on ethics and education would also have to address the theological and economic rationale for sustainable communities and universal human rights presented, for example, in Herman Daly and John B. Cobb, Jr.'s (1994) award-winning book *For the Common Good* and Joel Spring's (1998) penetrating analysis of global economic injustices in *Education and the Rise of the Global Economy,* and would have to do so in the spirit of the critical theories of such diverse thinkers as Bill Ayers, Seyla Benhabib, Michelle Fine, Jeanne Brady, Cornell West, Michael Apple, Susan Edgerton, Cameron McCarthy, Douglas Kellner, Nancy Fraser, Dennis Carlson, Chandra Mohanty, Dan Marshall, Noam Chomsky, Michael Parenti, Abdullahi An-Na'im, Mahmoud Mohamed Taha, Patti Lather, Henry Giroux, Lois Weis, Howard Zinn, and so many other evocative social, political, and cultural thinkers. Our vision for a new educational ethics book demands a multicultural attitude that draws inspiration from James and Cherry Magee Banks (1997), Geneva Gay (1994), Leela Gandhi (1998), Peter McLaren (1997), and Sonja Nieto (1996), as well as a commitment to justice for those marginalized by gender and sexual orientation as explicated in the work of Audre Lorde (1984), James Sears (1992), Valerie Walkerdine (1997), Will Letts and James Sears (1999), Anne Fausto-Sterling (2000), Deborah Britzman (1995), Jonathan Silin (1995), Madeleine Grumet (1988), and William Pinar (1994, 1998). This list of scholars and activists is meant to be neither normative nor exhaustive; rather, it reminds us of a religious litany or spiritual mantra that immerses us in the power of the presence of a community.

No ethical stance would be complete without an investigation of aesthetic sensibilities, as exemplified in the intimate literary analyses in *The Arts of the Possible* by Adrienne Rich (2001), *The Reenchantment of Art* by Suzi Gablik (1991), *Creating Spaces and Finding Voices* by Janet Miller (1990), and "Evocative Autoethnography" by Carolyn Ellis (1997). These authors remind us that one of the most important ingredients in contemporary approaches to educational ethics is a sense of the aesthetic. The voices of Maxine Greene (1995, 2001), Sara Lawrence-Lightfoot (1983, 1997), Jean Clandinin and Michael Connelly (2000), and Carol Mullen and Patrick Diamond (1999) eloquently and dramatically reinforce this connection. The arts and narrative, we believe, are the heart of education. Without a passionate, prophetic, and perceptive heart, all ethical and educational systems eventually fail.

The more I (Patrick) pondered, the more I realized that writing a critical ethical analysis of education could be very dangerous. Such an analysis would challenge the simplistic fundamentalist notions of ethics that prevail in our society by revising traditional philosophies for a contemporary milieu. Additionally, the book must offer a truly ecumenical and liberatory theology. In this regard, it must affirm diverse religious spiritualities that seek peace, love, justice, transcendence, and personal transformation (Hahn, 1995) not only in the mainstream (yet theologically complex and diverse) Jewish, Muslim, Hindu, Buddhist, Christian, and Confucian traditions, but also with a genuine respect and acceptance of agnostic, Gnostic, theistic, atheistic, Wiccan, Unitarian, naturalistic, voodoo, Santeria, Baha'i, Jain, Sikh, Taoist, Quaker, indigenous, and pantheistic spiritualities or cosmologies as well. The book would have to challenge status quo political, religious, and socioeconomic arrangements in institutions such as schools, governments, corporations, churches, the military, the American Psychological Association, the American Educational Research Association, and universities that offer tenure to professors who write such books. The book should speak of ethics in ways that would worry some ethicists and their devotees, present new ways of hearing old wisdom, and use biography, autoethnography, and arts-based aesthetic imagination as its method.

In this context, we (Dana and Patrick) believe a book on ethics must include the stories of people involved with democratic projects that will blow our minds, unsettle our convictions, and demand that we proclaim our love of freedom loudly (Camus, 1960; Hillman & Ventura, 1992). We think of bold women like Dorothy Day, Rosa

Parks, and Helen Keller in this regard. Dorothy Day, a white American journalist, often wrote that prophets must comfort the afflicted and afflict the comfortable. She was inspired in her youth to actively work for justice in U.S. society after reading Upton Sinclair's novel *The Jungle*. At the age of twenty she was arrested in front of the White House with a group of forty-one women protesting women's exclusion from the electorate. The women began a hunger strike and were later freed. Day is known today as the cofounder (with Peter Maurin in 1933) of the Catholic Worker movement, a network of hospitality houses for the poor. Day often said that the class structure is our making and by our consent we must do what we can to change it.

Rosa Parks, who refused to obey the Montgomery, Alabama, law that supported segregation on city buses, is also a source of bold, prophetic inspiration. Rosa Parks was not a tired old woman who couldn't get to the back of the bus. Prior to her arrest, Parks was secretary and advisor to the NAACP. She had tried to register to vote on several occasions, even when it was impossible to do so, and she had been evicted from several buses for refusing to move from the "white only" sections. Rosa Parks was not only tired from "spending a full day working . . . on clothing for white people," but she was also sick of being mistreated by the racism, segregation, and Jim Crow laws of the time (Zinn, 1995, p. 442). Like Ida Wells Barnett, Ella Baker, and Mary McLeod Bethune, Rosa Parks placed her life in jeopardy as she fought for racial justice.

Like Rosa Parks, Helen Keller's political activism is often ignored. Keller was more than a blind and deaf woman fighting for those with physical disabilities or a humanitarian working for those neglected by society, as many history books and popular films (such as *The Miracle Worker*) portray her. Instead, Keller was a social radical and a member of the Industrial Workers of the World (IWW). She helped found the American Civil Liberties Union (ACLU), and she was involved in various demonstrations for women's suffrage. Keller would often visit sweatshops, factories, and crowded slums to gain a better understanding of class struggle. These experiences shaped her activism and inspired her work for broader social justice. Keller argued that blindness was often due to accidents in unsafe factories employing the poor or inadequate medical care. In addition, many poor women had to become prostitutes to feed their families, and they often developed syphilitic blindness (Loewen, 1995).

Other sources of critical prophetic energy and ethical inspiration include iconoclastic artists, Greenpeace activists, independent filmmakers who explore taboo subjects and expose social injustices; Planned Parenthood volunteers; Mrs. Grayson from around our block who has dedicated her blood, sweat, and paycheck to providing food to homeless families; Amnesty International investigators who expose torture and defend political prisoners; Mitch Balonek, the Toledo teacher who refuses to administer biased standardized tests; Peace Corps and Americorps workers; rape counseling and suicide crisis center volunteers; the Reverend Sterling Lands and Stella Roland, leaders of the East Side Social Action Coalition of Austin, who work tirelessly for students in neglected and underfunded schools in low-income neighborhoods in predominantly African American and Hispanic communities; gay and lesbian religious leaders like the Reverend Mel White and his allies in churches like the Metropolitan

Community Church and the United Church of Christ; Sierra Club members; journalists like Molly Ivins and Ellen Goodman who investigate and expose fraud; Doctors without Borders; and the firefighters, police officers, and medical crews who rushed to the burning World Trade Center in New York on September 11, 2001. Many of these social workers and cultural visionaries use their oppositional imaginations to actually threaten some of the "best practices" and "sacred cows" that dictate educational and social terrains (see Culclasure, 1999; Rapp, 2001a, 2002b; Zinn, 1995, 1997). World Trade Organization demonstrators, civil rights activists, Vietnam War protestors, and subversive artists and musicians provide insightful threads into the democratic aims to which we could be committed. What connects these ethical agents are their penetrating social analysis, their unwavering convictions, their rebelliousness, and their radical democratic visions. Their experiences encourage us to ask ourselves whether we, too, are more obligated to achieve justice and democracy through peaceful non-violent action than to obey the law.

Acquaintances of Tolstoy often commented that as a teacher he was able to "fire minds to white heat" in which "electric sparks were striking into the depths of souls and setting in motion all kinds of thoughts and plans and decisions" (Troyat, 1967, p. 309). In this book we are attempting to prick the consciences of educators, and indeed all citizens, by emphasizing the direct intentions and prophetic spirits of such inspiring people as Eugene Debs, Eve Ensler, Mary Harris "Mother" Jones, Chief Seattle, Sojourner Truth, Sari Nusseibeh, Fatima Mernissi, Ismail Ragi al-Faruqi, Jane Addams, Nelson Mandela, Rigoberta Manchu, Caesar Chavez, Martin Buber, Morris Dees, Ralph Nader, Abdul Ghaffar Khan, Gandhi, and Ida Wells Barnett.

We want readers to ask penetrating and probing questions. Can a decent society exist if citizens humbly obey all laws, even those that violate human health and welfare and survival of life on the planet? If governments proclaim democracy while supporting organizations and nations guilty of murder, torture, terrorism, and blatant human rights abuses? If less than 10 percent of the global population controls and consumes over 90 percent of all resources, and if 5 percent of the population owns 95 percent of the wealth? Is this just? At what point will it be unjust? If minimum wage is $10,700 a year for a full-time worker in the United States and half the new jobs are produced at minimum wage, can justice be served? And if justice does not exist for all global persons, will there ever be hope for peace for anyone? A bumper sticker best expresses our conviction: "If you want peace, work for justice!"

We believe that a book on ethics must include the inspiring stories of prophetic voices that offer countertestimony to the realities of conventional wisdom, the hegemony of the American Dream, and the dehumanization of the New World Order (see Rapp, 2001a, 2002a, 2002b). Unauthorized histories and oppositional imaginations are predominantly found in people located outside conventional memory, mainstream media, and authorized historical accounts. The following litany of a few of the alternative prophetic and oppositional voices reminds us of the multiple representations that inspire action for justice: magazines like *Mother Jones, Sojourners,* and *UTNE Reader;* music by Bob Dylan, Rage Against the Machine, Alejandro Escovedo, Sweet

Honey and The Rock, Ruben Blades, Pink Floyd, Patti Smith, Jackson Browne, Goodie Mob, Cee Lo, John Trudell, Tracy Chapman, Ani DeFranco, Los Lobos, Pearl Jam, Mercedes Sosa and Silvio Rodriguez of Nueva Cancion, Miles Davis, Joan Baez, Melissa Etheridge, Marvin Gaye, Joanne Shenandoah, Pete Seeger, John Lennon, Harry Chapin, Nas, Chris Reynolds, Utah Phillips, and Peter, Paul and Mary; artwork, architecture, and photography by Judy Chicago, Paul Robeson, Maya Lin, Robert Mapplethorpe, Chris Offili, Gordon Parks, Angelina Pozo, Philip Johnson, Edward and Nancy Kienholz, Sebastiao Salgado, Stephen Chapman Crane; books such as Richard Wright's (1940) *Native Son*, Daniel Guerin's (1998) *No Gods No Masters*, Alexander Cockburn and J. St. Clair's (2000) *Five Days that Shook the World*, Saul Alinsky's (1969) *Reveille for Radicals*, Jeremy Rifkin's (1985) *Declaration of a Heretic*, Burg and Feifer's (1972) *Solzhenitsyn*, Upton Sinclair's (1948) *Flivver King*, Peter Glassgold's (2001) *Anarchy*, Virginia Woolf's (1929) *A Room of One's Own*, Howard Zinn's (1995) *A Peoples' History of the United States*, Kenzaburo Oe's (1985) *Nip the Buds, Shoot the Kids*, and Rachel Carson's (1962) *Silent Spring;* performances by The Guerrilla Girls and the plays *Rent, Bent, The Vagina Monologues, The Laramie Project,* and *Angels in America;* and films such as *Silvia* (USA), *Pixote* (Brazil), *A Lesson before Dying* (USA), *American History X* (USA), *Son of the Shark* (France), *The Blue Kite* (China), *The Mission* (Brazil), *My Life as a Dog* (Sweden), *Vukovar* (Croatia), *Green* (USA), *Lone Star* (USA), and *Europa, Europa* (Germany). These films, texts, lyrics, photographs, and artwork abound in images of culture, ecology, dislocation, and justice that relate directly to our work as educators. Although limited, this list gives us a sense of the enormous body of counternarratives in popular culture that promote social justice and action.

We are inspired by these aesthetic sources, as well as by our experiences in homeless shelters, soup kitchens, prisons, cinematic film festivals, HIV/AIDS counseling centers, health clinics for the poor, gay–straight alliances (GSA) in high schools, Peace Action marches, labor rallies, sanctuary churches, Holocaust museums, and rape crisis centers. We use these as our basis for discussing good societies, social justice, and the ethical choices before us.

What makes teaching and writing about ethics in this way challenging and dangerous? First, there are so many culturally embedded understandings of ethics that any discussion of applied ethics or morality can easily degenerate into hostile debates and ad hominem attacks. Second, there are many conflicting philosophies of ethics: rule-bound deontological systems that insist on legal interpretations of morality; natural law theories that expect human behavior to conform to universal laws of science or religion; situational ethical systems that judge moral decision making differently in each unique context; utilitarian systems that search for ways to promote the greatest good for the greatest number of people (or animals or natural sites); existential philosophies that stress the importance of the freedom and responsibility of individuals above essential and universal moral norms; and postmodern theories that reject modern methods of coercive normative regulations in political practice and the philosophical search for absolutes and universals, while still remaining firmly committed to moral concerns such as human rights, social justice, peaceful cooperation, ecological sustainability, community solidarity, personal responsibility, and democratic participation. Third, critical analyses and philosophical investigations are discouraged by political, educational, and religious authorities. If citizens begin to investigate social, political, religious, and educational systems, then the status quo economic, bureaucratic, and political power arrangements will be called into question—probably even undermined—by uncovering inadequacies, injustices, hypocrisy, and fraud. Fourth, those with power seldom encourage critical investigation. More often than not, power elites in business, the military, corporations, labor unions, schools, religious institutions, and government agencies silence the voices of opposition either overtly or covertly. As we will attest through our personal stories, people are routinely fired, humiliated, harassed, denied promotion and tenure, transferred, condemned as sinners, or even killed if they behave outside of the cultural norms established by the dominant power brokers or if they become a protestor or whistle blower. Ralph Nader's exclusion from the political debates in 2000 exemplifies this phenomenon. Even labor union leaders and progressive government officials become uncomfortable when Nader challenges the Taft-Hartley Act of 1947 or initiates investigations to protect workers and consumers. The Enron debacle in late 2001 revealed that many people across the political spectrum are entrenched in campaign finance and investment scandals.

In thinking about the dangers of writing a critical educational ethics book, we began to recall some of the resistance that I (Patrick) had encountered while teaching the "Ethics of Leadership" doctoral course at Ashland University of Ohio in the summer of 1998. The cohort consisted of fourteen graduate students, all of whom were white, middle-class administrators in public and private schools in northeast Ohio. I was assisted in teaching the course by two colleagues and friends from the Ashland Theological Seminary, Drs. Gene Gibbs and Luke Kiefer. The three of us held some divergent interpretations of ethical systems, but we were resolutely committed to exposing the doctoral candidates to the diversity of the field of ethics in an academically rigorous and intellectually stimulating milieu. After several class sessions that focused on philosophical ethics as summarized previously, a field experience in applied ethics was held in Cleveland in which the students interacted with professionals and practitioners who were dealing with controversial ethical issues in the schools.

Beginning with a breakfast roundtable discussion and ending with presentations over dinner, a total of eight speakers met with the students in relaxed settings in various locations throughout the city. One panel featured Bert L. Holt, director of Cleveland Scholarship and Tutoring, a program that administers the controversial educational voucher experiment for the state of Ohio that was argued before the U.S. Supreme Court in 2002, and Lee Lundblad, who coordinates the implementation of the voucher program for the Catholic Diocese of Cleveland. These women presented the arguments for and against vouchers and offered the doctoral students the opportunity to examine the program in detail. Questions about equity, transportation, accountability, distribution of funds, church and state relations, and the academic progress of students were all discussed in this session. A second presentation was made by Judy Montgomery, media specialist at Hayes Elementary in Lakewood, Ohio, who had recently been honored with a statewide award for outstanding public service as chair of GLSEN (Gay Lesbian Straight Education Network), and Leslie Sadasivan, a registered nurse and mother of four children from Strongsville, Ohio. Leslie had recently suffered the loss of her fourteen-year-old gay son, who committed suicide. Robbie was a freshman at St. Ignatius High School in Cleveland, a prominent Jesuit institution. Following this heart-wrenching discussion, the group traveled to St. Ignatius to learn about the ways that issues of suicide, homosexuality, community relations, crisis management, and the counseling of gay students are handled at this school. We were graciously hosted by the president, Fr. Robert Welsh, and the principal, Richard Clark, for a roundtable discussion about the social, religious, political, and emotional impact of Robbie's suicide on the school community. Later that evening, Dr. John A. Weaver of the University of Akron, a scholar who specializes in cultural studies related to media and technology, and Dr. Beverly Reep, the superintendent of Westlake public schools, led the final panel presentation. Westlake public schools had recently settled a lawsuit concerning the First Amendment rights of students who set up web pages. The high school suspended a student for publishing what the school considered slanderous depictions of the band teacher (whose name is Raymond) on the student's home page titled *RaymondSucks.Org*. The student gained notoriety with feature stories on *Inside Edition* and other nationally syndicated news shows. He eventually won the lawsuit and a $30,000 settlement, and was reinstated in the school and in the band class. The professor and superintendent discussed with the doctoral candidates the ethical implications of this and similar cases related to technology.

All of the speakers discussed the complexity and ambiguity of ethical decision making, providing a learning laboratory for examining and critiquing the philosophy and practice of educators in each unique situation. Needless to say, the follow-up discussion with the doctoral students at the next class meeting was intense and provocative. Everyone had strong opinions and a variety of conflicting reactions to the leadership style and decision-making process of each guest. It was not until a few months later that I discovered further complications had resulted from this field experience. A few students registered strong complaints to Ashland professors and administrators about the appropriateness of some or all of these sessions and the postmodern philosophy that informed the process. Some of these students reacted from positions of apparent homophobia, sexism, racism, and religious intolerance.

Because Ashland is historically affiliated with the Brethern Christian Church, the controversial topics offended a few doctoral students who believed that the open-ended discussion of these issues violated the mission of the university. A few were particularly incensed that they had to listen to presentations by an openly lesbian media specialist and a Catholic priest who was sympathetic to the plight of gay students. One or two others were startled that the Jesuit priest did not share their interpretation of their bible. One questioned why I would invite a grieving mother to speak about her gay son's suicide. A few were unsettled by the discussion of Internet pornography and interpretations of First Amendment rights. Finally, one student was also indignant that a doctoral course would spend time exploring the complexities of applied ethics rather than the certainties of traditional theological (i.e., conservative Christian) ethics. Battle lines were drawn in the cohort group, and several students came to me to report that the matter had been debated vigorously among the group. Eventually the complaints from these students and a few professors made their way up to the board of trustees. The provost contacted the dean of education and the director of doctoral studies and informed them that I would not be invited to teach the course the following summer because my philosophy, as understood by the board of trustees, conflicted with the mission of the university. This was despite the fact that I had been granted tenure by Ashland University the year before and had been nominated by the faculty for the Taylor Excellence in Teaching Award that same year. In the litigious atmosphere surrounding educational administration, it does not surprise me that there was not an opportunity to discuss my philosophy, syllabus, and teaching methodologies with the university administrators.

Arguments were later put before the provost by the director in favor of my continued association with the program, especially in light of the positive response of the majority of the students on course evaluations and the reputation of my courses in the community. After all, how could a few disgruntled students interrupt the academic freedom and departmental autonomy of an entire university? Should not an ethics course for doctoral students in educational leadership explore the difficult and controversial issues that school administrators must face? The provost eventually agreed with the director, and my contract was honored for the next summer session. It soon became evident that the next summer's "Ethics of Leadership" seminar would be my last teaching experience at Ashland University. Dana Rapp, a second-year Ashland professor, would audit the class, review the course materials, and prepare to teach the course the following summer.

Although this scenario caused anxiety for many people, it also sparked important discussions about ethics, education, justice, university administrative practices, academic freedom, and the complex and conflicting missions of private and public universities in a pluralistic society. This experience also permitted us (Dana and Patrick) to discover the extent to which our histories, passions for social justice, and approaches to teaching ethics are similar, perhaps to the continuing dismay of some people in the Ashland University community.

Much of the renewed inspiration for moving forward on this book came in July 2001, when we brought together students from Ashland University (where Dana was an assistant professor teaching the "Ethics of Leadership" course) and Ursuline College of Cleveland (where Patrick was a visiting professor teaching a course titled "Wisdom Leadership") for a field experience and discussion pertaining to education, ethics, and aesthetics at the Cleveland Museum of Art. It was here that the Ashland doctoral students and Ursuline graduate students were exposed to the art and philosophy of Anselm Kiefer, Judy Chicago, Georgia O'Keeffe, and Pablo Picasso. We lectured on aesthetic criticism and autoethnographic investigations of Jackson Pollock's personal brilliance and tragic life as viewed in the 2001 award-winning film *Pollock* (see Slattery, 2001). Educators Paul Passano and Becky McElfresh talked with us about their art and how it influences their work as teachers.

Over dinner we further explored how racism, terrorism, ecological destruction, gender inequity, and homophobia were manifest in our hearts and in society, but absent in our educational agendas and curriculum materials. The emotionally heated dialogue inspired several students to express their pain, confusion, fear, and denial related to these issues. Personal narratives were frequently met with sympathetic tears and occasionally with verbal and confessional defensiveness. However, most of the graduate students drove home that night with a renewed sense that issues of justice and democracy were much more important than the decontextualized administrative dilemmas that are often the focus of courses in educational ethics. Several students also conveyed to Dana how their resurfacing feelings, experiences, and blind spots on these issues could hardly be explained or expressed through impersonal ethical rules, scripts, or recipes. Their exposure to the arts earlier that day, they said, propelled them to more fully explore and expose their ties to the extraordinary ethical dilemmas before them. This reaffirms our conviction that ethics and aesthetics must be united holistically in order to honestly address complex moral issues.

Professors of ethics have always struggled to balance open academic investigation with the theological beliefs of students and the university community. This struggle is important, and there is always the danger of overstepping boundaries or creating inappropriate discomfort for students. Academic inquiry, especially surrounding controversial topics, must be carefully planned and sensitively executed. However, we believe that this practical difficulty does not warrant silence, even by newly hired principals or by untenured faculty, at a time of biological and chemical terrorism, religious extremism, pandemic disease, worker exploitation, and increasing disparities of wealth.

One of my (Patrick) ethics professors in graduate school was Charles Curran, a Catholic priest and author of numerous influential books on moral theology, who is now a professor at Southern Methodist University in Dallas. Curran's theology was questioned by the Vatican in the 1960s, and he was eventually fired from his teaching post at the Catholic University of America in Washington, D.C., despite support by students and faculty. Curran (1986) wrote an excellent response to these controversies in a book titled *Faithful Dissent,* in which he attempted to explain that one can remain faithful within a religious tradition and still present dissenting views in university courses and public forums. This democratic principal, which we will explore in detail in Chapter 5, was also widely misunderstood following the September 11, 2001, attacks in New York City and Washington, D.C., in the attempt to threaten and silence voices of critique in the United States. Attorney General John Ashcroft led the charge to dismantle civil liberties after the September 11 attacks—except, predictably, the proliferation of handguns and weapons. Benjamin Franklin and other leaders over the years have cautioned that if we relinquish our *liberties* in times of conflict and fear with the hope of gaining *security,* we will certainly lose *both.*

A case that made national news was the firing of a philosophy professor who included a lecture on pornography in his ethics class. *The Chronicle of Higher Education* reported on the incident: "The professor wanted to see if students could tell where art ends and pornography begins, something difficult to do just by reading articles" (Schneider, 1999). The report concludes by asking what will happen when professors of ethics refrain from talking about sensitive topics such as pornography, stem cell research, cloning, bioengineering, corporate fraud, campaign finance reform, environmental racism, sexual identity politics, or other challenging topics. It seems to us that a professor who teaches ethics must explore these topics in detail, presenting all valid research, including dissenting philosophies and the historical complexity of the issue. Without such penetrating analysis a course in ethics is removed from the social, scientific, theological, and political dynamics of the human community and becomes a platform for indoctrination, prejudice, or (possibly worse) silent disinterest. Of course, ethics professors themselves must also be cautious to present multiple perspectives on controversial issues so that they do not perpetuate narrow interpretations.

Over the years we (Dana and Patrick) have realized that we are emotionally and philosophically invested in similar issues and questions: Should we not risk introducing important but controversial topics in our courses? Should we pamper students so as to avoid negative evaluations and administrative confrontation? Do we address only those topics that conform to the narrow prejudices of outspoken and politically connected students and administrators, and refrain from introducing material that might dislodge their sedimented perceptors and expand their thinking? Do we refuse to invite leaders and educators from marginalized populations to speak to our students? Must we give equal time to racial bigots, Holocaust deniers, white supremacists, intolerant religious leaders, patriarchal sexists, abortion clinic bombers, violent homophobes, and international terrorists? Must professors in private or religious institutions—or, for that matter, in public institutions dominated by leaders of reactionary or narrow-minded fundamentalist communities—avoid any investigation of ecumenism, postmodernism, ecofeminism, environmental racism, heterosexism, unexamined patriotism, Internet pornography, stem cell research, cloning, or any theory or idea that does not explicitly reinforce the dogma of these power brokers in the institution or community? Should professors take a religious loyalty oath, as some religious institutions require, and as Catholic bishops proposed in 1999 for theology professors at Catholic universities? Should all professors take a political loyalty oath like the one mandated in California in the 1950s? Should elementary, middle-school, and secondary teachers explore only safe topics so that students and parents do not complain? Should controversial books and ideas be banned from schools, universities, and professional conferences? Our answer is an emphatic "No!" However, we remain vigilant to protect the rights of all students while presenting multiple perspectives that are committed to justice, compassion, and ecological sustainability.

We will, of course, always look for ways to improve our courses. We will search for additional books from a variety of sources to include in our syllabi, more meaningful research projects to assign to our students, more stimulating lectures to present in our classes, and more compelling people and experiences from which to develop a stronger ethical fortitude to address injustice. However, we will not alter the academic rigor and intellectual investigation because of the prejudices of a few. We enjoy teaching ethics and appreciate the engaging response of the vast majority of students. But we are reminded that prophetic teaching that investigates controversial issues in applied ethics is a dangerous enterprise.

Despite the risks and conflicts involved, I (Patrick) wanted to write this book. I should not be hesitant or fearful about speaking my convictions, I thought. It is time for me to write a book on educational ethics, a topic that I have studied in graduate school and researched carefully for years, and that I am passionately committed to. I have many life experiences and insights that could be instructive for others. No, I can't possibly write a book on educational ethics, I debated with myself. I am only forty-seven years young and my experiences are limited. What could I add to the discourse? As a privileged white male, is it even realistic to expect that I could interrupt and problematize my white, patriarchal, middle-class world context in order to offer fresh insights and countertestimony? I am too cautious, vulnerable, and uncertain to write the book. But then again, I thought, I must write it. I have an uncanny ability to clarify difficult concepts with students. I am driven by an insatiable desire for justice, compassion, and ecological sustainability. I have spent most of my adult life reading about eschatology and searching for meaningful educational philosophies that could address global conflicts. I need to write a book on ethics that will give teachers and students hope in the face of growing despair, cynicism, violence, and war.

If I write this book, I thought, I will have to address controversial topics and propose alternative perspectives on issues that will certainly upset some people, like those who employ me and maybe even my mother! What would happen if I started writing in an autobiographical mode now? And who would believe me anyway? Sometimes I do not even believe my own southern gothic tales of my life growing up in New Orleans and later teaching in the Louisiana Cajun bayou country. The stories are sometimes so outrageous that the popular Louisiana authors Anne Rice or James Lee Burke could incorporate the events into their fiction. No, I could not possibly write this book, I thought to myself. It would be too controversial, too personal, and too emotionally draining.

At the same time, I felt compelled to write this book. Racism, sexism, heterosexism, historical amnesia, ethnic bigotry, economic and ecological degradation, cultural marginalization of those who are different and unique, physical and emotional abuse, hate crimes, war, and religious fanaticism are exploding globally and threatening life, liberty, peace, and the joy of making a difference in the lives of others. Everyone must speak out for justice and radical democracy. Didn't I demand as much of others in my youth as I protested the war in Vietnam and signed petitions for environmental causes? It is our duty—our calling—to write and speak with conviction.

Like Patrick, I (Dana) often go through bouts of anger and confusion when it comes to living, teaching, and working for a more just society, as well as writing about it. How can I ethically justify my work within systems, institutions, and structures that appear to ignore conditions in which a small minority of the population controls most of the wealth; schools and communities are more racially divided than they were before *Brown v. Board of Education;* U.S. citizens have three to six weeks less vacation than workers in other industrialized countries for the same wages; 38 percent of the U.S. population is at or below the poverty level if it were adjusted for inflation; half the new jobs are produced at minimum wage (that is, about $10,700 a year); 5,000 people between the ages of fourteen and twenty commit suicide each year; women earn 75 percent of what men do for similar work; at least 20 percent of kids go to school hungry; and an environment with clean air and water is a luxury? More important, how can I work with students at all levels to dismantle conditions of poverty, racism, ecological destruction, and hatred at a time when many people appear overworked, spiritually disconnected, politically demoralized, and in desperate need of escape? How do I relate to friends and family whose SUVs guzzle natural resources; whose lawn mowers and snow blowers pollute the air; whose children play in parks poisoned with toxic herbicides and pesticides; whose porches are built to extend to their private backyards and not to public community sidewalks; whose consumer products are often made by children in unsafe working conditions; who relate more to Katie Couric and Matt Lauer of the *Today Show* than to their own families; whose kids will go to schools in drug-free zones in which 33 percent of the students will be on Prozac, Ritalin, or other legal medications (often either unnecessarily or for the convenience of parents, teachers, or administrators); and many of whom still believe that Christopher Columbus was a hero?

I recognize that those of us who are concerned about these issues are having to address them within communities and institutions that are increasingly obedient to industrial models of effectiveness and homogenized curricula. I know that at Ashland University, for example, the curriculum for teachers and administrators is rapidly changing to address the new state report card system in which colleges of education are ranked by the percentages of students who pass written exit exams. More and more faculty meetings focus on how we can become more accountable to state mandates and help greater percentages of preservice teacher education students pass exit tests. Not only are faculty encouraged to use the technological language of information transmission, discrete skills, dispositions, and benchmarks, but also the university is increasingly seeking to hire and tenure people who promote this language of merit and accountability. This is the same anti-intellectual and creativity-neutering "reform" agenda that is destroying public schools and the work of teachers and administrators. Although some university administrators convey to me that my discussions of race, class, gender, ecological destruction, global inequities, and homophobia in my classes are needed, it is becoming increasingly evident that there is less time and support for me to address these issues. Outside accrediting agencies, like the Ohio Board of Regents, are consumed with the idea of direct implementation to such a degree that a few of my colleagues believe that ethics will not even be offered at the doctoral level in a few years.

Ashland University is not the only college of education in which this is happening. Public schools and colleges of education around the country are building technological and administrative bases that align with state and corporate agendas that directly and indirectly focus our work away from deeper issues of social injustice. It is an increasingly dangerous moment with many pitfalls and possibilities. My greatest fear is that educators at all levels will continue to concede to the undemocratic, culturally imperialistic, and economically ravenous forces that profit from the overly inward turn toward civic disengagement (see Rapp, 2002b). My greatest hope is that we can transcend the often overwhelming pressure to temper our teaching convictions and domesticate our political rebellion.

Although many of us affirm the gravity of these issues, we appear stuck in a soup of professional calculation more than prophetic spirit. Perhaps too many of the benefits of the free market and the state have become our own. Maybe we are tired of fighting for justice. Perhaps our vision of justice has been educated and professionalized out of us. Maybe we have internalized an archetype of personal consumption to a level that forbids social covenant. For whatever reason, not one of my colleagues has supported me in faculty meetings when I suggest that we refuse to accept the results of exit exams as the primary basis for evaluating our success or failure with students. No faculty member has refused to attend in-services orchestrated by testing companies. No faculty member has publicly stated that peace, justice, ecological sustainability, empathy, and spirituality are essential aims of our work with preservice teaching and administration candidates. I am not aware of any professor of education in Ohio that has walked hand in hand with students and parents who are protesting high-stakes tests. I have seen too few professors publish newspaper editorials that decry poverty, homelessness, racism, and corporate domination as they are manifested in state educational and social policies. Is it me? Am I naive? Are most of us, myself included, kidding ourselves when we think that our efforts with students are leading to a more just world? Are issues of poverty, corporate exploitation, child labor, and hate crimes important enough for educators to mobilize and act? Do we want our children and our grandchildren to inherit a healthier world in which clean air and water are a given, disparities of wealth are not so extreme, quality health care is a guarantee, people can enjoy some leisure time, and there is a definite lessening of spiritual disconnection? Aren't these issues worth fighting for? How many people will have to be raped, exploited, poisoned, or emotionally destroyed before we act? How many of us are willing to do more than just talk about Gandhi's idea of noncooperation as valid political action? One of my primary purposes for writing this book is to better understand how far I am willing to go in my teaching and activism for justice.

But we (Dana and Patrick) may run into trouble with authorities. I (Patrick) am forty-seven and I (Dana) am thirty-six as we write this book and prepare it for publication. We have partners, children, and aging parents to worry about. We have academic careers to consider and mortgages to pay. Tenure and promotion are just around the corner. We have dreams and plans for our lives. In the Hebrew scriptures in the Book of Joel it is written that "Sons and daughters will prophesy, young men and women shall see visions, and their elders shall dream dreams." Is it possible for us to accurately and thoroughly investigate race, class, and gender issues? How will our positionality, privilege, and prejudices impact our writing—and is it even possible for us to deconstruct ourselves? What are we to do?

I (Patrick) signed a contract pledging to submit the ethics and education manuscript. I invited my friend and colleague, Dana Rapp, to be my coauthor. I have known Dana for only three years, but I know he is passionately committed to bringing issues of social justice to the forefront of education, as well as to his own institution. His community activism, teaching, and writing explore a range of issues from poverty, homelessness, arts-based protest, globalization, and oppositional imagination. Dana's convictions arise out of his deep concern that the adults of today have a responsibility to ensure that the next generation will live in a healthier social, political, ecological, and spiritual world. Our recent experience together at the Cleveland Museum of Art proved, once again, that we share a passionate commitment to dismantling injustices in the world. Now that we have joined together in this project, we believe that it is our responsibility as educators to speak prophetically and act politically for justice, peace, and democracy. We recognize the complexity of negotiating the terrain of ethical issues as two privileged white males. However, we also believe that our critical theories compel us to live in the margins, work for agency and justice, and nurture a language of possibility. We hope that you will join us in our teaching convictions to challenge and rupture dominant educational practices as you read this book.

We can think of few issues as important as ethics and education in our contemporary global society. We hope that this book will contribute to the ongoing dialogue about virtues, character education, religion and schooling, environmental education, the politics of the curriculum, the causes of violence and terrorism, racial and ethnic diversity in schools and the curriculum, the moral life of teachers and students, peaceful cooperation in a global society, and ethical living in our local communities. We explore ethics by foregrounding the social construction of reality, postmodern irony, poststructural complexity, cosmological ambiguity, hermeneutic analysis, and the contribution of critical theory to justice, compassion, and ecological sustainability in our contemporary society. We do this using autobiographical narrative rather than a technical research methodology. We do not position ourselves as passive observers of ethics nor as dispassionate intellectuals explaining competing ethical systems. We carefully promote a critical postmodern philosophy, and we do this while examining and deconstructing our own social constructions using tragic and humorous examples from our own life experiences and classroom practices. However, we are most concerned with providing inspiration and insights that propel us and others to not only "keep hope alive," as Jesse Jackson so eloquently intones, but to act boldly at a time when social justice and democracy appear to be in decline. These are our teaching convictions.

1 Autobiography and the Self: The Search for Ethical Meaning

Ethics and a Day in the Life of Patrick Slattery

I begin writing this chapter on a fairly typical weekday at the end of an exhausting fall semester. I begin my morning routine before 7 A.M. by throwing on faded blue jogging shorts and a well-worn LSU sweatshirt, doing a few stretches and push-ups, jotting down the highlights of my dreams on a bedside tablet, and giving my thirteen-year-old son Joshua an extra wake-up call for school. As I stagger blurry-eyed to the kitchen to boil some water and select cereal, Josh rolls over and falls back asleep. Grape Nuts or Grape Nut Flakes? Are the bananas still green or have they ripened overnight without becoming mushy? A good banana means the nuts; a green or mushy banana means plain flakes. Today the flakes win. I call Josh again, this time in a serious tone. It is 7 A.M. and he bolts to the living room, plops down on the sofa, and tunes into ESPN for a half-hour of sports highlights. I walk outside to get the *Austin American Statesman,* which I will skim later tonight for local music and film events, and the *New York Times,* which I will devour with breakfast from cover to cover, except for the Business Day section. It is now 7:35 A.M., and I am getting nervous. In ten minutes, the bus arrives, but I am hoping to drive Josh to school if he is late. The drive affords us special time to talk about important global issues, adolescent development, and my experiences as an eighth grader in 1966. It is also a wonderful opportunity for father–son bonding. Knowing all of this, Josh seldom misses the bus.

It is now five minutes until the bus arrives, and Josh is watching the replay of the replay of the play of the day on CNN. Josh shouts, "Dad, sign those papers on my desk." I want to stick to our rule that all papers must be signed at night before bedtime. I worry about which is most important: signing papers for teachers, fostering responsibility in Josh, or training Josh to be organized the night before? Maybe we should change the rule, I ponder as I sign the papers. I shout back to Josh, "Get dressed, eat your breakfast, brush your teeth—and don't forget your vitamin and the key!" Somehow he gets it all done and gathers up his books and the papers I just signed. As he rushes for the front door, I call out, "I love you, boy. Study hard!" Then, with a serious smile on my face, I ask, "Hey, where's my hug goodbye?" Josh feigns a symbolic embrace and rushes out, mumbling with a semblance of true affection as he shuts the door, "Love ya too. Bye." This moment makes family life and parenting not only bearable but memorable. The serenity of the postevacuation morning routine energizes my spirit.

The water is now boiling and screaming for attention. As I move to the kitchen stove, I realize the importance of selecting just the right cup from the shelf above the sink to set the tone for this day. After all, I intend to write about ethics, education, and my life journey this morning. As I gaze up at our cup collection, ignoring the hissing water, I know that I am not in a *New Orleans Mardi Gras: Laissez Les Bons Temps Rouler* mug mood. The University of Alberta *Ewe of Eh* cup is much too cold for a warm December morning in Texas. I sentimentally settle on my deceased maternal grandmother's favorite, the *Irish Blessing* mug with rich dark coffee stains on the rim. As I shut off the gas burner and fill Mama's cup with steaming hot water, I add one tablespoon of vinegar and one tablespoon of honey. This familiar morning brew helps elicit the finer details of last night's dream and fill in the missing clues on my yellow bedside tablet. My friend and Jungian analyst, Richard Chachere of Lafayette, Louisiana, taught me the intricacies of recording and interpreting my dreams, and my mother, Pattie C. S. Burke of Scottsdale, Arizona, gave me the recipe for vinegar and honey tea that she learned from her Native American medicine man years ago at the Turtle Island Project in Phoenix. When taken before brushing, the tea flushes the vital healing enzymes that have accumulated in the mouth overnight back into the digestive system. The tea also soothes the psyche and digests the dreams. There is a strange anima/animus tension going on here that I do not fully understand yet, even after seven years of this tea-dream ritual. Last night I dreamed again about driving my deceased father's blue '64 Chevy Impala with the red dented driver's side door. Richard and Pattie both want me out of that car. I stubbornly remain psychically attached.

My thoughts drift back to the summer of 1970 when I was a sixteen-year-old senior-to-be at De La Salle High School in New Orleans. My best friend Kirk Diez and I asked my father if we could borrow his Impala. As he handed over the keys, Dad reminded me to be home by the midnight curfew. I hesitated. Kirk glared at me and whispered in my ear, "Ask him now." I stammered while gathering up the courage to plead our case. "Can we borrow the car for a bit longer please, sir?" Dad casually replied, "How long? Until one o'clock?" It was now time to pop the big question. "Well, Dad, it's summer, and I'll be a senior next year and Kirk will be a junior. We're getting older, and, as you know, we're very mature for our age." "Yes, yes!" he impatiently urged us on. "Can we borrow the car for two weeks to go camping in Colorado?" Almost without a flinch and much to our astonishment he said "Sure. Just be careful." A few days later Kirk and I were off on an unforgettable adventure through Texas, New Mexico, and Colorado. The old Impala actually made it from New Orleans to the Rocky Mountain National Park near Boulder and back south again without a hitch.

Today is Thursday, December 17, 1998, and I have the time to record my dreams and casually read the *New York Times*. I can even ruminate about the strange image of my father's '64 Chevy Impala in my dream last night. Being a university professor provides the luxury of writing and researching in my home office occasionally, and the morning ritual is essential for getting my mind, body, and spirit ready for the task. As I settle in to my office and boot up the computer, I deliberately and confidently gather my books and research materials and prepare to write. But the morning news weighs too heavily on my heart; I cannot yet jump into the technicalities of philosophical ethics. So here I am, blank computer screen, stacks of research documents, several notepads full of references, textbooks from my ethics course, and a neatly organized desk prepared for the academic task. I am ready to begin a chapter on critical ethical issues and education. Nothing is happening; words of wisdom elude me. Writer's block grips my psyche. How can I possibly write about ethics and education on a day like today?

The headline in the *New York Times* still screams in my ears: "Impeachment Vote in House Delayed as Clinton Launches Iraq Air Strike; Cites Military Need to Move Swiftly." The *Times* reports today that this attack on Iraq is the biggest since the 1991 war and that Republicans are bitterly split over the timing of the attacks. Is this a legitimate and unavoidable military action, as the president claims? Or is this a contrived event—reminiscent of the recent film *Wag the Dog* in which a fictional president stages a war with the help of his Hollywood cronies to deflect attention from a sex scandal in the White House—in which President Clinton is desperately trying to avoid an impeachment vote at all costs? Pictured on the front page of the *Times* today are three photos: President Clinton reading a prepared text from the Oval Office about the U.S. military action in Iraq, a color image of a fire and huge explosion in Iraq, and Robert L. Livingston, the United States representative from New Orleans and the new Speaker-elect of the House of Representatives who is preparing to replace the outgoing Newt Gingrich, angrily criticizing the president while announcing that the GOP had reluctantly voted late last night to postpone the impeachment debate in the House.

My mind drifts back to Bob Livingston's office fifteen years ago. I was chaperoning a student tour of Washington, D.C., and during a free afternoon I stopped by Bob's office for a visit. Not only was Bob Livingston my representative, but also his half-sister is married to my first cousin. (Everyone in south Louisiana is related, even if they don't acknowledge it. Although I was a registered Democrat, I always voted for Bob. Family loyalty overshadowed political affiliation. Or was it the self-interest of influential political connections that trumped personal beliefs and civic responsibility?) During my visit with Bob Livingston, a beeper sounded calling all representatives to the floor of the House for a vote. He invited me to walk with him. As we took the elevator to the basement for the tram ride from the office complex to the House, he inquired about my opinion on the issue under consideration. I had the impression that he was undecided about how he would vote, but maybe he was just trying to gauge my temperament on the issue. Today I can no longer recall the specific topic, but I do remember feeling inadequate to offer an informed opinion. So much for my opportunity to influence a vote in Congress or impress my cousin-representative!

As I look at the images in the *New York Times* today, I wrestle with the complexity of the issues involved. I am much more informed now than I was as a young teacher-chaperone in Washington, D.C., in the early 1980s, though I am still uncertain at times about appropriate solutions to complex global problems. As I ponder the beauty and fragility of our global community, our natural environment, and our individual lives, the image of the fires in Iraq sickens me. How will future generations remember this day—assuming that the earth will be capable of sustaining future generations? What kind of world am I creating for Josh and my two teenage daughters, Michelle and Kayty, as well as all the children of the earth? I worry about the ways in which the media, the military, and politicians are attempting to manipulate my emotions and opinions. One part of me is angry at Bill Clinton's recklessness, betrayal, manipulation of a young woman intern, and alleged illegal cover-ups; another part of me is revolted by the invasion of his privacy, assumptions about the nature of the liaisons, and the hypocrisy of the Republican morality police. On the one hand, I abhor war and indiscriminate violence, but on the other hand I refuse to remain idle and silent while a terrorist dictator tramples over the lives of innocent people. No more silence in the face of an emerging Hitler, Stalin, or Mussolini. Is this another Vietnam or another fascist assault on humanity? I always thought I was a passivist dove. Am I now a militaristic hawk? What sense do terms such as *dove* or *hawk* make in this complex postmodern world today, anyway?

I want the partisan bickering in Washington, D.C., to end. I do not want the pseudo prosecutor Kenneth Starr or the ex-confidante Linda Tripp to reveal any more details of intimate conversations or liaisons. To be honest, however, I occasionally find it irresistible to peek at the titillating material in the tabloids. I have never bought one of these horrid magazines, but I must confess that I have read an article once or twice while waiting in a long line at the grocery store checkout. In the midst of the presidential sex scandals, I worry more about the war in Iraq. I do not want Saddam Hussein to terrorize and threaten the Kurds, Kuwaities, or humanity any longer. But I also wonder whether I am a part of the problem. How do I contribute to the wasteful materialism of oil consumption, ecological degradation, racial discrimination, and cultural imperialism of the United States that also terrorizes and threatens the global community—probably even in Iraq? How have I been manipulated by the media and the politicians? We certainly understand that the war in Iraq is about protecting oil supplies and material wealth for global corporations and their rich stockholders in the United States. How else can we explain our lack of interest in genocide, civil war, ethnic cleansing, and ecological destruction in Rwanda, East Timor, Congo, Sri Lanka, and other global hot spots? Are we on the verge of a resurgence of cultural colonialization and hegemony by the United States?

This morning I worry about human nature and my own human frailty. Whatever happened between Monica Lewinsky and William Jefferson Clinton, is it necessary that this morality play unfold in the public arena? I am sex scandal weary. What virtues are required for leadership—by Bill Clinton or Bob Livingston? Are these the same virtues required of a college professor, college student, or any other citizen? Would my moral behavior, or the lives of any ordinary citizen, meet the test of public scrutiny? And today I must ask this most important question: Must global and personal conflicts always escalate to violence, terrorism, war, or even impeachment? I have read many research reports by ethnographers and anthropologists who contend that communities of peaceful cooperation and ecological sustainability have existed in human history and in the natural world. Can these communities teach us their values? Is there any way to achieve lasting peace for all of humanity?

In the 1960s and 1970s, I would sing along with the popular protest folk songs and ballads: "Give Peace a Chance," "Imagine," "Ohio," and "Where Have All the Flowers Gone?" Are massive bombing attacks in Iraq really necessary? Who is being killed and maimed by such bombings? Should Clinton be impeached if he lied about having sex with "that woman"? The headlines and my own questions batter at my mind.

But I now realize that December 17, 1998, is actually an excellent day to write about critical ethical issues and education, for ethics is not simply a tidy system of rules of behavior. Nor is it an unambiguous code of moral conduct, religious virtues, and civic responsibilities. Ethics can be understood only in the context of the messy and ambiguous struggle to live meaningful and consequential lives in the midst of human aspirations, desires, frailties, and shortcomings. Our moral dilemmas necessarily include all dimensions of our lives: political maneuvering, intimate relationships, economic endeavors, ecological sensibilities, religious practices, social and personal conflicts, health and welfare concerns, peace and war, career planning, entertainment and recreation, disease and death, technology, the arts, spirituality, and personal desires. Ethics involves every dimension of living and being in the world. Education is the process of teaching and learning for growth in mind, body, spirit, and psyche in order to effect positive social change for justice in the world. Thus, educational ethics explores and informs all life processes, seeking peace, justice, wisdom, understanding, democratic communities, compassionate relationships, ecological sustainability, aesthetic sensibilities, and prophetic vision. In short, ethics is the substance of daily living and decision making and not simply a list of rules and regulations. Ultimately, ethics is a search for hope to continue the journey beyond December 17, 1998—or any day—and into every moment of our lives. This is the philosophy of educational ethics that informs this book.

Ethics and a Day in the Life of Dana Rapp

I can't explain why I rose early on July 21, 2001, especially because I was emotionally and physically exhausted. The day before I had driven 250 miles from northwestern Massachusetts to Philadelphia, where I picked up my partner, our three-year-old Madeline, and our two-month-old Heron. We then drove another 450 miles to our home in Wooster, Ohio. Not only was I fatigued from driving a rattling and wobbling 1983 Volvo wagon with two fidgety young ones, but I was also drained from a grueling two weeks of guest lecturing at the Massachusetts College of Liberal Arts Educational Leadership Academy. I was counting on Monday July 21 as a twenty-four-hour respite before beginning to teach the course Ethics of Leadership for Ashland University doctoral students. I even had the nerve to ask Kathy, who was equally exhausted, to keep the curious Madeline out of my room until at least nine o'clock the next morning. Thus, I was a bit stunned when I found myself walking down the hall steps, past our unpacked bags of laundry and books, and into the kitchen, where I flicked on a light at 5:45 A.M. I was even more struck when I walked outside to get the newspaper and spotted John, our next-door neighbor, getting into his mother's Ford Explorer for his morning ride to the day care center. I flinched when I noticed that John was wearing a baseball uniform with the number 58 on the back. John's mother, Mary, must have thought it peculiar, perhaps bizarre, that I was standing in my white boxers on our brick walkway not more than twenty yards away. I am not sure if I was half asleep, still awake, or both. My dreams were with me, however, and their multilayered nuances in those brief moments must have frozen my instinct to move back toward the front door and into the house.

Kathy and I often worried that eight-year-old John and his six-year-old sister Sally lived more than sixty hours a week in the homes of their nanny and various sitters. We rarely saw them during the day and, if we did, it was never with their parents. Mary would wake John and Sally at 5:30 each morning, throw some processed food in a lunch box, and drop them off at the sitter du jour, where they would live until Mary picked them up at 7 P.M. As John was getting into the Explorer today, I wondered what he thought about his way of life. Was this the way things had to be? Was it fun to go to sitters? Was he destined to live in constant flux forever? Did he secretly despise his parents? Would he raise his children with the understanding that his experience was both healthy and "natural"?

I reflected on my conversations with Rob and Mary. They told me that they both worked sixty hours a week so that they could own a second house, two Ford Explorers, a luxury speedboat, and a summer time-share vacation plan for a week at Disneyland. Rob traveled out of state and was rarely home during the week. When I did see him, it was usually on Saturday evening after 6 P.M. when he was cutting the lawn. Rob had an unusual concept of relaxation, rejuvenation, and recreation. I never saw him throwing a baseball with John or Sally, telling enriching stories to them on the way to a nearby park, or making mud pies with his children in the backyard. In fact, Rob confided to me one evening that his children stressed him out almost as much as his job, which he said he hated. When we did see or hear Rob, it was usually while he was cutting his lawn; he often said that he did yard work to temper his road rage. "Cutting, edging, blowing, trimming, and spraying chemicals is my therapy," he told me on more than one occasion.

As sweet, caring, energetic John climbed into his mother's Ford Explorer at 6 A.M. that morning, I shook my head in amazement. What is it about U.S. institutions and corporate America that propels midlevel managers like Rob to become so angry and alienated? How different would his life be if he had six to eight weeks of vacation like people in most other industrialized countries? How did Rob and Mary come to be consumed by patriotic materialism and hedonistic spirituality? Did their church pastor condone and support their lifestyle? Why did Rob destroy his soul for personal and ecological exile? Should I tell my children that Rob and Mary are successful? Will John and Sally grow up to neglect themselves, their ancestry, their communities, and their natural environments to the extent that Rob and Mary have? And how can neighbors, educators, and families interrupt the corporate mentality that manipulates and demoralizes people to the extent that they become angry, controlling, and self-destructive? Is this the American dream or the American nightmare?

As John and Mary drove down Grant Street, I quickly realized that it was the number 58 on John's jersey that had led me to pause in my boxers in front of the house. While I lectured at the Leadership Academy, 58 had taken on a special significance for me and some of my students. As I slowly moved toward the front door of our home and eventually to the kitchen for peppermint tea, my mind traveled back to my recent experience in Massachusetts when my students and I took personal, autobiographical, and creative risks in discussing ethics. The students were shocked when I walked in the first day and my first words to the class were, "The one thing I request of you at this point is that we write the syllabus on the last day of the course and that we not speak of grades until the second week." Disbelief emanated in the body language and facial expressions of the students, most of whom had attended the academy the year before. They expected me to follow protocol by filling their time with lectures, notes, quizzes, and tests on educational dilemmas, ethical formulas, and professional anecdotes. Immediately, several people dismissed me as a flake, a pushover, or a sixties throwback. It was obvious that more than a few students were terrified at the thought that the structure and assessment of the course, as well as the passion, imagination, and emotion, would have to come from the entire group and not the professor alone.

I waited for a verbal response from at least one of the twenty adults before me, most of whom were building principals and veteran teachers much older than I, but only silence and polite submission followed. Still, I refused to pass out a syllabus. I worried that Ellen, my friend and the director of the Leadership Academy, might be uncomfortable with my methods. The silence continued. These adult educators sat like obedient schoolchildren whose sense of direction and passion could only erupt with permission.

As I tried to read their thoughts, feelings, and inhibitions, I noticed that our silent pause had brought the group's breathing cadence into synchronistic unity. Chests and stomachs were moving in and out in tandem. Suddenly, the silence broke when a young woman from New York City rather forcefully exclaimed that ethics scared her. Another student demanded an explanation. Anita responded that a course on ethics intimidated her because it had the potential to be personally terrifying.

She described how her experiences with racism as a black woman raised outside the United States and now living in New York City created thick walls of defensiveness. Anita wept as she spoke to the mostly white European American audience. "Many of you just don't know. You don't know what it's like to have your children pulled over by the police because they have brown skin. You don't know what it's like to have a cop's gun pointed at your head and being called 'nigger' in front of your kids all because the cop couldn't believe that a black woman could afford a BMW. He thought I stole it. What he stole was my children's innocence and my integrity. He stole my ability to ever pass a BMW again without wanting to rage. You get where I'm coming from?"

I didn't say anything. Ten minutes into the course and one student was crying, while several white people were already thinking, "Fuck, another class where we have to listen to those blacks whine about past injustice." A few students were seriously considering how to convince Ellen to allow them to switch to another section of the ethics course. "Thank you for sharing your experience, Anita," a middle-aged white woman from Brooklyn said. "It must be so hard to discuss and to live with these issues." Immediately hands flew up across the room from men and women of all colors, experiences, and backgrounds. A fire was lit—or maybe it was reignited, reenvisioned, and reimagined. Some people had questions for Anita about racism, but most were intent on relating their stories of suffering and hope. More tears flowed and hearts beat faster as some students left their chairs and hugged one another. Others sat in their seats awkwardly, not sure how much emotion or empathy they were willing to express publicly. After this penetrating moment of emotional, creative, and soulful replenishing, I decided to speak.

"What do you think?" David asked me before I could string together a few thoughts. "About what?" I responded. "About this class, about what just went on. About ethics. You planned this, didn't you?" Before David could finish his series of questions, Joan piped in, "What are we going to do next? When are we going to discuss ethics? This isn't ethics. This is therapy, and I didn't pay all this money for therapy." Karen, an outspoken black woman from Albany, interrupted Joan to announce, "What are we going to do next? I'll tell you one thing, Joan. I want you to hear more of Anita's stories. I want you to feel her pain. I want you to hear me, and I want to listen to you. Don't you get it? This is ethics. It's raw emotion; it's personal pain. It's the development of empathetic, intuitive, and imaginative convictions." What more could be said, I thought to myself, and wished that an artist could capture in some small way the passion, the creative energy, and the beauty in our classroom at this moment. After another short pause, I smiled and thanked the class for sharing their autobiographical experiences and said, "Let's continue after a short break." Before we could leave, Karen said, "I think I know what you are up to, and we just had our break."

As I sat before the unopened newspaper on our kitchen table, I dreamed of the many smiles, hugs, tears, and connections formed at the Leadership Academy. I thought about how we explored our personal convictions and ethical issues related to racism, sexuality, corporate crime, patriarchy, heterosexism, exploitation, healing, hope, resistance, addiction, spirituality, peace, and ecology through dance, poetry, music, charcoal sketches, short stories, and comedy—some improvisational, some planned—at homeless shelters, rape crisis centers, churches, the local Wal-Mart, and a cooperative farm. The shades of Rosa Parks, James Hillman, George Sessions, Aldo Leopold, Che Guevara, Adrienne Rich, the physicians of Muddfai, Mother Jones, Angela Davis, and Winona LaDuke often sat with us in our circle as did visitors, stories, artifacts, and myths from Yemen, Somalia, Jamaica, Puerto Rico, and Hungary. Often our discussions began and continued beyond the three and a half hours formally scheduled each day. Conversations flowed into and out of the cafeteria and restrooms, into phone calls home to loved ones, into the smoky lounges of nightclubs, where students would often congregate to blow off steam, and into our awakening dreams. We began each class by discussing possible points of departure for ensuing conversation and performance. Students shared their passions, fears, and imaginary landscapes that arose in their dorm rooms the night before. Some read poetry or offered colored-pencil compositions they had sketched while ruminating in the early morning hours; others discussed how they took a creative risk and visited a biker bar, a gay nightclub, or a poetry reading at an offbeat coffeehouse.

Our stories sometimes elicited defensiveness. Many of the white, European American students, for instance, continued to be offended by an outspoken Latino man who was not shy in expressing his belief that "most white people just don't get it. It's not about the past; racism is in the present. I live this stuff every day. Do you know how afraid I was when you took off without me at the lake? Do you know what kinds of looks the white people gave me when I walked by them? Did you notice? Do you understand?" Stories of oppression and discrimination were often received with sympathetic recollections of family racism, alcohol abuse, gender bias, religious persecution, and trauma. Some white, Christian, heterosexual men even expressed this sentiment: "I'm listening and, although I cannot understand your pain completely, I want you know that many of us and our families are suffering at the thought of having to come to terms with our own complicity in your suffering."

The newspaper remained on the kitchen table in its plastic wrapping. The sun was now appearing through the windows to the east of the house, and I could hear Cody, our dog, tap dancing on the hardwood floors as she made her way to my side to ensure that I had not forgotten to fill her bowl. However, I couldn't get the Leadership Academy experience or John's jersey out of my mind. I began to reflect on the significance of the number 58 and the mystery surrounding it. With a second cup of tea in my hand and Cody on her way back to bed after eating, my imagination drifted to my experience with Bell, a thin and passionate African American woman from Queens, New York, with beautiful cornrows. I found it strangely disturbing, perhaps unnerving, that a middle-aged white guy like me who had never experienced the daily pains of legal and social racial apartheid could find her autobiography and history strikingly familiar. Bell's empathy, compassion, and deep appreciation of others' pain somehow connected us. Although I can't speak to the origins of Bell's desire to feel and heal others' suffering, I can speak to my own. My early childhood images of seeing a gun held to my mother's head by my biological father have shaped who I am and my connection to Bell. At night when I dream, I can smell the musk of coal on my ancestors' coats, and I can hear it in their lungs as they trudged home after being told there no longer was work for them in the mines of Brynamon, Wales. The residual effect of my great-great-great-grandfather's anger, unrest, and discontent at economic exploitation resides not only in my dreams, but also in the crevasses of my imagination and the pores of my physical body. Some may call this phenomenon a thorn, a mad spot, or even a trauma. I remember thinking quietly, as other students were talking this summer, "Here is a link between you and me and our ancestry, Bell. My family's oppression was related to your family's oppression. My anger is your anger. My rage will be your rage."

I had made a half-hearted commitment to avoid thinking about my experience at the Leadership Academy before returning to Wooster. So much for that thought. It was now 6:45 A.M., and I was still at the table with my memory unleashed. There was no way I could go back to sleep. I glanced quickly at the paper; I no longer looked forward to reading the *Akron Beacon Journal,* or even the *New York Times,* because I thought George W. Bush was so inept and misguided. Was it possible for him to be even more destructive of the environment and the economy than Ronald Reagan? Within six months of taking office, Bush had already refused to support the Kyoto Accords on global warming, supported drilling for oil in pristine Alaskan wilderness, advocated lower standards for air and water pollution, proposed that the United States quit the SALT Treaties on nuclear proliferation, and refused to support treaties that would limit the production of biological weapons. He had also advanced demoralizing high-stakes testing for schools, provided tax refunds that supported the wealthiest Americans at the expense of middle-class and working people, crippled the campaign finance initiative, advocated only superficial changes in voting procedures, argued against a patients' bill of rights, supported an easing of workplace safety measures, and sought to raid the budget surplus and social security to fund corporate and military welfare. Each day has been a new nightmare as President Bush acts to roll back ecological, political, environmental, and social justice initiatives on a massive scale.

What horrible news would the papers report today? What other damage could be done? I also wondered how the U.S. public could allow such behavior to persist. Whereas some conservative cultural and political supporters were suggesting that Bush would restore integrity and morality to the White House, I was arguing that he was committing crimes against the environment and democracy. Does the destruction of the earth and the creation of tax laws that benefit the super rich reflect integrity and morality? When the government callously denies healthy coverage to children and vetoes legislation to punish hate crimes, is this ethical? No, I thought, I'd better not pick up the paper this morning. I'll take a shower and then head down to Woogles Bagels with Madeline for breakfast, but I'm not going to dedicate whatever mental energy I have to the political maneuvering of George W. Bush—especially on a day in which I planned to relax.

This feeling reminded me of the the feeling I'd had when I awoke on Wednesday, July 5, one of my days off at the Leadership Academy. Ellen had thoughtfully scheduled classes so that each professor taught for two days and then had the next day off to relax. She was also considerate enough to purchase extra tickets so that faculty could attend the Fourth of July James Taylor concert at the beautiful Tanglewood Music Center. James is always extra special at Tanglewood, and that night was no different. With "Carolina in My Mind" on the tip of my tongue, I took comfort in knowing that I could sleep late, take a twelve-mile hike in the early afternoon, and then read and prepare for class in the evening.

At the kitchen table, my mind rehearsed the hike. I drove about ten miles from campus to the state park at the base of a mountain. It was a perfect day to hike; there was a cool breeze, it was sunny, and temperatures were not expected to exceed seventy-five degrees. The park was also nearly deserted. My pace that morning was quicker than usual for reasons that still elude me. In two hours, I had hiked several miles up a steep trail, and within forty-five minutes I would reach the top of the mountain. The thick pine forest that engulfed me at the base of the mountain gradually gave way to open vistas of the valley below and the Berkshires to the south and west. The deeper blues on the horizon rapidly lost their prominence to the more aggressive ominous blacks and grays of a front moving in from the west. As I walked farther, I noticed that my senses were awakening. The cries of birds, the scent of moisture, and the cold tones of the fast-approaching storm intensified. Sensory reflections were soon matched by a sudden and powerful feeling of guilt, fear, and trespass. I couldn't explain it. "Half a mile more," I thought, "don't lose it now. You want to reach the top." A path soon lured me off the road and into the woods. A misty rain accompanied a cold, haunting breeze. My memory and imagination raced uncontrollably, as if to keep pace with my increased panting on the steep ascent. The woods had always comforted and restored me, especially when I was hiking alone, but not this time. What was it about this place? All of a sudden, as I left the steep wooded path and entered a grassy knoll a hundred yards before the summit, I was overtaken by a force that brought my hands together in a tight clasp. Within seconds I was on my knees, bowing, praying, succumbing, weeping, and paying homage to a force/presence/memory I still cannot begin to comprehend. Dreams and visions collided with pain, emptiness, ecstasy, and fantasy. Yet I felt a sweeping blankness, as if what was working to disturb was also seeking to release. I lifted my moist and muddy hands from the ground to my face and, after several minutes, my legs lifted me up. Rather than walk up toward the summit, I felt the urge to move downward and inward without hesitation. I no longer marveled at the thought of viewing the valley from the top of the mountain. In fact, before I knew it, I was sprinting down the path toward the road. The sun reappeared and the rain stopped, but the pace of my running continued. My feelings of dread and remorse waned, but the tingles in my neck and spine lingered, even as I recall these events on July 21.

I returned to campus vowing to visit the mountain on my next day off, only this time I would drive to the top. Fortunately, Mike Mullman, a friend I have known for twenty years, had made plans to visit me at the institute and agreed to join me. On the way to the summit, Mike and I reminisced about our youth and talked about plans for a beer that evening. It was a beautiful early evening, slightly cool with a wonderful red sunset. Mike and I left his car in the parking lot close to the top of the mountain and approached a place where several people had gathered for various rituals. The wind picked up as we ascended, and I felt again the strange physical and mental symptoms of anguish, dread, and remorse. These feelings intensified until I began to run toward Mike's car to escape. We weren't far from the area where I'd had the powerful experience a few days before. Mike was startled but understanding and immediately drove us down the mountain and into town. Although my symptoms were subsiding, and I knew Mike was a fairly sympathetic guy who wouldn't completely write me off as a lunatic, I knew I couldn't begin to relate what had happened to me on the mountain to a person who, by all visible measures, had not been affected in the least.

In class the next morning, my imagination was elsewhere. After a few minutes, Helen said that she wanted to use some of Billie Holiday's songs for the poetry jam she was putting together. Bell mentioned that she had a few Billie Holiday CDs and that Helen was welcome to borrow them. I asked if I could borrow one or two of Bell's Billie Holiday's CDs for myself. "Of course, Dana. Come on by to—" Before she could announce her town house number, I, for whatever reason, blurted out, "Let me guess. You live in townhouse 58, don't you?" I don't know what prompted me to guess, or why I chose the number 58. There were 150 town houses in our complex, and I had no idea where Bell lived. Bell was equally caught off guard, and she was visibly moved when she uttered, "Yes, it is 58, how did you know?"

Later that day between classes, Bell and I happened to meet in the courtyard by the library. As I sat down next to her, she turned slightly and said, "I want to talk to you about a recent experience. Maybe it's worth bringing up in class." I was stunned as Bell began to explain how she had been overcome by anguish, distress, and a mysterious presence on a recent hike with friends. "It was evil, Dana. I can't fully explain it, but it was evil. No one else felt it. I thought I was having an anxiety attack. I did a little research. The mountain is situated on an Indian burial ground, a very sacred place, a place of intense meaning for both the living and nonmaterial spirits. Roads, buildings, and paths have desecrated not only the lands of Native Americans, but also their most holy places of worship. I think I was feeling the wrath of a restless ancestry." "Bell," I said, "I have to tell you something."

It is 7:15 A.M., and I still have not opened the paper or taken a shower. Maybe I can get back to bed after all. I don't hear Kathy, Heron, or Madeline stirring, and, uncharacteristically, not one of my neighbors has begun to tame the lawn with their obnoxiously loud mowers and leaf blowers. As I returned to bed, I continued to think about my relationship with Bell, Mike, John, the number 58, my mountain experience, and my summer class. How would my understanding of ethics be different if I had not met Bell? How was my understanding of oppression, genocide, and hegemony inten-sified through my mystical and emotionally disturbing hiking experience? Why did these events have a lifetime of meaning for me now? And why did I feel that my quiet, intuitive connections with John, Bell, and my ancestors in Wales had enhanced my un-derstanding of and commitment to act for social justice? When I awoke again, my alarm clock read 11:58.

Understanding Autobiography and the Self

Our approach to ethics and education in this book may seem unusual and unortho-dox—possibly even unacceptable—for those who expect a dispassionate, analytic, or reasoned scholarly investigation of moral issues and ethical systems. Others may find our autobiographical style and social activism uncomfortable, too intimate and personal for a textbook. These are legitimate concerns we address below. However, others may find our autobiographical approach refreshing and stimulating, believ-ing that passion and life history provide a rich meditative context for a textbook. Be-cause we also use an autobiographical approach in teaching our classes, we are aware from student evaluations of the perils and possibilities of using narrative life histories and autobiography in the classroom. However, we believe that the benefits outweigh the dangers, especially when a clear understanding of the complexity of autobiography guides the process. Therefore, we now discuss autobiography in some detail.

Some of the earliest expressions of interest in using autobiographical meth-ods in educational research can be traced to the article "Working from Within" by William Pinar (1972), in which he cites the abstract expressionist painter Jackson Pollock to suggest that teachers and students might work from inner sources of in-sight and imagination. Pollock was once asked by a reporter to explain why he did not use subjects from nature to create his paintings, as other artists had done through-out the history of art. (Recall that Pollock was famous for splattering paint—as well as broken glass, dirt, coins, and cigarette butts—on his canvases. At the height of the popularity of abstract expressionism in the late 1940s, *LIFE* magazine ran an article in which critics argued that "any monkey" could throw paint on a canvas, but this would not constitute good art. This is just one example of how Pollock, arguably the most widely renowned American artist of the twentieth century, was sometimes ma-ligned and ridiculed.) Pollock responded to the reporter's question about subjects from nature with his now famous retort, "I do not paint scenes from nature because I am nature."

Was Pollock trying to be cynical, bold, egotistical, or evasive? Probably not. Jackson Pollock truly believed that nature could best be experienced and expressed au-tobiographically, from within, and thus his painting tapped an inner source for ex-pression. This was also William Pinar's proposal for educational academic writing. Pinar explored "synthetical moments" and used them in his writing in ways inspired by Pollock. Pinar explained synthetical moments in his book with Madeleine Grumet, *Toward a Poor Curriculum* (1976) as follows:

> We cannot solely rely on the imagination, however artful its expression, or reports of psychological problems or philosophic accounts of experience. Some synthesis of these methods needs to be formulated to give us a uniquely educational method of inquiry, one that will allow us to give truthful, public and usable form to our inner observations. It is this search for a method I am on now. (p. 5)

The method Pinar and Grumet describe is committed to self-conscious conceptualization of the temporal world:

> It is therefore temporal and conceptual in nature, and it aims for the cultivation of a developmental point of view that is transtemporal and transconceptual. From another perspective, the method is the self-conscious conceptualization of the temporal, and from another, it is the viewing of what is conceptualized through time. So it is that we hope to explore the complex relation between the temporal and the conceptual. (p. 51)

The first step is the regressive moment in which one returns to the past as it impinges on the present. The present is veiled because the past is manifested in who we are and what we do in the existential now. Pinar and Grumet propose that we enter the past, live in it, observe ourselves functioning in the past, but not succumb to it. Because the focus of the method is educational experience, special attention should be given to schooling, books, teachers, and other pedagogical experiences and artifacts. We regress to the past but always with an eye toward a return to the present and to the next step, the progressive moment. The word *progressive* derives from *pro*, meaning "before," and *gradi*, meaning "to step, go." Here we look, in the language of existentialist philosopher Jean Paul Sartre, at what is not yet present. We imagine a future, envision possibilities, and discern where our meditative images may appear to be leading us. The next step, the analytical moment, describes the biographic present, exclusive of the past and future but inclusive of responses to both. According to Pinar and Grumet (1976), "Bracketing what is, what was, and what can be, one is loosened from it, potentially more free of it, and hence more free to freely choose the present" (p. 60). This bracketing allows us to juxtapose the past, present, and future and evaluate the complexity of their multidimensional interrelations. After the analytical moment, a synthetical moment puts the three steps together to help inform the present. Pinar and Grumet (1976) conclude:

> The Self is available to itself in physical form. The intellect, residing in the physical form, is part of the Self. Thus, the Self is not a concept the intellect has of itself. The intellect is thus an appendage of the Self, a medium, like the body, through which the Self, the world are accessible to themselves. No longer am I completely identified with my mind. My mind is identified as a part of me. (Descartes' "I think, therefore I am" is thus corrected.) Mind in its place, I conceptualize the present situation. I am placed together. Synthesis. (p. 61)

We share William Pinar and Madeleine Grumet's enthusiasm for working within and exploring the self through autobiographical narratives. The approach, briefly described above, guides in part our study of critical ethical issues and education in this book.

Poststructural investigations problematize notions of self-formation, multicultural understandings of difference, the politics of recognition, and autobiography. As Pinar and Grumet explain, the notion of an individual subject has been called into question as these provocative images and themes emerge in philosophical literature: the disappearance of subject, the death of the self, and the disappearance of the author. These themes interrupt and problematize modern notions of the cohesive subject and the conscious self, challenging us to look at the world without the disposition of textual authority and without any subjective intervention by the power of language (Foucault, 1972b; Barthes, 1975; Burke, 1992). Some have suggested that language forms do not assert anything; rather, language reveals the tentativeness of all discourses, universal and totalizing discourses in particular, and demonstrates the essential insufficiency of words for expressing truth. Critics argue that the loss of universal rationalism and a turn toward the unreliability of the unconscious—as well as the subjectivity of autobiography—will entail the loss of all ability to distinguish good from evil and the beautiful from the grotesque, which can only lead to relativism, nihilism, tyranny, anarchy, and the end of civilization as we know it.

In this contested terrain, we must ask: What is the self? What wisdom can we glean from philosophers, poets, ethicists, and artists about the nature of the self? What useful information or insights can emerge from the projects of educational writers exploring ethics using autobiography and narratives? Investigations of the self have often centered on romantic notions of an ideal or perfect form, modern notions of embodied structures that define the essence of the individual person, or psychological notions of latent identity controlled by an ego or superego waiting to be gradually uncovered or healed. Some scholars propose a Hegelian dialectic to negotiate a true self. Here the self is situated between the lost and lonely individual (The Minimal Self) and the romanticized ideal individual (The Imperial Self) and capable of inherent narrative unity (Lasch, 1984). Recent discourses reject these conceptions of the self and challenge us to either reconceptualize our understanding of the self or give up the quest for the holy grail of self-awareness because the self does not exist.

Postmodernism views the self in terms of a multiplicity of ironic and conflicting interdependent voices that can be understood only contextually, ironically, relationally, and politically. Poststructuralism goes further and rejects the notion of the self because there is no cohesive and consistent self; the search for the true and lasting self is a metaphysical dead end. Whereas postmodernism proposes a radical eclecticism of "both/and," poststructuralism rejects the project to delimit in any way by contending that the self is "neither/nor."

Nietzsche (1968) concluded in *The Birth of Tragedy* that we have our highest dignity in our significance as works of art. In light of the Nietzschean and poststructural critiques, let us consider the work of the Belgian surrealist René Magritte.

Magritte's painting *La Trahison des Images* (Treachery of Images), popularly known as *Ceci N'est Pas une Pipé* (This Is Not a Pipe), and Michel Foucault's (1983) commentary on Magritte's painting in his book *This Is Not a Pipe,* provide an aesthetic insight into the poststructural philosophy of the self.

Recently, I (Patrick) visited the Los Angeles County Museum of Art. I stood before Magritte's *Trahison des Images* with the large scripted words *Ceci N'est Pas une Pipé* below the almost photographic image of a smoker's pipe on the 3'-by-4' canvas. Many visitors passed through the gallery as I meditated on this painting. Some paused for a moment of confused appreciation and others glanced quickly as they passed at a distance. As I observed the viewers and their multiple responses, one young couple particularly intrigued me. Locked in an intimate embrace, the young man was forcefully explicating the meaning of Magritte's painting to the young woman. His logic and her intuition were not in sync. Finally, in frustration he insisted, "It says *This is Not a Pipe!*" I could not resist the urge to turn to the couple and interject, "Mais non! Il dit *Ceci N'est Pas une Pipé.*" Of course, the words on Magritte's painting, like my purposeful response, were in French and not in English. Various translations of the French word *pipé* also allow for several playful interpretations such as "This is not a joke." The couple was startled by my playful comment and walked away perplexed.

Surrealism, the school of painting associated with René Magritte and Salvador Dali, among others, challenges the assumption that art—or any aesthetic artifact or text—is a one-dimensional portrayal of reality. Magritte's paintings startle the viewer and demand a reexamination of a host of assumptions, including those about space, time, dimensionality, relationality, and, of particular interest here, notions of the self and the unconscious. Surrealism provides an opportunity for viewers to reconsider their own preconceptions of familiar objects and experiences by presenting reality in new and often disturbing ways. Some surrealistic work, especially that of Joan Miró, is called automatism because ideas are expressed as they flow forth unfettered by logic or conscious structure. Surrealists sought meaning in destruction and hope in rebuilding—a reflection of their social context in the interwar years of the 1920s and 1930s. Surrealists established a context for Jackson Pollock and other abstract expressionists who portray an inner world of energy and motion. Stephen Polcari (1991) writes:

> Pollock's statement that he painted with visible energy and motion, organic intensity, memories arrested in space, and human needs and motives is a near-manifesto of Bergsonian vitalism. For Henri Bergson, life is striving, a need for invention, a creative evolution. Through the human body, vital movement courses and pursues moral life. Bergsonian philosophy describes an organic consciousness in harmony with Pollock's (and Thomas Hart Benton's [Pollock's mentor]) implicit understanding of natural action. For Bergson, life is imbued with organic consciousness, a sense of spirituality beyond mere biological or physical determinacy. Organic consciousness is seen in continuous movement. [As Pollock writes,] "Consciousness is co-extensive with life . . . , matter is inertia. . . . But with life there is free movement." (pp. 53, 256)

Here, visual efforts unite time and space, and Pollock reflects this journey into the unconscious in his search for generative forces and cycles of human existence. No longer does a symbolic figure or a mythical god represent the potency, vitality, fertility, and transformative power of the world and the self. Abstract forms and relationships represent this vitality for Pollock.

Both Jackson Pollock and René Magritte reflect a disgust for their times and a distrust of traditional practices. They were both products and cultural critics of their social milieu. Social and personal conflict provide nourishment for the aesthetic expression. The self is no longer a mirror image of reality; rather, it is a challenge to the very assumptions of totalizing images, boldly announcing, "This is not what it appears to be!" As noted earlier, when asked why he did not paint pictures of nature, Pollock responded, "I am nature." The canvas, nature, life, and self all merge in a phenomenological encounter, a visceral rather than a visual experience. The irony of a person proclaiming not to be a self is as startling to the casual observer as Magritte confronting a viewer in the museum with the words *Ceci N'est Pas Une Pipé* on his painting of a pipe.

Michel Foucault (1983) comments on Magritte's painting in his book *This Is Not a Pipe* on three levels: First, the drawing you recognize as a pipe is not substantially bound to nor does it cover the same material as "a pipe"—that is, the word from your language made up of pronounceable sounds that translate the letters you are reading as *pipe*. Second, "this," meaning the statement arranging itself beneath your eyes in a line of discontinuous elements, of which "this" is both signifier and the first word, is neither equal to, nor could substitute for nor adequately represent, "a pipe"—that is, an object whose possible rendering can be seen above the text because it is inaccessible to any name. Third, "this," as understood as the entire assemblage of the written statement and the drawn text, is not compatible with "a pipe."

Foucault's commentary on Magritte's painting parallels our deconstruction of traditional notions of the self in order to reconceptualize the purpose of teaching and the meaning of texts—including this one on critical ethical issues and education. When we reject a unifying rational narrative in favor of the complexity and multiplicity of the unconscious, and conclude, in the spirit of Magritte, that "This Is Not a Self," we are asserting three possible levels of irony: First, this physical assemblage of chemicals in a three-dimensional form does not constitute "a self," a unique spiritual, emotional, biological, and psychological entity that is irreducible to a mere physical form. Second, "this," meaning a logical or rational statement about the nature of the self, cannot constitute the meaning of "the self," for to so describe would delimit and obfuscate the complexity of the whole being. Third, the dual assemblage of both our physical entity and the attempt to construct the spiritual and psychological dimensions of this assemblage together cannot constitute "a self," for in the construction a new self does not emerge. Must we now conclude that there is no self? Is the reconstitution of the notion of self possible? Are there multiple interrelated selves? What is the "self" that we excavate and express in this educational ethics book? Let us explore further.

To study the self is "to forget the self" (Buksbazen, 1977). To forget the self is to detach oneself from nature and at the same time to be enlightened by all things in nature.This paradox is the heart of Zen. The way of Zen is a way to an end, but there is no end. The way is an end in and of itself. It is precisely such efforts to "free" oneself from oneself that makes one's work one's own; we find ourselves when we get away from ourselves.

In *This Is Not a Pipe*, Foucault (1983) pictures this process as an exercise of disengaging himself from himself in his "fragments of an autobiography," through "writings" that try to alter his way of seeing things. Foucault emphasized the power of sight to subvert the homogenizing drive toward the "same" that is implicit in naive linguistic versions of representation. The disciplinary power of the gaze and any search for essentializing immediacy are Foucault's primary concerns. Likewise, these are our concerns as educators and authors. In order to uncover meaningful data and enhance understanding of educational ethics, we must deconstruct the disciplinary gaze that so profoundly seeks to direct our consciousness, our life, and, in effect, the artifacts we produce as citizens, teachers, writers, artists, or researchers.

The traditional recognition of the individual self in Western cultures is at the center of society; relationships are considered by-products of interacting individuals. Curriculum and educational practices are built around improving the minds of individual students. However, after the advent of existentialism, phenomenology, and structuralism, the notion of self and "things in themselves" were called into question. Language and the structure or systems that shape our understanding of ourselves and the world were modified. The truth about oneself has in the West been "a condition for redemption for one's sins" or as "an essential item in the condemnation of the guilty" (Foucault, 1993, p. 201).

According to Lacan's revision of Freudian psychoanalysis, the subject does not think; rather, language thinks and speaks the subject. In Foucault's account, generic "man" only came into being as the subject of knowledge in the 1800s. In Hegel we find that a conception of subjectivity is described as developing through history toward a comprehensive self-knowledge, and a conception of history is described as a process through which spirit progressively comes to know itself. Subjects occupy the roles of the empirical object of knowledge, with the elevated subject—the human person—as the condition of possibility for that knowledge. Foucault contends that the human person as a subject and an object of study simultaneously initiates the destabilization of structure and of subject itself. And this is exactly the destabilization that Jackson Pollock visually demonstrated. It is also the (dis)juncture of autobiography. The goal is to free the self from the petrified connections forced onto the self by a repressive society or normative behaviors. This is exactly the political and social project begun by Magritte and the surrealists, a project that reached a crescendo in Jackson Pollock's abstract expressionism. This is the basis for the social and political projects in schools and society that inform our study of ethics in this text.

Returning to the paintings of Jackson Pollock, it is undeniable that surrealists such as Magritte were the catalysts for his abstract expressionist work. In 1947 the art critic André Breton wrote: "There are three major goals of Surrealism: the social liberation of man [sic], his complete moral liberation, and his intellectual liberation" (Gershman, 1974, p. 80). Surrealists sought freedom of thought, speech, and expression. Pollock actually applied the surrealist philosophy directly to his painting. He was committed to the idea that the creative act is a process by which the artist defines her or his inner experiences and inner values. The finished work of art was conceived as a form analogous to the artist's inner experience of the world, which included the work itself being created. This experience is what the painting means, and this meaning is stimulated by the very act of making the painting. In sum, the form of the work evolved as the appropriate articulation of an experience that occurred because the work was being made.

Pollock began his work without any specific idea of how it would come out. During the creative process, artist and medium each affected the other so that as the work took form, its meaning emerged. The creative act, therefore, was considered an ethical process during which the artist defined herself or himself by means of the actions taken in the process of painting. Thus, Pollock constantly reinvented the art of painting by relying on spontaneity to stimulate the direct expression of inner experience. However, unlike the surrealists, Pollock also insisted on a role for conscious choice as the work progressed in order to address any compositional problem that occurred during the process of painting:

> When I am in my painting, I am not aware of what I am doing. It is only after a short get acquainted period that I see what I have been about. I have no fears about making changes, destroying the image, etc. Because the painting has a life of its own, I try to let it come through. It is only when I lose contact with the painting that the result is a mess. Otherwise there is pure harmony, an easy give and take, and the painting comes out well. (qtd. in Chipps, 1971, p. 548)

Pollock's process is a model for our study of ethics and education through autobiography. Our writing flows from the same aesthetic sensibilities presented by Jackson Pollock. It also emerges from the surrealist manifesto and finds fruition in abstract expressionism.

I began a psychoanalytic journey similar to Pollock's in the early 1990s with Richard Chachere, my Jungian therapist in Louisiana, with my own desires and demons lurking within. Unlike Pollock, I did not sketch improvisational drawings from the unconscious; rather, I produced narrative vignettes of my nightly dreams. On my initial visit, Richard instructed me to record my dreams on a bedside tablet as soon as I awoke each morning. As I had never been consciously aware of my dreaming, I assumed that nothing fruitful would come of this exercise. In fact, I was skeptical about the prospect of remembering anything significant each morning. I was a busy school administrator, and I often tossed and turned at night worrying about discipline hearings, budget shortfalls, board meetings, and schedule changes. However, my willingness to begin Jungian therapy at a time of stress and trauma, along with the power of the suggestive influence of a respected therapist, elicited a life-clarifying first dream. This is what I wrote on the yellow bedside tablet the morning after my first session:

> A tiny baby was wrapped tightly in a blanket. His hair was thick and black; his skin was dark. He was sleeping soundly in a newborn crib in a doctor's office. As I entered the spacious office, the doctor—who had curly hair and resembled a principal in our district named Claude—rose to greet me affectionately. We stood near the baby—my fourth child, a son named Peter Slattery. The baby boy looked beautiful, but the doctor cautiously explained that Peter was born with a strange new disease. I quickly asked the doctor, "Will he be able to hear?" The reply from the doctor was affirmative. "Yes, Peter will be able to hear and understand." I then inquired, "Will he be able to run and play and hold a job when he gets older?" "Yes, of course!" the doctor adamantly replied, but added, "Peter will not be able to speak." I cried and the doctor tried unsuccessfully to comfort me, and then he opened the *New York Times* to a full-page advertisement devoted to this new childhood illness. I leaned forward and saw graphic photographs and diagrams of fetuses with captions explaining muteness. I was devastated. As the doctor put his arm around me, we took two steps down into an adjacent room—it was the living room of my childhood home in New Orleans. The deacon of my church greeted me in the living room; he consoled me as I wept. I regained my composure and then quoted from the Christian Bible to the doctor and the deacon: "God never tests us beyond our ability to endure."

I awoke from this dream in a cold sweat, deeply moved and profoundly disturbed. I was married at the time, and I shared this dream with my wife over breakfast and pondered the meaning of these strange images. We had three small children, and we were actively trying to get pregnant with a fourth child. We had, in fact, already selected the name John in hopes of having a son. My immediate reaction to the dream was twofold: First, the dream was a warning that we should not have a fourth child— even though the name in the dream was Peter rather than John—because the boy would be born handicapped. Second, the doctor, deacon, and school principal in the dream represented my responsibility as a compassionate educator to be supportive of people in distress.

Over the coming months, Richard taught me several Jungian concepts such as active imagining, symbolic representation, individuation, archetypes, anima and animus, collective unconscious, shadow figures, and mandala drawings (Jung, 1962; Storr, 1973). As we discussed the dream together and explored the mythic symbols in the dream, I reevaluated my initial interpretation. These new insights derived from the unconscious began an important healing process in my life. I also concretely understood for the first time the power of the unconscious and the importance of working within. Anthony Storr (1973) concludes:

> One of Jung's central ideas was that modern [persons] have become alienated from the mythopoetic substratum of their being, and therefore their lives lack meaning and significance. The task of analysis is to put [persons] in touch once again with "divine ground," as Aldous Huxley would have called it, by means of analyzing the subject's dreams. (p. 36)

Such alienation is the focus of the early work of William Pinar. It is most interesting that both Carl Jung and Jackson Pollock figure prominently in Pinar's educational research, particularly in his analysis of Pollock's painting *The White Cockatoo* (Pinar, 1991). His first study, "Sanity, Madness, and the School," was an effort to portray the milieu of schools by emphasizing the unseen and unspoken dimensions of life in schools and the seemingly inescapable experience of losing oneself there. Pinar explains that much of his research is an effort to elaborate strategies for the educational researcher to work from within (1991, p. 245). Pinar writes, "Like modern painters, my students and I have come to feel that we rarely need to refer to subject matter outside ourselves. We work from a different source. We work from within" (1972, p. 331).

Pinar links Pollock's abandonment of realism and representational painting (Rohn, 1987, p. 122) to his own abandonment of mainstream empirical and statistical research (Pinar, 1991, p. 246). Relinquishing realism allowed Pollock to become more self-conscious about the very process of painting and the generation of each stroke or line. Pinar compares his research to Pollock's style:

> In an infinitely more primitive way, leading to an incomparably more modest result, I have explored the uses of autobiography in the effort to comprehend curriculum, devising the method of *currere,* which allowed [the researcher] to become more self-conscious about the "strokes" and "lines" etched into the personality by curricular experience (and vice versa). My point here is to suggest to you that the processes in which Pollock was engaged, processes that begin with the relinquishing of so-called realism and representation and end in abstract dynamics of color, shape, and texture, allow us to see anew and to understand anew. Such is the high purpose of art, and such is the high purpose of scholarship. (Pinar, 1991, p. 246)

Pinar's "high purpose" of art and scholarship accurately describes the goal of our educational investigation of ethics. The purposes of art and writing are combined to create a powerful dynamic that allows us to understand complex layers of the educational process. Not that other research and other textbooks are incapable of such noble work. Rather, exploring poststructural notions of the self in educational contexts through the arts by foregrounding the excavation of the unconscious provides an alternative method for arriving at fresh new understandings.

I (Dana) have always been fascinated and disturbed by my dreams. I remember waking up as a five-year-old in the middle of the night and hearing the sound of footsteps and seeing images of a distant and burly figure moving toward me. Even when I pulled the covers over my head and hid underneath the pillows, the sounds of the plodding walker were vivid. My first real experience with trying to understand the unconscious occurred at this time. Although I was relieved to know that the footsteps came from the sound and reverberation of my heartbeat as I lay my ear on the pillow, the image of the distant and shadowy walker haunted me. I remember thinking that it probably had something to do with my parents' recent separation after a marriage marred by violent arguments, the physical abuse of my mother, and my father's determination that my mother would never gain custody of me. I also secretly hoped that the figure was a messenger from a distant time who had come to console me that the events in my young life had been experienced by children and adults from the beginning of human existence. As I thought more about this interpretation of my dreams, the sounds began to remind me less of footsteps and more of crashing waves hitting the shore in their timeless and endless rhythm.

Another powerful dream experience involved paralysis. In the early 1990s, I remember slowly coming out of a series of dreams, half conscious and half asleep. I could see the bedroom, paintings, and a table, but I was incapable of moving any part of my body except my eyes. It was one of the most terrifying episodes in my life. I lay in bed fully aware that my mind wanted my hand to move, even prodded it to move, but my hand remained paralyzed. I recall the intense frustration of being unable to scream for Kathy's assistance because I could not move my mouth. Many questions continue to resonate with me regarding these dreams. For instance, was my mind awake and my body asleep? Was I conscious or dreaming or both? Over time I came to partially, perhaps superficially, explain these dreams as reactions to a diagnosis I had received from a couple of doctors in the late 1980s. One doctor informed me that he thought I had multiple sclerosis but that the more serious and physically debilitating symptoms would not arise until a few years later. I was devastated. I immediately left his office and ran to the library where I scoured the shelves for articles on multiple sclerosis. What I found was not pleasing to a man in his early twenties who had been extremely active in sports his entire life and who had a sublime trust in medical experts. I read that MS was a neurological disease that in many cases results in the inability to use muscles to walk, talk, eat, and move. I reasoned, therefore, that some nuances of my recent dreams involving paralysis were the manifestation of my fears about developing multiple sclerosis.

My dreams have scared me in other ways. For the last eight years, I have been dreaming about different couples among our family and friends. Often these dreams reveal how one of the partners in the relationship isn't happy, or another is diagnosed with an unnamed, threatening illness. At first, when I awoke I would often relate to Kathy these horrible images and my own internal fears. To my amazement, several of these dreams became reality. Eventually, we no longer joked about the accuracy of my ability to foresee a divorce. Recently, I have tried to avoid dreaming about or analyzing many of my dreams that involve the happiness and health of others.

The power of the unconscious assumed new magnitude with the birth of our second child, Heron. In the last five years, I have been 100 percent accurate in predicting through my dreams the gender of seventeen children born to our family and friends. Kathy was aware of this record and asked me to confirm or disconfirm her maternal instincts regarding the gender of our new baby, which she had been carrying for two months. Part of Kathy's request came out of her playful desire to blemish my record and discredit my growing self-inflation. Another part of her, however, did not doubt the prophetic power of dreaming, and she was curiously supportive of my intuition. I told Kathy in September when she made this request that I would reveal my dreams about the gender of our child to her in Wales on New Year's Eve.

As it turns out, several months passed before I had my first dream of our second baby. I had an image of a small child, probably about three years old, standing beside me as I pointed at something in the valley below. We were huddled near the top of tall hill in a field where brown and gray grasses were weaving to and fro in a warm November breeze. No one was around. Both of us were peacefully smiling, and it was obvious that we felt quite content and secure in the quiet woods where we delighted in the songs of birds, the scent of pines, and the barely visible migration of animals. The child who stood next to me in this dream had no physical features or clothing that led me to determine the gender. A second vision came to me five weeks later. It was Christmas night, and Kathy, Madeline, and I had just returned from a long evening of feasting, fun, and celebration. We were staying at the old and majestic Angel Hotel in downtown Cardiff in Wales. With rich food and a little wine in our systems, Kathy and I both fell directly asleep within minutes of returning to our hotel room around 10 P.M. Sometime in the next two hours, I began to dream. I saw an image of a six- or seven-inch fetus kicking aimlessly while huddled in Kathy's stomach, and the child had a penis. I remember thinking to myself while I was having this dream that Kathy had been reminding me lately that New Year's Eve was only six days away. Now, I thought, I can tell her the image I saw. Eight-pound Heron Rapp, a boy, was born at our home on May 22, 2001. I am now certain that the image I had of the little child standing next to me on the hill was Heron. I am also confident in the power of dreams to predict, recall, uncover, relate, and reconnect us to the meanings, myths, and memories of the people with whom we live.

Two days before I had my dream about Heron I had spent the better part of a day in Brynamon, Wales, making etchings of gravestones of ancestors and others to whom I thought might be related. Brynamon is a small town of no more than fifteen thousand people located in the rolling hills and mountains of mid-Wales. Although the physical remains of my relatives have been buried for 150 years, I believe that my experience in the graveyards affected my unconscious and eventually directed my Christmas night dream. The dream of Heron and I perched on a hill has also reaffirmed my commitment to move with my family to an area where we can be enveloped by birds, animals, trees, streams, and mountains—someplace like Brynamon. The woods have always been soothing, calming, and nurturing for me, and I believe that the images I saw in my dream developed out of my need to commune with nature. Thus, I look at our future relocations, as well as my work as a teacher, writer, and researcher, as a returning more than a leaving.

Our understanding of dreams has matured and evolved over the years, and, as our narratives have demonstrated, we believe that dreams provide powerful healing insights. Although some psychologists and counselors encourage literal interpretations of dreams and visions—especially lucid dreams—Jungian therapists such as Joseph Henderson and Richard Chachere prefer to explore archetypal imagery emerging from the unconscious as expressed in psychoanalytic sketches and dream narratives. It is this symbolic imagery that informs our approach to ethics and education. The dreams we have described convince us of the healing power that flows from the artist–teacher working with(in) the unconscious, whether on a symbolic or a literal level. However, there is disagreement among artists and psychologists about the appropriate use of art therapy or psychoanalytic drawings. In fact, when Henderson published Pollock's psychoanalytic drawings in 1970 (after storing them in a file for twenty-five years), Lee Krasner, Pollock's widow, filed a lawsuit claiming that anything that goes on between analyst and patient must remain private. Although Krasner's lawsuit was dismissed, the conflicting comments by Joseph Henderson regarding the nature of Pollock's sketches as both art and psychological symbolism continue to generate lively debates in the art and medical professions (Cernuschi, 1992, p. 18). Despite the debates about the meaning and use of dreams, we believe that dream analysis is an important dimension of the process of understanding ourselves, students, and family, as well as ethics in our postmodern world.

Historical and Contemporary Approaches to Ethics

The first part of this chapter is devoted to exploring autobiography, identity construction, aesthetics, dreams, and the self. Throughout this chapter, we constantly connect these topics to narrative reflection. Without establishing an autobiographical context for our teaching convictions on ethics and education, the study of philosophical ethics remains a detached intellectual exercise. Moral decision making, educational policies, teaching practices, and personal value judgments do not occur in a vacuum; they are interwoven into the very fabric of our lives. Likewise, philosophical ethics and applied ethics are not separate disciplines. As we begin to explore theories of ethics in education, we continue to contextualize each philosophy within our autobiographical journey and the sociopolitical and cultural issues of the larger global milieu. Many traditional ethics texts often begin their investigation with an overview of ethical systems. We delay until now the study of ethical systems to be certain that the focus of this book is on justice, compassion, identity construction, autobiographical reflection, democracy, community, and ecological sustainability. Too often textbooks and teachers begin with a review of ethical systems without establishing a context for reflecting on such systems. We now review, discuss, critique, and contextualize four approaches to ethics: deontology, teleology, existentialism, and postmodernism.

Deontological Approaches

Deontological theories of ethics are rule-based systems that imply ethical obligations for all, with a stress on duty. *Deontology* is derived from the Greek words *dei* (necessity) and *ontology* (being), thus implying absolutist standards that cannot be questioned. For the deontologist, there is no higher authority than the rule or law. The source of the rule or law varies. Religious systems of ethics find the rule of law in the "will of God" as outlined in commandments and divinely inspired scriptures, as seen in Judaism, Christianity, Hinduism, and Islam. According to intuitionism, humans have an "inbuilt" sense of right and wrong that does not depend on rational processes. The rule of law is a natural state and a conscience is built into the human psyche. This conscience allows individuals to know and conform to the rules of law and religion. Traditionalism teaches that moral duty is what is expected by the culture of a particular people. Thus, social mores and expectations direct ethical decisions, and the conscience is shaped rather than built in. Rationalism states that morality is established by reason in regard to basic human obligations (the things we ought to do). Human emotions cloud reason and clearheaded logic. Thus, we must eliminate self-interest and fear in favor of behavioral imperatives. As set forth by the most famous deontologist, eighteenth-century philosopher Immanuel Kant (1724–1804), the "categorical imperative" has two criteria:

- *Universalization*—Act only according to that maxim by which you can at the same time will that it should become a universal law. This might be paraphrased as do unto others as you would have them do unto you.
- *Ontology*—Act so that you treat humanity, whether in your own person or in that of another, always as an end and never as a means only.

For Kant and other deontologists who subscribe to the notion of categorical imperatives, human beings are never instruments but always an end in and of themselves.

Critics of deontology contend that deontological systems of ethics can quickly become legalistic, inflexible, and unjust. First of all, the rules and laws are not always clear. Human interpretations—even of divine laws—are essential. Courts, constitutional conventions, and church councils meet regularly to interpret or amend laws. The human conscience has evolved and changed over time; acts that were once considered illegal or immoral in one civilization or social context have been accepted in another. For a child growing up in a Roman Catholic community in the 1940s or 1950s, eating meat on Friday was considered a major transgression against the law of God. Of course, this was not a major problem in south Louisiana, where eating seafood is a way of life. However, by the late 1960s the rules had changed, and today few Catholics abstain from eating meat on Fridays. But in an interesting twist of events, vegans and vegetarians do not eat meat at all and often advocate for the ethical treatment of animals. In the early 1970s as a student in California, I (Patrick) studied liberation theology and Catholic social justice encyclicals, and I became aware of the interrelationship between the destruction of the South American rain forest, political opposition to land reform for peasants in Central America, and the consumption of beef in North America. I stopped eating beef and pork not only on Fridays but also every other day of the week. My thinking about beef consumption has evolved over the years as I have gradually become a vegetarian. Church laws and practices have also changed. The same can be said of social regulations. For example, in my native Louisiana some forms of interracial marriage were not only illegal until 1978 but also remained a social stigma well into the 1990s in some rural communities. Critics of deontology can present hundreds of historical examples of laws and rules that have multiple interpretations in various communities, as well as laws that have changed over time. We examine this in more detail in Chapter 2 when we review hermeneutics.

Another problem deontological systems of ethics must address is the dilemma of what to do when rules contradict one another. Some would propose a graded system of rules whereby "save life" takes precedence over "tell the truth," and "report abuse" takes precedence over "obey your parents." However, once rules are graded by levels of importance, the rule is no longer absolutely applicable in every situation. Finally, other critics believe that deontology creates an atmosphere of adversarial law rather than a community of healing. Adversarial law mitigates against "caring" (Noddings, 1992) and "community" (Bauman, 1993).

Deontologists, obviously, disagree with the analysis of these critics, often contending that identifying contradictions does not negate the categorical imperative to treat human beings as ends in every situation. We once heard a deontological ethicist present this scenario to a college audience: Suppose a child was living with her biological parents but was being emotionally and physically abused on a regular basis. A judge intervenes and removes the child from the family and decides to place the child in a foster home. The only foster parents available are two lesbian women. The speaker argued that even if it could be demonstrated that these lesbian women would never physically abuse the child and that they were loving and compassionate people, the judge must not place the child in the home with the lesbian women. In fact, he insisted, it would be better to leave the child in her home with the abusive biological parents rather than place the child in this foster home. The speaker based his decision on his belief in the absolute law of parental rights and a religious law in his church prohibiting same-sex relationships. He argued that adherence to these fundamental laws is always in the best interest of the child, even if in the short term it may appear that a loving home with lesbian parents is better than a violently abusive home with the biological parents. How did this deontologist respond to questions of graded systems of morality? He answered without hesitation. If the Nazis knock at the door and ask if you have Jews hiding in the attic, you must not lie. Why? Because if you violate the law of truth telling, you may end up endangering others who will lose their lives or initiate other events that will result in unimagined evil. Individuals must not calculate the possible outcome of their moral decisions. Tell the truth in all circumstances, honor parental rights in all circumstances, and follow all of the commandments to the letter of the law in all circumstances, and good will overcome evil, the deontologist insisted. Deontology remains a dominant philosophy of ethics in many fundamentalist communities in the world, and deontologists believe that adherence to the categorical imperatives, religious commandments, and social norms must prevail in every circumstance.

Needless to say, there are many who reject deontology, calling it coldhearted, rigid, impractical, and biased, among other things. As a preservice teacher education student preparing for my first job as a high school teacher, I (Patrick) found myself in a deontological dilemma. During my interview with the principal in a K–12 rural school, I was asked if I would be willing to teach one section of eighth-grade speech in addition to two classes in my major area of certification, English, and two classes in my minor area of certification, mathematics. I was anxious to secure my first teaching position, so I enthusiastically agreed, and the principal hired me. I was elated. While preparing my classroom during the week before the school year began, a veteran teacher stopped by to introduce herself. We had a pleasant conversation, and I could tell that we would become fast friends. Before she left my room, she asked a question that caught me off guard: "By the way, the principal didn't assign you to teach the class from hell, did he?" I laughed hesitantly and replied, "No. He didn't mention anything about teaching a class from hell." She clarified that none of the tenured faculty agreed to teach the eighth-grade speech class because the students had assaulted a teacher the previous year, and two of the students were on probation for fighting and suspicion of drug dealing on campus. Everyone wanted to catch these criminals in the act so they could be expelled. I froze. "Why, yes, I have been assigned to teach the eighth-grade speech class," I mumbled.

For the next week, I panicked. I was not certified as a speech teacher, and I had taken only one speech class in college. I was so busy preparing lessons for my English and mathematics classes that I had time to read only one chapter ahead in the speech book. I tried to remain confident, hoping I could teach the so-called class from hell, especially because I was intent on impressing my new principal and succeeding in my first teaching assignment. As the first day of school approached, I was apprehensive, fearful, and excited all at the same time.

My morning classes were excellent, and as the day progressed I became exhausted. The last period of the day was eighth-grade speech. The best way to describe the situation is mayhem. It was like the turmoil in Michelle Pfeiffer's classroom in the movie *Dangerous Minds,* only I was not a female ex-Marine and no one was filming a fictional movie. This was a war zone. I suppose these students prided themselves on driving teachers away. For years they had been labeled failures, drug addicts, behavior disordered, and incorrigible by teachers and administrators. They were living up to the adults' expectations.

Looking back on the situation, I am not sure they really hated me personally. They resented the authority I represented. The ringleaders of the class were two older boys who had been retained many times in previous grades. "Mike" was black and "Scooter" was white, and they were both on probation. I was told that the entire staff was carefully monitoring Mike and Scooter in hopes of catching them at any infraction. The next incident meant expulsion.

After a few days of classes, I could understand why the faculty and administration were trying to catch Mike and Scooter to expel them. The two boys were sly and devious. I could see it in their eyes; I could feel it in their insults. They could curse, push, banter, and provoke right up to the limit. They also manipulated the younger students into doing much of their dirty work for them. Part of me supported the law-and-order approach of the school administration; clearly, my classroom would be a more pleasant environment without these two drug dealing, foul-mouthed, incorrigible criminals. Many teachers joked, with a spooky seriousness, that corporal punishment was not suitable for Mike and Scooter—only capital punishment would solve the problem.

Weeks went by and I grew more frustrated. I would go home at night confused and emotionally drained. I recalled reading in my undergraduate education classes that most new teachers do not last in the profession more that five years; the stress of teaching accelerates burnout. I never believed the statistics, and I loved teaching, coaching, counseling, and nurturing young minds and hearts. I was determined to be a compassionate and inspiring teacher, an academically challenging pedagogue, and an active extracurricular sponsor and coach. However, within a few short weeks I had developed a deep animosity toward some of my students. I kept wondering what was going on. My undergraduate teacher training program had not prepared me to deal with Mike and Scooter and other belligerent, angry students of diverse cultural backgrounds.

One Friday afternoon in the midst of my desperation, an amazing incident occurred. The lesson called for students to practice duet acting skits. The teacher manual instructed me to pair up students in cooperative learning dyads. Each dyad would then present a skit in front of the class. But no way was I going to relinquish what little control I had achieved with this group, even if the lesson called for duet acting practice. In fact, I had learned that it was best not to let the students speak in speech class, so I just lectured about duet acting techniques while most students slept or talked. A few conscientious students pretended to take notes while I pretended to teach. The week was almost over, and Thanksgiving vacation was only a month away.

I introduced the duet acting lesson with instructions on methods of staging, voice inflection, props, and enunciation. When I started to read the first selection from the textbook, "Little Red Riding Hood and the Big Bad Wolf," the class from hell howled like wolves, the boys made obscene comments about Red Riding Hood, and the girls hid their embarrassed giggles. Then Mike and Scooter shouted out something that caused me to reevaluate my teaching methods on the spot. In retrospect, my response to their question changed my philosophy of education. "Hey, teacher man, we'll do a duet acting skit for you, but not that 'Little Red Riding Hood' shit. We'll do 'Mike and Scooter and the Big Bad Drug Dealer.' " The entire class went crazy. They howled even louder and clapped in unison for their class heroes. I am not sure whether Mike and Scooter were serious, but I had a flash of either stupidity or genius and said, "OK, y'all come up here and perform for the class. Let's see what you can do."

I moved to the back of the room while Mike and Scooter swaggered confidently to the front. The class fell silent in anticipation. All eyes were fixed on the front of the room. Were Mike and Scooter going to perform or were they intent on embarrassing me, their novice teacher? The few conscientious students kept glancing back at me to be sure I knew what I was doing. Mike and Scooter adjusted themselves, cleared their throats, took a deep breath, and then performed a stunning rendition of a drug bust. They knew the gestures, the street language, the legal terminology, the intonation, and the inflections. Their improvisation, albeit clumsy in the moment, was a brilliant performance. The class burst into rousing applause that still rings in my ears when I recall this story. Then the bell rang and my class from hell scattered for the weekend.

The following Monday many of my eighth graders returned to class with duet acting skits they had dreamed up over the weekend at an overnight party with Mike and Scooter: "Alice in Drug Land," "Peter Eats a Wolf," "Goldie Locks up the Bears," and the like. Although I did not care for the innuendos, I was amazed that this unruly class was actually excited about participating. I worried that the principal might not like the curricular deviation, but no one had been in my classroom to observe yet, so I took a chance and let the kids create their own duet acting skits.

Although most of the skits were crude and awkward, Mike and Scooter had actually polished their piece nicely. I was impressed. So I asked them to bring props the next day and perform for the class. I sat in the back of the room to judge their duet acting skit. Everyone was attentive. Mike and Scooter used handcuffs, drug paraphernalia, police clubs, and rope to create a realistic drug bust scene. As Scooter pushed Mike up against the wall, slapped on the handcuffs, and started to search his crotch for drugs, the principal burst into the room, grabbed the boys by their collars, and shoved them against the blackboard. The principal had the imposing physique of a professional wrestler and wore cowboy boots and an oversized Texas belt buckle. As he slammed the boys into the wall, he yelled, "This is it. You knew you were on probation. This is your last fight in this school." We all froze in shock. My jaw dropped; I could not utter a word. As the principal began to drag Mike and Scooter out of the room, he noticed his new speech teacher, mouth agape, in the back row. The boys wiggled and complained that they were not really fighting. The principal looked to me for affirmation. I could only stutter, "It was a duet acting skit, sir." He turned beet red and told me to see him in his office after class. With great reluctance, he released the boys, growled at them, and slammed the door as he stormed out of the room.

The class from hell cheered wildly and shouted congratulatory comments like, "Great job, Mike and Scooter. Y'all showed him." Then they congratulated me for helping them embarrass "the principal from hell." I became their reluctant hero.

As I sheepishly walked into the principal's office after school, I was a nervous wreck. I wanted to tell him about my progress with these students. I wanted to beg him to let me continue with this experimental curriculum. I wanted to tell him that Mike and Scooter were good actors, albeit unconventional. Instead I listened to his sermon about school rules and said "yes, sir" when he told me to get back to the textbook and keep the brats quiet. He also reminded me that the entire staff wanted Mike and Scooter expelled for the sake of the other students and that it was my duty to help catch the boys breaking the rules.

I was torn. I knew that drugs were a serious problem in the school and community. I also realized that Mike and Scooter were probably the ringleaders and drug dealers. I believed that the orderly conduct of students was essential for good learning, and I knew that the rules of behavior for students were clearly stated in the student and faculty handbooks. In fact, I supported most of the rules. I wanted a safe and drug-free environment as much as the rest of the faculty, administration, board, and parents. But I also knew that I was beginning to reach these kids using unconventional methods. The drug skit provided an opening not only for good lessons on acting, but also for discussions about the consequences of drug and alcohol abuse.

I was young, and my new job was on the line, so I resisted the urge to challenge the school policy as articulated by the principal and board. However, a few weeks later an invitation arrived from the local university for my students to participate in an eighth-grade speech tournament. I asked my class if they would like to attend. "No way!" they laughed. "No way we'll go someplace with those speech nerds!" But from the back of the room, Mike and Scooter shouted, "We'll go." I was in shock. "Really?" I asked. "Sure, if we can do our drug bust skit."

I was caught. The principal had banned the skit from the curriculum. However, I took a risk and said, "OK, this isn't a classroom assignment. Just clean up the language and eliminate the drug paraphernalia, and I'll let you enter the tournament." Once Mike and Scooter signed up, the rest of the students all wanted to attend as well.

It was quite a sight to behold my unruly eighth graders dressed up in suits and skirts at the speech tournament. Mike and Scooter developed a cultlike following in each round of the tournament. Although all my other students were eliminated before the semifinal round, Mike and Scooter actually advanced to the final round. As they entered the auditorium for the final competition, they were in shock. They ran to me in protest: "It's not fair. One of the judges is a nun from the Catholic school!" I convinced Mike and Scooter to do their best and not worry about judges. The final round progressed, and at the awards ceremony Mike and Scooter won first place. Even the Catholic nun had voted for them.

I returned to school on Monday with the trophies. The principal had a tradition of reading over the public address system the names of all academic and sporting awards from the weekend. When I brought him the trophies, he looked at the names, frowned, grabbed the trophies, threw them in the trash can, and said, "Kids on probation cannot receive awards. Get back to your classroom." I was shocked and furious but still afraid to challenge the principal's authority. So I went back to the class empty-handed. Instead of hearing their names called out over the school announcements, and instead of receiving trophies to take home, Mike and Scooter lost their reward for an excellent performance. The class was furious. They refused to participate in speech for the rest of the year.

Although the students never blamed me personally, the class from hell reverted to their old behavior. I did purchase two new trophies at the end of the year and took them to Mike and Scooter at their homes. But the substitutes could never replace the original awards. They appreciated my gesture, I think, but it did not seem to mean much to them. I transferred to another school the next year, and I heard that Mike and Scooter were eventually expelled. Someone told me years later that they ended up in prison for drug dealing.

These events from early in my teaching career shaped my thinking about rules and laws. The principal was technically correct; the school board policy prohibited students on probation from receiving awards. The principal was also admired in the community for his vigilance in the enforcement of policies against drug and alcohol use. He adopted a deontological philosophy of absolute law and order for the good of the entire school campus. However, he also forfeited a possible chance to reform this class by looking at other alternatives to strict discipline and punishment.

These events remind us of the complexity of ethical decision making. Obviously, the deontological philosophy did not make sense in the circumstances of my speech class. As we review the next three ethical systems, let us think about alternative ways to approach discipline and punishment in schools and classrooms. Let us also consider the potential consequences of abandoning a deontological approach in favor of one of these other ethical systems. What are the possible positive outcomes of implementing these other ethical systems, and when might a deontological approach be more appropriate?

Teleological Approaches

Teleological systems of ethics derive their name from the Greek word *telos* (end or goal); they determine the morality of an action from the results it produces rather than the law that was followed. Thus, teleological systems are often called *consequentialist ethics.* If I do *A,* what will be the consequences? If I do *B,* what will be the consequences? Various consequences are evaluated in order to derive ethical systems and determine moral actions. In short, the goal of teleological ethics is to discover the best results.

As with deontology, there are a variety of teleological systems. Those systems that focus on results that are good for the individual are called *personal systems* of ethics. These include hedonism, acting so as to maximize pleasure; epicureanism, acting so as to avoid pain and mental anguish; and ethical egoism, acting according to what produces individual happiness and self-interest, for no one can know with certainty what will produce happiness in others. Even altruism can apply here. If altruism gives a person pleasure, then it produces a self-interest. So, if Mother Teresa derived pleasure from helping the poor and dying, then she was acting out of ethical egoism.

Those systems that focus on results that are good for others rather than for the individual are called *group systems.* Jeremy Bentham (1748–1832) was a leading proponent of this ethical stance. He ascribed to quantitative utilitarianism, an ethical stance that calls for the individual to act so as to maximize pleasure and minimize pain. Of course, this so-called hedonistic calculus assumes first of all that it is possible to calculate and measure pleasure and pain. John Stuart Mill (1806–1873) refined this position and developed what is called *qualitative utilitarianism.* This form of utilitarianism seeks to assure the greatest pleasure for the greatest number. Lifeboat analogies are often used to explain this ethical position. If the *Titanic* is sinking and there is only room for a limited number of people to be saved, who should be selected to enter the lifeboats? Women and children? The first-class passengers? Those most likely to survive? The elderly and infirm? Those with power and money? Random selection? Should families stay together? Bentham's utilitarian ethics requires that we calculate the maximum benefit with the least amount of pain and suffering. Mill's utilitarian approach would seek the survival of the largest number of people.

What concerns are raised by teleological systems that promote hedonism, epicureanism, ethical egoism, and utilitarianism? Should ethics focus on personal happiness, maximum pleasure, minimum pain, and the greatest good for the greatest number of people?

The first problem is that there is no solution to how to resolve conflict in egoism. What if the personal needs of one individual conflict with the personal needs of another? Second, how can we assess or anticipate the greatest good for the greatest number? Utilitarianism violates Kant's second principle of categorical imperatives, thus resulting in some people being used as a means instead of an end, and the rights of some individuals are violated in the name of the greatest good for the greatest number of people. Critics of utilitarianism contend that it forces the rights of individuals to be violated. They also point out that even in a democracy a tyranny of the majority is never permitted; the minority is always protected with inalienable rights that may not be superseded by the will of the majority.

The third concern with utilitarian ethics is how to evaluate the motive for an action. Unlike deontologists who insist on an absolute norm, utilitarians must evaluate the motive for an act. Although an individual may receive pleasure from an act, the motive may not be personal pleasure. For example, if an individual receives a reward for an act of heroism, did she or he perform the act to help a person in need or to receive a monetary reward or public recognition? Depending on the circumstances, either scenario could have been the case. Critics of utilitarianism contend that there is no way to judge with certainty the motives for any human action or the potential results of any ethical action. Behavior can be disguised to manipulate for selfish interests, and no one will know for sure how to calculate the intent of any action.

The final concern with utilitarianism is that numbers alone do not always tell us what the greatest good is. We must inquire into the nature of the persons involved. Do we value every life the same? Are Adolf Hitler and Mother Teresa of equal value? Is there such a thing as an innocent life that deserves one type of treatment and a criminal life that deserves, say, the death penalty? Can individual lives be judged differently? Who is more innocent? Who is to be condemned? These questions lead to the critique that utilitarianism can justify violating some human rights in the name of utility. And because our own self-interest and happiness are not clear and predictable, utilitarianism leads to a problem of accountability.

One of the more contentious social issues that relies on utilitarianism for guidance is euthanasia. Some countries, notably the Netherlands, have laws that allow doctors to assist terminally ill patients with medication that will lessen pain and hasten death. Some states in the United States, notably Oregon, have enacted legislation that allows medical doctors to do the same as those in the Netherlands. Attorney General John Ashcroft, representing a deontological philosophy, attempted to use his national office to overturn the assisted suicide law in Oregon in 2001. Some states, notably Michigan, have prosecuted and jailed medical doctors, such as the famous Dr. Jack Kevorkian, who have assisted terminally ill patients with suicide. Some have even called Kevorkian "Dr. Death" and labeled him a murderer. However, there continues to be a steady flow of terminally ill or severely suffering people who seek pain medication that will reduce their misery and potentially end their lives. Others specifically seek doctors who will help terminate their lives. Critics of euthanasia point to the many dangers of this practice: potential murder of the elderly and infirm by greedy or angry relatives; diminishment of the value of individual human life; rash decisions by ill or infirm people in moments of despair. Supporters of euthanasia laws also make strong arguments for assisted suicide: compassion for those who are suffering and dying; individual freedom to choose death with dignity; options for the terminally ill.

Some religious figures, such as Bishop Joseph Bernardin of Chicago in the 1980s, have publicly discussed their spiritual perspective on the process of dying. Bernardin is famous for writing about the "seamless garment of life" in which he argues for the sanctity of human life, thus leading him to oppose abortion, capital punishment, euthanasia, murder, war, and violence against human life in any circumstance. Bishop Bernardin himself valiantly fought a long battle with cancer. Although many admire the Bishop Bernardins of the world, others turn to utilitarianism to support their belief that each circumstance is unique and that decisions about medication, resuscitation, feeding tubes, organ transplants, and the like must be made by individuals in their living wills and/or in consultation with their doctors. When individuals are unconscious or incapacitated, family members and medical professionals often must make gut-wrenching life-and-death decisions. Family members may even vigorously disagree about the best course of action, thus revealing the astonishing complexity of ethical decision making.

The following narrative is based on a true story about a family that faced such an emotional crisis. This story is titled *Beloved,* and it provides insight into the frustrations and complexity of end-of-life decisions. It was written by my (Patrick) mother, Pattie C. S. Burke, many years after the death of her brother and my uncle, David Cotter. All of the names of the characters in the story have been changed except David's. As you read this creative nonfiction narrative, look for examples of the ethical systems we have discussed.

If Mother were still alive, this story would be stuck somewhere behind my lips. The truth of it would have killed her. Or, perhaps, she would have killed me, even though I was motivated to act on her behalf more than on his; to alleviate her despair rather than his; to preserve her physical and mental strength, rather than relieve the agony of his inability to have neither.

It was the first week of January. When Mother called, I was curled up in my soft polyester robe, sipping weak decaffeinated coffee and reading *The Arizona Republic.* I was finally snug at home, after having spent the holidays in the damp cold of north Louisiana.

"Beverly, you might want to think about coming back."

"What happened?" I felt the agony of those few seconds when people try to break bad news gently.

"Well, your brother's in the hospital. He came downstairs last night . . . "

"Mother, what is it?"

" . . . and said he was really sick. Wanted me to take him to the VA hospital right away."

"Is he okay?"

"He has pneumonia."

I relaxed my grip on the phone. Pneumonia is curable in a 47-year-old man. Even so, I realized that Mother needed me. I had two weeks of vacation remaining before classes started at ASU, so another week or 10 days away was doable.

"I'll call Delta and make reservations for tomorrow. Tell David I'm coming to nag him about taking care of himself."

When I arrived at the Shreveport Airport, Mother was in the front row of people waiting at the gate. Her frown was deep, even when she recognized me coming toward her. She didn't linger over our hug but grabbed my coat sleeve and hurried me toward Baggage Claim.

"He's in a coma. They took him to Intensive Care. Made me leave."

"How could . . . ?"

"He seemed better yesterday. Then, this morning the doctor said he wasn't responding to the medication. It all happened so fast."

When we reached the hospital, the nurse allowed us to see David, but only for 15 minutes. "Rules of the Intensive Care Unit," she said.

She led us to the first cubical and pulled the curtain back along its ceiling track. Mother rushed to David's bedside, held his hand and began to smooth his hair back from his sallow forehead. I walked slowly toward the other side of the bed, trying to absorb the reality of what had happened to my brother. His body was covered with a sheet that was pulled across his chest and tucked under his arms. Lengths of thin, worm-like tubes snaked across the sheet, carrying fluids into and away from his body. A larger tube filled his mouth. And his eyes—those pale blue eyes that disappeared into vitreous fluid whenever we queried him about the Korean War—those eyes were covered with white pads, concealing any secrets that might have been revealed.

I slipped between the bed and a variety of equipment, kissed my brother's cheek, and said words that didn't make a whole lot of sense: "It's me—your big sister. I want you to get well." I wanted to believe that he heard me when I said, "I love you," because we hadn't said that to each other in a long time.

Our 15-minute visit was over and, with the help of a nurse who promised to call immediately if there was any change, I was able to convince Mother that we should pick up a shrimp po-boy and go home for the evening.

The next morning we began a daily routine of hospital by day and dinner and home by night. A week later the doctor told us that there was no detectable brain activity, no hope. It would be merciful to let him go. Mother argued so vigorously that I was embarrassed.

"Don't tell me there's no hope." Her eyes narrowed, and teeth clinched as she stared into the doctor's face. "Look at his hand." She rubbed David's hand and it jerked—slightly, but it did jerk. "There's no way you can tell me there's no brain activity."

Doctor Hammond tried to explain that this was an involuntary movement, but as Mother had said, there was no way that he was going to tell her anything. No one could tell her anything, least of all her daughter. Her pastor, Father Francis, came that afternoon and gave David the Last Rites. She wouldn't even listen to him.

The next day the nurses in ICU brought in a chair so that Mother could sit beside the bed. They didn't limit her time with her son as they had before. I had brought a sketchbook and Castel drawing pencils, instruments to subdue the helpless anger that I was feeling. I stood against the wall behind Mother's chair and began to sketch. I drew the line of her hip balanced on the edge of the straight chair. My pencil followed her back, curved forward, shoulders hunched. I drew her hand holding his while she stroked the pallid, marble-like skin of his knuckles, anticipating the slightest movement, real or imagined. This was her beloved son—this was her *Pieta* with a ventilator.

I rushed out to the telephone booth determined to do something—anything. I placed a call to Father Francis. He agreed to meet me at three o'clock in Doctor Hammond's office. Maybe the words of a priest added to mine would carry more weight.

"I can't unplug the ventilator against your mother's will," Doctor Hammond said. "I've already stopped the drip medication, which is no longer beneficial, but there are some things that I can't do."

"But I'm his sister," I argued, "and I should be able to make a decision when my mother's incapable of comprehending the truth."

"I wish I could help you, but I can't do something that's both immoral and illegal."

"Doctor Hammond." Father Francis spoke so softly that we were compelled to listen. "Mercy is justice. Mercy is the greater morality."

At 2 A.M. the phone rang. David had died. When we entered the ICU, a nurse and two aides were standing around his bed. Mother never looked at the ventilator, with its plug dangling free near the floor.

A less tragic example of a utilitarian dilemma is found in the story of Rodrigo Rhodes, one of my (Dana) high school students in the spring of 1992. Rodrigo confessed to me that he had smoked pot on school grounds. Rodrigo and I had met for the first time eighteen months earlier when he transferred to the school where I was teaching. I was a first-year teacher at a private, single-sex boarding school that advertised: "Our faculty meets the needs of young men who are having academic difficulties in public and private schools through small classes, remediation, and an extremely structured schedule." Many students came to our school after having been suspended or expelled from their previous schools for nonviolent offenses such as tardiness, insubordination, and limited drug use. Rodrigo ended up at the school because his father was afraid that Rodrigo was too involved with his girlfriends and buddies and not concerned enough about his future. Rodrigo's grades were mostly Cs, Ds, and Fs at his Atlanta, Georgia, high school. Rodrigo was attending our boarding school against his will, and he definitely had no interest in following his father into a position as president of one of the largest banks in the United States.

Rodrigo and I hit it off immediately even though he racked up the highest demerit total in the school after two months. I found him to be an extremely creative ninth grader who loved to read and paint. I spent many nights in his room helping him with his homework and trying to prevent him from acting on the urge to escape what many of the students thought was an oppressive structure. "My demerits," he intimated, "are an attempt to get kicked out. I hate this place. It's a prison. I'm old enough to drive but I have to ask to go to the bathroom. The only difference between this place and the military is that we don't have to wear army uniforms and drink saltpeter." As it turns out, it was not the demerits that led to Rodrigo's expulsion in early November of his first year; it was marijuana.

I knew that many students—and several faculty—smoked pot, but I wasn't sure how involved Rodrigo was. I didn't believe it was an everyday thing for him. He was probably like many kids and smoked on Saturday afternoons or evenings on the mountain while he was hiking with friends. Nonetheless, Rodrigo and another first-year student were caught by Paul Jones, a faculty member who was known for spending his weekends following kids up the mountain in hopes of catching them smoking pot. Rodrigo was expelled by the disciplinary committee a few days after Paul found them.

The ethical dilemma arose for me several months later. Rodrigo's dad had won his appeal to have Rodrigo reenrolled the next year. With the threat of military school lurking, Rodrigo returned for his sophomore year with a "yes sir!" attitude. He had struck a deal with his father that if he received all As and if he were a model citizen for a year, he could return to Atlanta for his junior year. Rodrigo definitely acted differently from the first day he returned. He was on time to his classes. He was in his room with lights out when the dorm monitors demanded it. He studied hard and made the dean's list the first semester. And, as far as I knew, Rodrigo stayed away from smoking pot.

Rodrigo and I had a trusting relationship. We would often talk in his room about girls, parents, and what he would be doing if he were at home. Somehow he trusted me enough to express his fears about the future, his sexual inhibitions, and his dislike of faculty and school policies. He also trusted me enough in March 1992, the second semester after his return, to confess that he had smoked pot on the mountain the night before. "I had to tell you, Mr. Rapp. I feel like shit. I've only smoked pot twice this year. Once in November and once last night. No one saw me."

I was stuck. According to the code of ethics for students, pot smoking, especially for second and third offenses, meant immediate expulsion. Our school made it explicitly clear to faculty that we were to have a zero tolerance policy when it came to drugs. "If we let one kid get away with drugs, every kid will get away with it," Steve, the faculty advisor to the Disciplinary Committee, would say. I knew that if I told Steve about Rodrigo's latest incident, Rodrigo would be expelled and probably shipped off within a week to a military school in Georgia. Rodrigo would hate military school and he would do anything to get kicked out, even if it meant something more drastic than cursing at faculty or smoking pot. I also knew that our school had been nicknamed "Reefer Ridge" by parents, teachers, and students at other schools as a way to express their lack of respect for our commitment to helping kids who needed second chances. Images were often more important than reality when it came time for parents to select schools. Our school's enrollment had dropped dramatically a few years earlier after a drug bust at the school, which was covered extensively in the media. So, as a school community, we were trying to shed the "drug haven" label into order to get enrollment back up to nonemergency levels.

I was at a loss as to what to do. If I went to the Disciplinary Committee with Rodrigo's confession and he were expelled, wouldn't it send a clear signal to other students and the outside community that our school was changing for the better? Wouldn't other kids get the message and quit smoking pot if their friend was kicked out? Wouldn't I be acting in the best interest of students, the admissions office, alumni affairs, and even the children of faculty who lived on campus if I worked to get a drug user out of our midst? I also thought that if I turned in Rodrigo, my status as a first-year teacher would be greatly enhanced in my colleagues' eyes. Maybe it would mean I could have a role on the Disciplinary Committee or the prestigious Honor Committee. And, if I assumed a role on one or both of these committees, not only would my professional career be enhanced, but I also might be able to work within the committees to develop rules and policies that would be more supportive of future Rodrigos.

On the other hand, I couldn't imagine that Rodrigo would ever graduate from high school, much less military school, if he were expelled. I've known fathers who have kicked their kids out of the house after being expelled from our school, and some boys even ended up living on the streets as a result. Moreover, Rodrigo had come so far. He had gone beyond what was expected by his father and many of his teachers in terms of grades, attitude, and demerits. Should I risk his future to advance my career or the image of the school? Is Rodrigo different than Sam, Bob, or Eli? Should I trust that Rodrigo has not smoked pot three times a week in the last month and that his recent bad choice is not a patterned one? Do I owe more allegiance to the school, to Rodrigo, or to myself?

Ultimately, no adult would ever know of Rodrigo's confession to me. I decided not to turn him in, because I feared that Rodrigo's life would take a turn for the worse if he were expelled. I decided to go with my intuition and proceed on the basis that I could see how an overly competitive father and a severely structured living environment could lead young men to occasionally smoke pot as an escape. I never revealed this decision to any of my colleagues because I feared that many would not understand my actions, and a few might even use it in an attempt to have me fired. I wonder what Rodrigo is doing now.

Existential Approaches

Existential ethics is a philosophy committed to personal obligation for the good that cannot be decided by appealing to deontological rules or by anticipating utilitarian consequences in the future. Rather, the "right" can only be identified when an individual confronts a particular situation. Ethical actions and decisions can vary from person to person, from context to context, and from time to time—even for the same person. Existentialists often contend that existence precedes essence (a phrase credited to the premier French philosopher of the twentieth century, Jean-Paul Sartre) and thus individuals require freedom in order to act, but always with responsibility for the other. Existentialists rebel against the idea of the essence and universal ethic of the human person. An effort is made to humanize the ethical process because dehumanization is what allows genocide, war, holocaust, slavery, classism, child abuse, sexism, homophobia, and racism to flourish.

There are many varieties of existential ethics. The term *situation ethics* was coined by Joseph Fletcher (1905–1991), who argued that the only rule in ethics is to act in a "loving way." The loving thing to do has to be decided in each individual case. Based in some ways on the book of Romans, Chapter 13, in Christian Scripture, Fletcher argues that if an individual truly acts out of love, then he or she will do what is best in every circumstance.

Relational ethics is often articulated by Christian neo-orthodox theologians (often influenced by Martin Heidegger's work *Being and Time*) such as Karl Barth and Dietrich Bonhoeffer, and other theologians such as Reinhold Niebuhr and Richard Niebuhr and the Jewish philosopher Martin Buber. Relational ethics advocates that one do "what is fitting" in order to be true to one's character and responsible for one's actions and their consequences on others—what Buber calls a sense of "I and Thou." Relational ethics strongly emphasizes actions that acknowledge our relational bonds with other people.

Virtue ethics shifts the focus from what one should "do" to what one should "be." Character formation is stressed rather than rules for deciding actions. The virtues to be pursued are determined by the "narrative community" to which one belongs. Lawrence Kohlberg's hierarchy of morality focuses on virtues and character formation as integral to moral development. However, Carol Gilligan (1982) exposes the gender bias in Kohlberg's research that used only male subjects, and she challenges the universal hierarchy of moral development in her book *In a Different Voice*.

Another existential approach is called *ethics of ambiguity* by Simone de Beauvoir (1908–1986). She proposed that a way out of existential absurdity, which leaves one paralyzed in the face of tyranny and injustice, is through the notion of ambiguity. The ethics of ambiguity allows us to act for justice even in the midst of uncertainty about ethical systems and outcomes. She challenged Sartre's contention that the essence or meaning of things is not predetermined by any outside force, because meaning is constructed by men. The response to this from de Beauvoir was "by men, and that is the whole problem!" The world does not contain any transcendent meaning; we make up meaning as we go along, filtering the world through language. Thus, de Beauvoir started to question whether the role of social conditioning in limiting freedom might not be more severe than Sartre said it was. Later thinkers (such as Michel Foucault, whom we examine in the section on postmodern approaches) agreed and amplified this doubt. In her most famous book, *The Second Sex* (1948b), de Beauvoir contends that people are brought up in a world defined by men and that women are defined by men. She doubts the freedom of women to break away from the definition by men of women as secondary if women never encounter any other possible definitions.

As we have examined in detail, a central element of existentialism is the notion of time. Ethical decisions are made in the moment. For some, such as Jean-Paul Sartre in *Being and Nothingness,* the moment is disconnected from past and future and thus absurd. For others, such as Søren Kierkegaard and Simone de Beauvoir, time is proleptic, integrating past, present, and future, and offers the possibility of meaning and hope.

The critics of existentialism claim that Fletcher's situational ethics created ethical relativism and hedonism. They point out that there is a difference between the commitment of love and ethical relativism. Another critique is that the moment is not always clarifying. It can be difficult to make ethical decisions in a crisis or in the midst of competing concerns because events become disconnected from the whole of life. What are the complex factors that influence ethical decision making? How influential is language in defining and manipulating human beings? These and other difficult questions (the focus of Chapter 2) sometimes make us want to retreat into the safety and security of deontological rules and laws. For some, existential philosophy is not a system of ethics at all, but rather a commentary on the angst of the human condition in the modern world. Postmodern ethics, the subject of the next section, seeks to find a way out of this dilemma to address the concerns of the critics of deontology, teleology, and existentialism.

We experience existential dilemmas every day that we work with students. For instance, Paul, a fourth-grade teacher and friend of mine (Dana), has recently felt extremely torn between what he sees as the potential essences and aims of education and what he feels forced to do in the classroom. Paul believes that education, especially in the elementary school years, should involve extended opportunities for exploration, creativity, imagination, and play. He neither dismisses what have come to be known as the 3Rs, nor the potential for developing new frameworks, community-generated curricular standards, and evaluation. Paul does object to what he refers to as an overzealous, irrational, socially naive, and manipulative educational agenda that permits almost no leeway or voice for teachers and students.

Up until this year, Paul had convinced himself that the politicians and CEOs who devised Ohio's educational reform structure were motivated by socially responsible intentions. But after years of witnessing his students suffer through periods of hunger, homelessness, environmental racism, and now curricular alienation, Paul believes the so-called reformers have devised a system to legitimate these conditions, not ameliorate them. More and more, Paul feels he is betraying his students and his conscience when he follows administrators' orders to neglect outdoor experiments, discussions of local history, and even recess in favor of "teaching to the test." As a student of mine and Patrick's at Ashland, and as a visual artist, Paul is aware of the potential for curricula to unleash exploration, autobiography, spiritual development, and the imagination. Therefore, the recent movement toward a homogenized curriculum with emphasis on high-stakes tests—a "whitewashing," as Paul sees it—is a crime against the creativity, spirit, and intelligence of children. In just two years, Paul has witnessed and experienced many of the side effects of the standards and accountability agenda. Students and teachers are more stressed out and silenced, creative and passionate people are leaving teaching, students are placed on antianxiety and antidepression medication, students are throwing up on testing days, there are more fights at his school, administrators are at war with teachers over high test scores, and teachers have vented their frustration on students. Paul believes that what is happening in his school is both unjust and absurd.

In a recent discussion in a graduate course, Paul raised these issues through a series of questions: Is it possible that the better I do according to state standards, the greater damage I could be doing to students? Is it my role to enact and enforce a state and district curriculum that is more harmful to children and their communities than beneficial? Is it fitting for me to lie, pretend, and convince many of the Hispanic, African American, and eastern European children before me that our educational system is fair and just? What happens if I stop teaching the manipulative state curriculum altogether and work with students in ways that are supportive, healing, and caring? When will administrators catch on? Will I be fired if they find out? What will schools in the future look like if adults like me do not take a stand now? Will I be doing the greatest good for the students I work with if I take a public stand and refuse to administer the tests? What is justice? And to whom do I owe the greatest allegiance?

I was convinced that Paul was going to emotionally and physically explode as I watched and listened to him wrestle with this ethically precarious situation. I also suspected that he would make a public "stand before the tank" and risk his position as a second-year teacher. In the last month or two, however, Paul has decided to hold back. "I'd love to speak out now," he says, "but I don't have tenure, and money is tight. I can't afford to lose my job and be blackballed by other districts." Paul has stated that his decision has less to do with rules of right and wrong and more to do with trying to balance a situation that would affect his students, his family, his career, and his health. He continues to ponder whether the benefits of risking a public statement and being fired outweigh the costs of not being there for the students he loves. "I'd hate to think that my replacement would be some unnurturing automaton who is addicted to Target Teach and high-stakes tests. It would kill the kids," he says.

Paul also says, however,

> I will work to quietly subvert the system by talking with students about the racial, social, and class biases of our curriculum and tests. When administrators come to my door and ask what strands and tenets I am following, I will rattle off some very behavioristic names and numbers to appease them, and then I'll close my door and try to support the children as much as I can in ways that let them be children and expose their

self-worth and personal histories. I will also continue to write editorials to the newspaper about the dehumanizing effects of the curriculum on children in this community, and I will use my artwork to prick the consciences of other teachers, parents, and professors—hopefully to fire them up, especially people who are tenured and in positions to speak and act out. In the future, I hope to be as public in my displeasure and refusal as Mitch Balonek in Toledo—the teacher who refuses to administer tests and who has picketed his central office because they have not acknowledged the evil conditions and effects of testing on students.

At the same time, Paul believes that the longer he remains silent and refuses to take a stand publicly, the greater the possibility that he will never act. "I know that most lasting changes—changes in human rights and dehumanizing conditions—have been brought about and initiated by people willing to risk their lives and their careers. I am almost there, but I don't feel the immediate situation, for me or my students, is right."

Postmodern Approaches

Postmodern ethics is the fourth and final system to be introduced in this chapter. Writings about postmodernity are contentious, and thus, like existentialism, no single definition is possible. Some contend that postmodernism has led to the "demise" of ethics and a substitution of aesthetics—a freedom from oppressive duties, commandments, and absolute obligation in a postdeontic age, where there is no excess and a demand for tolerance. Others contend that the postmodernist rejects modern methods of coercive normative regulation in political practice as well as the philosophical search for absolutes, universals, and foundations in theory while being committed to moral concerns such as human rights, social justice, peaceful cooperation, individual conduct and collective welfare, and ecological sustainability (Bauman, 1993, p. 4). These issues need to be seen and dealt with in novel ways.

French philosopher Michel Foucault (1926–1984) paved the way for Bauman and other postmodern ethicists. He took apart the phrase "knowledge is power" and analyzed it, studied it historically, and put it back together. He was interested in knowledge of human beings and the power that acts on human beings and influences their behavior. He began by asking what would happen if we doubt that we have any knowledge of "absolute truth." What then will "knowledge" mean? Maybe knowledge would become the majority power of rule and opinion. Could a minority impose its idea of the truth on the majority? Would physical coercion and mental manipulation be used to demand conformity? People who construct "the truth" are deciding matters that define all of humanity. If they can get enough people to believe them, that may be more important than some unknowable truth. Foucault was concerned with the methods people use to coerce others. How do they use this power to create belief? How do they use power to claim to be knowledgeable? How is this power used to know more about individuals than they know about themselves?

Foucault contended that power works through language. Language not only describes and defines human beings but also creates institutions to regulate human beings (e.g., hospitals, schools, factories, prisons, churches, courts). The social sciences categorize people into "normal" and "abnormal." Foucault was interested in finding out historically what constituted madness, criminality, perverted sexuality, and illness. Some philosophers have assumed that "normal" and "ethical" are universal concepts that have remained the same over time. Foucault examined historical documents and deconstructed this assumption. He found that definitions of *normal* and the treatment of abnormal persons have varied over time and place. And how was the "abnormal" understood? Only through the ideas of the "normal." In other words, normal people study, question, and become obsessed with the abnormal and eventually begin to regulate the abnormal people using their power to control. This operates in the same way as racial identity through negation rather than affirmation, which we discuss in Chapter 3.

The persons considered abnormal are silenced because they do not have the knowledge of the truth. Foucault wrote,

> We must see our rituals for what they are, completely arbitrary things. . . . [I]t is good to be dirty and bearded, to have long hair, to look like a girl when one is a boy (and vice versa); one must put "in play," show up, transform, and reverse the systems which quietly order us about. As far as I am concerned, that is what I try to do in my work. (p. x)

For Foucault this resistance isolates the individual and creates "special cases," which do not allow for generalizations. In his book *Discipline and Punish* (1979), Foucault tells the tale of power relations and oppression in an inquiry into prisons and forms of punishment. He contends that discourse (i.e., anything written or spoken using signs) has a role in power relations and that the seeming abstractions of discourse do have material effects on people's bodies because language is inscribed in our bodies. Thus, technical specialists work together to establish their field of study, dominant ideas, and specialized language. In effect, these ideas shape and structure our society. Foucault notes that words can be ameliorative and pejorative and that fields of study change (i.e., natural history becomes biology). Genealogies are formed—a series of infinitely branching and proliferating ideas without logic or order (p. 80). The complexity of genealogies is guided by accident, error, and opinion. Before the 1800s, for example, discipline was accomplished through public torture. After 1800, discipline became regulated and controlled. Foucault wanted to understand why this social change took place. He found that authorities worried that crowds were becoming unruly. Philosophers began to say that the desire to cause pain was not civilized.

Foucault documents the movement in the early nineteenth century toward punishment as regulation in prisons. This was accomplished in six ways:

1. **Spatialization:** Everyone has a place and with compliance can move to a better space.
2. **Minute control of activities,** especially by the use of timetables.

3. Repetitive exercises: Standardization and sufficient repetition were found to create automatic reactions to stimuli.
4. Detailed hierarchies: Each level keeps watch over the lower ranks.
5. Normalizing judgments: Continual analysis of whether the person disciplined deviates in any way from the normal. Punishments and rewards are given. This works on the inside of the person (i.e., in the madhouse, inmates work their way through wards for appropriate and sane behavior).
6. The panopticon: An architectural design for prisons in which the prisoner is isolated and observed at all times by a single person at a central tower. The panopticon is lighted so that inmates can see neither the observer nor other inmates.

The result? A docile worker who becomes reformed in prison to become an automaton for a capitalist factory. The recidivists return to prison and actually provide an advantage for the "normal" society. How? Those who do not accept the prevailing ideology imposed by the panopticon remain abnormal and can be kept away from the normal indefinitely in the prison system. Although Foucault's analysis of discipline and punishment in society deals specifically with prisons, the analysis can be applied to any institution that seeks to control those judged to be abnormal.

Reread Foucault's analysis and think about Mike and Scooter in the earlier story. Consider your own experiences in schools and classrooms. A major concern expressed by postmodernism and deconstruction is the marginalization and oppression of individuals by metanarratives of normalization. As we continue to examine the autobiographical nature of educational ethics, many more examples of such oppression will emerge.

Zygmut Bauman is one of the leading scholars of postmodern ethics. He believes that modern ethical thought and legislative practice operate under the twin banners of universality and foundations. According to Bauman, universality stood for the exceptionalist rule of one set of laws, and foundations stood for coercive powers of the state that rendered obedience to the rules sensible expectations (1993, p. 9). The moral thought and practice of modernity was animated by the belief in the possibility of a nonambiguous and nonaporetic (a contradiction that cannot be overcome or a conflict that cannot be resolved is aporetic) ethical code. While some may contend that the code has been found, modernists who recognize that the final code has not been found nonetheless expect that it will be discovered eventually. It is a disbelief in such a possibility that gives rise to the postmodern and the theories that Bauman articulates in the book *Postmodern Ethics*.

Elements of Bauman's postmodern perspective on ethics include the following:

1. Humans are morally ambivalent, and we need to learn how to live without guarantees of a perfect society or a perfect human being.
2. Moral phenomena are inherently "nonrational" and do not fit a "means–end" schema. They are not regular, repetitive, or predictable.

3. Morality is incurably aporetic. Few, if any, choices are unambiguously good. Most choices are made between contradictory impulses, and most moral choices, if acted on, lead to immoral consequences (e.g., domination, oppression, annihilation).
4. Morality is not universalizable. This does not endorse moral relativism and a nihilistic view of morality. Rather, the universalization of morality has silenced the moral impulse.
5. Morality is and is bound to remain irrational. The social management of morality is a complex and delicate operation that cannot but precipitate more ambivalence than it manages to eliminate.
6. Given this ambiguous state, the moral responsibility of being "for the other" precedes being "with the other" and is the first reality of the self.
7. Thus, for Bauman and others, postmodern ethics does not propose a relativism of morality nor a "do nothing" attitude. Rather, a positionality of "for the other" compels a moral stance.

A concrete example of an attempt to explicate the postmodern ethical stance is found in the publication "Catholics Speak Out," which was printed in the *New York Times* during the 2000 presidential election. I (Patrick) was one of the signers of this full-page ad that appeared in the *Times* to alert politicians to the fact that many people of various faiths support a more existential and postmodern approach to critical ethical issues. The text read as follows:

> The joys and the hopes, the griefs and the anxieties of the people of this age, especially those who are poor or in any way afflicted, these too are the joys and hopes, the griefs and anxieties of the followers of Christ (Pastoral Constitution on the church in the Modern World, Gaudium et Spes, Vatican II). There has been a lot of talk about the "Catholic vote." Now is the time for Catholic voters to talk. We agree with our bishops on many issues, but not all. For most of us, no single issue—including abortion—dominates our choices as voters. Our approach is deeply rooted in the gospel and the social justice teachings of our church. We believe that Congress, the President, and the People must work together to develop policies focusing on the common good, to protect our Earth, and to address the growing disparity between rich and poor people. That means we are looking for action on the following issues: **Universal Health Care**—Make quality health care accessible to all, regardless of income level. It is a human right, not a commodity; **Education**—Guarantee access to quality public education for all our children by equalizing school spending across boundaries, so children from poor districts have an equal chance. A well-educated citizenry is essential to democracy; **Social Security & Medicare**—Place Social Security and Medicare on a sound footing. Do not privatize Social Security. Our safety net shouldn't depend on Wall Street; **Gun Control**—Require child- and theft-proof locks, buyer screening, licensing, and registration. Nobody's "right to bear arms" should take precedence over the right to live; **Campaign Finance Reform**—Enact real campaign finance reform. Ban soft money and require full financial disclosure. Our democracy is threatened; **The Death Penalty**—Adopt a moratorium on

the death penalty. A system driven by fear and vengeance is not life-affirming, especially when poverty, racism, and laws that limit appeals and deny competent counsel often determine who lives or dies; **Civil Rights**—Support full civil rights for gay, lesbian, bisexual, and transgendered persons. Prevent discrimination and crimes against people because of their race, creed, gender, or sexual orientation by adopting hate crimes legislation and broadening laws barring employment discrimination. End racial profiling and police brutality; **Reproductive Health**—Support programs that make contraceptives, including emergency contraception, easily accessible to women and men here and in poor countries. Signers of this ad hold a wide range of views on the morality and legality of abortion, but we all seek to reduce its frequency. Catholic opinion is not monolithic on this subject; **Living Wages**—Make the minimum wage a living wage. Nobody can live on $5.15 an hour; **Environment**—Invest in research and development for clean energy. Expand mass transit. Fund programs that clean the water, preserve the forests and wetlands, and limit urban sprawl. The Earth must be respected and cherished as the source of life; **Globalization**—Support fair trade, not unbridled "free" trade. Significantly reform the World Bank and the International Monetary Fund. Cancel the debt of developing nations; **Immigration**—Enact fair immigration policies that protect workers and safeguard asylum seekers, including women fleeing practices such as genital mutilation and "honor" killings; **Drug Policy**—Reduce demand for drugs by providing treatment on request for drug users. Demilitarize drug policy. Billions spent on guns and helicopters in Colombia cannot remedy poverty and hunger. The Latin American region needs a mini-Marshall Plan, not a mini-Desert Strom; **Arms Control**—Ratify the nuclear test ban treaty. Drop the unworkable "Son of Star Wars" missile defense system that dramatically increases international tensions and drains our country's resources. Resume reduction of nuclear stockpiles; **Military Spending**—Stop funding discredited military programs such as the F-22 fighter and the aircraft carriers that even the military does not want. Use the money to pay a living wage to military personnel, and fund domestic and international aid programs that focus on people and the environment; **Cuba & Iraq**—Lift the economic sanctions against Cuba and lift the sanctions that restrict food, safe water, and medicine to Iraq. Action on the behalf of justice and participation in the transformation of the world fully appear to us as a constitutive dimension of the preaching of the Gospel ("Justice in the World" Synod of Bishops). (Catholics Speak Out, 2000)

This text reminds us of the myriad complex issues that must be addressed in the global community. Citizens in wealthy and industrialized nations have a particularly urgent responsibility to study and address these issues. Individual responses to each of these issues may vary, but the "Catholics Speak Out" text reminds us that thoughtful citizens are investigating these topics carefully and proposing specific action from a postmodern perspective. This document reflects the postmodern demand for justice, compassion, and ecological sustainability. However, in the political arena, disputes arise among leaders who may be committed to a different political philosophy or a different understanding of ethics.

The postmodern ethical stance was summarized by the Center for a Postmodern World (1990) in the following declaration, which urged humanity to address critical ethical issues and to transcend modernity in ways that include the following features:

A post-anthropocentric view of living in harmony with nature rather than a separateness from nature that leads to control and exploitation; a post-competitive sense of relationships as cooperative rather than as coercive and individualistic; a post-militaristic belief that conflict can be resolved by the development of the art of peaceful negotiation; a post-patriarchal vision of society in which the age-old religious, social, political and economic subordination of women will be replaced by a social order based on the "feminine" and the "masculine" equally; a post-Eurocentric view that the values and practices of the European tradition will no longer be assumed to be superior to those of other traditions nor forcibly imposed upon others combined with a respect for the wisdom imbedded in all cultures; a post-scientistic belief that while the natural sciences possess one important method of scientific investigation, there are also moral, religious and aesthetic intuitions that contain important truths that must be given a central role in the development of worldviews and public policy; a post-disciplinary concept of research and scholarship with an ecologically interdependent view of the cosmos rather than the mechanistic perspective of a modern engineer controlling the universe; and finally, a post-nationalistic view in which the individualism of nationalism is transcended and replaced by a planetary consciousness that is concerned about the welfare of the earth first and foremost. (p. 1)

The Center for a Postmodern World regards the cosmos as an organism rather than as a machine, the earth as a home rather than as a functional possession, and persons as interdependent rather than as isolated and independent. This introduction to some of the concepts of this manifesto reveals the dramatic paradigmatic shift in thinking that is required in order to introduce these ethical concepts into social, political, and educational discourses. Therefore, it is not surprising to us that there has been intense resistance to the postmodern ethical stance. We present another narrative that explicates this philosophy further.

I (Dana) recently ran into an ethical dilemma at our local YMCA. Each day when I exercised on a treadmill or step machine, Peter Bond, one of the attendants in the workout room, would engage me in a short conversation. Peter was a fifty-one-year-old man with a fascinating history. He had developed a strict regimen of long-distance running, homeopathic medicine, and positive thinking to overcome and live with a diagnosis of Hodgkin's disease at age twenty-six. He had an amazingly unique way of listening to and caring for people that undoubtedly grew out of his experience with Hodgkin's. People from all over town knew the name Peter Bond, not only because he was a friendly face at the YMCA, but also because Peter was one of those rare people who gave of himself to help others. People in their seventies and eighties would telephone Peter at all hours of the night if they lost their medication or if they needed a ride to the hospital. He would shovel their sidewalks for free and walk their dogs. I also watched Peter deliver newspapers for ailing elementary school carriers on more than one occasion. This ethic of care and compassion also carried over to Peter's job at the YMCA.

I became aware that Peter opened up the weight room at 5:30 A.M. several times a week, even though the YMCA officially opened at 6:00 A.M. He arrived early, he said, because several professional people had told him how hectic their schedules were. He gladly agreed to support their busy lifestyles even though he received no financial reimbursement. I began to ask Peter more questions about his history at the YMCA. He informed me that he had been working there about twelve years and that the YMCA management had communicated from the beginning that they would not pay him if he decided to open the facilities early or keep them open later. When I pressed him about his salary and benefits, Peter was hesitant. After several minutes of my badgering, Peter admitted that the Young Men's Christian Association payed him $6.75 an hour and kept his hours at thirty-four a week intentionally to avoid paying him health benefits. Maria, a single mother of two who swept the floors, cleaned the bathrooms, and vacuumed the hallways of the YMCA, conveyed a similar story. Like Peter, Maria often worked more than thirty-four hours a week in order to meet the demands of her job, yet she was never reimbursed. Maria also shared that she had to pick up another job at night to subsidize her YMCA income and to pay for her children's medical and dental bills. I knew that Peter's and Maria's stories were not unusual. In fact, millions of hardworking U.S. citizens do not have health care coverage and do not receive liveable wages. Many are working two or three jobs just to put food on the table and pay the rent. I knew Peter and Maria definitely fit into this category. What would happen if Peter needed emergency surgery? Does he avoid medical checkups? What happens if Maria's oldest child needs dental care? Who is home at night with Maria's children as she slaves away at a second job to pay the bills? Is this my responsibility, I wondered? Would I be willing to pay more than $250 for my membership? Would other members be willing to pay as well? What was the YMCA's responsibility to its employees or the responsibility of a Christian institution to people in general?

I decided to write a letter to the director of the YMCA to express my concern as well as my willingness to work toward creating a better system of support for Peter, Maria, and other YMCA employees. I heard nothing. After a month, I sent another letter and called several times. No response. While I was trying to make contact with the management, the YMCA employees began to express their concern to me that the management was encouraging them not to speak with me, or anyone else, about their salary or benefits. They feared retaliation to a certain degree, and a few employees, such as Maria, said they couldn't afford to lose their jobs. I asked Peter and Maria what I should do. "How can I support you?" I asked them. There weren't many answers and there still aren't. I tried speaking with a number of YMCA members about the predicament of YMCA employees, but many were resistant. Most were professionals whose jobs provided them benefits. Several suggested that Peter and Maria find other jobs if they weren't satisfied. When I asked them who would open up the weight room early each morning, one man in his early forties commented, "No problem. We can easily persuade someone else to do it." I thought about writing a letter to the local newspaper or sending out flyers that elucidated the importance of providing benefits to employees, but I decided not to because it might jeopardize Peter's and Maria's positions. Finally, after not being given an opportunity to meet with management, after relatively no success trying to convince members to raise their fees, and after feeling that I was on the point of endangering Peter's and Maria's major source of income, I decided to cancel my membership. In a letter to the management, I outlined the reasons for my decision and the history behind it. I made them aware that I understood that the provision of health benefits was not a minor one in terms of financial cost. I also expressed my belief that although the YMCA might not have the funds to provide or support health benefits for its employees, it had a responsibility to try to develop creative options and solutions. I questioned the extent to which the YMCA was honoring the Christian nature of its mission. "How can an organization that calls itself Christian not work for those who do not have insurance and who are barely making ends meet, especially when they are in your own organization?" Before I signed my name, I added, "I find it impossible to support an organization, especially one with a community service history, that is not willing to serve, work for, and support its own people."

It has been a year since I have exercised at the YMCA. I'm still uncertain if I made the most responsible decision for Peter and Maria. I wonder what would have happened if I had remained a member and used my encounters with other members in the gym to educate them about Peter and Maria's plight. Would more than a handful of people have agreed to support my initiative to raise membership fees? Would Peter and Maria have felt even more insecure in their positions if I had gone against their wishes and continued to pressure management? I don't know the answers to any of these questions. I did meet Maria in a grocery store a few months later, and we chatted for a few minutes. She intimated that the management was still suspicious about the questions I had raised, so suspicious that they are being careful to hire employees who will not bring the issue of health benefits to their attention or that of members. Maria did thank me at the end of our conversation for considering the struggles of her and her family. "Although on the outside we didn't accomplish much, it is nice to know that others care enough to fight for me." I'll always remember Maria's words. They stick with me when I listen to cashiers in supermarkets, bank tellers, waitresses, hotel cleaning people, and anyone else who has felt the brunt of economic marginalization. I know I have a responsibility to the Marias and Peters of the world, but I am never certain how to go about acting for or with them.

Paul's ethical quagmire about his school's formal curriculum can help us understand postmodern ethical positionalities. Paul, if you remember, contends that the state curriculum his district is enforcing renders both teachers and students powerless, as well as dehumanizing them. Paul knows that most of the students in his class cannot relate to the experiences, histories, and languages of the white, European American kids in the books and handouts he is required to use. Paul believes that those who will benefit the most from the current state curriculum are not his students but those students who come from economically privileged communities. Paul articulately argues that standards and testing are a mask for deeper social, economic, political, spiritual, and cultural injustices, and he ultimately keeps coming back to the question, "How can I act morally within an immoral structure, system, and educational framework?" When I hear Paul's stories and questions, I make many connections with my own life and work. As a professor, I am witnessing many of the same de-skilling and dehumanizing pressures of outside accreditation, state report cards, and canned curriculum at Ashland University that Paul is facing at his elementary school. I am being encouraged more and more to link our experiences and discussions in my doctoral course on ethics and leadership to accrediting standards and "real world" objectives and activities. I feel the squeeze of larger political, economic, and social forces that seek to break me down, define my agency, control my passions, repress my joys, rebuild me, and survey me in the image, a universal one, of a "normal" teacher of ethics. I feel that I am being encouraged and rewarded to abandon my intuitive knowledge, my experiences, my languages, and my positions of dramatic power in favor of "theirs'." I relate to Paul in that I believe that I am slowly and subtly being trained to police myself and my colleagues through a series of standards built on guilt, repetition, and an obedience to a mission that extends beyond Ashland University and maybe even the National Council for the Accreditation of Teacher Education (NCATE).

The extent to which I am already serving this mission is never clear. What is certain, however, is that moral decisions have taken on extended levels of complexity for Paul and me. Although Paul knows that standardized tests are harmful to many of the Hispanic and African American students in his fourth-grade class, he also is aware that if his students do not pass the tests, they will not move on to fifth grade, and if they are retained, they have a much greater chance of dropping out of school in junior high. Paul also recognizes that a few outspoken African American parents have demanded that test scores be raised in his school at all costs. Their reasoning, as I understand it, is that keeping track of tests scores will lead to greater vigilance over the quality of educational opportunities for marginalized groups. Paul has listened as mothers and fathers admit that although they know that test-prep and Target Teach curricula are racist and harmful to the creativity, intelligence, and interests of their children, at the same time they are willing to risk a loss of history and culture for the possibility that their son or daughter will graduate from high school and attend college. In light of these unjust and absurd realities, some teachers who work with poor students and students of color have gone so far as to help their students cheat on high-stakes tests in order to help them graduate. They cite numerous studies that point to racial and class biases inherent in the tests as well as in teachers. Each of these teachers believes that he or she is acting in and for the best interests of their students in the face of absurd social, political, economic, and historical processes that seek to subdue and eventually normalize both students and teachers.

Conclusion

This first chapter has taken us on a journey through many complex ideas related to ethics and education. In reviewing four prominent systems of ethics, we do not want to leave the impression that you must select one of these approaches as the final authoritative position on ethics. Obviously, we believe that the postmodern approaches of Bauman and Foucault offer much promise. We also believe that Simone de Beauvoir, Martin Buber, Søren Kierkegaard, and other existentialists offer compelling ethical insights. And there are times when we find deontological rules or the utilitarianism of teleology more appealing when making difficult moral decisions. The apparent clarity of these systems is sometimes soothing, especially when we are conflicted about a decision and need a quick solution. We do not believe it necessary to make a commitment to any one particular ethical system. Rather, it is important to understand the distinctions between the various approaches as we attempt to use ethical systems to inform our moral decisions and value judgments.

In the next chapter, we explore hermeneutic interpretation and eschatology. And then in Chapter 3, we take a closer look at the connection between ethics and aesthetics, which we introduced in this chapter. Hermeneutics and aesthetics will help us make sense of the complexity of educational ethics before we return to the philosophy of ethics as applied to contemporary ethical issues following the September 11, 2001, events and the financial debacles of Enron, WorldCom, and other corporations in 2002; this we discuss in Chapters 4 and 5.

In the process of investigating educational ethics, we reiterate our fundamental notion that ethics cannot be separated from our autobiographical journey or from aesthetics. The complexity of our lives makes the study of critical ethical issues and education an imprecise science at best. However, the process of struggling to understand the complexity of our lives is for us the beginning of wisdom. This process must foreground a proleptic understanding of time and an engagement with identity politics as an integral step in the development of educational ethics. Chapter 1 provides a context in which to evaluate these important issues. However, more remains to be said about these topics as well. As we move to Chapter 2, we continue to contextualize our philosophy of ethics within our life experiences. We encourage you to do the same.

2 Eschatology, Interpretation, and Hermeneutics: The Struggle for Understanding

An Eschatological Foundation for Ethics: Narratives of Hope

Eschatology is an essential component of any understanding of ethics that seeks to provide hope for the global community in the midst of war, terrorism, ecological deterioration, ethnic hatred, pandemic disease, and political corruption. I (Patrick) first encountered the word *eschatology* in a theology course taught by professor Mary Minella at St. Mary's College of California as part of a graduate theology consortium in the San Francisco Bay area in 1977. *Eschatology* sounded so esoteric and haughty. At the time, I could never imagine using the word, much less ever understanding what it meant. However, Professor Minella had the uncanny ability to make even the most esoteric concepts accessible and intelligible. In my graduate program, I became fascinated with various notions of eschatology and soon discovered that this word was very helpful in understanding many important life questions.

E*schatology* is synonymous with *hope for the future*. But this definition is deceptively simplistic. In order to introduce the complexity of eschatological notions of ethics, and in order to connect our intellectual and autobiographical journeys to the study of eschatology, we first contextualize eschatology. We begin with two tragic stories about our fathers that forced us to probe the meaning of despair and of hope. The first narrative, by Patrick, is the story of a suicide, one of the thousands of suicides that occur daily across the planet. The second narrative, by Dana, is the story of a violent parent and painful divorce, another difficult trauma faced by many children and adults in our society. Where can we find hope and comfort in the midst of so much self-destruction and abuse? This fundamental question guides our exploration of ethics in schools and society.

Two years before encountering the study of eschatology in my (Patrick) graduate program in California, my father died of a self-inflicted gunshot wound to the heart. I was a twenty-one-year-old undergraduate at the College of Santa Fe in New Mexico on that fateful day. Just as baby boomers and their parents remember the exact events in their lives on November 22, 1963, the day President Kennedy was assassinated in Dallas, and just as their parents and grandparents remember the exact moment they heard that Pearl Harbor had been attacked by the Japanese on December 7, 1941, and just as our children will vividly remember the tragedy and trauma of September 11, 2001, my father's suicide on March 19, 1975, is indelibly imprinted on my consciousness. For my entire adult life, I have been trying to understand my father's alcoholism, his occasional violent outbursts, and his eventual suicide. Every time I hear about a suicide, a murder, a school shooting, or a violent act by a depressed, angry, or alcoholic individual, I ask myself the same two questions: "What happened to this person's sense of hope?" and "How could educators, counselors, clergy, and family members have intervened to prevent this senseless tragedy?" In one way or another, this entire book continually returns to these questions. As teachers, authors, parents, partners, researchers, activists, and artists, our lives and our work continually intersect with the study of eschatological philosophy. But we get ahead of ourselves and our first narrative.

On the twentieth anniversary of my father's death in 1995, I wrote a long reflection in my personal journal in which I tried to capture the essence of my eschatological questions. Following is this journal entry, which I titled *March 19 on the Kisatchie Bayou*. After this journal reflection, we return to our discussion of eschatology to make some connections between ethics, education, and hope.

March 19, 1995. I am sitting on a sandy bluff overlooking a rushing river in the Kisatchie National Forest. I have stripped to my shorts, soaking up the glorious sunshine. The torrential rains of the past week have turned the normally placid Kisatchie Bayou into a maelstrom. The events of recent months occupy my mind. My thoughts drift to Langston Hughes' poem *I've Known Rivers* when he confesses that his soul has grown deep, like rivers. Camping along the river nourishes my soul, but sometimes I feel that I am drowning in the maelstrom.

I pour some coffee and recline next to the river. I listen to my inner voice. As I prop up my feet on the edge of the bluff, I gaze at my three children splashing in the rapids. Their innocence is refreshing. I inhale deeply: steamy chicory coffee, fresh pine needles, and bayou humidity. I cough again. The flu bug has persisted for weeks, and my doctor diagnosed bronchitis on Thursday. He also said that my heart might be congested. I know this to be true, so I had to come camping at Kisatchie this weekend. It is March 19.

St. Joseph's Day, March 19, 1975. It has been twenty years since my father's death. My kids are almost teenagers now, too young to remember but old enough to know the truth about their grandfather. I grew up with so many family struggles and so much dysfunctional behavior that I am determined not to repeat the cycle with my children. I have been thinking about generational dysfunction and wondering if there is anything to it. What can I do to recognize the patterns if they exist?

For the past several months I had been planning to spend this weekend with my children in New Orleans retracing those fateful steps before my father's death in 1975. I envisioned driving across the Crescent City Connection bridge while describing the heroics of my brother as we derailed our father's plan to jump into the Mississippi River. I would walk with my kids past the bar on Chartres Street in the French Quarter where my brother Kevin and I, two frightened young men, finally cornered dad and slipped a sleeping pill into his bourbon. I would tell my kids about their grandmother's call to the police. "My husband is running through the French Quarter barefooted threatening to kill himself!" Silence on the line. The exhausted dispatcher sighed with incredulity, "Doll. It's Mardi Gras night. We have a thousand barefoot drunks in the Quarter threatening to kill themselves!" We knew we were on our own.

I imagined finishing the story with my children over a Cajun meal at K-Paul's Louisiana Kitchen, a few doors down from the bar on Chartres Street. After some gumbo and crawfish we would drive up Saint Charles Avenue to my childhood home on General Pershing Street. This is where my 1975 adolescent Mardi Gras ended and my adult Lenten journey began.

We had managed to coax our weary father home from the Quarter later that night. He collapsed in his bed. After midnight Kevin and I tied up my father in his bedsheets and carried him to the back seat of his '64 Chevy Impala. He awoke from his drunken stupor long enough to stare me down and inflict a guilt wound that still aggravates, "What the hell are you doing? My oldest son—Don't you love me?" I did love him. I knew he needed help. Somehow we mustered the courage to take action this time. Along with my brother, my mother, and two friends, I drove my father, bound and angry, to the Coliseum House psychiatric hospital down Saint Charles Avenue.

I had planned to end the March 19 pilgrimage with my children in Metairie Cemetery, that historic and hallowed ground where President Jefferson Davis of the Old Confederacy was originally entombed. In the midst of the massive monuments and elevated tombs of Civil War generals, flamboyant politicians, carnival kings, voodoo queens, and the other royalty of the Big Easy, we would recite Saint Joseph Day prayers at dad's crypt. I had even thought of inviting the Jesuit priest who celebrated the funeral Mass at the imposing Holy Name of Jesus Church in 1975 to join us. It would be a fitting memorial for the twentieth anniversary. Yes, I had also planned to tell the kids that their grandpa got a Mass even though he shot himself. We had been a Jesuit family for generations, and the political connections always made a difference. The Catholic stuff still haunts me for some reason.

I was an undergraduate student majoring in English at the College of Santa Fe in March of 1975. I had flown back and forth between Albuquerque and New Orleans innumerable times during the previous year for one crisis or another. I always worried about my father, but this time I returned to college with more security since he was safely committed in Coliseum House. Mardi Gras had been exhausting, and I prayed on the plane that the hospital would cure his alcoholism and depression once and for all.

On our tour of New Orleans I also planned to tell my children that their grandfather was a popular administrator at Hotel Dieu, a large Catholic hospital whose name translates "House of God." The Daughters of Charity, a Catholic religious order of nuns with large winged habits and famous in the history of the city of New Orleans, loved him. He knew the hospital system well, and on March 19, 1975, he used the system to secure a pass from Coliseum House. He went directly to a gun dealer on the old Airline Highway and bought a cheap pistol. I would tell my children that my dad called me in my residence hall in Santa Fe to say goodbye. It was an enchanted New Mexico afternoon, and I had just returned from lunch when I received the call. I tried desperately to dissuade him from shooting himself. "Have you talked to the Jesuit priest? Maybe he can help you?" My father complained about my persistence. "God is the only one who can help me now," he insisted. Then silence. Then . . . a single bullet to the heart.

As the anniversary of his death approached, I had a change of heart. Today I am looking at my kids playing in the Kisatchie Bayou. They don't need to relive the horror. Richard, my Jungian friend, was right. Camping in the Kisatchie Forest is the best place to be this March 19 . . . and forever more! "Why do you keep honoring the memory of what that bastard did?" Strong words. Tough memories. Sound advice. It still gives me heart congestion.

As time goes on my children will continue to ask questions about their grandfather. I will tell them that he was a respected hospital administrator, a great baseball coach for his sons, a violent alcoholic at times, an avid golfer, and a tormented man when he died at the age of 49. They can ask me all of their questions when they are ready, and I will respond candidly and with compassion. However, today we are refreshed and soaking up the brilliant sunshine on a sandy bayou bluff in the Kisatchie National Forest, oblivious to the anniversary of death. We delight in the rushing rapids, coffee with chicory, the gentle gulf breeze, and the solitude of the forest.

My thoughts turn toward my three beautiful kids splashing with wild abandon in the bayou below. I sip my coffee. I smell the pines. *Joie de vivre!* It is a glorious sunny afternoon, not March 19. My soul continues to grow deep like the rivers.

I continue to explore the meaning of these events in my life, and my understanding grows deeper with every recollection. The tragic experiences of our lives can either be suppressed or explored, repressed or healed. How we deal with the tragedies, joys, and circumstances of our lives is the stuff of ethics. How we respond to these life events determines, in part, our moral response in other circumstances. As we search for the meaning of life's tragedies, growth and understanding become possible. John Dewey (1938) writes about such growth in his book *Experience and Education:*

> Traditional education did not have to face this problem [of utilizing a wide variety of experiences in the curriculum]; it could systematically dodge this responsibility. The school environment of desks, blackboards, a small school year, was supposed to suffice. There was no demand that the teacher should become intimately acquainted with the conditions of the local community, physical, historical, economic, occupations, etc., in order to utilize them as educational resources. A system of education based upon . . . experience must . . . take these things constantly into account. The tax upon the educator is another reason why progressive education is more difficult to carry on than it ever was in the traditional system. (p. 40)

Dewey reminds us that a progressive approach to education that foregrounds experience is taxing on teachers but essential for learning to occur. We agree. We also know that it is difficult to be engaged in critical analysis, interdisciplinary reflection, scientific experimentation, autobiographical introspection, comparative studies, and community activism. It is difficult to explore the stories of our lives. Many teachers and students believe that it is easier to avoid the complexities of experience by reducing teaching and learning to the memorization and codification of data, or inert information, as Alfred North Whitehead called it. John Locke coined the term *tabula rasa* to describe the mind of a student. Literally translated, *tabula rasa* means "blank slate," and Locke intended for children's supposedly empty minds to be inscribed with the knowledge necessary to lead moral and productive lives. In contrast to Locke's philosophy, John Dewey and other philosophers believe that students come to school with a plethora of social, cultural, religious, and intellectual experiences, some good and some tragic, that can be used productively to construct knowledge, address community problems, heal painful memories, understand global issues, and contribute to the aesthetic imagination and scientific investigation of concrete phenomenon.

The notion of prior experience as a legitimate source of knowledge construction in schools and classrooms allows us to think about ethics as a life process rather than a static set of rules or procedures to be memorized and applied uniformly in each new situation. It also helps to foreground in any discussion of ethics and education this fundamental question: "How can individuals keep hope alive in the midst of the difficult challenges of daily living?" Without a sense of hope, it seems to us, all other questions become moot. However, religious conceptions of hope that defer all gratification to some distant place after death, as well as materialistic conceptions of hope that demand instant gratification of the body, mind, or spirit, both contribute to the problem of malaise, terror, anger, anxiety, and defeat that plague modern society and lead to suicide—either instantly with a gun or slowly with drugs, alcohol, or some other form of anaesthetization—or murder—either instantly with a lethal weapon or slowly with verbal or psychological attacks. Relentless assaults on human persons degrade us all and strip the human community of justice and hope.

If hope is delayed until after death, as some believe, then we live in fear, resignation, or the paralysis of delayed expectations and constant anticipation. We are more likely to become intolerant and vengeful and less likely to take action for justice and peace. Consider Ijaz Kahn Hussein, a college-trained Pakistani pharmacist who joined the jihad holy war in Afghanistan in 2001 with forty-three other men—forty-one of whom were killed. He concludes, "We went to the jihad filled with joy, and I would go again tomorrow. If Allah had chosen me to die, I would have been in paradise, eating honey and watermelons and grapes, and resting with beautiful virgins, just as it is promised in the Koran. Instead my fate was to remain amid the unhappiness here on earth" (Burns, 2002, p. 1). Many other religious people reach a similar conclusion, saying things like, "I am in the world and not of the world" and disdaining anyone who does not accept their theology of a delayed parousia or defered happiness. They shun—and occasionally kill—the "evil and unsaved" people who espouse different beliefs or lifestyles. They assume that the world is evil and that only in a life after death will there be peace and happiness.

On the other hand, if hope is found only in immediate self-gratification in the present moment on Earth, we also are likely to succumb to greed, consumption, gluttony, lust, or violence. In both scenarios, we are less likely to work for social improvement and the needs of others because we are so culturally isolated and self-absorbed. But there is an alternative to these two conditions of delayed hope and realized hope: proleptic hope. Proleptic hope offers a way to access the strength to act for justice even in the midst of personal tragedies such as alcoholism and suicide or the turmoil of global events mentioned in Chapter 1: September 11, terrorism, the war in Iraq, or the presidential sex scandal. Proleptic hope offers a context in which to advance what John Dewey (1934b) called social consequences and values in order to counteract the malaise and despair resulting from tragedy.

Proleptic, of course, is another one of those unfamiliar or obscure words for many readers. Literary scholars and English majors will recognize this word as describing the moment in a short story or novel when the reader becomes fully cognizant of past, present, and future events all in one instant. It is the moment when all of the events of the narrative coalesce. Christian theologians have also used the word *proleptic* to describe the fullness of time—past, present, and future—in the person of Jesus Christ. We like to think of a proleptic event as any experience that transcends linear segmentation of time and nurtures holistic understanding. Have you ever had an experience in which time stood still? Not in the sense of being completely out of touch with reality, but rather a moment of clarity or understanding about your entire life: what you have done, where you are now, and what you will be in the future. As we noted in Chapter 1, William Pinar and Madeleine Grumet (1976) call this a synthetical moment. Some compare this notion to synchronicity in Jungian psychology, the Passover experience of the Jewish people, eating the Eucharist for Catholics and Episcopalians, reincarnation for Hindus, or moments of profound insight and aesthetic awareness for artists. The proleptic experience is difficult to describe because our language is embedded with dualistic notions of time (e.g., day and night, before and after, past and present, awake and asleep, beginning and end). We may have to suspend our modern notions of clocks, bells, calendars, and schedules and enter a holistic dreamtime state like the Aboriginal peoples of Australia in order to fully comprehend the meaning of the word *proleptic*. In dreamtime there is no distinction between what happens while we are awake and while we are asleep. Our night dreams are as real as our waking fantasies, and both are as real as the events of our day-to-day lives. Have you ever taken a nap in the afternoon and awakened only to be unsure about the time of day? In this suspended state, you often cannot distinguish the dream of a deep sleep from the present surroundings of your bedroom or couch. This experience is reminiscent of Dorothy in *The Wizard of Oz* as she awakes at home in Kansas at the end of the film and tries to explain to her family that they really were with her in Oz.

The proleptic experience has been described by many authors, theologians, and scholars in a variety of ways. The Jewish theologian Abraham Joshua Heschel describes the Jews as a people in whom the past endures, in whom the present is inconceivable without moments gone by. The Exodus, he pronounces, lasted a moment, a moment enduring forever. For Heschel, what happened once upon a time happens *all* the time. Author William Faulkner is famous for capturing the spirit of the South in the United States, and he writes that there is no such thing as the past because the past is still present. Anyone who has grown up in the South knows this experience to be accurate. Memories of the Civil War are not distant history—they are alive. The philosopher Alfred North Whitehead believes that the present holds within itself the complete sum of existence, backward and forward, that entire amplitude of time, which is eternity. In other words, all of eternity is experienced in each present moment. Lutheran theologian Jürgen Moltmann reflects on proleptic time in a similar way when he contends that the true present is nothing but the eternity that is immanent in time. The believer, for Moltmann, is the one who is entirely present in each moment. This is a difficult challenge for modern citizens whose lives are compartmentalized and scheduled to the minute.

In his most recent book, James Gleick (1999) describes modern technological gadgetry that is designed to save us time (e.g., cell phones, beepers, computers, e-mail) and the ways these devices actually complicate our lives rather than saving us precious seconds. It was originally believed, for instance, that electronic mail would save time so that we would not have to file, sort, and respond to paper memos. However, e-mail has actually doubled our workload for at least three reasons: the proliferation of e-mail messages that requires us to sort good mail from junk mail; the need to make duplicate paper copies of e-mail messages in order to file and save important communication and documents; and the intrusion of e-mail messages twenty-four hours a day into our lives. Some workers and some ordinary citizens never get any downtime from their technology connections. Being constantly "wired" and on call takes an exacting toll psychologically, even though technology has simplified cumbersome communication and improved organization in other ways. Engaging the notion of proleptic time does not require a rejection of modern technology. But it does force us to consider the psychological impact of technology on the way we live. Various moral dilemmas have been created by the modern technological world that demand a reevaluation of ethical systems for a postmodern age.

Gleick (1999) points out that linear notions of time force us to think in terms of the 1,140 minutes available every day, so we rush to make every second count. Directory assistance is automated, and in some cities the voice now says, "What listing?" rather than the old, "What listing, please?" in order to save a nanosecond. How often do you get frustrated by listening to a long answering machine message? "Door dwell" refers to the time it takes the elevator door to close once you have boarded. Door dwell typically lasts two to four seconds. Gleick asks his readers if they reach for the door close button on elevators anyway. Would you still reach for the button even if you knew that most building managers disable the door close buttons out of fear of trapped limbs and lawsuits? What would happen if we lived by the philosophy of Swami Vivekananda, who contends that time, space, and causation are like the glass through which the absolute is seen and that in the absolute there is neither time, space, nor causation. So what is time, anyway?

The philosopher Friedrich Nietzsche (1958, 1968) writes about time as "eternal recurrence" and contends that imposing the "character of being" on "becoming" is the supreme will to power. For Nietzsche, the fact that everything recurs is the closest approximation of a world of becoming to a world of being. Thus, our lives must be experienced as a journey and a process of becoming and not a search for a static destination. John Dewey applies this concept of becoming to education and concludes that the ideal of using the present simply to get ready for the future contradicts itself. Hence, the central problem of an education based on experience is to select the kind of present experiences that live fruitfully and creatively in subsequent experiences. In other words, our task is to experience the future in each present moment rather than simply getting ready for a nonexistent future. When students ask teachers why they need to study algebra (or any subject) and the teacher replies "Because you will need it in the future," the teacher has a misunderstanding of the notion of proleptic time. We must find a way to create meaningful connections in each present moment rather than imposing a rationale for delaying meaning and purpose. This is the proleptic task; it is also the urgent ethical mandate of contemporary living.

One of the most irritating comments we often hear at graduations, bar mitzvahs, confirmations, and other ceremonies of rites of passage is, "You are the future of the church, the future of the community, or the future of America." It should not be surprising that many young people refuse to engage in the social, cultural, religious, and political life of the community or to work for justice. The language of adults tells them to delay their participation until the future. It should also come as no surprise that most students are bored in classrooms, and many drop out of school when subject matter is not meaningfully connected to current events, life experiences, and personal autobiographies. High school dropout rates before graduation exceed 50 percent of the students in a few districts and hover around 25 percent nationally (Newman, 1997, p. 354). Unless students are self-starters with personal ambition or curiosity, teachers provide no meaning or purpose for learning when they tell students to study algebra not because it is interesting or applicable at the present moment, but because they may need it for classes or work in the future—a problematic claim because this is not always true. It is dangerous and counterproductive to separate the future from the present. We might even contend that it is unethical and constitutes educational malpractice.

Alfred Posamentier, professor of mathematics and dean of the school of education at the City College of New York, would agree. He contends,

> [We must] make math intrinsically interesting to children. We should not have to sell mathematics by pointing to its usefulness in other subject areas [or future occupations], which, of course, is real. Love for math will not come about by trying to convince a child that it happens to be a handy tool for later in life; it grows when a good teacher can draw out a child's curiosity about numbers and mathematical principles at work. The very high percentage of adults who are unashamed to say that they are bad with math is a good indication of how maligned the subject is and how very little we were taught in school about the enchantment of numbers. (Posamentier, 2002, p. A25)

This enchantment is an essential element of the ethical foundation of education that we propose in this chapter.

Author Virginia Woolf explained in the novel *The Years* the proleptic experience this way: "There must be another life, here and now, she repeated. This is too short, too broken. We know nothing, even about ourselves. We're only just beginning, she thought, to understand, here and there. She held her hand hallowed; she felt that she wanted to enclose the present and future, until it shone, whole, bright, and deep with understanding" (qtd. in Pinar, 1988, p. 151). This, ultimately, is one of the purposes of educational ethics: to enfold within each present moment the past, the present, and the future so that our lives will be illuminated with deep understanding. In the next section, we further explore the notion of proleptic hope to see how it can inform ethical decision making in a world too often filled with apathy, terror, suicide, war, and injustice. But first Dana recounts his story about his father.

Like Patrick, I continue to ask myself how my reactions to tragic events such as the violence on September 11, 2001, are influenced by my childhood memories of trauma. On a recent trip to California, Washington, and Oregon, I attempted to connect these various experiences with recollections of my relationship with my father. With each reflection came additional surprise and clues as to why Patrick and I have gravitated toward each other, this book, and our commitment to proleptic hope and social justice.

The most profound image I have of my father is the last—the day I informed the world that I, ten-year-old Dana, did not want to see my father again. It was the summer of 1975, and I remember that Lynn, my father's second wife, had arrived at 8:30 A.M. to pick me up and shuttle me to Norristown, Pennsylvania, where she had been living with my father for three years. These weekend visitations had begun after a horrific and lengthy custody fight. I was even called to testify against my father. After several years of litigation, he was eventually granted visitation every other weekend and one full week each summer. Lynn, whom I had grown to appreciate for her ability to forestall my father's temper, was definitely caught off guard by my posture, my eyes, and my pronouncement that "I am not going with you to see my father today or ever again." My action was definitely not prompted by my mother or stepfather. In fact, they appeared as surprised as Lynn.

It was obvious to my mother, stepfather, friends, coaches, and everyone who knew me that I dreaded the weekends with my father. I forced myself to rationalize my unpleasant experiences with my father by looking at them as opportunities. For instance, my father often took me to stay with his sister and her family near State College, Pennsylvania. Once, while I was in the basement playing with my thirteen-year-old cousin Eli, I heard the dead bolt on the door at the top of the steps lock. "What's going on?" I asked Eli. "Oh, those adults are just watching dirty movies and they don't want us to come upstairs. They'll let us out of here in a few hours." Before I realized what I was doing, I ran to the top of the steps, pounded on the door, and demanded to be let out of the basement. I was told to shut up by a number of adult voices shouting over the moans on the television. I screamed every vulgarity that a ten-year-old could think of until my father opened the door and commanded, "Go outside and play, and don't come back for two hours." I heard my aunt say to another adult in the audience, "What a pain in the ass that kid is." I remember thinking that if being a pain in the ass meant refusing to be quiet about captivity, pornography, and lying, then I wanted to be a pain in the ass.

Over time I managed to cope to some degree with my father's manipulative behavior—as well as his broken promises of new bikes, sports equipment, and miniature pool tables—through sanguine empathy more than anger. I didn't fear the temper of the man who had beaten my mother and held a gun to her head; I had no reason to believe that he was gutless enough to do that to me, no matter how much I provoked him.

A few years earlier I had secretly read my mother's diaries, which she had used in court for her divorce and custody fight, and I was disgusted and angered by her graphic descriptions of my father's abusive behavior. At the time, I held out a distant sense of hope that my father would learn to cope and nurture himself. I didn't despise him or feel uncomfortable accompanying Lynn to the Norristown psychiatric unit to visit him while he was being treated for depression, anger management, and probably drug addiction. In fact, today when I visit psychiatric hospitals with my students, I feel a certain unexplainable comfort in the smells, the stories, and the experiences of patients. Even at the age of ten I felt there was something penetrating and real about the haunting accounts lingering in the souls of those incarcerated—more so than in those I heard around the dinner table or at school. Like the characters in the film *One Flew Over the Cuckoo's Nest,* the bizarre stories, behaviors, reactions, and emotions of many of the "whackos" somehow made sense and led me to deeper understandings of life.

In retrospect, perhaps I knew that my stepfather, Bill, was providing much more love, stability, and compassion than my biological father ever could. Maybe I was disconcerted that my mother became distraught each Thursday and Friday before I left for my father's house; her anticipatory pain was too palpable. Maybe I feared that I would turn out like my father. Regardless of my motives, I felt a primal urge to boldly declare, "I've had enough!" These feelings have remained with me ever since. This is especially true at moments of uncertainty, social friction, and ethical tension, when out of conviction I need to take unpopular convictional stands.

Khoi Pham was one of my best friends in school. When I witnessed Khoi, a Vietnamese boat immigrant and junior high classmate, being kicked, punched, and called "gook" by a group of older boys, I remember having flashbacks of being locked in my father's cellar. "I have to get out," I said to myself as I rushed to fight with Khoi. It never ceases to amaze me how many times Khoi's image, our battles, and our friendship appear in my dreams and in memories when I try to respond to ethical injustice. Images from my childhood also come to mind when I try to fight against the horrendous ecological destruction of the earth. Whenever I see environmental degradation, I imagine my father holding a gun to my mother's head, and it deeply rattles my soul. Maybe this is the same feeling that EarthFirst! and Greenpeace activists experience. Maybe it's the same feeling Khoi had when he faced his attackers alone. Perhaps it is both. Nonetheless, getting out of locked cellars and away from pointed guns appears to have much less to do with escaping from the grave reality of spousal abuse and more to do with unleashing the hidden and mysterious intuitive fortitude that resides within each of us. It also has to do with helping others escape feelings of isolated entrapment and hopelessness by working to remove the psychic and social conditions in which they are bound.

To this day, I also continue to wonder why I feel little remorse at severing my relationship with my father. Why am I indifferent to memories of his cold response? I realize that my self-generated, self-induced, and self-congratulatory psychotherapy may have its limits and that my early detachment and cavalier reaction may be shells for deeper-rooted trauma and subsequent behavior. To be honest, at two or three periods in my life I have sought out places where my father and I had some of our more pleasant connections. In the spring of 1987, for instance, I wanted to locate the cabin fifteen miles outside of State College where my father and I often camped. I hadn't been there in years, but I knew the cabin was situated off a series of dirt roads on the edge of a mountain. I left State College without a map but confident in the power of childhood memories. After thirty minutes and twenty-five miles, I made a right turn just past a familiar tavern at the foot of an expansive hill. Houses, forests, junkyards, and back roads became strikingly recognizable, and they eventually directed me to the cabin. I stopped the car just long enough to verify that the image in my mind matched the sight before me. It did, and I turned around and drove back to State College with a feeling of contentment.

These events in my life have led me to believe that so many of our individual and collective experiences are related in timeless seams of harmony. Moreover, the process of self- and social exploration of our memories inevitably provides clues, insights, and possibilities for understanding everything from gay-bashing and racism in the faculty room to biological terrorism and nuclear threats in our global community. Coming to understand what might have led my father to never call, write, or otherwise attempt to contact me in twenty-five years is the basis from which I begin to decipher the complexities of poverty, classism, globalization, hatred, and the carnage of September 11, 2001. I have come to understand that neither the terrorist acts nor our responses to them can be understood by only examining the political present. Deeper and broader ethical understandings in light of September 11 can develop, however, out of our personal and collective recognitions of how guns, rage, abuse, and forgiveness have been manifested in our own lives. In sum, ethics involves a commitment to listening to our phantom selves within our historical contexts as much as it involves a commitment to hearing others.

Language and Interpretation

The stories of our fathers remind us of the importance of connecting memories to our study of ethics. In Chapter 1, we explored the complex and often controversial nature of the study of ethical systems and moral values. In light of the stories of our fathers, we now expand that discussion to hermeneutics, the study of methods of interpretation. Our autobiographical narratives contain many historical and contemporary nuances. Our narratives are embedded in the complexity of human language and linguistic theories, the intricacies of cultural codes and religious norms, the sociopolitical objectives of powerful stakeholders in various global communities, and the power of the insights of each individual autobiography. In diaries and narratives, individuals may also deliberately attempt to reveal and/or conceal specific information. All autobiographies, including the stories of our fathers, are selective; some memories are too painful to express, others are forgotten, still others are repressed. In such a climate, defining ethical systems, prioritizing human values, and assessing moral behavior has always been, and will continue to be, a contentious enterprise. Multiple and complex political, psychological, cultural, and social phenomena are involved in the process. In this section, we explore the relationship between interpretation and ethics in an effort to understand the ways in which human action and human communication are intimately interrelated. At the end of the chapter, we introduce six approaches to hermeneutics and investigate the various ways that philosophers and theologians have attempted to understand the art and process of interpretation, with attention to the complexity just described. We also include some specific applications of hermeneutics to schools and classrooms. We continue to use personal narratives to introduce these concepts, beginning with a lighthearted tale of international miscommunication.

When I (Patrick) was a fifteen-year-old high school ninth grader, my parents sent me to Europe for the summer to study culture and history. The American history teacher at my high school coordinated this trip for over one hundred students and faculty members from various schools in New Orleans, and I was one of ten students assigned to be chaperoned by a young English teacher. Our departure on a chartered flight from the New Orleans Moisant Airport directly to Italy was delayed six hours by inclement weather, and by the time we landed in Rome we had missed a full night's sleep and several meals.

Imagine the sight of one hundred hungry, giddy, sleep-deprived, and obnoxious pubescent teenagers arriving in a foreign country for the first time! We rushed through customs so that we would not be late for our first scheduled event, a "private" audience with Pope Paul VI in Saint Peter's Basilica. We had just enough time to drop off our luggage at the youth hostel and stop at an outdoor café in the piazza for a quick lunch before heading to Vatican City. I remember devouring the lasagna and sneaking several gulps of wine from a carafe at the center of our table. Every table had wine but no water, and the waiter did not seem to care that we were underage teens. Because our chaperone was delayed at the hostel, my classmates and I reveled in the freedom to imbibe. "When in Rome, do as the Romans!" we toasted in uproarious laughter, which quickly faded as our dour teacher entered the café to gather us for the bus trip to Saint Peter's. We hustled to pay our bills from our stash of Italian lira. Our chaperone was oblivious to our mild inebriation, and to the best of my knowledge he never discovered that we drank wine with our first Italian meal.

Arriving for our private audience with the pontiff, we were whisked inside the church to our seats directly in front of Bernini's massive altar. When we gazed around the majestic Basilica in awe, we realized that our "private" audience included several hundred people from all over the world. Our diminished sense of importance was bolstered somewhat when one of our classmates commented, "At least we got the seats directly in front of the pope's microphone." We figured it had something to do with being students from a Catholic high school in the United States.

The music of choirs, trumpets, and synchronized applause greeted the pope's arrival as he processed up the center aisle and took a position at the microphone directly in front of our pew. Fifteen hours earlier I had been a naive teenager who had never ventured beyond the borders of Louisiana except for a few summer vacations with my family on the beaches of the Florida panhandle and in the mountains of Tennessee. Today I was sitting a few yards from Pope Paul VI in St. Peter's Basilica with a pounding heart and an adrenalin rush shaking my body.

There was something else rattling my body; the Italian lasagna and illicit wine rumbled in my stomach with a wrenching twist. I realized that I was about to vomit on the floor in front of Pope Paul VI, the Holy Roman Vicar of Christ. I held the vomit in my mouth as my conscience demanded an honorable escape, but I was trapped in the middle of the pew between nine sweaty classmates and one prissy chaperone. My peers and our chaperone eyed me and demanded stiff silence. I could not open my mouth to explain. I slouched in my seat as the vomit began to drool down my chin and drip on my new seersucker suit. "God help me!" I begged to the crucifix above the altar.

Our chaperone finally noticed my distress and passed down the pew a small packet containing a cloth with rubbing alcohol, one of those individually wrapped wipes often found in greasy fried chicken restaurants back home. As I opened the packet, the fumes of the alcohol made me gag. The long arm of the chaperone reached out and pulled me across the pew. He whispered slowly and emphatically in my ear, "We are trying to listen to the pope; show some respect. Go find a bathroom and hurry back." I swallowed the vomit and set out into the Vatican looking for a bathroom. I didn't want to cry, so I wiped the tears from my eyes.

I rushed past statues of virgins, Michelangelo's *Pietà,* endless rows of prayer candles, and even a glass coffin displaying a deceased pope in my desperate search for the security of a bathroom. I was lost in the Vatican and getting more nauseated and disoriented with each step. Miraculously, I spied a sign at the end of a long corridor in bold red letters: *Infermiera.* The word registered. I ran to the nun behind a desk and pleaded, "I'm sick. I need a bathroom quick, please, sister." She shrugged her shoulders and responded in Italian. I panicked.

At the planning meeting for our study tour, each student received a pocket-sized folder with emergency information, language translations, currency exchange, and maps for the seven countries we would visit. There was also a pouch to hold our passport and another flap to hide our money. We were threatened with unspeakable consequences if we lost our folder or ventured anywhere without it. I reached into my back pocket, removed my folder, and nervously shuffled the pages looking for an appropriate Italian translation. I tensed, trying to hold down the vomit, but the sickness moved to my bowels. I found the Italian dictionary, but no word for *bathroom,* so I scanned the page and found the word *bad.* Doing my best charades imitation, I held my hands on my stomach, bowed my head, and closed my eyes. As I solemnly rocked my head back and forth, I pleaded with the little nun in my best singsong Italian: *"malé! malé! malé!"*

The elderly nun, only her ivory-skinned face exposed from the recesses of her starched black habit, looked at me with heartfelt empathy and grabbed my sleeve. "Yes! She understands I have a bad—*malé*—stomach," I sighed. She scurried down a long corridor, around a corner, and across a courtyard into an adjacent building. "Please hurry, sister, I'm sick," I moaned, fully aware that she could not understand a word I uttered. I was surprised I had not lost my lasagna lunch yet.

After an interminable run through the Vatican, we finally arrived at the bathroom. The nun pulled back a curtain and gently pushed me into the darkened room. I closed the curtain and searched in the dark for a light switch, but there was none. The room was actually a tiny closet, and there was no toilet. But it did not matter. Vomit and diarrhea soaked my new seersucker suit. Suddenly, a small window opened on the wall in front of me. I saw the silhouette of a priest and realized that I was in a confessional and not a bathroom. "Oh, my God, the nun thought I was bad with sins," I thought to myself in horror.

A quick whiff, and the priest slammed the confessional screen shut. I was alone in the dark again. I knew I had to get out of the confessional before the priest came around to scold me. In my adolescent Catholic confusion, I worried about arrest and excommunication. I took a deep breath, pulled back the curtain, and peeked out of the confessional. The nun was gone, but a woman was waiting in line to confess her sins. Our eyes met in horror; I froze for a split second in uncertainty before I darted out of the confessional, scrambled down the corridor, and slid around a corner in search of a place to hide. I do not know which made me feel worse, the anguish or the stench.

I was lost somewhere in the Vatican museum looking for an exit to St. Peter's Square, playing hide-and-seek behind statues to avoid tourists and guards. Most people were still in the Basilica listening to the pope, so I snuck out of the museum and found my way to the buses in the square without too much attention. The buses had formed a circle around one of the fountains, and I was able to sit alone next to the soothing sounds of the water. Once I was confident that no one could see me, I nervously removed my suit coat and frantically rinsed my clothes in the fountain water. I scooped some water in my hands and tried to clean my body. After I put my wet seersucker suit back on, I located my group's bus and curled up in embarrassment on the backseat and cried. I missed Pope Paul's sermon, but I have never forgotten St. Peter's Basilica, the Vatican confessional, and the fountain in the square.

I remember this story fondly today, even though it was the most embarrassing moment of my life. Although the narrative of my sickness in the Vatican may be too graphic for some readers, I enjoy this story because it dramatically exemplifies several dimensions of the problematic of human communication and linguistic interpretation that we want to discuss in this chapter. First, recalling the discussion of language by Michel Foucault in Chapter 1, words do not have a one-to-one correspondence with absolute meaning. Second, nuances and interpretations of words and ideas change depending on cultural conditions, the psychology of the speaker and the listener, political or religious ideologies, body language, voice inflection, and verbal tone. Third, words can have an ameliorative or a pejorative effect. For example, a word such as *awful* may have a negative connotation today, but in the nineteenth century it meant "full of awe and beauty" in some linguistic usages. *Bad* can refer to sins and stomach conditions—as well as good rap music! The meanings of words change over time and across cultures and personalities, sometimes for the better and sometimes for the worse. Fourth, we cannot assume that our understanding of a word or any human situation will translate to others with the same meaning we ascribe to it. In addition, we cannot assume that others will agree with our interpretations even if mutual definitions are established. This is true not only of words but also of ethical systems and moral actions. Does this mean that the search for ethics must be reduced to a relativistic acceptance of all utterances as equally valid and true? Does this mean that no ethical systems or moral values can be universally articulated? Is authentic human communication impossible? At the end of Chapter 1, we argued, along with Zygmut Bauman, that postmodern ethics does not have to result in nihilism, relativism, hedonism, or anarchism. Does the complexity of hermeneutic interpretation now preclude this possibility? We return to these important questions after we do the difficult work of exploring the various understandings of hermeneutics.

The story of the confessional experience in the Vatican also introduces the important notion of autobiography and subjectivity into the hermeneutic investigation. Interpretation does not exist in a vacuum. The meanings of words and ideas are not located in hermetically sealed containers. Understanding and interpreting are living processes that require a community of persons involved in articulating, sharing, clarifying, deconstructing, and reconstructing ideas. This is sometimes called the *hermeneutic circle.* The next section of this chapter begins to explore the complexities of hermeneutics in the context of community, autobiography, and subjectivity. This analysis may be challenging for some readers; the discussion may seem esoteric and confusing. However, remember that the following analysis seeks to explore the history of hermeneutics from a philosophical perspective in order to inform and enrich our discussion of concrete educational examples at the end of this chapter and throughout the rest of the book. Hermeneutics is an essential tool in the process of developing a critical educational ethics. We begin now an in-depth analysis of hermeneutics and subjectivity.

Hermeneutics and Subjectivity

An investigation of the interrelationship of hermeneutics and subjectivity in the educational context could move the discussion of schooling practices beyond methodological rules and principles of interpretation toward an understanding of interpretation committed to community conversation and the hermeneutic circle as proposed by Richard Rorty (1979) and Georg Wilhelm Hegel (1977). This understanding of the hermeneutic experience resembles the sequencing of events that befall a traveler; the details of the journey are utterly unknown in advance, and the process unfolds in a unique and unrepeatable sequence. This is the concept of experience that guides Hegel's *Phenomenology,* philosophies of *Bildung,* and the understanding of reading and interpretation in the work of Hans Georg Gadamer that we explore in this section. This understanding is distinct from empirical accounts of experience because it allows for self-consciousness and self-formation, not in the sense of invariant constructs of human consciousness, but in a poststructural sense of emergent, ambiguous, tentative, and eclectic identities. This is similar to our discussion of multiple identities in Chapter 1 in which we argued that there is no singular invariant human identity but rather ambiguous and eclectic identities. It is here that the discussion of hermeneutics and subjectivity find common ground.

Postmodern hermeneutic interpretation—an apparent oxymoron—is possible if grounded in aesthetic experience and subjectivity and if attentive to the Aristotelian sense of *applicato,* that is, grounding interpretation in experience. An educational experience that incorporates lived experiences called *Bildung*—without separating learning from its application to oneself, as happens in technical, managerial, and behavioral models—encourages interpretation within our subjective contexts. It is here that forms of self-encounter emerge in which teachers and students are aesthetically present to the subject matter they study in schools rather than assuming they possess or can possess all knowledge and can control it. Possessing subject matter reduces learning to the accumulation of inert information in preparation for meaningless standardized tests, a concept that Whitehead vigorously critiqued. We believe that schooling practices that emphasize the inculcation of inert ideas will continue unabated until the emergence of a hermeneutic conversation based on engaged experience and community action. This is the fundamental ethical proposal of this chapter.

The following classroom example may be helpful in understanding this concept. In the constant drumbeat of testing, accountability, and reform movements in the schools, the voices of human persons are often drowned out, stamped out, and extinguished. A reverent silence, empathetic listening, democratic conversing, and hermeneutic understanding become the first casualties of the accountability tidal wave in education. In our schools, classrooms, religious institutions, and civic spaces, we find that lived experience, active imagining, and social activism are too often replaced with inert information, empty rituals, self-promotion, and oppressive drudgery. I (Patrick) am reminded of an event that occurred in my son's middle school classroom a few years ago. We were living in Cleveland at the time, and Josh played hockey year-round in the local leagues. Hockey consumed his time and attention, and schoolwork was often a chore. Politicians and education bureaucrats in Ohio were demanding an ever increasing commitment to proficiency testing and accountability by principals, teachers, and students.

Josh's middle school was experimenting with a prototype test in art history. Many of my graduate students at the time reported that some Ohio art teachers were demanding that art be added to the battery of proficiency tests required in elementary and middle schools. Proponents of the art proficiency exam claimed that they wanted to elevate their subject matter to the level of math, reading, social studies, and science. However, I suspect they were also interested in protecting their jobs. It is much more difficult for a school board to justify a reduction in the budget for the art curriculum or an RIF (reduction in force) of art teachers if all students are required to pass an art history proficiency exam. In any case, there was a concerted effort by some educators to get the middle school students ready for the art test. On the one hand, I was pleased to see the renewed interest in the arts. On the other hand, I was horrified that the art curriculum was being manipulated for political and pre-scriptive purposes.

For better or worse, my son became a pawn in this art history pilot project. One art teacher serviced each grade level for the entire middle school with an "art on the cart" program. For one semester, the students would rotate schedules to view a series of slides and films and take notes on the life of an artist or sculptor, the date of birth and death of the artist, titles of specific works of art, artistic styles, and historical pe-riods. Some time was also devoted to hands-on arts and crafts. The good news is that Josh still has a creative self-portrait he completed in that class hanging in his room amid six NHL hockey posters, a Cleveland Indians flag, and other baseball and hockey memorabilia.

Josh's art teacher was enthusiastic about her program and committed to the art curriculum. She was also exhausted from the demands of teaching hundreds of students each semester throughout the school building. The lack of supplies in this predominantly low-income district made matters even worse. A few half-hour lectures each week in preparation for a criterion-referenced art test did not pro-vide the time or space needed for releasing the imagination. I suspect that the rigor-ous demands of the art curriculum took an exacting toll on this teacher's aesthetic sensibilities.

Josh came home one day and announced that his teacher showed a film about Georgia O'Keeffe and her painting *Cliffs beyond Abiquiu: Dry Waterfall* in class that day. He was unusually animated as he discussed this film. I was thrilled. Josh did not often actively participate in art class at school, and like most kids his age he seldom commented on school activities at home. In fact, he had been known to occasionally participate in silly middle school mischief. However, Josh had never been punished at school, for he is generally a mild-mannered and polite kid.

When Josh was telling me about the O'Keeffe film, he also mentioned that the teacher had reprimanded him for talking about the film. I was surprised and queried further. Apparently, while watching the film, Josh impulsively blurted out, "I saw that painting in the Cleveland Museum of Art." The teacher did not appreciate the disrup-tion. Further, she insisted that there were only paintings of calla lilies and morning glo-ries by O'Keeffe in the Cleveland Museum. She had been there numerous times, and she knew with certainty that O'Keeffe's *Cliffs beyond Abiquiu: Dry Waterfall* was not on display in the museum. She tried to continue with the lesson, but Josh interrupted again and insisted that he did see it in the Cleveland Museum of Art: "I saw it in a pri-vate room on the roof with some person who runs the museum. You know, the lady with all the money who buys the paintings. I think they call her the *creator.*" At this point, the teacher was frustrated by the interruptions and delays in the lesson plan. The class was howling in uproarious laughter, and Josh's remark was passed of as silly middle school mischief. When he came home from school that day, Josh was baffled that his teacher and the other students did not believe him. It was no big deal to him. Josh professes little interest in art (except the design of hockey logos), but he was surprised that the art teacher did not know that this special O'Keeffe painting was owned by the Cleveland Museum of Art.

In the hectic schedule of the art curriculum, the art teacher had little time for life experiences, listening, and conversing. She missed a wonderful teachable moment—like Aristotle's *applicato*—and one of those special opportunities to extend the lesson and enhance the learning experience for the entire class—like Gadamer's *Bildung*. You see, Josh was very familiar with Georgia O'Keeffe and her paintings. I am a volunteer museum docent, and my children have tagged along with me (often reluctantly) to museums all over the United States and Canada. Having lived in New Mexico in my youth, and having seen Georgia O'Keeffe when I stayed at a monastery in Abiquiu, I often talk to my children about this special time in my life. When I take my children to museums, I speak passionately about my experiences in New Mexico and my love for O'Keeffe's paintings.

One of the most influential O'Keeffe paintings in my life is *Cliffs beyond Abiquiu: Dry Waterfall.* The chief curator of the Cleveland Museum of Art, Dr. Diane DeGrazia, also loves this painting, and she displays it in her private office on the top floor of the museum. When I lived in Cleveland, I made special arrangements to visit Dr. DeGrazia's office with my children and my mother. It was an emotional visit, especially when my mother shared with the children that when she dies she wants her ashes scattered in the desert of Abiquiu along the Chama River that runs through the monastery and Ghost Ranch near O'Keeffe's home. It is here that my mother also painted in the desert. We have several of her oil canvases—including one of the Abiquiu desert—hanging in our home. We also have framed reproductions of the *Cliffs beyond Abiquiu* by O'Keeffe on prominent display in our home. Josh and his sisters Michelle and Kayty have been immersed in the artwork of Georgia O'Keeffe since childhood. While visiting the museum, my mother shared with the family this moving poem that she had written through a recreation of the persona of Georgia O'Keeffe:

Georgia O'Keeffe at Ghost Ranch
Far from Manhattan skies
scraped with girders,
pristine calla lilies and crimson
poppies cultivated on canvas,
I have found my place
with craggy cathedrals
beyond human influence.
Before these mountains were, I am
and I shall leave with them.
Our painting time together
disappears, then stays
frozen into ice I lay upon
waiting for the morning light to reveal
what came before, and is now
compelling me, create what is to be.

Even the death of bones
demands delivery of their pregnant past,
as the moon rises above the pelvis void
alive with cerulean blues
precisely planned,
as though my hand
defines reincarnation.
Now I stand like a moth
pinned by walking stick
to this sacred ground
in which I am eternally encased.
If you dare look with painter's eyes
you will see my wrinkles
forming the ash grey hills of Abiquiu,
ascending through pinks and ochers
of mountain strata.
I am bones building nature's skyscrapers. (Burke, 1998)

In addition to his grandmother's poem, another connection to the Georgia O'Keeffe landscape for Josh was our family trip to New Mexico the previous summer to visit the place where O'Keeffe painted, where his dad once lived, and where his grandmother's ashes may one day be scattered. During the visit to New Mexico, each kid was given time to explore the desert alone and walk along the river barefoot and in silence, imagining that they were an artist, explorer, Native American Pueblo teenager, or native child being initiated into the mystery of the desert landscape. These experiences were not reflected in the short video presented in Josh's art history classroom. Any video that ignores the lived experience of the artist, the particularity of the culture and place of her or his art, and an invitation for the viewer to enter into this aesthetic space misunderstands the significance of *Bildung,* art as experience (Dewey, 1934a) and the importance of application in the interpretive process. The art history lesson did not capture the depth of understanding Josh possesses about Georgia O'Keeffe and her desert landscape. His contribution was overlooked in the rush to complete the lesson. In fact, the art history proficiency movement is at times an obscene curriculum that stifles teachable moments, life experiences, listening, conversing, and hermeneutic understanding. Even the teacher appears to be disconnected from the art she loves and teaches. The curriculum has become what Whitehead accurately portrayed as inert ideas lacking enchantment and romance (Whitehead, 1929).

Current educational philosophies and structures often militate against teachers and students becoming actively engaged in releasing the imagination, critically analyzing ideas, experiencing romance or passion in the curriculum, and understanding our culture and society. The hermeneutic circle that seeks conversation and understanding is perceived as dangerous, for teachers and students might become engaged and empowered. They might actually bring the fullness of their life experiences into the curriculum. They might even begin to create Dewey's social consequences of value. The possibilities are endless; the resistence is immense.

Although some students in Josh's art history class may have memorized the information necessary to pass the experimental proficiency exam, all students lost an opportunity to listen and converse about Georgia O'Keeffe and Joshua Slattery in that middle school classroom. Such life stories create a context whereby the information will be remembered for a lifetime and not simply used for short-term recall on a test that is limited to names, dates, places, and titles. We believe it is a moral fault when we do not actively resist data transmission and inert curriculum in schools and insist that experience and application be foregrounded in the classroom. The Abiquiu desert story energizes our resolve to explore the ethics of curricular practices and the hermeneutics of subjectivity in schools and classrooms. A hermeneutic conversation and an affirmation of experience as *Bildung* then become not only possible but also transformative.

Linking Hermeneutics to Social Struggles

The attempt to make sense of the tragedies and uncertainties of contemporary society often paralyzes people in fear, despair, and malaise. David G. Smith locates hermeneutics in such social struggles, linking social upheaval and the need for interpretation. The hermeneutical task is not a technical one, solved by logic; rather, it is born in the midst of human struggle. It enables us to ask, "What makes it possible for us to speak, think, and act in the ways we do?" (Smith, 1991, p. 188). Smith sees the aim of interpretation not in an infinite regression or relativism, but in "human freedom, which finds its light, identity, and dignity in those few brief moments when one's lived burdens can be shown to have their source in [a] too limited view of things" (p. 189). The significance of this process may be in efforts to find the contradictions and injustices in the dominant culture so that we can try to change the culture and engage it transformatively. Thus, hermeneutics is a political process as well as a search for subjectivity. We argue that the empowerment of students in classrooms, as in the example of Joshua's art class, is the first step in creating an ethical hermeneutic conversation in education. The subject matter, a transformative autobiographical journey, and the quest for justice and understanding all merge in this process. This allows teachers and students to break free from bondage to inert ideas, mastery learning, information transmission, and rote memorization for tests.

Schooling has the responsibility to participate in the quest for critical voice, social justice, and individual transformation. Peter McLaren (1997) warns that education is a contested terrain that challenges singular hermeneutic interpretations or methodologies. In such a complex and conflictual milieu, some argue, schools must opt out of the social, political, and religious debates. However, we argue that educators must enter the cultural debates with a commitment to justice, compassion, liberation, agency, and ecological sustainability.

Unlike Stephen Arons (1983), who sees the political and religious debates as unresolvable parochial conflicts—and public schools as obsolete in such a climate— we believe that a hermeneutic conversation is an alternative mode of inquiry that affirms subjectivity and transcends apparently irresolvable conflicts. The hermeneutic conversation challenges the deeply entrenched parochialism, intolerance, violence, hopelessness, and anti-aesthetic worldviews that Suzanne Langer (1957) critiques as contributing to a society of formless emotion. We believe that a penetrating and vibrant aesthetic sensibility is possible.

Consider the apparently irresolvable conflicts over various religious interpretations of truth. The major faiths interact in the world, despite centuries of conflicts, crusades, inquisitions, holy wars, and colonial impulses. They have sent out missionaries, intermingled rituals, and even absorbed deities and holy days from one another. Afro-Caribbean religions such as voodoo that intermingle West African deities and Catholic saints are an example. In south Louisiana, it is not uncommon for folks to create an eclectic blend of Catholic, Caribbean, Wiccan, and African rituals in their personal spiritualities. In our teaching, we are committed to exploring these complex dimensions of local culture by linking hermeneutics to social struggles. This can be accomplished by teachers in any school or community if they carefully explore the context of their community and elicit the support of local historians, elders, healers, and artists to begin the process. We present an example of our teaching methodology as an example of how we engage in this process. Although our example may appear on first reading to be a unique exception, we believe that every teacher has the professional capacity and local resources to create similar public discourse experiences for a community-based curriculum.

Let us preface with some background. Professor Dwayne Huebner of Yale University discusses the nature of public discourse and community-based curriculum in the teaching and learning process in the book *Educational Activity and Prophetic Criticism* (Huebner, 1991), in which he contends that "education happens because human beings participate in the transcendent" (qtd. in Hillis, 1999, p. 396). With Huebner, we believe that education is a prophetic enterprise that seeks justice, curriculum is a public discourse that seeks transformation, and teaching is a moral activity that seeks compassion and understanding. Teaching is not simply a technical human enterprise; rather, it is a creative process of "healing, re-integration, re-membering, and re-collection" (Huebner, 1991, p. 1). Education happens when we are confronted by the "other" and an image of what we are not and yet remain committed to what we can become. Huebner writes, "Confrontation with the other brings us under question and enables us to shed the idolatrous self into which we have poured ourselves and which now contains us" (qtd. in Hillis, 1999, p. 397).

We are inspired by Huebner, and we believe that *university* teaching is first and foremost a cosmological enterprise directed toward understanding the *universe*. This was the classical conception of teaching from the Middle Ages through the Renaissance, a notion that has lost favor among technicists, empiricists, and vocationalists in the modern era. In our philosophy, university teaching and classroom pedagogy must not simply be directed toward preparing students for a career, although career advancement is sometimes an important concern. Rather, as we noted at the beginning of this chapter, teaching and learning must be an experience of life itself and not a preparation for a future life (Dewey, 1938).

In this spirit, I (Patrick) begin all of my classes with a reflection on a work of art that consciously foregrounds an issue of social justice related to the central theme of the course. The work of art may be a film, novel, short story, song, sculpture, painting, or poem. The purpose of the experience is to evoke—in the postmodern sense of eliciting a visceral response of disequilibrium and inquiry—an immediate and emotional connection to the theme of the course syllabus. For example, in my undergraduate teacher education course on social foundations of education, we begin the course by reading the novel and watching the film *A Lesson before Dying* by Ernest J. Gaines. This novel is set on a rural Louisiana plantation in the 1940s. The two central characters are Grant Wiggins, an African American teacher educated in California who returns to his home on the plantation to teach the young children, and Jefferson, a young African American man and school dropout accused of a murder he did not commit. Jefferson is condemned to die in the electric chair in thirty days, and Grant is reluctantly persuaded by Jefferson's godmother to visit Jefferson in jail and teach him to read and to walk like a man before his execution. The story explores the relationship between a teacher and a student and the complexities of social issues such as slavery, racism, capital punishment, inadequate educational opportunities for the rural poor, religion and schooling, and a host of other important topics. This novel and film elicit powerful discussions with my students, and they also prepare us for a field experience related to these themes later in the semester.

For our field experience, we visit several urban high school campuses. Each students spends half of the day at a wealthy, predominately white campus and the other half of the day at an underfinanced school with predominately poor children of color. At the end of the day, I take my students to a restaurant for a meal and discussion with the principals and several teachers from the schools we visited. During the dinner discussion, the students can explore the discrepancies they noticed during the day. At the next class session following this field experience, we discuss the novel and the field experience. Then we watch the film *Children in America's Schools* narrated by Bill Moyers and based on the book *Savage Inequalities* by Jonathan Kozol (1991). The students not only view the plight of students in schools in high-poverty communities in the film, but they also relate to the scenes because they have actually seen campuses from different socioeconomic contexts in their own community. Having had firsthand experience of the economic disparities, my students are much better prepared to explore the complexities of economics and education in our class discussions. We agree with author Ted Halstead (2002), president of the New America Foundation, when he writes:

> The much-hyped but disappointing bipartisan education bill that President Bush signed into law [January 8, 2002] reveals the extent to which both political parties are caught in a trap that prevents them from addressing the deepest problems in our elementary and secondary education system. The trap is a legacy of localism in school funding, which creates dramatic disparity in per pupil funding across the country. Schools in Mississippi spend an average of $4,000 a year on each student; in New Jersey, the comparable figure is more than $9,000—even after adjusting for differences in cost of living. This results

from our antiquated practice of financing schools primarily through state and local taxes, which translates vast socioeconomic differences between neighborhoods, counties, and states into vast differences in school funds . . . and traps students who live in the poorest neighborhoods into inferior schools with marginally qualified teachers, larger classes, and crumbling buildings. . . . Until our national leaders muster the courage to address the financing problem that lies at the heart of our educational predicament, America will remain stuck with an educational system that confines our options to little more than rhetoric and symbolism. (p. A23)

We observe these discrepancies everywhere. Despite the fact that there have been many school finance–related Supreme Court decisions in the past thirty years, including those in California (*Serrano v. Priest,* 1971), New Jersey (*Robinson v. Cahill,* 1973; *Abbot v. Burke,* 1990), New Hampshire (*Claremont School District v. Governor,* 1997), and Texas *(San Antonio Independent School District v. Rodriguez,* 1973), states continue to struggle with methods of ensuring equity and justice in school financing formulas. Some states have made honest efforts to reduce inequalities—usually with only modest success. Other states tolerate glaring problems in poor schools and school districts such as leaking roofs, inoperable fire alarms, toxic environments, noncertified teachers, outdated textbooks, lack of computers and equipment, faulty wiring, and deteriorating athletic fields. When we study these court cases and read Kozol's *Savage Inequalities,* our students understand the issues involved precisely because they have witnessed and explored the problem firsthand in the local schools.

In our undergraduate classes, we constantly connect art, literature, film, field experiences, and classroom discussions to issues of justice related to racism, violence, and economics in schools and society. We hope to inspire our teacher education students to address social and economic issues within their own contexts, and the only way to motivate activism for justice is to directly expose our students to these issues through the arts and field-based projects.

I (Patrick) use this same teaching philosophy in my graduate courses. When I teach Philosophy of Education, for example, I include a visit to an art museum in the course syllabus. The Museum of Fine Arts Houston and the Cleveland Museum of Art are two of my favorites. I spend an entire day with my students slowly walking through the museum, and we pause to consider the possible philosophical lessons inspired by certain works of art. Although I note parallels between the history of particular philosophical movements and schools of art, the primary purpose of the field experience is to evoke visceral responses to various works of art and to allow the graduate students to express their aesthetic understandings. Once the students become comfortable philosophizing in an aesthetic context, I challenge them to apply this methodology in a historical context. Sometimes this involves watching the film *Vukovar,* a dramatic and disturbing narrative about the 1992 Bosnian conflict. Sometimes I take my graduate students to the Holocaust Museum in Houston; I am always surprised by the number of students who have never visited the Holocaust Museum, The Museum of Fine Arts Houston, or any other museum in their lives. I remember one graduate student, a middle-aged football coach with four sons, who complained vigorously about having to visit an art museum. His first three sons were excellent high school and college athletes. The father was worried about his middle school son, who would not practice football and only wanted to paint and sketch. When I suggested that maybe his youngest son might enjoy art more than football and that I could recommend several art programs and summer workshops, the father became furious. His goal, he said, was to get his son away from art so that he could learn to be a man and not grow up to be a "sissy." I often worry about this football coach's son—as well as all young people in similar circumstances—who are forced to deny their talents, passions, and interests because of parental or social pressure to conform to narrow and prejudiced views of life and gender roles.

Consider another tragic story, this one about our friend Benjamin. As an undergraduate in a pre-law program at a prestigious university, he used an elective during his senior year to join the chorus. Benjamin had always enjoyed music; he sang in the church choir in elementary school and strummed the guitar in high school. He had always wanted to sing in the college chorus, but the demands of a rigorous program of study and family pressure to focus on his legal career prevented him from exploring his interest formally. His father insisted that grades remain a priority to ensure admission to the best law school after graduation. Benjamin's father resembled the drama student's father in the film *Dead Poets Society* who ruled his son's life choices and career options with an iron fist.

The choir director soon discovered that Benjamin had an outstanding voice. When Up with People, an international traveling music ensemble dedicated to ethnic understanding and world peace, visited the campus on a tour, the director encouraged Benjamin to audition for the group. He agreed, and at the beginning of the spring semester he received word that he had been accepted as a member of the troupe for the following school year. He would have the opportunity to perform and sing around the world. With years of rigorous study behind him and a high grade point average, Benjamin thought it time he did something personally meaningful and socially significant with his life before starting law school, at least for one year after graduation.

Elated by the invitation, Ben rushed home to tell his parents the good news. Some twenty-five years later, our friend is still bitter about his father's response. His father threatened to withdraw all financial support and close out a trust fund if his son dared to squander a year on such a ridiculous enterprise. His father considered singing a distraction that would remove his son from the real world of law and finance. To be sure, our friend is a wealthy and successful tax attorney today, but he still laments the fact that he failed to pursue his dream of traveling the world for a year promoting peace and understanding with the music ensemble. This story and the that of the football coach remind us of the persistent prejudice against the arts in schools and society and the urgent need to create a curriculum based on experience to counteract such bias. Arts and aesthetics is a neglected dimension of the education and life experiences of too many citizens. We believe that aesthetic ignorance is directly related to moral catastrophes. That is why we propose throughout this book the reconnection of ethics and aesthetics.

A particularly important field experience with graduate students that addresses prejudice and the arts is our walking tour of the statues on the University of Texas at Austin campus. Following our reading of selections from the texts *Lies My Teacher Told Me* and *Lies across America,* both by James Loewen (1995, 2000) and the book *You Are Being Lied To: The Disinformation Guide to Media Distortion, Historical Whitewashes, and Cultural Myths* (Kick, 2001), we visit the statues of the confederate generals and white slaveowners on the South Mall of the University of Texas campus. We talk about possible reasons why these statues were erected in the first place, and we consider the historical and political climate of Texas at the time. We then walk to the base of the tower to view the imposing statues of three U.S. presidents: George Washington, Woodrow Wilson, and Jefferson Davis. (Even white Texans are surprised that Jefferson Davis is venerated as one of the three most important U.S. presidents by the University of Texas.) We ponder why these white men receive places of honor at the base of the campus tower facing the Texas State Capitol, especially after reading Loewen's scathing critique of their complicity in racism and bigotry. Then we walk over to the newly installed statue (in 2000) of Martin Luther King Jr. on the East Mall of the UT campus and discuss the decades-long struggle to erect this lone statue of an African American leader. A dramatic moment on the walking tour occurs when we point to the surveillance cameras hidden in the oak trees. The students are visibly shocked. We ask the students why George Washington, Woodrow Wilson, and Jefferson Davis are surrounded by four statues of white male confederates and racists on the South Mall without surveillance cameras, but Martin Luther King Jr. stands alone on the East Mall under constant threat of vandalism? The visceral response of our students is intense—just as we intend—and elicits new teaching convictions.

My (Patrick) purpose in bringing Texas A&M students to the University of Texas campus—an hour and a half drive away—to deconstruct visual texts, statues, and other historical representations is threefold: First, I want my students to have a dramatic, visceral experience of the complexity of aesthetic representation. Second, I want my students to examine a specific example in Texas of James Loewen's historical analysis of campus statues from our class readings. Third, I want my students to understand deconstruction in a nonthreatening environment before I challenge them to deconstruct their own historical context back home at Texas A&M.

I am well aware of the rivalry between Texas A&M University and the University of Texas. The more "conservative" students at A&M in College Station make fun of the more "liberal" students at UT in Austin. When the College Station students recognize the racist representations on the UT campus in Austin, they are shocked and sometimes outraged. They tell me things such as, "I can't believe the hypocrisy of those 'tu tea sippers' [their derogatory name for University of Texas students]; they profess to be progressive, liberal, antiracist, and morally superior, but look at the racist symbols on their campus." Of course, I am tempted to add gently, "Yes, they are no better than you, huh?" But I hold my tongue. Instead, I bring my Texas A&M students back to College Station and ask them to take a closer look at the statues on our own campus. Suddenly we begin to recognize that the white men honored at Texas A&M also represent multiple historical complexities. We take a closer look at the sculpture of horses racing across a replica of the fallen Berlin Wall titled *The Day the Wall Came Down: A Monument to Freedom* by Veryl Goodnight at the entrance to the George Bush Presidential Library on our campus. Some of the phrases on the wall include: "Free, Free, Set Them Free, 11-9-89"; "Helmut Kohl—A True Friend"; "Art for Peace"; "You Can Vision—Reveille"; "'Tear Down This Wall'—Ronald Reagan"; *Frieren Fur Alles Wa_uf Dieser Erde Lebt."* Why are most of the words on the replica Berlin Wall in English and not in German? Why were these specific phrases selected, and where did the artist find these phrases? Who translated the phrases from German to English? Whose political purposes are served by the translation? Which phrases from the original Berlin Wall were invented, sanitized, or omitted for our replica on the Texas A&M campus? Was the artist censored in any way by the Bush family, the library staff, or the former president's own political views? The plaque tells us that "President George Bush's diplomatic skills enabled the hole in the Berlin Wall to become so large that all of Eastern Europe was set free from Communist rule. The Cold War has ended." Was President George Bush solely responsible for the fall of the Berlin Wall and the end of the Cold War? Historians have pointed to many complex factors involved in this process, including economic disaster in the former Soviet Union. Who should receive credit for the destruction of the wall? Maybe the people of Berlin? These questions are hermeneutics in action. Hermeneutics seeks interpretation and understanding of words and texts.

These questions bring us back to other omissions on campus. Why has there been such resistance to installing a statue of Matthew Gaines on the Texas A&M campus? Gaines was an African American Texas legislator who is credited with founding the land-grant institution in the nineteenth century that has become Texas A&M today. He is given full credit by some historians and incidental credit by others. Even though African Americans were not admitted to Texas A&M as students until the 1960s, Gaines played a role in the early development of our land-grant institution. Some people would like his image to join the all-white statuary club on campus. I do not believe that most of my students would be willing to seriously consider the case of Matthew Gaines, deconstruct the George Bush Presidential Library, or raise critical questions about the statues on our own campus without the initial experience of reading James Loewen's critique and viewing the statues on the University of Texas campus. My Texas A&M students are now in a better position to work for justice and antiracism, not only on other campuses but also within their own context.

Clearly, we consider the world and the local community our classroom, and the arts are our vehicle for exploring the terrain. Our goal is to challenge students to connect the subject matter of the curriculum to the lived world experiences of their surrounding community. We encourage our students to take a closer look at familiar objects and places such as schools and statues and deconstruct their historical and cultural symbolism. We challenge them to enter the hermeneutic conversation and critically analyze the interpretations of books, statues, and texts. Ultimately, we hope to inspire them to become prophetic voices for justice in schools and society, for we believe, as mentioned earlier, that education is a prophetic enterprise in search of justice; curriculum is a public discourse seeking transformation; and teaching is a moral activity that demands compassion and understanding. Teaching is not simply a technical human enterprise; rather, as Huebner (1991) writes, it is a creative process of healing, reintegration, remembering, and recollection.

Defining Hermeneutics

In light of our reflections on community experiences, learning through the arts, and hermeneutic inquiry, we are now ready to explore the meaning of hermeneutics itself. Many scholars, such as Roy J. Howard (1982), define hermeneutics as the art of interpretation. David Jardine (1992) writes,

> The returning of life to its original difficulty is a returning of the possibility of the living Word. It is a return to the essential generativity of human life, a sense of life in which there is always something left to say, with all the difficulty, risk, and ambiguity that such generativity entails. Hermeneutic inquiry is thus concerned with the ambiguous nature of life itself. (p. 119)

One of the questions educational ethics must deal with is this ambiguous and ironic dimension of interpretation in schools and classrooms: An unexpected question triggers an exciting and provocative tangent; the changing moods and emotions of individuals create a unique and often perplexing life/world in classrooms; the same methodology is not always successful with every group of students; hidden assumptions embedded in textbooks affect students in unpredictable ways; atmospheric changes in the weather alter the atmosphere of the school. Teachers cannot predict the ambiguous and ironic nature of life itself, especially in the classroom, and contemporary understandings of hermeneutics as an investigation into the ambiguous nature of being and knowledge can inform and enrich our teaching convictions. Thus, along with David G. Smith (1991), we argue that all discourses are interpretive hermeneutic endeavors.

Hermeneutics has a history of serious scholarship in biblical interpretation and nineteenth-century philosophical attempts to deal with the problem of how we understand the complex actions of human beings. Contemporary hermeneutics, as derived from the phenomenological philosophers Martin Heidegger and Edmund Husserl, acknowledges that discourse and dialogue are essential constituent elements of textual understanding. Understanding sets free what is hidden from view by layers of tradition, prejudice, and even conscious evasion. Although for Hans-Georg Gadamer these prejudices must be acknowledged as a starting point for hermeneutic inquiry, hermeneutic interpretation, for Heidegger, was moving toward understanding as emancipation from tradition, prejudice, and evasion. Recall the notion of multiple identities introduced in Chapter 1. All questions of interpretation must address the problem of prejudices and evasions, whether by starting the discussion by admitting your prejudices or by starting the process by seeking emancipation from your prejudices—or both.

Awareness of historical conditions and prejudices came to dominate hermeneutical understanding during the nineteenth century. Interpreters were understood to move within a hermeneutical circle that required the specification of historical conditions in textual interpretation. Hans-Georg Gadamer (1975) calls attention to pre-understandings that underpin interpretation. Gadamer terms the condition and the perspectives of interpreters their "horizons" and the act of understanding the sense of a text "the fusion of horizons." Through this fusion of horizons, the interpreter enters the tradition of the text and thus shares in the text's particular representation of truth. Gadamer (1976) writes about relationships in the hermeneutic circle that transcend the "technical sign-systems" of the modern age:

> Each [person] is at first a kind of linguistic circle, and these linguistic circles come in contact with each other, merging more and more. Language occurs once again, in vocabulary and grammar as always, and never without the inner infinity of the dialogue that is in process between every speaker and his [or her] partner. That is the fundamental dimension of hermeneutics. (p. 17)

Gadamer concludes by stating that genuine speaking, which has something to communicate to another human being and therefore is not based on prearranged signals but rather seeks words that reach the other human person, is the universal human task. This is the hermeneutic circle that educators must enter into in classrooms and on field experiences with students in order to facilitate and elicit genuine teaching convictions.

As an additional caveat, we must caution that hermeneutic inquiry has the potential to infuriate and incite those committed to traditional authoritative and bureaucratic structures. David G. Smith (1991) has written an eloquent and accessible summary of hermeneutic inquiry, and he offers the following insights into the mythological figure of Hermes and the hermeneutic tradition as a warning for educators in the postmodern era:

> Hermes, as well as being the deliverer of messages between the gods and from gods to mortals on earth, was known for a number of other qualities as well, such as eternal youthfulness, friendliness, prophetic power, and fertility. In a sense, all of these features are at work in the hermeneutic endeavor to this day, as the practice of interpretation attempts to show what is at work in different disciplines and, in the service of human generativity and good faith, is engaged in the mediation of meaning. There is one further aspect of Hermes that may be worth noting, namely, his imprudence. . . . Students of hermeneutics should be mindful that their interpretations could lead them into trouble with "authorities." (p. 187)

Hermeneutics can be dangerous, for it uncovers, interprets, clarifies, deconstructs, and challenges all fields of study, including models and methods of education and ethics that have been enshrined in sacred canons for generations. Examining the history and prejudices of the statues on your own school campus can be a very dangerous enterprise indeed.

A dramatic example of the dangerous conflicts that arise from hermeneutic analysis can be found in the various memorial events surrounding the fiftieth anniversary in 1995 of the destruction of Hiroshima and Nagasaki by United States' atomic bombs at the end of World War II. I (Patrick) joined my colleagues John Weaver of Georgia Southern University and Toby Daspit of Western Michigan University in an investigation of hermeneutics and the politics of memory construction at the Bradbury Science Museum in Los Alamos, New Mexico, where the bomb was developed, and at the National Air and Space Museum in Washington, D.C., where a historical display was being prepared by Martin Harwit, director of the museum, along with his staff: university historians Edward Linenthal, Stanley Goldberg, and Martin Sherwin; and military historians Richard Kohn, Herman Wolk, and Richard Hallion (Weaver, Slattery, & Daspit, 1998). Harwit believed that these historians would represent the various stakeholders and veteran organizations in the installation of the exhibit (Harwit, 1996). An attempt was made to examine the historical evidence related to the bombing of Hiroshima, including the various archival records that inform historians who research these events, not all of whom agree with the official U.S. position that the bombing was necessary to save American lives (Zezima, 2001). Instead, the proposed exhibit triggered an intense political backlash that resulted in the cancellation of the exhibition. Harwit's analysis of the cancellation is summarized at the beginning of his book *An Exhibit Denied: Lobbying the History of the* Enola Gay:

> *An Exhibit Denied* describes the planning and ultimate cancellation of an exhibition that nobody ever saw, but that nonetheless precipitated the most violent dispute ever witnessed by a museum. A national frenzy, fanned by lobbyists and the media, thwarted the Smithsonian Air and Space Museum's attempt to mount an exhibition featuring the *Enola Gay*, the B-29 bomber that had dropped the atomic bomb on Hiroshima. [The book examines] the decade long effort to restore the *Enola Gay*, the largest restoration project ever undertaken by the museum; recalls the help and support initially provided by General Tibbets and a small band of men he had commanded on the atomic missions to Hiroshima and Nagasaki; shows how a handful of World War II veterans became disillusioned and began to oppose the museum's display of the aircraft; and describes how these men succeeded in calling on powerful veterans' organizations, aerospace lobbyists, and congressmen for help in their cause. All the while, a separate drama was unfolding in Japan, where the prospects of an exhibition of the *Enola Gay* in a national museum in the heart of Washington raised an entirely different set of concerns. The book reminds us that James Smithson had founded the Smithsonian Institution for the "increase and diffusion of knowledge." In a democracy, predicated on an informed citizenry, the function of a national museum is to inform the public. In exhibiting the *Enola Gay,* the National

Air and Space Museum sought to depict the aircraft's pivotal role in twentieth century history—in all but ending World War II, but also ushering in a nuclear age that remains problematic to this day. This attempt was thwarted when congressional pressure forced the exhibit's cancellation. (1996, i–ii)

What was so controversial about this exhibit that it was attacked by Speaker of the House Newt Gingrich and removed by the United States Congress? As Harwit noted, the exhibit not only discussed the end of World War II, but also the lingering problems associated with the development of nuclear weapons and the impact on civilians when the bombs were dropped. The ethical fallout from nuclear proliferation must cause us to ponder and reflect on these issues. Unfortunately, powerful lobbyists and congressmen did not allow the public the opportunity to ask penetrating questions and examine the historical record in all its complexity. Earl Lee (2001) reminds us,

> When the Smithsonian Institution tried to put on the *Enola Gay* exhibit, the project came under considerable criticism from Veterans' groups which objected to graphic photographs of the human casualties of the atomic bombing of Hiroshima. Interestingly enough, an earlier exhibit on the use of the V2 bombs by the Nazis, including graphic photographs of the human devastation in London, did not provoke a reaction. The *Enola Gay* exhibit was . . . replaced by [a] more politically expedient exhibit. (pp. 77–78)

Museums, like school curriculum, are routinely used to advance a political agenda.

When the news of the controversy about the *Enola Gay* exhibit became public, we decided to travel to Washington, D.C., and to another exhibit at the Bradbury Science Museum in Los Alamos in August 1995 to interview participants, investigate the exhibits, and analyze the controversy. Our research attempted to frame a wider discussion about negotiation and contestation in museums and the ways in which counterhegemonic, nonlinear, and postmodern spaces may be created so that multiple hermeneutic understandings and dangerous knowledge can be constructed and deconstructed. We believe that museums must present multiple perspectives and various interpretations of historical, cultural, religious, and political phenomenon, even if it is painful to investigate and discuss dangerous memories.

The hermeneutic dimension of this research exposes the fact that the contents and the use of museums are contested and often co-opted for political purposes. They are also used spatially to project certain messages disguised as truth. Modernist notions of linear time from past to present to future are infused into museums when curators and boards view the museum as a repository of the past or vaults for preservation of high culture. We propose that the ways in which memories are created and constructed in museums can either advance knowledge, agency, and democracy or support narrow partisan perspectives. Despite memory manipulation by many, we believe that museums can be recovered as progressive sites for transcending hegemonic manipulation, for developing counterhegemonic responses, and for creating fresh understandings beyond both the hegemonic and counterhegemonic, as happened in the Bradbury Museum, which we discuss next.

The initial debate over the *Enola Gay* exhibit began when some veterans became outraged because they did not want the dropping of the atomic bomb remembered as controversial but rather as heroic. They believed "revisionist" historians were suffering from collective amnesia, forgetting facts and the context surrounding the actual event. The idea of collective amnesia, couched in the derogatory term *revisionist,* permitted the veterans to disguise their assumptions and beliefs as truth without problematizing their notions about important historical events. Moreover, it allowed them the opportunity to exercise their power to proclaim a crisis of knowing and learning and, eventually, to construct a solution to this crisis that fit their worldview. Memory creation implies that collective amnesia exists only as a rhetorical construct used to disguise one's power and justify one's social position and to determine who or what will be remembered or valued. We believe it is the duty of educators and museum directors to challenge hegemonic attempts to silence historical analysis. Martin Harwit stood firm in his conviction about the importance of providing the public with an opportunity to investigate Hiroshima and the *Enola Gay* with an eye toward the continuing struggle with nuclear proliferation and the dangers it presents to the global community. Unfortunately, the Smithsonian exhibit was denied by Congress and Harwit lost his job. Nonetheless, Martin Harwit provides a striking example of an ethical prophetic voice working for hermeneutic understanding through education.

The Bradbury Science Museum in Los Alamos was also embroiled in controversy when we visited in August 1995. This museum had decided not to address the problems associated with nuclear weapons and the complexity of the historical record about Hiroshima. Activists in Santa Fe pressured the museum to include these topics in the museum, however, and they eventually received approval to display several large panels depicting the effects of the nuclear bombs on the civilians in Hiroshima, along with some of the historical text that had been denied in Washington, D.C. Veterans groups protested this decision, claiming that it was insensitive to those who gave their lives for the United States and freedom to be subjected to "revisionist history" and images of dead and dying Japanese. The fact that many historians have questioned the "official" interpretation of the bombing infuriated many veterans. Not all historians agree that it was necessary to bomb civilian targets—or even use nuclear weapons—to end World War II. Other historians have reviewed the records carefully in the intervening years and discovered many other connections to the Soviet Union and postwar U.S. intentions. For example, was the decision to drop the bombs intended to warn the Soviet Union not to test U.S. authority and power following the war? We do not want to settle the historical debate here; instead we report on this struggle to allow a discussion of these alternative historical accounts in the museums. The activists argued that the U.S. public deserves to know the complex historical record and various hermeneutic interpretations. But, as mentioned earlier, hermeneutics threatens powerful people because it may not confirm their interpretations, which keep them in wealth or power. In the end, the small cramped corridor provided for the activists to

display several floor-to-ceiling panels was cut in half, and the veterans were given the other half for a military display with a traditional interpretation of the bombing of Hiroshima—despite the fact that this information was readily available and prominently displayed in several other venues. Nonetheless, the activists and veterans were required to share the small space, which did at least create additional opportunities for media coverage and dialogue.

I (Patrick) arrived in Los Alamos on a sunny August 6 afternoon in 1995 with my mother, stepfather, and children in tow. We toured the permanent science exhibits first, eventually making our way to the small corridor where the peace activists and the veterans had won the right to display their historical records and photographs. It was the fiftieth anniversary of the bombing, and U.S. veterans had gathered at Los Alamos along with several Japanese educators and some survivors of the explosion in Hiroshima. It was a profound moment. Dozens of elderly American and Japanese men and women were engaged in long pensive discussion about their experiences. My family and I were welcomed into the circle in the cramped hallway with both groups of survivors. Everyone was respectful, even in their disagreements about the historical record. I will never forget the moment when fifty years of history merged in human empathy as the elderly American military men and the frail Japanese bombing survivors extended peace signs and agreed that they wanted no more bombs.

I am so grateful that my children were a part of this experience. Kayty was eleven years old. My mother was also eleven years old in 1941 when she heard the news that the Japanese had bombed Pearl Harbor. In 1995, after our family experience in Los Alamos, my mother wrote the following poem describing her life as a young girl in Louisiana during World War II and how those memories were rekindled fifty years later at the Bradbury Science Museum in Los Alamos.

Seek the Realm of Peace
1941
Lazy Louisiana sunshine
shivers through December woods
a family drive on Sunday afternoon
crackling car radio
always out of tune
bombs blasting war
so peacefully.
How could this be a day of infamy?
Age 11 doesn't know the word
11 understands the deed.

12 draws the shades for blackouts
flips off lights
scans her battlefield
for fireflies disobeying curfew
then dreams them into marching men
a million miles away.

13 memorizes patriotic posters
Use less sugar and stir like hell
Lucky Strike green has gone to war
green dye-men die
black blood
prints their names each day.

14 snuggles against the console
with Roosevelt's fireside chats
she clings to words that cradle and comfort
F. D. R. casts his spell
all is well but not for long
his voice soon dies—no resurrection.

15 dreams of bright canteens
too young—she still can dream
of all the men who'd dance with her
kiss her lips
forget this war and all its slogans
all save one: Give 'em hell Harry.

Hell fell twice
as atoms split the generations

1995
50 years of faded dreams awake
as a postmodern pilgrimage to Los Alamos
conjures my ghosts
hidden in a half century of distractions.

We enter
through a gift shop
overstocked with toy men dressed for war
'Little Boy' and 'Fat Man' bombs
with all their deadly plastic playthings.

We see
beyond that room
not quite out of sight
a wall—one lousy little wall
to regurgitate it all
HIROSHIMA AND NAGASAKI
landscapes of nothingness
populated by skin
of melting bodies, faces fused.
BATAAN DEATH MARCH
tortured American
faces buried in the mud
of their inferno.

We memorize
with solemn eyes

compelled to digest the aged rot
of hideous past.

We hear
Japanese teachers with symbolic paper cranes and
American veterans with weight of all their wounds
resting on canes
politely exchange passionate discourse.

We stand
behind a blood red rope
and wait
as others mark on pages of a book
for all who look to see
ink bled from the heart.

My granddaughter 11
takes her turn with words
"We shouldn't have dropped the bomb."
11 understands the deed
perhaps that's all she needs
to understand.

I recall
my perception of war
at age 11
and my apprehension of wars that followed
and of the wars to come
I touch my son.

A Japanese grandmother bows
"Ah, BIG son."

Rising sun
proud
flaming red ball
beneath the mushroom cloud
that vaporizes infamy.

"Please, no more bombs."
Japanese words in broken English.
She presses a ceramic crane
no larger than a distant star
into my palm.

No more bombs
no more infamy
I touch her hand as we walk away
two grandmothers yearning for peace
our eyes shielded
against the harsh sunlight
of Los Alamos. (Burke, 1995)

From Modern to Postmodern Perspective on Hermeneutics

Modernity has been characterized by a search for an underlying and unifying truth and certainty that can render the self, the cosmos, subjective experiences, and historical events as coherent and meaningful. Some of our college students bring this desire for absolute truth to our classrooms, and they are confused by our critique of unifying truth and absolute certainty. However, most of our students eventually come to appreciate the postmodern perspective that the human condition and the cosmos are irreducible and irrevocably pluralistic, existing in a multitude of sovereign units and sites of authority, with no horizontal or vertical order either in actuality or in potency. In this environment, knowledge and truth are contested, constructed, tentative, and emerging. As we discussed in Chapter 1, even the self is decentered and multifaceted.

As we noted in the previous section, hermeneutics has a history of serious philosophical scholarship that attempts to deal with the problem of how we understand the complex actions of human beings and multiple interpretations of texts. Heidegger and Husserl contended that discourse is essential to understand what is hidden from view by layers of tradition, prejudice, and even conscious evasion. Like Hermes—messenger and trickster—many contemporary educators revel in the irony that the official interpreter can also be a cunning deceiver. This reminds us that layers of meaning, prejudice, and intention surround all artifacts, thus necessitating a hermeneutical study to expose not only the irony of deception, but also the implications of historical analysis. Contemporary historical, textual, aesthetic, and autobiographical interpretation all acknowledge this double-edged dimension of clarity and ambiguity. However, unlike modern empiricists who demand unbiased certainty and rational scientific proof, the ironic is celebrated by postmodern scholars who recognize that ambiguity is integral to the human condition and the natural world. Contemporary hermeneutics affirms the primacy of contested subjective understanding over inert objective knowledge and conceives of understanding as an ontological rather than an epistemological problem. In other words, knowledge and data alone cannot provide answers to challenging life questions; understanding is embedded in the difficult ontological struggles of day-to-day living in a complex world. This is why Hermes the messenger and deceiver becomes a metaphor for interpretation in postmodern theory.

In this milieu, the focus of hermeneutics shifts from inert and objective data to the community of interpreters working together in mutually corrective and collaborative efforts to understand texts and contexts. The entire educational experience is open to reflection because everything requires recursive interpretation. Without this perspective, Hermes the trickster continues to deceive, and modern men and women—including some of our students—naively believe that knowledge and data give them access to absolute truth. This in turn obligates them to convert or destroy those who refuse to share their beliefs.

This dilemma plays itself out regularly in school districts and state education agencies during the textbook adoption process. Many scholars have investigated the politics of textbooks and textbook adoptions and reminded us that no material is value-free (Kumashiro, 2003) and textbook adoptions are debates about ideology, power, and the control of ideas (Apple & Christian-Smith, 1991; Apple, 1992). Let us consider a few examples of this process and then link textbook adoption issues to hermeneutics at the end of this section.

Conservative politicians and parents often call for "back to the basics" in the school curriculum with structured, orderly classrooms and a focus on reading (phonics), writing (grammar), and mathematics (computation skills). Some even propose including sectarian Christian prayers, traditional "family values," and patriotic citizenship lessons in the curriculum. Others insist on specific "value neutral" materials in the schools so that parents can teach values in the home. Finally, the call for "back to basics" for some also means a return to traditional Greek, Roman, and European literature with an emphasis on the Great Books of Western culture.

When we examine the historical development of educational curricula, we find that different subjects, books, and lessons take prominence in different time periods. Thus, the call for "back to basics" in the curriculum raises questions not easily answered, despite the fact that those who propose a "traditional" or "basic" curriculum and textbooks assume consensus on the meaning of these words.

In Plato's ideal society, individuals received an education that matched their assigned social role of either worker, warrior, or intellectually elite philosopher-king. Early education for children ages six through eighteen included music and gymnastics. But music included the areas of letters, reading, writing, choral reading, and dancing. Later, Plato's students received instruction in the library classics, censored so as to emphasize poems and stories promoting obedience to authority, courage, truthfulness, and emotional control. Many politicians ascribe to Plato's philosophy today. Former U.S. Secretary of Education William Bennett is an outspoken proponent of classics in the curriculum, and he carefully selected, edited, and even revised the stories in his best-selling *Book of Virtues* to reflect the political and moral values he promotes for all U.S. children (Bennett, 1993). Over his loud calls for morality and values, it can be difficult for the casual reader to detect the political manipulation behind Bennett's work.

When we examine William Bennett's books *The James Madison High School* (1987) and *The James Madison Elementary School* (1988), we find an overview of his ideal curriculum for all U.S. students. He outlines both the courses he believes all students should take and a description of precisely what should be included in the lesson plans. A closer examination reveals several layers of hermeneutic interpretation in Bennett's curriculum. The four-year English curriculum includes introduction to literature—American literature, British literature, and world literature—with the following proposal for tenth-grade American literature:

> Students read a careful selection of American fiction, drama, and poetry. A good syllabus designed to spotlight that distinctive American achievement in literature might include Franklin, Irving, Hawthorne, Poe, Whitman, Twain, Melville, Dickinson, Faulkner, Wharton, Hemingway, O'Neill, Fitzgerald, Frost, Ralph Ellison, and Robert Penn Warren. Regular writing assignments are made and continued emphasis is placed on clarity, precision, and frequent revision. Students are given increasing experience in classroom speaking. (1987, p. 13)

Bennett outlines the major authors to be included in the American literature curriculum. Why are there only two women on the list? Why only one African American? Where are the Hispanics? Where is the voice of Native Americans? Where are the transcendentalists? Why does Bennett exclude the nineteenth-century literary giants Thoreau and Emerson? It happens that the political views of the transcendentalists conflict with the conservative politics of William Bennett. Might this explain the oversight? Contemporary African American authors such as Langston Hughes, Maya Angelou, Ernest Gaines, Toni Morrison, and Alice Walker are absent from Bennett's book list because he is committed to a view of the classics as a time-honored tradition—a tradition formed by those with the power and influence to create it. The author Jonathan Kozol often writes about this problem.

Kozol (1967) published his first book, *Death at an Early Age,* as a result of his experiences as a beginning language teacher among disadvantaged African American children in Boston's public schools. Kozol tells the story of his frustration with dilapidated facilities, overcrowded classrooms, and outdated textbooks. None of the authors William Bennett recommends in American literature reflects the contextual experiences of the students Kozol taught. Moreover, there were not enough books to go around, and the books that were available were damaged and missing pages.

Browsing through a Boston bookstore, Kozol caught sight of a collection of poems with a picture of an African American poet on the cover. He purchased the book for his class. He wanted to show the students what a new book looked like, and he also wanted them to see that African American poets exist, as none were represented in the textbooks. Kozol found himself fired for "curricular deviation," having read Langston Hughes's poem that asked what happens to dreams that are deferred: Do they shrivel and die, like raisins in the sun, or do they explode? Kozol related how one particularly angry young woman who had resisted him throughout the course asked to borrow the book and memorized the poem. The poetry of Langston Hughes transformed the students and Kozol's classroom, but it also disturbed the school authorities, who were afraid of what might happen if poor children of color began to read "radical" poetry. Because Hughes's poetry did not appear in the curriculum guide or district syllabus, Kozol was fired. He went on, of course, to write a library of inspiring books about such topics as the lack of education for the children of the homeless and migrant workers, the politics of literacy in the United States, and the savage economic inequalities of U.S. schooling. The works of Jonathan Kozol remind us that schooling is hardly a politically neutral activity. William Bennett's curriculum ignores the importance of multicultural literature, the contextual experiences of students and teachers, and the political consequences of censoring and editing the curriculum.

Supporters of Bennett's curriculum might respond that he includes world literature in the senior year of high school. But his curriculum includes only Western literature and, *"depending on the instructor's knowledge and interests,* a small number of works from Japan, China, the Near East, Africa, and Latin America" (1987, p. 13; emphasis added). Bennett reduces world literature to a limited canon of works from Greece, Rome, and Europe—a strong bias toward Western culture. He tosses a bone to "world" literature by including "a small number" of works from all of the eastern and southern hemisphere cultures. His worldview and political ideology permeate—we might say "infect"—his curriculum. It seems a bit naive to assume that teachers who have been exposed only to a classical curriculum have "knowledge and interest" in literature from Japan, China, Africa, or Latin America. But Bennett is not naive. He designed his curriculum to accomplish specific political ends with the suppression of diversity, human experience, and the contextualization of schooling. Hidden within proposals for "back to the basics" and classics in the school curriculum are efforts to impart a political, religious, and cultural ideology.

Bennett is not alone in this process. All texts contain ideologies and cosmologies. Is this unethical? Not necessarily. Our concern in this chapter is to alert educators to deeply embedded values within textbook selections and curriculum materials. Once the values are recognized, then the community can enter into an honest, transparent, and democratic discussion about these values, always with an eye toward greater inclusion and diversity. The values can also be deconstructed to find complex contradictions and ambiguous applications. For example, obedience to parents and authorities is a prominent theme in Plato's *Republic* and Bennett's *Book of Virtues*. But must a child obey an abusive parent? Must a citizen respect and adhere to an immoral public policy? If not, when is it a higher virtue to resist or protest? Recall the four ethical systems presented in Chapter 1. There are multiple complex responses to these questions that make absolute predetermined value judgments impossible.

One of the underlying tensions in the debates about curriculum and textbooks revolves around the philosophical purposes of education. Dewey often asked, "Is education a function of society or is society a function of education?" In other words, is the purpose of schooling to replicate and support the status quo—the sociopolitical, cultural, and economic arrangements in the nation sponsoring the schools—or is the purpose of schooling to expose injustices in society such as racism, sexism, economic disparity, and environmental degradation? We agree with Dewey that the purpose of schooling is the latter—to create experiences and learning environments that will lead to positive social consequences and values for personal growth and global justice (Dewey, 1934b). During the Great Depression, educational philosopher George Counts (1932) asked, "Dare the schools build a new social order?" In other words, do we have the courage and fortitude to address social problems in the global community? Counts proclaimed loudly, "Yes, we must build a new social order!" We believe that the message of George Counts and John Dewey is as pertinent today as it was in the 1930s. Another related question probes the function of the university: Is the purpose of a university to train students for a profession and prepare them for economic advancement and career development, or is the purpose of a university to provide a broad liberal arts education to prepare students for lifelong learning, community service, professional ethics, cultural appreciation, and personal growth? Obviously, we believe the latter. However, we also believe that it is possible to accomplish both functions: to prepare students for the world of work and to prepare students for an intellectual life dedicated to the betterment of humanity and personal growth. The schooling experience can be very different depending on the philosophy of education that guides the process—especially if one of these two functions dominates the philosophy of the administrators and faculty.

Another way of thinking about this philosophical debate is to question whether schools should be instruments of social control or agents for social adaptation. Should schools emphasize lessons that advance cultural assimilation and political compliance or experiences that advance critical analysis and personal agency? As we discuss shortly, the textbooks and media we select for student consumption and the ideas we include in the textbooks and lessons plans are directly related to our perceptions about society. They are never value-neutral.

In some schools and classrooms, educators allow power brokers to attain their goals by pretending to promote equality under the guise of such value neutrality. Tragically, the accountability measures and standardized curriculum touted as politically neutral and culturally equitable actually produce the stratified workforce corporations and employers demand. Scholars call this process "hegemony." Peter McLaren defines hegemony as the maintenance of control less by the use of actual force than by subtly coercive social practices in churches, government, the mass media, the family, and the schools that eventually win the consent of individuals. These individuals, McLaren concludes, are unaware that they have given their consent to those in power and, as a result, participate in their own oppression. When schools, for example, teach rugged individualism or manifest destiny—the myth of individual achievement—the dominant culture ensures that economically, culturally, or racially marginalized students who fail at school will blame themselves. In other words, such students are taught to accept their subordination (McLaren, 1994, p. 182). When these students find themselves unemployed or in low-paying dead-end jobs, they blame no one but themselves, an attitude that nicely serves the corporate power brokers because it blinds workers to the injustice of a system that needs the majority of the population working in low-paying dead-end jobs without health insurance, retirement plans, or workplace safety protection.

With their power to control information and manipulate public opinion, especially through school textbooks and curricular materials, politicians and corporate leaders convince average citizens that an economic system built on job stratification, gender pay inequities, and class differences actually serves their interests. In recent decades, such leaders have convinced the public of some strange ideas indeed. For example, corporate-backed politicians in the Reagan era convinced a majority of Americans that tax decreases for the richest citizens would "trickle down" to improve the economic lives of the poor. The George W. Bush administration is attempting to do the same thing in the early twenty-first century. These politicians have convinced many Americans that regulations designed to stop U.S. companies from moving their factories to other countries and leaving hard-working Americans unemployed were superfluous. We were supposed to believe that business and industry would police themselves and care for the environment. U.S. workers who invested in company 401(k) retirement accounts even trusted the corporations—until Enron went bust in 2001 and the faithful workers lost their jobs, their health insurance, and their retirement accounts. Incredibly, after the savings and loan scandal of the 1980s, the political campaign financing scandals of the 1990s, and the bankruptcy of Enron in 2001, many U.S. citizens still naively believe that the Bush tax cuts and deregulation of the oil and gas industry will advance the U.S. economy, protect the environment, and support average workers. Politicians even wanted us to believe that companies such as Enron, which avoided paying income tax for four years between 1996 and 2001 by hiding losses in foreign subsidiaries, should receive tax breaks as part of the 2001 government economic stimulus package. We contend that such blind acceptance by the general population of self-destructive policies can be traced back to schooling practices that discourage critical thinking and the hegemony of textbooks that present students with limited information. People become, like the workers in low-paying dead-end jobs, enculturated into the unethical corporate, political, and financial system that is manipulating and betraying us. We are committed to challenging such practices, deconstructing the biases in textbooks, and exposing ethical lapses that undermine democracy and justice. We encourage a critical hermeneutics in the interpretive process in education, as explained in the following example.

This is a story of a controversy about U.S. history textbook in the Hudson, Ohio, public school district in the mid-1990s. History textbooks are, of course, at the forefront of debates internationally as scholars challenge the way that many texts distort history, glorify national heroes while ignoring their complexity and character flaws, or disseminate narrow nationalistic propaganda. Japanese textbooks obfuscate the complicity of military leaders, soldiers, and politicians in horrendous acts during World War II such as the massacre of civilians in the Chinese city of Nanjing; Chinese textbooks glorify nationalism in order to repress political dissent; German textbooks ignore the complexity of widespread public participation in the theft of Jewish assets and support for Nazi atrocities in the concentration camps during the Holocaust; Pakistani *madrasa* schools operated by the Taliban interpreted the Koran with anti-American and anti-Western distortions; Saudi Arabian Wahhabi Islam textbooks portray women and non-Muslims negatively and incite discrimination; Belgian textbooks sanitize the devastation wrought on the people of the Congo by King Leopold's colonization of central Africa in the late nineteenth century and early twentieth century; Korean texts denounce Japanese imperialism but gloss over collaboration by the nation's elite with Japanese colonial authorities in the early twentieth century; British textbooks elide the consequences of centuries of global colonization; Russian textbooks glorify communism but ignore the brutality of Stalin; French texts omit information about collaboration with the Nazis or injustices in Algeria; museum guidebooks overlook the plunder of art during wartime and the theft of indigenous artifacts that established the museum collection; and denominational religious catechisms ignore multiple biblical interpretations and cover up financial scandals, the moral failures of clergy, and forced proselytization by missionaries.

Despite outrage at blatant historical distortions in these texts from other nations, Americans appear unwilling or unable to address the shortcomings, silences, and distortions within their own textbooks. U.S. textbooks, for example, often tiptoe around the Vietnam War, the Civil War, and the American Revolution, preferring to anoint a few heroes and list the dates of battles and treaties rather than examining these difficult periods in-depth, so as to avoid stirring up any lingering racial, cultural, or political divisions from the past. Earl Lee (2001) explains:

> In theory, one of the main functions of public education is to help create a citizenry that understands the functions of government and is able to make informed judgments about how public policy will affect future generations. But at the same time there are powerful commercial interests who see an informed citizenry as a direct threat to corporate power. These corporations would rather have a citizenry that is easily influenced to accept whatever message is given by the corporate-controlled media. For this reason, they find many topics in textbooks to be particularly dangerous, including the Revolution and the Civil War. The possibility that the people might view government as an instrument of the public will, much less take up arms to oppose entrenched power, is a dangerous idea that [they believe] must be squelched at all levels. One of the most blatant frauds found in textbooks is the idea of a "democracy." All students are taught . . . that America is a democracy. However, anyone who bothers to objectively examine our system of government can quickly see that it is a republic, not a democracy. (p. 74)

How often do we explore notions of democracy, public will, dissent, and restitution in our history textbooks? The silencing of democracy occurs in Mexico, Canada, the United States, and any nation that attempts to indoctrinate, assimilate, or placate the citizenry with patriotic fervor, political subservience, passive compliance, or benign neglect of history in order to advance its political, social, religious, or economic goals.

A faculty and administrative textbook search committee in Hudson, Ohio, attempted to address this hermeneutic dilemma of historical interpretation when the teachers and administrators proposed adoption of the textbook *The American People* for the Advanced Placement course in U.S. history in their district in 1996. The school board rejected this proposed textbook, and their reasoning was applauded by the local chapter of Excellence in Education, a culturally conservative organization, in the following community news release:

> At its June 17, 1996 meeting, the Hudson Board of Education rejected *The American People,* a new textbook that the school administration proposed for AP History. [The vote was two opposed to adoption, one in favor of adoption, and two abstentions. Three favorable votes are required by Ohio state law for adoption.] One board member stated that *The American People* presented a revisionist view of history written in the spirit of political correctness [and] is deficient in its coverage of American patriots and heroes, American technology and science, and the foundation of our republican form of government [while] overemphasizing the roles of our nation's minority groups and portraying them as perennial victims. Another board member denounced the book as giving a revisionist and negative view of America and that the authors attempted to reinterpret history, making some historical events less important and others more important, to meet an educationally elite and politically correct social agenda. Several people spoke favorably of the text. These included parents, high school students, a high school history

teacher, and a history professor from Cleveland State University. The book was defended for its multicultural coverage of our history, with a strong emphasis on minorities, women, and the environment. It was stated that the book is widely used across the country in high schools and colleges, and that it gives good coverage to material that is included on the AP test for college. We applaud the School Board for deciding not to accept this text. *The American People* book needed to be rejected because of its unbalanced, revisionist coverage of our history. To our knowledge, this is the first time that a Hudson Board has ever turned down a textbook proposed by the administration. (Hudson CEE Explorer, 1996, p. 1)

What issues so infuriated the board members who did not support this textbook? Seven objections were listed in the news release: (1) The emphasis on social history is too heavy and the reporting of traditional public history is diminished; (2) U.S. history is viewed as a story of victimization; (3) U.S. history is portrayed as a class struggle—the rich versus the poor; (4) The basic foundations of U.S. government are not covered in sufficient detail; (5) There is little in-depth coverage of American heroes and patriots; (6) Scientific and technological information is minimal; (7) The positive role of religion in our heritage is slighted.

The response of the teachers and administrators who supported adoption of this textbook included the following citations from professional reviewers:

1. Social History—The chronology of facts and events about minorities as presented is interesting and useful. Modern textbook writers have expressed great concern about past deficiencies in minority history, and *The American People* has made a concerted effort to overcome these deficiencies. More than any other text on the market, Nash [the lead author] demonstrates that women, minorities, and non-elite groups have a history; 2. Pedagogy—The pedagogical features of *The American People* are outstanding. The comparative chronologies are very thorough and give students an order about important events. The chapter-opening vignettes personalize history for students by presenting accounts of individual experiences of people involved in some phase of history. The Recovering of Past Essays are one of the Nash text's best features. Presentations of such topics as the movies, public opinion polls, popular music, political cartoons, and television are written in a style that relates to young people; 3. Balance—One of the greatest strengths of the Nash text is its balance. Students need equal doses of social and political history, which very few texts, outside of the Nash text, provide. It is a well written, thorough text that gives good coverage to social history as well as more traditional topics, and because it is well illustrated and includes vignettes and exercises that make history come alive, it is very enjoyable [for students]. (Hudson Portfolio, 1996, pp. 1–3)

An informative exercise would be to compare and contrast two articles about social studies standards in U.S. education and the nature of history textbooks. In order to understand the various positions in this debate, we recommend reading the culturally conservative position in Lynn V. Cheney's (1994) "The End of History" in the *Wall Street Journal* and the politically progressive response by Robert Cohen (1996) in the journal *Social Education.* The political debates about *The American People* in

Hudson, Ohio, are a reflection of intense national debate about hermeneutics and history textbooks. There is much at stake in these debates, and ethical responses to global events today are shaped in many ways by the manner in which we approach historical interpretation in schools, classrooms, curricular materials, and textbooks.

A few weeks after the initial rejection of this text, the district administrators presented additional information to the school board in a meeting covered by the national news media, and *The American People* was adopted for use in the schools. Patti Picard, the assistant superintendent for curriculum and instruction in Hudson who made the presentation to the board, concluded that educators must recognize the complexity and political dimensions of the textbook adoption process and be prepared to work diligently to address the multiple concerns that are raised about history standards, curricular practices, and textbook reviews. Having reflected on these specific examples of hermeneutic interpretation in the first part of this chapter, we now examine specific applications of hermeneutics that will help to contextualize these narratives.

Classroom Examples of Synthesis and Wide-Awakeness

A graduate student in one of my (Patrick) classes who studied the concepts presented in this chapter appreciated my perspective, but she could not imagine implementing these ideas in her own classroom. Her principal demanded daily lesson plans with specific outcomes tied to the state proficiency tests in math, reading, science, and English as outlined in the district curriculum guide. Her tenure depended on how well her students performed on these tests, and her pay scale followed a merit system that rewarded compliance with the traditional program. She resented the environment this system created, but she saw no realistic possibility of deviating from the planned curriculum. Moreover, her students behaved so disruptively and their participation was so sporadic that she doubted they would accept a contextual and experiential curriculum. In short, she considered postmodern hermeneutics too idealistic and impractical. But for her final course project, she decided to explore the possibilities.

Because the district did not test social studies, and because most teachers skipped the thirty-minute social studies block to spend more time on the "important" tested subjects, she decided to experiment with her relatively safe social studies curriculum. She videotaped her lessons for the two-week unit on deserts. Instead of writing lesson plans in advance with specific objectives and evaluation requirements, she introduced the lesson much as Dana did at the Massachusetts Leadership Academy, discussed in Chapter 1. She made this simple statement: "Today we begin our next unit in social studies. Our topic is deserts." Bored and distracted faces appeared on the video. A few prepared to take notes. Others sat in respectful silence waiting for instructions. Then she dropped her bombshell: "I do not know very much about deserts. I have never been to a desert. We are going to have to figure out how to learn about deserts together." Immediately, one student raised his hand. "I went to a desert in California last summer." He described his trip enthusiastically, but he struggled to remember the name of the desert. Another student suggested they look at a map and find its name. The class moved to the map. Another student pointed to Africa and said that her father once went hunting on a safari. "What's a safari?" another student asked. The student described her father's trip, and then the class consulted a dictionary to find a definition. Over the next few days, the students decided to divide themselves into groups to investigate deserts. One group selected animals of the deserts, and they made a small-scale model of a desert and a safari. Another group drew maps of the various deserts of the world. Other groups investigated plant life, human habitation, and survival in the desert. A few students joined the girl whose father went on a safari to look at his photos and conduct an interview.

The teacher reported that she had never seen such enthusiasm for a unit of study in her entire career. Students who formerly presented severe behavior problems emerged as group leaders. Another group of students went to the library every day at recess to find more information about their topics. The teacher became convinced of the power of the hermeneutic circle when she completed this experimental project. The maps and models of deserts were displayed in the corridor and caught the attention of other teachers. We suspect that this teacher will now find ways to resist a steady dose of the traditional approach to curriculum and instruction in the future. This was one teacher's attempt to implement the things she had learned in her graduate class on hermeneutics and postmodern theory. She began to shift her way of viewing education as she deconstructed the modern curriculum in her school district. This is the first step in creating an educational ethics for justice based on experience and activism. Let us consider another example.

Tom Schwandt was the first person to introduce me (Dana) to the possibilities and dangers of postmodern hermeneutic study and, like Patrick's student, my work will never be the same. I was enrolled in Schwandt's Philosophy of Social Science seminar during the spring semester of my initial year as a Ph.D. student in the educational policy studies program at Indiana University. The experience threw me for an assortment of personal and professional loops. At first, I saw no importance in studying or debating issues of objectivity, grounded theory, reality, and existentialism. What relevance did they have to my life as a teacher and administrator and my future ambitions to be a professor of educational leadership? I had never heard of Geertz, Gadamer, or Habermas. Where are the Sergiovannis, the Fullans, the Demings, and the Deals, I thought? How can this course help me become a better professor of educational leadership? What does this have to do with the "real world"? As it turns out, the discussions that arose in Schwandt's class around these subjects have changed me forever. I say this not only in terms of how I approach written texts, but also in terms of how I approach each social situation or teaching context.

There were moments in Schwandt's class when much of the clarity in my life appeared contrived and my work seemed superficial. Suddenly, things that had been lucid and concrete became gray and kaleidoscopic. Questions of "how" slowly evolved into "why," and my self-assurance morphed into self-doubt. I began to ask many questions: "What do you mean, that reality is socially constructed? How can truth not be verifiable? Does reality itself not exist?" My defensive questioning was soon overwhelmed by feelings of personal insecurity. I became unsettled and quiet. I wondered if my experiences were that much different from others', and if so, whose experiences were more valid and real. Maybe many of the universal definitions and absolute truths I had learned in my youth were comfortable and attractive to me because I had never been exposed to other ways of viewing the world. Perhaps my position in the world as a white, male, heterosexual, athletic, and economically privileged American was creating and limiting my realties. I began to realize that my motivations, aspirations, and values are not divinely appointed but socially constructed. Eventually, I began to ask, "Who am I, and why do I value the things I value?"

Schwandt's teaching convictions and personal encouragement challenged me to investigate and deconstruct textbooks, media, and ideologies, whether economic, social, spiritual, sexual, or political. I cautiously accepted the postmodern position articulated by Robert Fowler: "Reading and interpretation is always interested, never disinterested, always significantly subjective, never completely objective; always committed and therefore always political, never uncommitted and apolitical; always historically bound, never ahistorical" (Aichele et al., 1995, p. 14). I was consumed with Louis Althusser's caution, "There is no such thing as an innocent reading" (qtd. in Aichele et al., 1995, p. 5) and the questions that I pursued in relation to it. Jacques Derrida influenced my burgeoning fascination with the possibilities of deconstruction, desacrelization, and decolonization:

> Deconstruction was not destruction, in other words. Rather, it was a dismantling of structures (philosophical, cultural, political, institutional, and above all and from the start textual) that was designed to show how they were put together in the first place. . . . Deconstruction seeks out those points within a system where it disguises the fact of its incompleteness, its failure to cohere as self-contained whole. . . . This amounts neither to destroying nor dismantling the system in total, but rather demonstrating how the (w)hole, through the masking of its logical and rhetorical contradiction, maintains the illusion of its completeness. (qtd. in Aichele et al., 1995, p. 120)

Fowler, Althusser, and Derrida challenged me to ask penetrating ethical questions about education and historical criticism: How does history get told in schools? Who is empowered to do the telling? What perspectives are ignored and erased? Am I comfortable with my privileged social situation or am I willing to change it? In the economic realm, what is the bottom line? What does the construction of the notion of a bottom line do to the poor? Who is relegated to the margins of society? Whose interests and power are my interpretations serving? How can a text liberate and bring about positive social change? Can the reading of the text expose injustices related to race, class, religion, neocolonialism, gender, and sexual identity? Who is represented? Who is excluded, silenced, and absent? How long have I been living in a historical amnesia? Why didn't my teachers before Schwandt help me explore these important questions? (Aichele et al., 1995, p. 303).

The hermeneutic process that I initially found so repugnant in Schwandt's class ultimately captivated me. I began to search for analysis and insights on issues related to poverty, hunger, ecology, relationships, sex, love, identity, and spirituality. The uncertainty that arose with each new question caused me to appreciate my partner, who was willing to grow with me to deeper levels of ambiguity. This was especially true when we both began to question our beliefs regarding the dominant religion in our society, Christianity. What is a good Christian? Are we born into original blessedness, as Matthew Fox (1990) contends, or into the original sin of traditional theological notions? Was Jesus a fictional character, did he exist, and does it really matter? Why have many Christians developed an addictive fascination with the sins of the body? Why do some continue to insist that homosexuality is a sin and cause so much pain and injustice for gay, lesbian, bisexual, and transgendered (GLBT) persons? Why do some religious people gloat over and glorify their accumulated privilege and love of money? Why do our churchgoing friends defend war, vengeance, and the loss of life? What is the sociopolitical significance of Jesus' transformative life and ignominious death? What was Jesus' political stand? Was he a radical and a zealot who advocated the violent overthrow of the Roman imperial government? Was he made a scapegoat for teaching against the dominant ideology? Was he an advocate of nonviolence similar to Gandhi's *satagraha,* truth or soul force? (Aichele et al., 1995, p. 293).

I wonder if I am willing to deconstruct my own religious, social, political, and sexual realities. I am comfortable investigating the media and government images of war that are meant to both entertain and indoctrinate us. I am also eager to interrogate and destabilize the myths and values that have structured my white, middle-class view of professionalism and education. I seriously question, however, as does Kathy, the extent to which I have the courage to honestly engage in deconstructing the social structures and privileges that accrue to my heterosexuality. Sexual orientation and gender identity are often the points at which many progressive and compassionate people, such as Candida, who you will learn about later, jump ship. My experience with deconstruction has forever made me more "wide-awake" to my complicity in injustice and my obligation to articulate what is good and what is ethical in schools and society. I am particularly committed to deconstructing heterosexism and homophobia, the topic of our next section.

Teaching Convictions on Gay and Lesbian Issues and Religion

In this section, we contrast traditional theological hermeneutics and conservative philosophical hermeneutics with reflective, critical, and poststructural approaches to hermeneutics on the topic of gay and lesbian issues in education. We present a series of challenging narratives that deconstruct heterosexism and homophobia in schools and society. We propose that a postmodern approach to ethics offers opportunities not only for justice for gay, lesbian, bisexual, intersexual, and transgendered persons but also, by extension, acceptance of all marginalized persons in contemporary schools and society.

Queer theory and other investigations of the legitimacy of identities and the power relations that oppose multiple identity formation—as well as investigations of anti-identity positionalities—have emerged as important areas of study in the academy. We suspect that the investigation of the effects of power on individuals and communities may be one of the more important theoretical trends of the postmodern era. The effects of power on the objects it represents (Ellsworth, 1997; Rouse, 1987) are associated with two different theoretical lines of research: identity politics, movements that represent the empowerment and civil rights agenda of groups marginalized by their racial, gender, sexual, physical, and other identities, and queer theory, philosophies that investigate notions of identity by "refusing normal practices and the practice of normalcy," by "exploring those things that education either dismisses or cannot bear to know," and by "imagining a sociality unhinged from the dominant conceptual order" (Britzman, 1995). On the one hand, queer theory can be understood as deconstructing and protesting the idea of "normal" behavior; on the other hand, it can be understood to emphasize diverse forms of individual and social identity and the ways gender itself is constructed. Queer theory actually problematizes identity politics because identities are shifting and fluid, not confined by labels such as straight, gay, lesbian, or bisexual. Thus, naming identities serves the political cause of normalizing. In either case, queer theories and identity politics have become forms of contemporary research advocating for multiplicity and diversity at the heart of any research question.

Recent interest in queer theory has led to a proliferation of writing and research in this vein. My (Patrick) own political and personal activism recently led me to participate in the ALLY training program at Texas A&M University, a support program for gay, lesbian, bisexual, and transgendered students. Faculty, administrators, staff, and students—gay and straight, as well as those who resist binary identities—are all invited to become ALLIES, and a plaque is provided for them to affix to their office or dormitory door to indicate a supportive and safe environment for information or conversation on GLBT issues. During my first semester at Texas A&M in 1998, I did not notice any ALLY plaques in the education building. When I registered for the spring training workshop, I encouraged some of my colleagues to attend with me. To my pleasant surprise, many did. By the spring semester, ALLY plaques were displayed in the education building on several office doors, including that of the dean of education and other administrative staff. A simple invitation met with a generous response.

The positive reaction of many of my colleagues in education was in stark contrast to the strong heterosexism and homophobia that is evident on our campus and all campuses to varying degrees. Last semester I spotted a tee-shirt worn by a few undergraduate male students on campus that read: "No Fags: A Tradition from the Beginning." This message reflected the anger of some students—and maybe some form of unconscious self-analysis—following a public incident at Bonfire (a sacred campus ritual that came to national attention in 1999 with a fatal collapse of the structure and death of twelve students) that resulted in the president of the university apologizing for antigay remarks made by a star football player. This ignited a round of letters to the editor in the student newspaper for the next several months, including the following:

> 1 Corinthians 6:9–10 states, "Do you not know that the wicked will not inherit the kingdom of God? Do not be deceived: Neither the sexually immoral nor idolaters nor adulterers nor male prostitutes nor homosexual offenders nor thieves nor the greedy nor drunkards nor slanderers nor swindlers will inherit the kingdom of God." It's pretty simple, huh? It is in the bible after all. . . . So, when two men or women come to a church to be wed in holy matrimony, it cannot be done. God will not recognize it, and He will not tolerate it. That is why the church cannot accept homosexuality. Now, I ask you, why is it so hard to see that homosexuality is wrong? It is straight from the Scriptures. It is the word of God, and God's word cannot be compromised. (Harris, 1999. p. 6)

There are many hermeneutical and linguistic problems evident in this letter, not the least of which is the fact that divergent exegetical interpretations and contradictory congregational practices are often derived from the same Christian Scriptures—the contents of which vary from translation to translation. If all drunkards and slanderers are included in the condemnation, then most college students are in big trouble! Even words such as *homosexuality* are not found in most translations of this passage. In short, a comparative study reveals that there is no single "bible" and no standard translation of the various Christian bibles or other sacred texts. Of course, there are also many other sacred and philosophical texts all vying for wider legitimization and acceptance, such as the Koran, the Torah, the Book of Mormon, the Tao Te Ching, the Humanist Manifesto, the Hindu Scriptures, the Bhagavad Gita, and the Gnostic Scriptures. If there are multiple interpretations of these various texts, how can legitimate inspiration and guidance be uncovered or constructed? This is one task of hermeneutics.

I (Patrick) recently had dinner with a graduate school administrator of a private university. We have been colleagues and friends for years. He identifies himself as a born-again, politically conservative Christian. We share some common philosophical and pedagogical perspectives, but we have politely avoided debating controversial theological and political topics about which we certainly disagree. Our last conversation was an exception. He asked me bluntly, "I know that you have studied theology and that you are committed to spirituality, so I cannot understand why you allow discussion of gay and lesbian issues in your books and in your classes. Clearly, the Bible says homosexuality is a sin."

I choked on my food. How does one respond? I thought for a moment about discussing diversity, academic freedom, postmodern eclecticism, tolerance, gay bashing, the contribution of gay and lesbian poets and scientists, Matthew Shepard,

Melissa Ethridge, Ellen Degeneres, Walt Whitman, Stonewall, or anything but religion in relation to homosexuality. It is often a no-win situation. However, I decided to tackle the hermeneutic question head-on this time. I was growing weary of polite disengagement.

I recalled a recent scandal reported on the front page of the local newspaper concerning my colleague's Christian denomination. In fact, I remembered that his congregation had a schism over this scandal. So I tried this approach: "I heard that your congregation divided recently when your popular pastor was fired after he announced that he divorced his wife." My friend nodded in agreement. "Does your bible condemn divorce?" I asked. He nodded again. "Did your church board overturn the decision to defrock the pastor for violation of church law and biblical injunctions?" "Yes, they did," he replied. He continued enthusiastically, "A prominent Christian theologian was hired by the church to resolve the question. The theologian explained to the board and later to the congregation the cultural and social context for the biblical injunction against divorce." My colleague then summarized the theologian's historical analysis. "The biblical scholar told us that at the time of the writing of Scriptures many men were abandoning their wives without providing a decree of divorce. The women were then left destitute and unable to remarry. Once our board understood that the Bible condemned only the sin of not providing a decree of divorce, then they decided to reinstate our pastor. Those that disagreed with this decision split off and formed their own congregation. Our pastor is a good man, and we love him. He did the Christian thing by providing the decree of divorce. This is what the Bible requires."

The theologian hired by my colleague's mainline Protestant church used traditional hermeneutics to investigate the cultural and social context of a scriptural text, and then he translated the intention of the prohibition against divorce in a modern context. There has been an evolution in thinking about the very concrete statements in Christian bibles that prohibit divorce. Practices have changed; popular pastors have been reinstated in some conservative Christian congregations. Biblical interpretations are fluid and culturally conditioned on issues as diverse as divorce, dietary regulations, sacred rituals, clothing, ministerial leadership for women, usury, and sexuality.

An excellent film we use in our classes titled *There Is a Wideness in God's Mercy* (Soulforce, 2000) addresses this topic thoroughly and thoughtfully. The film features an interview with the prominent theologian, pastor, and author Reverend Lewis Smedes, who describes the complexity and multiplicity of biblical interpretation in various contexts. Another teaching tool we use is a popular Internet letter sent to antigay radio personality Laura Schlessinger that exposes the hermeneutic dilemma. The tongue-in-cheek letter dramatically demonstrates the problem of using texts of any kind to generate infallible truth statements. This letter might best be described as a poststructural and postmodern hermeneutic response to heterosexism. Dr. Laura, as she is popularly known, stated on her radio program that homosexuality is an abomination according to Leviticus 18:22 and cannot be condoned in any circumstance.

The following response was posted anonymously on the Internet as a challenge to her position:

Dear Dr. Laura:

Thank you for doing so much to educate people regarding God's law. I have learned a great deal from your show, and I try to share that knowledge with as many people as I can. When someone tries to defend the homosexual lifestyle, for example, I simply remind them that Leviticus 18:22 clearly states it to be an abomination. End of debate. I need some advice from you, however, regarding some of the specific laws and how to follow them. (a) When I burn a bull on the altar of sacrifice, I know it creates a pleasing odor for the Lord (Lev. 1:9). The problem is my neighbors. They claim the odor is not pleasing to them. Should I smite them? (b) I would like to sell my daughter into slavery, as sanctioned in Exodus 21:7. In this day and age, what do you think would be a fair price for her? (c) I know that I am allowed no contact with a woman while she is in her period of menstrual uncleanliness (Lev. 15:19–24). The problem is, how do I tell? I have tried asking, but most women take offense. (d) Leviticus 25:44 states that I may indeed possess slaves, both male and female, provided they are purchased from neighboring nations. A friend of mine claims that this applies to Mexicans but not Canadians. Can you clarify? Why can't I own Canadians? (e) I have a neighbor who insists on working on the Sabbath. Exodus 35:2 clearly states he should be put to death. Am I morally obligated to kill him myself? (f) A friend of mine feels that even though eating shellfish is an abomination (Lev. 11:10), it is a lesser abomination than homosexuality. I don't disagree. Can you settle this? (g) Lev. 21:20 states that I may not approach the altar of God if I have a defect in my sight. I do have to admit I wear reading glasses. Does my vision have to be 20/20, or is there some wiggle room here? (h) Most of my male friends get their hair trimmed, including the hair around their temples, even thought this is expressly forbidden by Lev. 19:27. How should they die? (i) I know from Lev. 11:6–8 that touching the skin of a dead pig makes me unclean, but may I still play football if I wear gloves? (j) My uncle has a farm. He violates Lev. 19:19 by planting two different crops in the same field, as does his wife by wearing garments made of two different kinds of threads (cotton & polyester blend). He also tends to curse and blaspheme a lot. Is it really necessary that we go to all the trouble of getting the whole town together to stone them (Lev. 24:10–16)? Couldn't we just burn them to death in a private family affair like we do with people who sleep with their in-laws (Lev. 20:14)? I know that you have studied these things extensively, so I am confident you can help. Thank you again for reminding us that God's word is eternal and unchanging. Your devoted disciple and adoring fan.

This letter reminds us of the difficulty of selecting passages from any text to assign absolute interpretations. This is especially repugnant when people use interpretations to justify persecution and marginalization of people because of race, religion, ability, class, gender, or sexual identity. Why have so many people accepted illogical and unjust interpretations of texts (whether the Koran, Christian Scriptures, Hebrew Scriptures, or Gnostic Scriptures)? The study of hermeneutics and theology is essential in order to understand the various genres that are used in these texts such as mythology, allegory, embellishment, and parables, and to recognize that the meaning of all texts changes over time in various historical contexts based on social constructions of ethics, aesthetics, and morality. One of the most dangerous phenomena occurring throughout the world is narrow interpretation of sacred texts and the arrogance of those who profess to know the truth. We seek to deconstruct narrow and unjust applications of hermeneutics.

I (Patrick) am reminded of two other events, one from 1998 and another from 1959, that further explicate our philosophy. In 1998 the dean of students at a Christian university told me that he reluctantly prohibited a gay and lesbian group from meeting on campus because the president and board of trustees told him he would be fired if he allowed any discussion of homosexuality or the formation of any groups for gay and lesbian students on campus. Further, the board wanted to remove the word *diversity* from the mission statement for fear that some would think that gays and lesbians might be included. Faculty were intimidated, reprimanded, and even dismissed if the topic of sexual orientation was discussed in classes. GLBT students, if discovered, were immediately expelled (even if they abstained from intimate or sexual relations). The dean wondered if the library would soon be purged of books by gay and lesbian authors, poets, and scientists. Or perhaps, historical or psychological books that included chapters on homosexuality. Or research that did not conform to the biblical interpretations of the president and board. Or non-Christian authors. He worried about where the silencing would lead next. In the short term, the dean decided to ignore his conscience and comply with the university, but a few years later he resigned and moved to an inclusive and affirming college.

In 1959, I (Patrick) was a first-grade student in New Orleans. Ruby Bridges was also a first grader in a nearby school. All campuses were in turmoil as Ruby courageously faced the angry mobs of white parents chanting, "Two, four, six, eight, we don't want to integrate!" They yelled and spat at her as she walked into her classroom with federal marshals. I overheard many angry adults shouting insults in those dark days. I was wide-eyed and impressionable, and I vividly remember this statement being repeated again and again, "The Bible says that slaves must be obedient to their masters. What right do niggers have contaminating our schools? The Bible says that niggers are offspring of Enoch and must keep in their place!" The phrase "The Bible says" reminds me of intense hatred and bigotry in both 1959 and 1998.

Fortunately, there is hope. Otherwise, why would we continue our research to create a just and compassionate society? There is a growing body of scholarly literature that deconstructs gender and orientation bias (i.e., Britzman, 1995; Sears, 1992; Letts & Sears, 1999; Scroggs, 1983; Fausto-Sterling, 2000; Pinar, 1994, 1998; Kumashiro, 2003; Macgillivray, 2002). It is important for this information to be disseminated to a wider audience.

Having studied theology formally for a graduate degree in the 1970s and informally for scholarly publications over the past twenty-five years, I (Patrick) am particularly interested in an analysis and deconstruction of decontextualized theological arguments that are perpetuated in letters like the one cited by the Texas A&M student.

I have been criticized in the past for including chapters on theology in my books. Some of my colleagues contend that there is no room for dialogue with religious bigots and modern-day zealots because they always reduce theological discussions to the authority of canonical texts and submissiveness to a politically hegemonic religious ideology that is often unjust. Others argue that my postmodern ecumenical theological perspectives—inspired originally by Hans Kung (1988)—undermine all religions and spiritualities by stripping them of their unique faith claims, making them inappropriate for academic discourse.

We are not persuaded by either argument. In fact, we believe that such disengagement perpetuates injustice. We must enter the debate forcefully and compassionately. All of our curriculum theorizing, critical theories, feminist theories, identity politics, queer theories, multicultural theories, and postcolonial theories are jeopardized if they do not include theological deconstruction and an openness to liberation through an ecumenical humanism and spirituality. Likewise, theological studies that exclude critical hermeneutics, cultural studies, and political activism have lost their prophetic voice (Dewey, 1934b). We even suggest that a mutual engagement of theology and critical/cultural studies is part of the formula for a peaceful resolution of conflicts not only in Yugoslavia, Afghanistan, Northern Ireland, Rwanda, Haiti, Kashmir, Tibet, East Timor, Congo, and Chiapas, but also on U.S. soil following the September 11, 2001, events. We also believe that homophobia and heterosexism are rooted, in part, in narrow interpretations and misrepresentations of canonical religious texts. With William Pinar (1999), we may be able to move beyond the political domination of the Christian churches and "imagine [that] these final months of the millennium are also the 'last days' of the Christian period and the beginning of a truly new age in which authentic spirituality humanizes rather than maims and kills" (p. 42). If so, then a critical engagement in theological discourse may be more than quaint; it may be essential. We address this topic in more detail in Chapter 3.

As I (Patrick) look back on some of my earlier publications, I must reevaluate my naiveté at times (e.g., Slattery, 1995). I have assumed a generosity of spirit similar to that of my Texas A&M colleagues who joined the ALLY support group. Maybe I omitted the fact that the ALLY members are a tiny fraction of the campus population. Maybe religious intolerance runs so deep that dialogue is impossible. Maybe my administrator friend is unwilling to listen to hermeneutic analysis except when it meets his personal needs to reinstate a popular pastor. Maybe the dean of students at the Christian university is too intimidated to speak up for the gay and lesbian students for fear that he may lose his job. Maybe we all assume too much goodwill. Maybe William Pinar's authentic spirituality that liberates rather than maims and kills is still another millennium away. Maybe the rash of vandalism to the office doors of professors who display ALLY signs is an indication of the intensity of hatred that exists on campus. Despite the odds, we continue to affirm the possibility of a critical and constructive postmodernism that includes an ecumenical theology and liberating spirituality.

When vandalism or gay bashing occurs on our campuses, we choose to address it rather than ignore it. When a math professor in my (Patrick) department who is president of the College Station PFLAG (Parents, Families and Friends of Lesbians and Gays) recently had his office vandalized because of his ALLY sign, I joined other faculty members in offering this resolution to be displayed in our department office and classrooms and included in our course syllabi:

> The Department of Teaching, Learning and Culture (TLAC) does not tolerate discrimination, violence, or vandalism. TLAC is an open and affirming department for all people, including those who are subjected to racial profiling, hate crimes, heterosexism, and violence. We insist that appropriate action be taken against those who perpetrate discrimination, violence, or vandalism. Texas A&M University is an Affirmative Action and Equal Opportunity institution and affirms its dedication to non-discrimination on the basis of race, color, religion, gender, age, sexual orientation, domestic partner status, national origin, or disability in employment, programs, and services. Our commitment to non-discrimination and affirmative action embraces the entire university community including faculty, staff, and students.

This statement met with the unanimous approval of my colleagues, even though one person suggested that we simply affirm the university diversity policy without any specific mention of GLBT. When pressed for an explanation, the reason presented was that specifying one group could lead to a long list of diverse groups to be affirmed, including "left-handed, skinny, and blue-eyed people." This critic also stated that some religious people might be offended by a statement of support for GLBT persons. I pointed out that "left-handed, skinny, and blue-eyed people" are not subjected to vandalism, discrimination in employment, and marginalization because of their condition. Likewise, Matthew Shepard in Wyoming and our own Texas A&M graduate Paul Broussard had been brutally murdered for being gay. Left-handed people are not victims of hate crimes. Finally, I challenged those who base prejudice on religion to reexamine the history of religious intolerance, which we do in detail in Chapter 3.

The examination of religious intolerance must begin with a study of hermeneutics that allows for a careful deconstruction of concepts such as "*The* Bible" and "*The* Word of God." In our society, this in itself is a dangerous enterprise. With my devout (mostly Protestant Christian) students, I always begin our study of hermeneutics and religion with two simple questions: "Have you ever heard of the Dead Sea Scrolls?" and "Have you ever heard of the Nag Hammadi Scrolls?" My students unanimously respond in the affirmative to the first question and in the negative to the second. This is as good a place as any to engage my students in a hermeneutical analysis for social justice. As the lecture unfolds, there is always an audible gasp as students are exposed to information that challenges their taken-for-granted cosmology.

Let me briefly explain. As mentioned earlier, I spent a year in a Roman Catholic novitiate sponsored by a congregation in Santa Fe, New Mexico. Most of that year was devoted to silent reading, meditation, and reflection. (What a luxury! I would love to have another year of uninterrupted reading and meditation in the high desert of the Land of Enchantment.) For a short part of that year, I lived in a Cistercian and Benedictine monastery in Abiquiu, New Mexico, where I stumbled on a book that changed my life. Like the monk in Umberto Eco's novel *The Name of the Rose,* the discovery of this mysterious manuscript unveiled secrets that astonished me. I would never again look at the world through the same lens. My religious cosmology was problematized, just as my students' cosmology is challenged in my education courses today.

The book, of course, was a translation of the Nag Hammadi library of Gnostic Scriptures discovered in Egypt at about the same time as the Dead Sea Scrolls. "Why," I purposely ponder in my embellished southern drawl, "were these scrolls from Nag Hammadi hidden from public analysis but the canonical scrolls of the Dead Sea widely disseminated and studied?" In my lectures, I read samples of both libraries before discussing the history of hermeneutics. I point out that we have never fully resolved the debate about the canon of Judeo-Christian Scriptures, as is most evident in the ongoing theological debate about deuterocanonical—or as Protestants today insist, apocryphal—books of "*the*" Bible. (The King James Bible in the nineteenth century and some Protestant bibles of the twentieth century still contain the Apocrypha, but only as holy literature and not inspired Scripture.) In short, my point is that canonical, duterocanonical, apocryphal, and Gnostic texts and their interpretations are contested not only by those working outside of a religious traditions but also by scholars and theologians within various sects and denominations. My friend's congregation split over the interpretation of divorce decree. Women are ordained in some congregations but not in others. Gay and lesbian pastors are ordained in some mainline churches like the Disciples of Christ and the United Church of Christ and prohibited in others. I always enjoy reading to my students portions of the Nag Hammadi scrolls that closely resemble traditional Judeo-Christian texts, noting that it is sometimes difficult to decide on authenticity and authorship.

I remember taking a theology class in Berkeley in the 1970s from Raymond Brown, the internationally renowned biblical theologian. I asked him whether any of the Nag Hammadi scrolls or any future texts that may be discovered in Egypt, Greece, or the Negev could ever be included in canonical Judeo-Christian scriptures, even if, for example, they could be authenticated by all biblical scholars as legitimate documents. An example might be "The Third Letter of Paul to the Corinthians," for which we have internal and external evidence of its existence. He answered in the negative, indicating that hermeneutics alone cannot authenticate a document; ecclesiastical approbation is required. And because the canon of Scripture was closed at the end of the Council of Trent, future changes are impossible. So much for the hermeneutic circle!

Returning to the student letter about "the word of God," we are struck by the fact that various official interpretations of the exact same passage in other Christian bibles do not include the word *homosexual.* All translations reflect cultural, linguistic, and political motivations. For example, the New American Bible (Roman Catholic) uses this litany: "No fornicators, idolaters, adulterers, sodomites, thieves, misers, drunkards, slanderers, or robbers will inherit God's kingdom." We see in Chapter 3 the problems associated with various interpretations of the word *sodomite.* From Foucault (1986a, 1990) in *The History of Sexuality,* we learn about the creation of "homosexuality" as a discursive and social concept for surveillance and regulation in the nineteenth century. Our purpose here is not to produce a complete historical exegesis. (For interested readers, we recommend in addition to Foucault's books the texts *The New Testament and Homosexuality* [Scroggs, 1983] and *What the Bible Really Says about Homosexuality* [Helminiak, 2000] as a good overview of the problem of interpretation on this topic.) Rather, we seek to problematize, deconstruct, and reevaluate decontextualized and uncritical sociopolitical positions based on fundamentalist use of texts to prove an absolute truth within a particular narrative tradition.

Scroggs (1983) divides theologians into two camps: those who believe that the Christian Bible opposes homosexuality and those who believe that the Christian Bible does not oppose homosexuality. In the first group, there are five different positions taken by theologians, congregations, and denominations: (1) The Bible opposes homosexuality and is definitive on what the church should think and do about it. Thus, ordination of homosexuals and same-sex marriages are prohibited; (2) The Bible opposes homosexuality, but it is just one sin among many (e.g., the list in 1 Corinthians 6). There is no justification for singling out homosexuality as more serious than other sins castigated in the Bible. Thus, ordination (and in some cases, same-sex marriage) for homosexuals is permitted; (3) The Bible opposes homosexuality but the specific injunctions must be placed in the larger biblical context of the theology of creation, sin, judgment, and grace. This position is divided into two subgroups, those who argue from the position of creation and see homosexuality as a deviation from the male and female sexual union, and those who argue from the principle of love and support wholesome and edifying human relationships of any kind. Thus, the believer is free and called to responsibility to make *independent* judgments about what counts as "human relationships which affirm life and love"; (4) The Bible opposes homosexuality but is so time- and culture-bound that its injunctions may and should be discarded if other considerations suggest better alternatives. If Leviticus and Paul are addressing situations so foreign to our own times, there is no reason to apply those judgments, and thus ordination and same-sex unions are possible; (5) The Bible does not oppose homosexuality, only homosexual acts. This is the position of the Roman Catholic Church and some other denominations. Thus, heterosexuals and homosexuals may be ordained as long as they pledge celibacy to the local bishop.

Scroggs (1983) then discusses how these five interpretations affect church law and community practices in many denominations. Obviously, there have been many changes in church discipline and congregational practices since the publication of this book in 1983, with some pastors and Christian churches becoming more affirming of homosexual members, same-sex marriage, and the ordination of gay and lesbian pastors. There are obviously widespread differences in church practices and theological positions.

The second category consists of those theologians and congregations who do not believe that the Bible opposes homosexuality: (1) The Bible does not oppose homosexuality because it does not speak of true or innate homosexuality but rather only of homosexual acts by people who are not homosexual; (2) The Bible does not oppose homosexuality because the texts do not deal with homosexuality in general. For example, the word *sodomite* has no contemporary scholarly translation and must be judged a mistranslation. The actual prohibition was prostitution and not homosexuality in general. In both of these cases, these theologians and pastors argue that it makes no sense not to allow homosexuals to serve as ministers and to marry. Scroggs (1983) presents the multiplicity of interpretations and practices in Christian denominations and theological seminaries. Although legal prohibitions may exist in the wider society, the practices within Christian churches vary dramatically. It is this variety of understandings that must be allowed to enter the hermeneutic circle and inform those who are unaware of the various interpretations and church practices.

Studying the specific case of the Nag Hammadi library and then applying the hermeneutic process to other textual problems is enlightening for some students and disturbing for others. Some students and scholars embrace the invitation to enter the hermeneutic circle; others retreat in bafflement or anger. It amazes us that more than any other issue we include in our syllabi, a careful hermeneutical study that includes deconstructing notions of gender, sexual orientation, and identity constructions generates the most hostile response. Without intending to elide the continuing tragedy of racism and classism, and without blurring the boundaries of race, class, ability, orientation, ethnicity, and gender, we are convinced that the civil rights issues exposed by queer theory and identity politics must continue to be foregrounded in our teaching, research, and social activism. This is one of the most important ethical and civil rights issues of our time, and if we can overcome prejudice based on gender identity and sexual orientation, we believe that many more doors will open for human rights in multiple other areas. We explore some of these other issues as we continue our analysis of critical ethical issues and education in upcoming chapters. For now, all of us should ask ourselves why gender, sexual orientation, and identity issues are so controversial and divisive in schools and society. A study of queer theory can help us evaluate the complexity of the competing notions of identity politics and enlarge the hermeneutic circle, hopefully to include an ecumenical theology, an authentic spirituality, and an active social conscience in the process.

Many courageous young people are blazing a trail for social consciousness and political activism. We think here of Brandon Fitzgerald, a high school senior who formed a Gay Straight Alliance (GSA) in his high school in Cleveland in 2001. Brandon, like so many other GLBT students and their straight allies, has taken the lead in educating administrators, teachers, and parents about the needs and contributions of gay youth. The GSA movement in high schools is proliferating, providing education and hope for thousands of young people. Brandon did not form the GSA without struggle. Only one year earlier, he came out to his classmates and teachers in a dramatic way. Brandon asked for permission to read a poem at a school assembly during his junior year, along with other students who were planning skits, poetry, and narratives for this assembly. Brandon was given permission by the moderator to read this poem:

> *Locked away minds of rainbow flags . . .*
> *Faces hidden beneath paper bags . . .*
> *Confused kids rolled away in body bags,*
> *'Cause everyone else always called them fags.*
> *They are the few, and they are often the crazed.*
> *They are mere mortals of life's twisted maze.*
> *They are fish in black water.*
> *They are the victims of history's ongoing slaughter.*
> *Years upon years*
> *My face drowns in tears.*
> *I shouldn't have to hide in fear*
> *Or fade into shadows and disappear.*
> *For me each day is a rainy day,*
> *In a world where being different is somehow not okay.*
> *Don't try to make me go away,*
> *'Cause I am who I am and that includes being gay.*
> *(Fitzgerald, 2001)*

Brandon's maturity and courage inspire us. But, as he states in his poem, life is not easy for those who are different from the culturally stereotyped norms. Others are not as fortunate, because hate can also kill. Reread Brandon's poem while listening to lesbian musician and entertainer Melissa Etheridge's song "Scarecrow," a poignant tribute to Matthew Shepard, the University of Wyoming gay student who was beaten mercilessly and left to die tied to an isolated ranch fence post. Matthew's only offense was being gay, his murderers' only excuse homophobia and hatred.

Unfortunately, Matthew's fate is not an isolated event. Professor John Aston has studied gay bashings and murders and reports that the typical high school student hears antigay slurs 22.5 times a day; 69 percent of youths perceived to be either gay or lesbian experience some form of harassment or violence in school, with over half of these (45.9 percent) experiencing it daily; and over one-third of youth reported hearing homophobic remarks from faculty or school staff (Aston, 2001b). In addition, Aston cited a 1993 Massachusetts Governor's Commission on Gay and Lesbian Youth study that reported that 85 percent of teachers oppose integrating gay/lesbian/bisexual studies within their curriculum (Aston, 2001a). Psychologist Karen Franklin's landmark study found thrill seeking, peer dynamics, and societal permission and encouragement as the primary motivations for antigay assaults (Franklin, 1997). If societal permission seems to be overstated, consider the response in Dallas by the Constitution Party of Texas (CPT) that led a protest of the Texas legislature's consideration of bills to protect gays and lesbians. The *Texas Triangle* reports:

> The men protesting, one who brought his five-year-old son to the event, believe homosexuality should be illegal, and ultimately punishable by death. They base their belief on the book of Leviticus in the Bible. "Well, we know punishing homosexuals by death would be extremely hard in today's society," said Larry S. Kilgore, the Dallas/Ft. Worth chairman of the Constitution Party. "But we hope that we can drive it under ground so in about twenty or thirty years, the punishment can fit the crime. ("Protesters," p. 7)

The attitude that it is permissable to kill not only gays and lesbians but also Jews, immigrants, and other minorities is promoted by several political groups, churches, and websites today. Just glance at the website www.americannaziparty.com to get a chilling glimpse of the hate rhetoric. We show two films to our students to impress on them the seriousness of this ethical nightmare: the dramatic fictional account of teenagers in Los Angeles in the film *American History X*—a must-see for all educators concerned about hate crimes—and *Licensed to Kill,* a documentary that interviews men in prison who killed gays and lesbians. One of the frightening aspects of both the fictional and the documentary films that must give critical educators pause is that the permission to murder is rooted in biblical interpretations, church sermons, and hate-filled rhetoric learned in educational settings. Our teaching convictions must direct us to counter hate speech in all its manifestations. Ignorance of the pervasiveness of this problem and silence in the face of hate crimes or hate speech are moral failures of educators and citizens that amount to complicity in the crime.

John Aston (2001b) followed up on Karen Franklin's research with a case study of one gay assailant in Houston, Texas, titled "Deconstructing Heterosexism and Homophobia in Schools":

> This investigation focuses on the internal and external factors that led to Jon Buice's murderous assault along with nine of his adolescent peers on a gay man, Paul Broussard, in Houston on the night of July 4, 1991. The study examines the societal sense of permission to harass and assault those who violate gender norms, with a particular focus on the role of schools as passively and sometimes actively contributing to a sense of permission. . . . This case study shows that Jon was more typical than atypical of young male adolescents in our highly gendered and patriarchal society. He was driven by thrill seeking and peer dynamics to attack societally-permitted targets rather than by any knowingly antigay ideology. The members of Jon's school and community may make convenient scapegoats of Jon and his companions, but this study indicates that we are all implicit in such acts, and ends with suggestions about ways to end our school's complicity in such grim oppression. (p. iii–iv)

Our teaching convictions must arouse educators to examine their complicity and silence on gay bashing, teasing, and violence against minorities and those perceived as different in schools and society. Aston's recommendations must become an integral part of teacher education workshops, administrative policy, and classroom practices. These recommendations include:

> Establish and maintain gay-straight alliances, where students and staff, whether gay or straight, could get together for mutual support and understanding without being branded or labeled as one or the other. Include [GLBT] issues in the curriculum. Sadly, such [curricular materials and] alliances, I found, are frequently against school and/or district policy. Indeed any mention of homosexuality, whether in sex ed., health, history, or any other subject, is frequently not allowed. Stop the antigay language, even when kids say "that's so gay" . . . I would never again let another bit of such "language" go unchallenged, so help me God. I would speak up, and out, and add my voice to all those who seek full civil rights and liberty for the GLBT community. Finally, I would no longer remain silent, or in any way equivocate. (Aston, 2001b, p. 71)

Can all educators take such a positive ethical stance? We hope so!

We conclude this section with a poignant story that summarizes the difficulty of this topic. In my third semester of teaching, I (Dana) received a call from a woman who wanted to enroll in my inquiry seminar Education and Pop Culture. Inquiry seminars are the culminating experiences for master's students of curriculum and instruction. Most of the time, professors and students develop semester-long seminars out of the negotiated interests of about fifteen people. In the case of Education and Pop Culture, a student named Candida was excited about pursuing many issues—race, class, gender, aesthetic inquiry, religion, identity, multiculturalism, and ecological sustainability—that she had passionately discovered in another professor's course. Candida conveyed on the phone that God was the driving force behind her commitment to love, care, and work for justice. "That is why I loved Dr. Smith's course so much. I cried when I knew he was leaving for another university. You appear to be trying to raise similar issues. Dr. Smith was a saint, a scholar, a loving man, a wise man. He was the most influential person in my fifty-six-year-old life. He was the most spiritually grounded and aware man that I have met. What a prophet. He changed my life." "Wow," I thought, "this Professor Smith must have been an amazing shaman to be able to effect the fundamentalist Christian, Candida, to such an extent. What praise!"

I secured Candida a position in the seminar, and I was looking forward to seeing how this passionate woman's agenda for social justice and love would influence and connect with the values and practices of students who were not so outward in their Christian beliefs. I didn't have to wait long, as one of the first sentences out of Candida's mouth almost knocked me off my chair. Within the first hour of our first meeting, Candida had announced that homosexuality was a sin and that she could never understand, respect, trust, or love people with gay, lesbian, bisexual, or transsexual identities. "How can I trust anyone who is going to hell?" she asked. Our conversation soon shifted to the issue of sexual orientation and identity as several students spoke up to condemn Candida's animated disgust. But Candida was not moved by our three-hour-long conversation and testimony; her tone, comments, and body language indicated complete disdain even for the word *homosexuality*. Candida was an anomaly. She spoke frankly and passionately about her experiences with racism. She decried patriarchy in her church relationships and within the contexts of theological development. She was appalled at the growing disparities of wealth in the United States. And she had written a collection of poems about her reaction to the raping of natural environments. I could see how her concerns would align her with Dr. Smith and why she would continually raise his name in the spirit of her rekindled faith and social activism. Dr. Smith's philosophies occupied our discussions on more than one occasion. In fact, two hours into our last meeting of the semester a few students became aware that I might bump into Professor Smith at a conference in San Diego. A card was circulated and signed by ten students of all ages, colors, and economic backgrounds, and I was asked to hand-deliver it to him. Before we knew it, our seminar time had elapsed and it was time to leave. Candida was the last person to shake my hand and say goodbye. "I want to thank you for a wonderful course," she said, "but, more important, I need you to pass on my sincere, loving, and divinely respectful praise and allegiance to Dr. Smith." Candida began to cry. "He'll never know how much he meant to me." "Of course I will, Candida. He would love to know how much you love him and how important his class was. I'll be seeing him and his partner John in San Diego, and I'll pass on the message." Candida's mouth dropped. She appeared frozen for a split second, but her tears intensified as she ran out the door and toward her car.

I have not heard from Candida since, and I wonder how she has reconciled this experience. I wonder how she compares what she has heard from parents, neighbors, friends, ministers, and educators with what she believes to be true regarding Dr. Smith. Will she read and interpret her Bible differently when it comes to sexual orientation? Will she continue to believe that Dr. Smith is going to hell? How will she respond to gay and lesbian students on her block and in her classrooms? And how will Candida use her growing understanding of Dr. Smith and his sexual orientation, this opportunity for "wide-awakenness," as a basis for deconstructing other conventions in her life? We all need such jolting experiences in our lives!

Conclusion

We have introduced a range of philosophical definitions and concepts in this chapter to elucidate a broader context of how ethics has historically been envisioned and taught. We encourage you to continue to cycle back through our discussion of language, interpretation, subjectivity, and hermeneutics and reconsider the possibilities, connections, and pitfalls of the paradigms. We also ask that you use these notions as a basis for understanding why we propose an alternative paradigm for the study of ethics and education in the next chapter.

In Chapter 3, we further develop Maxine Greene's (1995) concepts of imagination and wide-awakenness as they relate to creating richer "cohesive wholes" by discussing the power of the arts to unleash our subjective and aesthetic imaginations. Autobiographical and academic reflections on arts and artists are interwoven with discussions of spirituality, hope, and theology as a basis for exploring and developing ethical platforms for social justice. As you read the next chapter, we ask that you reflect on how your exposure to the arts has shaped your identity as well as your theological and teaching convictions. Also consider how our lives, our children, our spirituality, our architecture, and our ethical decisions would be improved if the arts became an essential element in our daily lives.

CHAPTER

3 Aesthetics and Theology: The Passion for Justice

We teach undergraduate and graduate courses in ethics, aesthetics, philosophy of education, leadership, and the social foundations of education. In all of our courses, no matter what the theme, religion always emerges as one of the most important and controversial topics, not only because the social and cultural implications of religion and schooling are intensely debated in the media, courts, and churches, but also because all educational issues are significantly interrelated with theology and ethics. Our students interpret our lectures and readings through the lens of their own theological or philosophical beliefs, and thus we are acutely aware that everything we teach is filtered through a theological lens. Religion permeates school curricula, albeit hidden and suppressed at times, and we risk great peril if we ignore it. In a speech in Austin at the LBJ Presidential Library, Bill Moyers contended that after September 11, 2001, theology and religious pluralism may have replaced race and ethnicity as the most critical social issues confronting U.S. society and the global community (Moyers, 2002).

The history of education is intimately linked to religion internationally in curious and complex ways: the influence of Confucian philosophy in Chinese schools; Puritan morality in early American textbooks; the development of private religious academies in the United States and Canada; the primacy of religious conversion of indigenous peoples by colonizers and missionaries in Africa, Latin America, and the Middle East; Catholic crucifixes and statues in public school classrooms in Italy and other predominantly Roman and Orthodox countries; religious education release time programs for Mormons in some public school districts; Jewish religious instruction in the kibbutz in Israel; Islamic religious instruction in the Koran in the schools of Pakistan; literary references and allusions to sacred texts in art, music, and literature courses; and creation mythologies blended with evolution in science classrooms. Examples of the intersection of religion and schooling extend beyond prayer at football games or the display of religious holiday symbols. Theological questions are at the very heart of every aspect of life in schools.

The litany of historical factors that have influenced public school curricula and university programs of study causes grave concern for some. Stephen Arons (1983) has even contended that religious conflicts are unresolvable parochial matters, and therefore public education must be eliminated and replaced by various private schools

131

where parents and families can choose the value system that best reflects their theology. We disagree with Arons. Democratic public spaces, especially public schools, offer the best hope for mediating the apparently unresolvable conflicts over religion in our world today. We cannot ignore, banish, or erase diversity, especially the various religious, spiritual, and theological beliefs in the global community. For example, Americans now understand that the Taliban schools in Afghanistan and Pakistan have a direct impact on global events half a world away. Likewise, Israeli Jews and Palestinian Muslims who share the same land—where even the most sacred Temple Mount and Dome of the Rock are physically located on the same land—must continue to struggle for peaceful coexistence. The same can be said for Catholics and Protestants in Northern Ireland; Hutus and Tutsis in central Africa; Byzantine, Roman, and Orthodox Catholics and Muslims in the former Yugoslavia in Bosnia-Herzegovina, Croatia, Serbia, and Kosovo; or Catholics and Muslims in Indonesia and East Timor. The same is true of violent fundamentalists of any religious preference in the United States. For example, consider the following message distributed by takeaction@act. actforchange.com on December 6, 2001:

TREAT THE ARMY OF GOD AS A TERRORIST ORGANIZATION
It is way past time for the Justice Department to recognize that violent anti-choice organizations exist rather than treating each murder and threat as isolated crimes by individual disaffected men. Yesterday, federal authorities apprehended Clayton Lee Wagner, a self-described "anti-abortion warrior" who claimed responsibility for sending hundreds of letters and packages professing to contain anthrax to women's reproductive health clinics across the U.S. and also announced his intent to kill 42 clinic workers in the next few weeks. We applaud law enforcement for capturing this fugitive, who Attorney General Ashcroft described as a "domestic terrorist." However, Wagner and others like him do not act alone. Now is the time to target the organization that enables Wagner, and men like him, to carry out violent acts against innocent people.

Terrorism and violence are not restricted by ethnic, national, religious, or ideological boundaries. Oklahoma City bomber Timothy McVeigh was a white, Christian, middle-class American. It might surprise many people that of the 169 anti-U.S. attacks reported for 1999 by the U.S. State Department, Latin America (particularly Colombia and Peru) accounted for 96, western Europe for 30, Africa for 16, the Middle East for 11, Eurasia for 9, and Asia for 7 (Abunimah, 2001). Despite these numbers, the State Department considers the primary terrorist threats to the United States to be from South Asia and the Middle East. Ali Abunimah (2001) provides an extensive review of this data that portrays the complexity of perceptions of terrorism:

The U.S. State Department report makes disturbing assertions that may fuel anti-Muslim prejudice in the United States and around the world. The [report] appears to cast any Muslim person fighting any battle, for any reason, as an "Islamic extremist." It also uses the Arabic words "jihad" and "mujahidin," which have very specific definitions, as synonyms for terrorism. Is it not possible to imagine that a Muslim in Kosovo or Chechnya [who have U.S. support] could be engaged in a legitimate battle? I certainly think the United States would have thought so when it provided substantial state sponsorship to groups in Afghanistan and when it designated such people "freedom fighters," using them to fight against Soviet intervention. (pp. 114–116)

Terrorism and violence plague the global community, and biased misrepresentations and uninformed generalizations perpetuate ethnic divisions and injustices. This is particularly disturbing when done in the name of a religion. The world continues to learn the difficult lesson about the absurdity of separating people into isolated pockets of indoctrination that can breed hatred and violence, whether it is the Army of God, Jerry Falwell, Rabbi Meir Kahane, Khalid Mohammad, Osama bin Laden, or the Taliban. In hindsight, we now know that Stephen Arons was deadly wrong in his 1983 book.

In this chapter, we do not review the history of religion and schooling; others have summarized this topic quite successfully in other texts (Ravitch, 1999; Wald, 1987). Rather, we explore ethics and aesthetics to suggest alternative ways of viewing schools and society in order to ameliorate the current tension between and among various faith communities. We advocate for a broad ecumenical acceptance of diverse peaceful and nonviolent theological perspectives—in the spirit of Gandhi's *Ahimsa,* to do no harm—and a rigorous study of world religions, native cosmologies, human spiritualities, indigenous mythologies, and other cultural expressions of immanence and transcendence. The absence of these topics in the school curriculum contributes to misunderstandings and insensitivities at best, and neocolonialism, murder, and terrorism at worst. However, pluralism and ecumenism are dangerous and unacceptable to those who insist on religious purity and the conversion of nonbelievers. The existence of diverse theologies, spiritualities, religions, and cultures frightens some people, but such diversity is at the heart of the ethical perspective we espouse in this text. Ecumenical dialogue and acceptance is essential in our pedagogy, and pluralism is the hallmark of a true democracy.

In the mid-1990s, we observed a dispute in a midwestern public school located in a city established by zealous white Protestant missionaries in the nineteenth century. The local public school was built in the 1920s and included a large portrait of Jesus Christ hanging in the entrance foyer. Even after the 1962 U.S. Supreme Court rulings that barred the Lord's Prayer and daily reading of Bible passages in public school classrooms, this small school district continued the practices of Protestant Christianity without protest. In the 1990s, a large metropolitan area expanded around this small community, and it quickly became a bedroom suburb. A large Muslim mosque was built in the city. African American and Hispanic families bought houses in formerly all-white neighborhoods, and many wealthy white Protestants fled to outer ring suburbs. In time, several new families began to complain about the prominent painting of Jesus Christ in the public school. Some wanted it removed. Others wanted to add alternate religious portraits on the wall. The white Protestants insisted that the painting of Jesus—and that painting alone—was a historical artifact representing the traditions and culture of the community, and it must remain. The immigrants and non-Protestants argued that the traditions and culture of the white Protestant community were repressive and insensitive to the multiple ethnicities and religions now represented in the school. The battle lines were drawn, and the dispute ended up in court for a decision to either remove or retain the painting of Jesus.

Because of our connections with administrators from the school district who were students in our graduate program, we had the opportunity to meet with some of the plaintiffs and defendants in this case. We suggested an alternative to the either/or dilemma. We reviewed with them Supreme Court cases that allowed for teaching about religion in the public schools as long as proselytizing or evangelizing does not occur. For example, in *Lemon v. Kurtzman* in 1971 the Supreme Court ruled that government law or practice was constitutional if it met all three of the following tests: (1) the government act that bears on religion must reflect a secular purpose; (2) it may neither advocate nor inhibit religion as its primary effect; and (3) it must avoid excessive government entanglement with religion. Thus, we argued that in order to fully appreciate and understand art, music, literature, history, science, and social studies, the school district must find a way for students to legally study religious imagery, mythology, allusions, and metaphors from sacred texts, church patronage for the arts, political theocracies, and a host of other related topics and do so in the spirit of the Supreme Court rulings.

We also related stories of friends and former students who had been ostracized and belittled because they belonged to a minority religious faith. We reminded our audience that Native American spirituality was practically obliterated by ruthless Christian politicians and evangelists. We told the story of a Jewish friend who was forced to clean blackboards every afternoon from October to December in his public elementary school while the majority Christian teachers and students rehearsed for the Christmas pageant in the auditorium. He reported to us that his family did not celebrate Christmas, and he grew up thinking that his religion was deficient because he was the only Jew in his school and he had to wash the blackboards while the other children sang and performed. We also taught the school leaders about the Catholic Councils of Baltimore in the 1840s. The Catholic bishops decided to start their own school system rather than subject the Catholic minority children to the Protestant prayers and proselytization in Horace Mann's common schools. Persons of minority religions have suffered greatly in U.S. schooling and U.S. society, and fear of the impossibility of legitimate neutrality causes many people to insist that we remove all vestiges of religion from public schools and government institutions. Persons from majority religions are often ignorant about the ways in which religion can coerce, marginalize, and intimidate minorities. Minority rights is a core principle of democracy but one that is often trampled on by the power and arrogance of the majority. Minority rights must be protected for the sake of all citizens because, if for no other reason, the majority will one day be the minority—as happened in this small midwestern town.

We worked tirelessly with both sides of this debate and proposed the following compromise. Because the painting of Jesus was positioned on a large wall that extended down the entrance corridor, and because there were no other objects on this wall, we proposed the following: "Commission several theology professors, religious leaders, and community members representing various philosophies to create a series of portraits and photographs depicting all of the world religions, cosmologies, and philosophies (including agnostics and atheists), starting with those represented in the local school community. Next to each painting or photograph place a short statement about the history and theology of this religion, cosmology, mythology, or philosophy. There would be space to constantly expand the collection of photos and statements within a rotating display. An ecumenical panel of democratically elected leaders would oversee the project. The exhibits would have to conform to the Supreme Court guidelines in the *Lemon v. Kurtzman* decision and refrain from critiquing other religions or nonbelievers." This proposal expressed our hope that the students would benefit academically from exposure to the history, theology, art, and literature of various world religions and cosmologies and that the community could begin to overcome decades of isolation and bigotry. We also believed that a first-rate artistic mural would inspire students, teachers, and parents to explore ecumenism and live with more tolerance and acceptance in the community.

Unfortunately, all sides in the debate rejected our modest proposal. Why? The majority Christians along with a few devout believers of other faiths did not want their children exposed to philosophies that contradicted their strict interpretation of sacred texts. The minority Hindus, Catholics, Muslims, Mormons, Jews, Buddhists, pantheists, and Wiccans did not trust the majority Protestant Christians to fairly represent minority perspectives, even with a democratically elected board and an ecumenical panel of theologians. Some other parents in each group did not want any mention of religion in the school, fearing that misinterpretations were inevitable and that confrontations would escalate. They preferred to relegate all discussions of religion and theology to the home and church. (Recall Stephen Arons's proposal.) Those who identified as atheists, agnostics, and other philosophical orientations worried that the definition of religion would be so narrow as to exclude their beliefs and spiritualities. This turned out to be a prophetic insight. When someone suggested that Voodoo of Haiti, New York, and New Orleans, Wicca of North America, and Santeria of Cuba and Latin America should also be included in the displays, many people of all faiths recoiled in horror. The majority condemned these religions as "Satan worship" and their adherents as practitioners of "human sacrifice," expressing a genuine fear that their children might be abducted, dismembered, or eaten in evil midnight rituals. We tried to calm the audience with a discussion of the history and significance of these sacred and compassionate religions, but the audience remained rigid in their historically inaccurate interpretations and cultural stereotypes. We personally have many wonderful friends who practice Wicca, Voodoo, and Santeria. We have studied these religions, and we have occasionally worshiped with our friends. We have even lived in communities with large numbers of adherents (e.g., New Orleans). Human sacrifices and evil rituals have never been a part of their beliefs or practices. Dangerous and derogatory stereotypes emerge from media misrepresentations and malicious denigration by antagonists. As we observed the reactionary ignorance of the school community, we were reminded of the hysteria in Massachusetts that led to the Salem witch trials and the murder of many innocent people. Ignorance and hysteria still prevail in contemporary society.

In order to counteract such ignorance, we often bring a copy of a large number of sacred texts, political manifestos, and philosophical treatises to our classes and pass them around the room as we begin our study of philosophy. Students are suddenly confronted with how little they know (and hopefully also how much they have to learn) as they look at reproductions of documents such as the Magna Charta, the Universal Declaration of Human Rights, the Humanist Manifesto, the African National Congress Charter, the Bill of Rights, the Declaration of Sentiments and Resolutions, the Dadaist Manifesto, the Manifesto of Surrealism, the United Nations Charter, the Tao Te Ching, the Kabala, the Hindu Scriptures, the Koran, Christian Scriptures, the Gnostic Scriptures, and the documents of Vatican II.

Some students dismiss all of these religious, artistic, and political manifestos except for the ones they have chosen to accept as true. Students sometimes become angry when confronted with historical contradictions, multiple hermeneutic interpretations, probing questions, and eclectic philosophical analyses. Like many modern citizens, they are uncomfortable with uncertainty and ambiguity, preferring instead absolute and unquestioned truth. Other students, however, recognize the ways they have been conditioned and indoctrinated by religion, textbooks, the media, family, and/or the government (recall Foucault in Chapter 1), and they welcome the opportunity to expand their understanding.

Returning to our story of the portrait of Jesus, the reaction of the audience, like the reaction of some of our students, to other religious perspectives confirmed our worst fears: many citizens are ignorant, bigoted, and intolerant. Prejudice against minority religions will escalate unless we engage in intensive cultural and historical analyses and ecumenical approaches in schools and other social institutions. When the U.S. military added Wicca to the list of officially sanctioned religions in 1999 that could be practiced by military personnel and soldiers on bases, many conservatives reacted in disbelief. Some pastors said they could no longer encourage their young people to join the military. Senator Bob Barr of Georgia led a vocal but unsuccessful campaign at Fort Hood in Texas to ban Wicca religious ceremonies from the base. While fear, ignorance, and parochialism dominate the thinking of many citizens, reflective educators must continue to work for justice through ecumenical inclusion of all philosophies and theologies in the school curriculum. Although our compromise proposal for ecumenical inclusion failed, the litigation was successful in court. The portrait of Jesus was removed. The wall remains empty today, and an educational opportunity has been lost. We agree with activists who contend that silence equals death. It happened in the Holocaust when too few spoke out against Nazi atrocities. It happened during American slavery when too few joined the abolitionist movement. It happened during lynchings and even recently to James Byrd Jr. in east Texas. It happened to Matthew Shepard of Wyoming, Paul Broussard of Houston, and many other gay men and lesbian women who have been beaten to death because of their sexual orientation. Religious intolerance has killed millions of people in the course of human history. Who is speaking out against prejudice and demanding civil rights for all? In this chapter, we explore a new aesthetic vision of theology and schooling that may offer hope for a compassionate, informed, and ecumenical curriculum to overcome this cycle of hatred, ignorance, silence, and death. We shall overcome one day soon.

Religion and Government: Deconstructing Patriotism

In the wake of September 11, 2001, American flags, patriotic symbols, and national music proliferated in communities throughout the United States. On the one hand, these symbols provide comfort as they reflect our grief and anguish over the loss of innocent life. On the other hand, patriotism and nationalism can be used to silence dissent and strip away human rights. Patriotic zeal was evident in news reports, at sporting events, and on automobile windshields. Classrooms became particularly important venues for reciting pledges and supporting the war effort, while at the same time controversies about free speech and historical analysis plagued schools and universities. The visual and auditory landscape of the United States invaded the consciousness of a frightened citizenry. However, what initially appeared to be a uniform response to evil deeds became more complex on closer examination. The *Arizona Republic* newspaper (Benson, 2001) printed an editorial cartoon with a sketch of a child sitting at a school desk saying, "I pledge allegiance to my conscience, not some flag driven collective group-think in America, and to the first amendment for which I sit, one vote, individual, constitutional, with liberty and free expression for all." Utah Phillips (DeFranco & Phillips, 1999) expressed a different sentiment when he recited a pledge of allegiance to the flag of multinational corporations and the ethic of corporate profit and greed without government regulations, with monopolies and underpaid labor for all.

What is happening here? Shouldn't all citizens of the United States and other democracies join in a unified pledge of allegiance in response to a clear and present moral danger? Who or what is the evil perpetrator of terrorism and injustice? Is it unpatriotic to challenge government policy, deconstruct the history of the United States in classrooms, refuse to recite a pledge, problematize national symbols, or criticize the president's policies? What is the appropriate moral response to global events in the wake of September 11? Can the U.S. government racially profile and harass innocent Middle Easterners, Muslims, and "others" who appear suspicious, and still claim to be a democracy, a beacon of liberty, a defender of freedom and justice? Can ethics guide us in a time of trauma and uncertainty?

Another pledge that is recited at many Christian schools has become a part of the national debate over school vouchers. Students at Calvary Center Academy in Cleveland recite this pledge every morning: "We pledge allegiance to the Christian flag and to the Savior for whose Kingdom it stands, One Savior, crucified, risen and coming again with life, liberty for all those who believe." Calvary is one of fifty-one religious schools that receive public funding as part of the Cleveland Tuition and Scholarship program, which was reviewed by the Supreme Court in 2002. A federal appeals court ruled that the Cleveland program violates the First Amendment's separation of church and state. Should public funds support schools that mandate this pledge? What is the appropriate relationship between religion and government?

Robert Jensen (2000) in his book *Writing Dissent: Taking Radical Ideas from the Margin to the Mainstream* deconstructs these pledges and argues that pledges and patriotism mask the global connectedness of all human persons:

> I believe there is a light shining out of September 11, out of all that darkness. It is a light that I believe we Americans can follow to our own salvation. That light is contained in a simple truth that is obvious, but which Americans have never really taken to heart: We are part of the world. We cannot any longer hide from that world. We cannot allow our politicians, and generals, and corporate executives to do their dirty business around the world while we hide from the truths about just how dirty that business really is. We can no longer hide from the coups they plan, the wars they start, the sweatshops they run. For me, all this means saying goodbye to patriotism. (Jensen, 2000, p. 5)

Jensen does not reject democracy, freedom, friends, family, or his home. He rejects blind allegiance to the actions of a nation-state in a global community. He argues that we must be able to echo the words of Eugene Debs—which were echoed from Marcus Aurelius and others before him—that "We have no country to fight for; my country is the earth, and I am a citizen of the world." He concludes that we must stop trying to redefine the word *patriotism* to make it more palatable and move forward to address the global issues of poverty, hunger, environmental degradation, disease, terrorism, and war. How can we make this shift in consciousness when patriotic urges dominate the landscape and allegiance to state and religion is normalized through regulated and mandated practices in schools and society? Consider the next example.

We attended a professional conference in early November 2001 at which all participants were told to stand and recite the following pledge before two large American flags prominently displayed in the ballroom: "I pledge allegiance to the flag of the United States of America, and to the republic for which it stands, one nation under God, indivisible, with liberty and justice for all." This pledge was not a part of the Declaration of Independence nor the U.S. Constitution; rather, it was written by clergyman Francis Bellamy for a children's magazine, *Youth's Companion*, in 1892 for the purpose of solidifying a national consensus on the 400th anniversary of Columbus's voyage to the Americas. Public school children first recited the pledge as they saluted the flag during the National Public Schools Celebration on October 12, 1892 by order of President Benjamin Harrison. The National Flag Conferences of the American Legion expanded the original wording in 1923, and in 1942 Congress made the pledge part of its code for the use of the flag. The last time the Supreme Court ruled on the Pledge of Allegiance was during World War II in June 1943. The West Virginia State Board of Education had mandated the pledge as a daily activity, and any student who failed to comply was charged with insubordination and expelled. For religious reasons, Walter Barnette, a Jehovah's Witness, refused to allow his children to salute the flag and say the pledge. In a 6–3 decision, the Supreme Court ruled in his favor in 1943. In 1954, at the height of investigations into loyalty to the United States during the Senator Joseph McCarthy communist hearings on Capitol Hill, Congress added the words "under God," which were not part of the original pledge. Religious leaders had argued before President Dwight Eisenhower that the U.S. pledge needed to be distinguished from similar orations used by "godless communists." What is the motivation for reciting this pledge today? What does it mean? Is there really a deity that favors one nation or one army over another? How can the global community move beyond war and nationalism to address justice? What is the role of dissent in a democracy? Recently, a federal court in California ruled that the pledge could not be recited in public schools because the phrase "under God" violates separation of church and state laws and the First Amendment prohibition of establishment of religion. Congress immediately recessed and some went to the Capital steps to recite the pledge. Future Supreme Court rulings are inevitable.

At our conference, all participants stood in compliance and recited the 1954 pledge in rote unison. We were silent, curious, and dumbfounded as the audience sat down after the pledge and continued with the meeting agenda, apparently unmoved by the recitation. This event made no visible impact on the audience, and the meeting progressed without any reference to the global events that had inspired its recitation. What was going on here? The aesthetic environment had been jolted, but no one responded. We, of course, were taking mental notes and later asked participants many questions about this event.

As critical postmodern educators, we are sensitive to the symbols of patriotism because we have experienced abuses in the past as a result of unquestioned allegiance to governmental or religious leaders. For example, clandestine and illegal support by U.S. lawmakers—and their wealthy corporate benefactors who are interested in making political and economic fortunes—for regimes that blatantly abuse human rights and trample democracy in Iran, Nicaragua, Afghanistan, the Dominican Republic, Saudi Arabia, Kuwait, and Haiti, to name but a few, are abundant in U.S. history. Vietnam, Cambodia, and Laos are places of death and deceit forever etched in the memory of the baby boom generation. Consider the following editorial in *Mother Jones* by Roger Cohn:

> Perhaps we, as a nation, will begin to recognize that we cannot ignore the legitimate needs and grievances of people in other parts of the globe, whether they be on the West Bank or in East Timor. We cannot keep supporting autocratic governments in the Middle East or Africa or Asia simply because they guarantee a flow of cheap oil or sweatshop-made swimsuits. We cannot promote globalization without making sure that it benefits, rather than exploits, the poor. We cannot keep driving our SUVs and turning up the heat without recognizing that we are suffocating the planet. (Cohn, 2002, p. 4)

Cohn concludes that we must seize this current moment by connecting with the grief and resolve of those who have suffered because of September 11 with an emerging maturity to develop a more hopeful and compassionate role for the United States in the twenty-first century. Let us consider a story related to the Vietnam War era.

When the four Kent State students were murdered by National Guard troops on May 4, 1970, I (Patrick) was a high school student in New Orleans. I was approaching my eighteenth birthday and the prospect of being drafted and sent to Vietnam. I remember intense conversations with friends about the options available to young American males in the late 1960s: enlisting in the military, fleeing to Canada, joining the campus protests, patriotically supporting Nixon, registering for the draft but seeking a deferment, declaring ourselves conscientious objectors, mutilating our bodies in some way to make us ineligible for the draft, joining the National Guard with the politically connected rich kids, securing a college deferment, trusting that the lottery draft system would select our birthday last, or just ignoring the inevitable.

Ignorance was not an option for me. I was caught up in the political fervor of the times, and I generally favored nonviolent resistance and political activism. I remember musing aloud to my grandmother at Thanksgiving dinner in 1969 that if I were drafted I might consider fleeing to Canada. She was stunned and livid. Mama, as we affectionately called her, scolded me and recited a litany of family members who had valiantly served their country in various wars: Uncle David in the Navy during the Korean War, Uncle Joe who was shot down over Belgium in World War II, and even the great-grandparents who fought at the siege of Vicksburg during the "War of Northern Yankee Aggression," as she called it.

The family history lesson did not change my position on Vietnam. However, the photograph on the front page of the newspaper on May 5, 1970, solidified my political perspective. The haunting image of Mary Ann Vecchio, the fourteen-year-old runaway from Florida, kneeling in anguish by the body of Jeffrey Miller on the Kent State campus made an indelible impression on my psyche and galvanized my resolve to join the Vietnam protests. That single photograph clearly articulated the tragedy and failure of U.S. politics and the military involvement in Vietnam that had been a vague confusion in my mind before May 4.

I have visited Kent State University many times, including during the twenty-fifth anniversary memorial, when Vecchio returned to the campus for the first time to meet John Filo, the student who took the famous photograph. As I spoke with Vecchio in the parking lot where Jeff Miller and the other three students died, time merged into a synthesis of insights that affirmed my continuing commitment to social justice. For many of us who experienced the turmoil and confusion of the 1960s, John Filo's photograph became a catalyst for igniting our critical consciousness for social change. Interestingly, former Secretary of Defense Robert McNamara published his memoirs about Vietnam just before the twenty-fifth anniversary memorial at Kent State. In his book, he finally admitted the mistakes that were made and the cover-ups that were approved. Although he offered an apology, he did not take any action to address the wrongs committed. While Peter, Paul, and Mary sang *Blowin' in the Wind* (a folk anthem of the 1960s), the mother of one of the murdered students spoke to the crowd and tearfully begged McNamara and others to step forward to identify the persons who gave the command to shoot and the soldiers who fired the fatal shots at her son. To this day, no one has spoken out; all that remain are hollow apologies. Once I realized that Nixon and the National Guard would shoot and kill student demonstrators my age, any hope of blind allegiance or forced patriotism was lost forever. Let us now return to our present dilemma concerning patriotism and see if there are any lessons to be learned today.

Current enemies such as Osama bin Laden and the Taliban were once U.S. allies in the fight against the Soviet Union in Afghanistan. They were the recipients of millions of dollars in CIA funding. Sadam Hussein also enjoyed our support when he was fighting Iran, but once he invaded Kuwait and threatened oil companies and the flow of oil to the West, we attacked him in the 1991 Gulf War. Clearly, the United States regularly turns a blind eye toward oppression and antidemocratic practices in places such as Saudi Arabia and Nicaragua when it serves the interests of the power elites in Washington. Friends and enemies are not always readily identifiable.

The long history of double standards, political deception, and illegal activities in U.S. history, such as the Iran-Contra scandal of the Reagan White House, the invasion of Haiti by the Woodrow Wilson White House, and the Vietnam War of the Johnson White House, cautions us to resist blind patriotism. We agree with Senator J. William Fulbright (1969) of Arkansas who called such maneuvers "The Arrogance of Power." Shortly after September 11, we witnessed a parade of about one hundred men in their thirties and forties marching on the state capitol in Austin, Texas. They appeared to be a combination of working-class and middle-class citizens from various ethnic groups. The men wore army fatigues and white tee-shirts with American flags printed on the front and back, and each carried a large sign that read "God Bless America." As they marched in lockstep precision, they shouted again and again in unison "We're number one! We're number one!" This is but one frightening example of how religion has been hijacked in the aftermath of September 11. War and peace have been reduced to a football game with a cheerleader chant. Some U.S. citizens assume that God is on their side and justify all sorts of horrors in the name of religion. Of course, so does the Taliban and so did the Crusaders and Inquisitors!

The history of humanity is replete with examples of religious crusades, inquisitions, wars, torture, embezzlement, murder, theft, and terrorism executed in the name of God, Allah, Jesus, Abraham, Buddha, Mao, Hitler, Stalin, Nixon, Confucius, or "our" flag. Andrew Sullivan (2001) wrote a provocative article in the *New York Times* magazine following the September 11 events titled "This *Is* a Religious War" in which he claimed, "The Osama bin Ladens of the world—like the leaders of the Inquisition and others before them—demand that all embrace absolute faith. Individual faith and pluralism were the targets Sept. 11, and it was only the beginning of an epic battle" (p. 44). Understanding the theological roots of our current global conflicts and the history of world religions is essential. We must envision another way of relating to one another in a theologically diverse global community, without either attempting to annihilate or assimilate those who profess different belief systems—no matter how bizarre or convoluted their religion may appear—as long as peace and pluralism guide those theologies. This message must be heard and acted on by Muslim fundamentalist Taliban, Jewish fundamentalist Zionists, Christian fundamentalist evangelists, and any other extremist group that uses theology, cosmology, or political theory to perpetuate injustice and deny human rights in the name of religion. In this chapter, we explore aesthetics and theology in an effort to uncover a new way of being in the postmodern world beyond violence, terrorism, colonialism, religious intolerance, patriarchy, heterosexism, racism, ableism, and ethnic hatred. We believe that an investigation of aesthetics and theology provides important ethical insights for a world in crisis. Pluralism, peaceful nonviolent activism, and democracy are fundamental to our ethical vision in this chapter. However, the very nature of the way we relate to each other as human beings and the way human beings relate to the natural world also figure prominently in our cosmology.

Although we often deconstruct the theology and aesthetics of various religious, political, educational, and cultural institutions and challenge unquestioned allegiance to flags and bibles, we also appreciate the values of democracy, pluralism, justice, and compassion that can be found in U.S. history and world religions. As Jacques Derrida (1972) has written, "Nothing of what I have said had a destructive meaning. Deconstruction has nothing to do with destruction. That is to say, it is simply a question of being alert to the implications, to the historical sedimentation of the language we use—and that is not destruction" (p. 271). Some may accuse us of intolerance toward religion and disrespect for nation-states. Some may even contend that our critiques are misplaced, distorted, treasonous, or sinful. However, our goal is not to disparage any religion, cosmology, nation, or person. Rather, we seek to deconstruct historical sedimentation and interrupt textual interpretations so that we can move beyond the unexamined cultural and religious stalemates that prevent the global community from envisioning alternatives to terrorism, colonialism, abuse, and the like.

An example may be helpful. I (Patrick) was attending a Roman Catholic Mass at our church in Ohio with my son Joshua in 1995 during the presidential campaign season. Bill Clinton was running for reelection, and several Republican contenders were maneuvering for the nomination to challenge him. During the sermon, our elderly pastor instructed the congregation to vote for Patrick Buchanan because he was the only Catholic in the race and he was opposed to abortion. Under other circumstances, I might have simply ignored the obnoxious political commentary in church, but I had just read a front-page story in the New York Times with my coffee that morning describing a covert fund-raising meeting between Buchanan and David Duke, the Ku Klux Klan Grand Wizard and racist politician in Metairie, Louisiana. I was attending LSU as an undergraduate in 1971 when Duke began his activism by preaching white supremacy and racial apartheid in Free Speech Alley near the student union. I was once even confused with David Duke in a news report in The Reville, the LSU student newspaper, while serving as campaign manager for Duke's rival candidate in student government. Thus, I had a long-standing antagonism toward Duke's philosophy, and the priest's comments about supporting Buchanan, a candidate who was raising funds and meeting with David Duke, infuriated me.

I wanted to vocally repudiate our pastor's sermon and walk out of church in protest. Josh could sense my agitation and urged me to be quiet and not make a scene. His teachers and classmates were sitting in the pews behind us. So, instead of walking out, I turned to Josh and said with an emphatic tone: "Not everything a priest says is true." The lady behind us dropped her rosary beads. Several parishioners peered at me sternly, but I remained unapologetic. At that moment, I recalled my own Catholic education when I was Josh's age. The nuns taught me to elevate the priest on a pedestal with the saints and angels, and I was admonished to respect everything uttered by the infallible pope and his priests. It the early 1980s, this theology crashed for many Catholics when Father Gilbert Gauthier of Louisiana was arrested and found guilty of sexually molesting four young altar boys in his church over a period of several years. Gauthier was the first publicly convicted priest pedophile in the United States, and he was sent to prison in Angola, Louisiana. At the time, I was a principal of a school near the community where these events occurred. The tragedy of the rape of the young altar boys was exacerbated by the bishop's attempt to minimize Gauthier's actions and deny the boys' accusations. Eventually, Bishop Frey's cover-up was exposed in court, and the jury recommended a huge financial judgment against the Roman Catholic Diocese of Lafayette. It is incredible that this same scenario repeats itself again and again, most recently in the trial and conviction of Father John Geoghan and arrest of Father Paul Shanley in Boston in January of 2002, and the endless stream of sexual abuse cases in the Catholic church through the next several months.

The boys did not report Father Gauthier's sexual abuse in church—nor Father Geoghan's touching at swimming pools and even in their homes during nighttime prayers—until many years after the events because their parents and teachers had instilled in them a blind allegiance to and respect for the priest. Gauthier was the same man who frightened the young boys by telling them they would go to hell and their parents would die if they reported what had happened. This often happens in cases of sexual molestation and rape; victims are psychologically manipulated into blaming themselves or remaining silent. In order to dispel any stereotypes this story may reinforce, we remind readers that statistically the majority of pedophiles, rapists, and child molesters are not priests but rather heterosexual male relatives or acquaintances of female victims. But no matter who the perpetrator, the victims suffer a lifetime of shame, anger, and guilt. The trauma of rape and abuse is pervasive in our society, and the victims of Father Gilbert Gauthier, Father John Geoghan, and Father Paul Shanley have suffered immeasurable damage.

When I uttered my caution to Josh in our church in 1995, I was doing more than disagreeing with my pastor's sermon about voting for Patrick Buchanan for president. I was reminding my son—and all who could hear me—that pastors are fallible and that we should never accept their instruction without question. Of course, this is equally true for Baptist youth ministers, Boy Scout leaders, high school coaches, Methodist deacons, and college professors, some of whom have also been found guilty of sexual abuse, child endangerment, and sexual harassment. Popular televangelists Jimmy Swaggart and Jim Bakker have also deceived their followers. Abuse and injustice are often hidden behind theological doctrine, religious zealotry, family loyalty, and political patriotism. Once citizens or church members relinquish their ability to question authority, trouble religious practices, deconstruct theological interpretations, problematize political motivations, and investigate historical events, they open themselves, their children, and society at large to devastating deception and tragic abuse. All truth statements must be challenged, deconstructed, interrupted, troubled, and problematized, and this was my message to Josh. We expand our philosophy by exploring aesthetics because we believe that the arts provide the best resource for understanding this important ethical imperative.

As we begin searching for aesthetic insights in art, music, and literature (among many other art forms) to inform our ethical imperative, let us begin by reading the lyrics of a popular song by Woody Guthrie (1998) titled "This Land Is Your Land." This song has been used by many politicians, including President George Bush at prominent campaign and inauguration rallies in 1988, to inspire patriotism and a sense of theological entitlement in the spirit of American manifest destiny. However, only the first three verses are included in rallies. Read the verses of the entire song and ask yourself why the other verses are always omitted. Have you ever listened to the entire song? What messages are too uncomfortable for patriotic sensibilities and political posturing?

> *This land is your land, this land is my land,*
> *From California to the New York Island;*
> *From the Redwood forest to the gulf stream waters,*
> *This land was made for you and me.*
>
> *As I was walking that ribbon of highway,*
> *I saw above me that endless skyway;*
> *I saw below me that golden valley;*
> *This land was made for you and me.*
>
> *I've roamed and rambled and I followed my footsteps*
> *To the sparkling sands of her diamond deserts;*
> *And all around me a voice was sounding:*
> *This land was made for you and me.*
>
> *And the sun came shining, and I was strolling,*
> *And the wheat fields waving and the dust clouds rolling,*
> *As the fog was lifting a voice was chanting:*
> *This land was made for you and me.*
>
> *As I went walking, I saw a sign there,*
> *And on the sign it said "No Trespassing."*
> *But on the other side it didn't say nothing,*
> *That side was made for you and me.*

In the shadow of the steeple I saw my people;
By the relief office I seen my people;
As they stood there hungry, I stood there asking,
Is this land made for you and me?

Nobody living can ever stop me,
As I go walking that freedom highway;
Nobody living can ever make me turn back;
This land was made for you and me.

The power of Guthrie's lyrics is diminished when his message is truncated. Cultural apologists, celebrationist historians, and political conservatives are afraid to address critical social issues such as those exposed in this song. Poverty, greed, and the history of Native American peoples are tragedies of monumental proportions. Eliminating their memory in songs and textbooks compounds the devastation and perpetuates the injustices. The continued pollution of the land and destruction of the natural landscape is another tragic result of our ignorance and repression. We have seen this happen again and again in textbook-banning controversies in school districts and museums throughout North America and globally. Examine a list of non-adopted textbooks, banned texts in schools, banned books in libraries, censored artwork in museums, and banned music on radio stations, and you will often discover important and inspiring literature, art, photography, and music, as well as some of the most penetrating scientific and historical analyses. Music, film, poetry, photography, dance, literature, and other art forms can stir the imagination, challenge the social order, and advance the cause of justice, but when the voices of poets and prophets are silenced, an atmosphere of repression, fear, and ignorance takes over. Consider the history of burned books, banned artwork, and repressed ideas in Hitler's Third Reich. Humanity has not learned the tragic consequences of censorship. Education for emancipation and justice must not bow to controversy. In fact, open and honest investigations are the hallmark of ethics in education. As we contend throughout this chapter, ethics is inseparable from aesthetics. We cannot understand the ethical imperative outside of the aesthetic context that includes a rigorous theological investigation.

Aesthetic Imagination for Justice

We believe that aesthetic vision, creative imagination, and a passion for justice are in short supply in our contemporary society. In fact, institutions such as schools, churches, businesses, and governments—despite organizational leaders' rhetoric of creative problem solving, critical thinking, bold reform initiatives, social transformation, and individual redemption—often contribute to the very inertia and malaise that render the prophetic voice impotent. This is not a new revelation or insight. John Dewey, for example, noted this problem when he wrote in *A Common Faith,* at the height of the Great Depression in the early 1930s, that the churches had abandoned their prophetic voice (1934b). While the churches preached a gospel of love and compassion, they ignored the plight of the hungry, destitute, and jobless. This in part led to Dewey's rejection of the eschatology of his early theological training. Similarly, we find that educational leaders have abandoned the voice of imagination, leading us to reevaluate our early educational training in melting pot egalitarianism and scientific management. We are on a search for a new ethics for education characterized, in part, by an aesthetic and theological vision for social change.

We are concerned about voice, especially the prophetic voice of imagination that contributes to positive social change. As mentioned in Chapter 1, Michel Foucault claims that knowledge and power are intimately linked and that the power of language serves a normalizing function in society. Therefore, it is not surprising to us that prophetic voices and artistic imagination are marginalized in schools and society. One of the ways this is accomplished is by silencing the artist—sometimes a self-inflicted silence of conformity and comodification, and at other times a bureaucratic silencing by forceful imposition and program elimination. We seek to recover and reaffirm the voice of the artist as prophet in schools and society. Our goal is the reenchantment of the arts at the heart of the curriculum.

The modern experience has rendered many persons hollow and voiceless. In this state of paralysis, we have become unable to act with passion or compassion, listen with empathy, or even imagine a world beyond our emptiness. Somehow, students and citizens become hollow, stuffed, and hardened. Prophetic poets, visual artists, dancers, actors, lyricists, filmmakers, and novelists challenge us to investigate and not ignore despair, injustice, and paralysis. Some would argue that artists merely reflect cultural prejudices and elitist tastes; others would insist that artists shape culture and presage social change. Perhaps it is best to assume that both are possible. However, in our vision of ethics and education, the latter will become the norm.

As we experience the despair and malaise of the modern world, especially following the events of September 11, possibilities for a new ethical vision of education emerge when we are willing to hear the voice of those calling us to create a different kind of community. These voices of imagination are present today. Like the *Cueca Solo* performed publically by the wives, mothers, and daughters of the "disappeared" in Chile, prophetic artists yearn for recognition and justice. Listen to the song "They Dance Alone" on the CD titled *Nothing Like the Sun* by musical artist Sting for a poignant reflection on the dances of the *Cueca Solo*. Voices of imagination, particularly as expressed through the arts, continue to "disappear" from the schools and society. But though these voices may be suppressed, they have not been eliminated. The visionary educator must seek them out amidst the cacophony of competing interests on urban street corners, on experimental stages, in independent films, in music-filled coffeehouses, in alternative newspapers, at poetry slams, and in sweaty garages turned music or art studios. Urgent political, social, ecological, and spiritual concerns are being discussed and debated on campuses and in church halls as well. These discussions often intersect with the arts in remarkable ways, as we investigate in the following sections.

The Art of Edward Kienholz and Nancy Kienholz

When Edward Kienholz began his work in the 1950s, his style was likened to that of the Beat poets who "raged against a nation that by all outward appearances was content with itself and ostensibly relieved of the burden of self-reflection" (Raskin, 1996, p. 38). During this time, Americans were reacting to the launch of the Soviet satellite *Sputnik* and its implications for education and national defense interests. McCarthy-era anticommunist sentiment at an apex, our national attention turned to an external enemy as we sought to rid the world of communism. Deep personal reflection, however, led some visionaries to examine the apparent contradictions between our overt national policies and the actions undertaken by our newly developed military–industrial economy. Were we really concerned about the liberation of human beings or had we come to understand ourselves in the context of the economic advantage of the business of war? Unfortunately, we continue to ask this same question in 2002. Edward Kienholz exposed such contradictions ingrained in the American consciousness of the 1950s and 1960s, and his prophetic art inspires ethical reflection in our current global crisis.

Edward Kienholz and Nancy Kienholz began to work collaboratively in 1972. Inspired by their shared vision of the prophetic nature of their work, they created assemblages to express their outrage with child abuse, war, poverty, religious hypocrisy, sexism, and violence against Native Americans and other indigenous and minority cultures. They also probed the decay of the human spirit in the modern age. Their sculptures were created with common household objects and discarded industrial materials—as if to say that injustice is everywhere in our day-to-day lives. This highlighted the irony of their themes, as seen in the major retrospective of their work in 1996 at the Whitney Museum in New York City. The museum presented a collection of striking images designed to both reflect and deconstruct the human condition (Hopps, 1996).

One of Edward Kienholz's earliest creations, completed in 1959, reflects the condition of the archetypal American male. This sculpture, titled *John Doe,* was constructed with a store display mannequin cut in half at the waist. The two halves were placed back to back on a baby stroller base. The penis was severed and stored in a drawer below the stroller. A carved section of the man's chest forms a hole that contains a wooden cross instead of a heart; a stovepipe connects both sections of the body leading to the cross. The sculpture portrays the American male as a bifurcated hero; he is depicted as limbless, powerless, heartless, and impotent. The emptiness of his existence—void of emotional, sexual, or spiritual passion—shocks the viewer and forces a reevaluation of macho male media images. When we view slides of this artwork with our students, the males initially react defensively, arguing that this is an outdated stereotype. They contend that men are no longer macho, spiritually empty, and vacuous. Then the women begin to speak, affirming the macho image and, yes, even the sexual immaturity and repression. The male students are shocked that the women affirm the Kienholzes' critique of men. The artwork opens a dynamic space for communication and reflection about the nature of gender, sexuality, spirituality, and passion.

Jane Doe, John Doe's counterpart, fares no better, and the women are also afforded an opportunity for self-reflection. She is constructed with the head of a child's female doll attached to a small chest of drawers covered by the lace-laden skirt of a bridal gown (Hopps, 1996). The absence of arms adds to her defenseless and passive stance. As the body takes on the appearance of a table, the relationship between feminine nature and the act of service is dramatic. The three drawers—representing three stages of womanhood—are covered with the lace wedding gown, requiring the viewer to lift the skirt of the woman-turned-service-table in order to reveal her inner humanity. Such imposition on and exploitation of women is all too common. The viewer becomes voyeur and must now confront her or his own complicity in exploitation and subjugation. Unlike our male students who react with anger toward *John Doe,* the women initially react with shock and sadness as they view *Jane Doe.* The intensity of the image forces a self-analysis that is often painfully honest.

The images created by the Kienholzes enabled them to assume the role of prophet and challenge those who view their art to consider important social issues such as gender roles, violence, and subjugation. The use of common materials to construct images of exaggeration effectively communicate the struggle inherent in various critical causes. Because the images are sometimes disturbing, particularly their series on child abuse, the artists are able to engage the imagination and evoke the emotional connection and response necessary for lasting impact. Adding to this response is the three-dimensional nature of the work. This dimensionality allows the observer to interact with the piece and step away from what Suzi Gablik calls the subject–object separation found in much contemporary art. Not only does the observer become a participant, but also the dimensionality of the work allows movement into the space of the tableau, thereby evoking, in the postmodern sense, an intense and ironic juxtaposition (Gablik, 1991; McElfresh-Spehler & Slattery, 1999). We recommend viewing the work of Edward Kienholz and Nancy Kienholz.

The Art of Anselm Kiefer

Anselm Kiefer, a German citizen born at the end of World War II, addresses political and social issues of this century in his large canvases. He challenges his German contemporaries—indeed, all modern women and men—to ponder and deconstruct those aspects of twentieth-century German history that many would like to forget. Kiefer is attentive to the complexity of memory construction and antimemory deconstruction that we discussed in Chapter 2 (Weaver, Slattery, & Daspit, 1998). Gilmour (1990) explains the purpose behind Kiefer's artistic approach to memory:

> Kiefer moves beyond modernism by violating its taboos against representation, narrative, and historical allusion and by the decisive ways in which he employs art to confront reality. At the same time, he raises fundamental doubts about the received world view of

modernity. Although the avant-garde were radical in their criticism of the art world, Kiefer's challenge extends further toward the roots of modern humanity's outlook. He does so by turning the canvas into a theater of interacting forces that exposes tragic conflicts engendered by modern life. By synthesizing the traditional and the modern, the mythological and the rational, the simulated and the real, Kiefer achieves a puzzling and provocative mixture of elements that inspire us to reconsider our assumptions and formulate our visions anew. (p. 5)

For example, Kiefer's *Lot's Frau,* completed in 1989 and found in the collection at the Cleveland Museum of Art, depicts a barren and scorched landscape with two sets of converging railroad tracks at the horizon. Constructed with a substructure of lead mounted on wood and overlaid with canvas, the work evokes images of abandonment, suffering, and deep loneliness. Above the horizon explode huge white puffs of what might be smoke or clouds or human ashes.

This painting challenges us to look back at tragedies of the twentieth century such as the Holocaust and environmental disasters. The viewer becomes like *Lot's Frau*—Lot's wife—who looked back on the cities of Sodom and Gomorrah as they were being destroyed in the biblical story. Traditional religious authorities have assumed that she was cast into a pillar of salt for her disobedience to a vengeful God who had commanded that Lot and his family leave the city without turning around. But here is another interpretation. Yes, Lot's wife ignored the patriarchy to look back in compassion and love at the friends and family she had left behind. In the agony of her exodus, she would not erase the memory of her loved ones. In looking back, she is transformed and becomes the salt of the earth, not as a punishment, as traditional patriarchal theology has assumed, but rather as a model of the prophetic vision—for salt is the substance of wisdom in alchemy and in biblical literature. Kiefer is even known to have mixed salt, ash, and semen in the paint, assuring us that there is life, healing, and preservation in the backward glance and in uncovering the unrecognizable. It is the attempt to erase the memory, to walk forward without looking back and becoming salt, that is most dangerous. Without healing salt, Lot's semen produces a dysfunctional progeny that eventually self-destructs at the end of the biblical story—the part of the narrative that most preachers ignore.

Kiefer's art calls us to become the pillar of salt for an earth on which global communities have repeatedly burned and bombed their cities, scorched the earth, and obliterated innocent people for centuries. Gilmour (1990) concludes:

Kiefer's palpable grasp of the powers of imagination enables him to fulfill one pedagogical task of postmodern art: teaching us the importance of the habitat of the earth. His refusal to forget the consequences of war, the threat of nuclear destruction, and the negative outcomes of technology keeps being projected, in his Theater of Cruelty staging, against the symbol of the earth. But even more than that, this artist brings fire to the earth, which purifies our vision of the abstract images of nature and history that stand at the root of so many of these consequences. His visionary sketch of the habitat for postmodern humans recalls us to the elemental relationship we have to the earth, to its place within the cosmos, and to previous human cultures who have understood so well the limits of human powers. (p. 175)

Kiefer allows us to enter the landscape of ecological concern in the broadest sense. He challenges our most intuitive and rational assumptions about our relationship to the earth and to one another. As our imaginations are engaged through our interaction with his art, the voice of imagination and change can emerge. The call is compelling; the response is vital.

Kiefer offers the opportunity not only to deconstruct memories of violence and destruction, but also and especially to elicit fresh understandings of the positionality of the self in relation to memories. We now take a circuitous route back to Kiefer through the work of bell hooks, Jean-Michel Basquiat, Friedrich Nietzsche, and Michel Foucault.

bell hooks has written about the 1992 retrospective of the work of Jean-Michel Basquiat at the Whitney Museum of Art in New York City. With the release of the Julian Schnabel (1996) film *Basquiat,* there is a renewed interest in the life of this widely misunderstood artist. hooks (1993) writes:

> It is much too simplistic a reading to see works like *Jack Johnson,* 1982, *Untitled (Sugar Ray Robinson),* 1982, and the like, as solely celebrating black culture. Appearing always in these paintings as half-formed or somewhat mutilated, the black male body becomes, iconographically, a sign of lack and absence. . . . In Basquiat's work, flesh on the black body is almost always falling away. Like skeletal figures in the Australian aboriginal bark painting, . . . these figures have been worked down to the bone. To do justice to this work, then, our gaze must do more than reflect on surface appearances. Daring us to probe the heart of darkness, to move our eyes beyond the colonizing gaze, the paintings ask that we hold in our memory the bones of the dead while we consider the world of the black immediate, the familiar. To see and understand these paintings, one must be willing to accept the tragic dimension of black life. . . . Basquiat's work gives that private anguish artistic expression. (pp. 71–72)

This anguish described by hooks also permeates Kiefer's paintings. As Basquiat confronts us with the naked black image, Kiefer confronts us with the naked ravages of postwar terrain. The body is diminished for Basquiat; the landscape is barren for Kiefer.

The backward glance illustrated in Kiefer's painting transforms our lives. As with Nietzsche, this takes us to the point of becoming more of what we are not so as to free ourselves from the limits of what we live. We do this in order to illuminate that which has remained unrecognizable. Nietzsche (1968) writes about "dangerous books" and concludes,

> Somebody remarked: "I can tell by my own reaction to it that this book is harmful." But let him only wait and perhaps one day he will admit to himself [sic] that this same book has done him a great service by bringing out the hidden sickness of his heart and making it visible. Altered opinions do not alter a man's character (or do so very little); but they do illuminate individual aspects of the constellation of his personality which

with a different constellation of opinions had hitherto remained dark and unrecognizable. (p. 15)

Nietzsche's "dangerous books" parallel the "dangerous looks" described in relation to *Lot's Frau*. It is our challenge in museums and classrooms to create spaces in which the dangerous can prod us to construct and reconstruct memories that can illuminate aspects of our autobiography and our culture that have remained hidden or unrecognizable. We share examples of this process at the end of this chapter.

bell hooks (1993) contends that Basquiat's work delineates the violence that results when the culture and traditions of a people are erased. Sodom and Gomorrah have been the scapegoats for colonization and hegemonic domination for too long. We must look back with the heroine of the biblical narrative, Lot's wife, and become the pillar of life-giving salt for the earth. hooks (1993) concludes, "The erasure is rendered all the more problematic when artifacts of that vanishing culture are comodified to enhance the aesthetics of those perpetuating the erasure" (p. 72). Thus, the memory of Lot's wife is comodified for a conservative religious hermeneutic, and Sodom and Gomorrah remain fixed in the collective memory as evil and decadent. That image has been perpetuated to support violence of all sorts, including most often an illogical condemnation of homosexuals. Kiefer, Basquiat, and hooks refute this vanquishing and challenge such destructive interpretations.

It is in this spirit that we often take our students to visit *Lot's Frau* in the Cleveland Museum of Art. The response of David, an eighteen-year-old first-year student, is typical of the reaction of those students willing to deconstruct linear notions of time and space and look back, look within, and look forward in a single glance. After meditating before this painting for almost an hour, David insisted that he felt the very real presence of the Holocaust as he stood there. He told us that for the first time in his life he truly understood the Holocaust, and he was haunted by the intensity of Kiefer's desolate landscape. Why, he asked us, was the memory so haunting? Why did he feel so present in this desolate landscape?

Early in the next semester, David contacted us to say that over the winter break he had discussed his experience at the museum with his devoutly Christian parents. David's glance had uncovered a purposeful erasure of a family memory, the death of Jewish ancestors in the Holocaust. His parents for the first time revealed to him that their parents were children of Jewish parents killed in the Holocaust. David, like Lot's wife, found himself in the imagery of smoke, clouds, salt, and ashes on Kiefer's canvas. David is not unlike many of us who discover ourselves within the phenomenological lived experience. This story reflects our vision of ethics and aesthetics. We must re-member our bodies and re-connect our lives if the colonization and erasure are to be resisted and overcome. Literally, we are holistically a part of the global landscape and the historical event; the aesthetic experience allows us to enter the process of healing and understanding.

Like Foucault's notion of "simulated surveillance" that engenders the kind of blind obedience that regulated Lot and persuaded him not to look back, the force that causes museums and classrooms to refuse to challenge sedimented perceptors and explode colonizing structures of power also regulates our bodies and imprisons our minds. Most tragically, it also stifles the aesthetic imagination and silences the creative urge. The artwork of Anselm Kiefer deconstructs educational, political, and social structures that have created such surveillance and sought to extinguish the passion for justice.

A Postmodern Perspective:
Ethics and Aesthetics

The branch of philosophy known as axiology consists of the examination of both aesthetics and ethics. What we are proposing in this chapter is a reintegration of both. The study of goodness and the study of beauty were long held to be inseparable—so inseparably linked that they formed the axis of values and morality. Modernism, however, has tended to separate aesthetics and ethics into distinct disciplines, no longer viewing them as contributing to each other. Such bifurcation, in our estimation, is at the heart of the loss of imagination, vision, and prophetic voice. Nel Noddings (1995) provides this insight:

> The Enlightenment brought with it the wonderful idea that human beings might have a hand in their own destinies, that an adequate ethic would make life better here and now, and that human beings are subjects, agents—not just vessels for divine intervention. The Enlightenment brought the promise of freedom from the authority of the church and an invitation to human beings to exercise reason in the conduct of their lives. (p. 141)

Along with this freedom came an elevation of human reason, which led to the Cartesian mind–body dichotomy and eventually to the bifurcation of ethics and aesthetics. In the attempts to create systems of ethics, modern philosophers have sought to eliminate moral uncertainty and provide a rational vision for the ideal society. Within the emergence of rational deontological proposals has come the gradual elimination of the aesthetic component in the ethical project. Our postmodern project seeks to reunite ethics and aesthetics. This, for us, is an important first step in the development of voices of imagination for a new education founded on justice, compassion, and ecological sustainability.

Existential philosophy has undermined the hegemony of reason, substituting, as with Sartre, absurdity for reason. Nietzsche (1968) concluded that the ultimate meaning of human existence was to be found in the aesthetic experience. In this sense, aesthetics is elevated over ethics. In her description of the dilemma of modern art in the context of the ethics–aesthetics bifurcation, Suzi Gablik (1991) writes that "it is perfectly true that moral purpose falls outside the scope of modern aesthetics just as surely as it falls outside the scope of scientific methodology—both are mute about responsibility, and artists today are not provided with any sense of the social or moral importance of their role" (p. 140).

Some blame postmodern ambiguity for this dilemma, arguing that ambiguity leads to absurdity, apathy, and inaction. Simone de Beauvoir (1948) counters this assumption: "[We must not] allow the liberating movement to harden into a moment which is acceptable only if it passes into its opposite; tyranny and crime must be kept from triumphantly establishing themselves in the world; the conquest of freedom is their only justification, and the assertion of freedom against them must therefore be kept alive" (p. 11). In *The Ethics of Ambiguity,* Beauvoir critiques metanarratives of the nature of the social condition and deconstructs totalitarian doctrines that raise up beyond the individual "a mirage" of the universal. Beauvoir challenges utopian and utilitarian visions of ethics, contending that the individual must assume freedom in the creative and constructive moment in the face of the absurd so as to counteract the attempt by tyranny, terrorism, and crime to subvert freedom. Zygmut Bauman (1993) expands on Beauvoir's concept when he explains that "what has come to be associated with the notion of the postmodern approach to morality is all too often the celebration of the 'demise of the ethical,' of the substitution of aesthetics for ethics, and of the 'ultimate emancipation' that follows" (p. 2).

We concur with Beauvoir and Bauman and propose further that this notion of paralysis and absurdity results from the modern bifurcation of ethics and aesthetics, not from postmodern notions of uncertainty. Just as Beauvoir would lead us to struggle with the ambiguity inherent in the world, we must struggle to find a way to weave again the tapestry of an axiological view that unites aesthetics and ethics. The reenchanted voice described by Gablik offers such a perspective on the reunification of ethics and aesthetics. A constructive postmodern philosophy encourages us to utilize this reunification to promote social consequences of value, as in the examples reviewed earlier. We must be about the task of allowing our appreciation of and involvement with the aesthetic to inform our examination of ethics. Conversely, we must allow our exploration of ethics to inform our understandings of aesthetics. This holistic reunification drives our understandings of a new education within the sociopolitical context.

The Nature of the Aesthetic Voice

The prophet is one who calls and inspires others to attend to matters of great significance. It is here that theology begins to intersect with aesthetics. The development of the prophetic voice is a process integrating psychological, spiritual, cognitive, and emotional aspects of our being. This process of evoking vision in others is very much dependent on an inner awakening, a realization of a personal capacity to perceive and affect the world. Modernism certified the behaviorist view of human development and limited our capacity to be agents of change. If we are merely the result of our circumstances—direct causal links to events of the past—for the most part we lose the ability to influence our own development. Gershon and Straub (1989) refer to this as a model of pathology in which our focus is on the elimination of a negative nature. The result is the very bifurcation of the human soul that we seek to empower. In effect, we are battling ourselves in the attempt to become empowered. In contrast, empowered individuals open before them unlimited possibilities in the envisioning process as they embrace that which Jung called the shadow. Thomas Moore explains that our work in psychology would change remarkably if we thought about it as ongoing care rather than as the quest for a cure. Problems and obstacles offer a chance for reflection that otherwise is precluded by the swift routine of life. Care of the soul observes the paradox whereby a muscled, strong-willed pursuit of change can actually stand in the way of substantive transformation (Moore, 1992). The arts play a vital role in both the enlivening of the soul and in the development and communication of vision. Moore suggests that the life of the soul requires a different language, one that is expressed in images. Therefore, with the artists of every culture rests the burden of the prophetic voice (McElfresh-Spehler & Slattery, 1999).

The imagination plays a huge role in the development of voice and vision. Through the imagination, we are often able to conceive of a reality different from the one we are currently experiencing. Maxine Greene (1995) writes about the importance of the imagination in the empowerment of individuals: "A space of freedom opens before the person moved to choose in light of possibility; she or he feels what it signifies to be an initiator and an agent, existing among others but with the power to choose for herself or himself" (p. 22). In regard to developing the voice of the young, she continues: "Acknowledging the difficulty of moving the young to bestir themselves to create their own projects or find their own voices, I nevertheless believe that we must make the arts central in school curricula because encounters with the arts have a unique power to release the imagination" (p. 27). The development of the imagination empowers us to conceive of possibilities and social consequences of value (Dewey, 1934b). In order to do so, we must have an understanding of proleptic time. Modernism has given us a linear sense of time that results in cause-and-effect relationships. As we explained in Chapter 2, proleptic time views the present as coexisting with both the past and the future in a holistic experience. Events of the past continue to live in present experiences. Picasso (1971) spoke of the power of art created in the past to continue to create new meanings and understandings:

> A picture is not thought out and settled beforehand. While it is being done it changes as one's thoughts change. And when it is finished it still goes on changing according to the state of mind of whoever is looking at it. A picture lives a life like a living creature, undergoing the changes imposed on us by our life from day to day. This is natural enough, as the picture lives only through the man [sic] who is looking at it. (p. 268)

As the past continues to influence the present, so does the future. It is not predetermined and remote; the future is very much a part of our current experience as we engage in the process of creating the future. For some, this involves the process of envisioning. We are aware that our capacity to imagine a different future is the beginning of this process. John Dewey (1938a) reminds us: "The ideal of using the present simply to get ready for the future contradicts itself. Hence, the central problem of an education based on experience is to select the kind of present experiences that live fruitfully and creatively in subsequent experiences" (p. 28). A significant sense of empowerment arises from the awareness of one's capacity to envision, engage, and create the future in the present moment.

The Postmodern Reply: Time and Aesthetics

Although we investigate the importance of "creating spaces and finding voices" in the educational process, as Janet Miller (1990) has so aptly written, the preponderance of materials and programs that emphasize the technical rationality of our work as educators continues to stifle and silence the voices of imagination. Neil Postman (1996) in *The End of Education* warns that we must be attentive to more than this technical rationale:

> In considering how to conduct the schooling of our young, adults have two problems to solve. One is an engineering problem; the other, a metaphysical one. The engineering problem . . . is essentially technical. But it is important to keep in mind that the engineering of learning is very often puffed up, assigned to an importance it does not deserve. . . . I suggest that without a transcendent and honorable purpose schooling must reach its finish. (pp. x, 3)

We concur with Postman. If schooling is simply technical, it has reached its end and is incapable of contributing to solutions to the social, spiritual, and ecological problems of our communities. But we are not resigned to the end of education. Rather, we believe that empowering the voices of imagination through the arts will contribute to a renewal of the metaphysical dimension of our work. We advocate for such a posture.

It is important to infuse a postmodern perspective into our discussion of time and aesthetics. Here is how the author Umberto Eco (1991), from "Postscript to *The Name of the Rose*," explains the notion of time in postmodern thinking:

> The postmodern reply to the modern consists of recognizing that the past, since it cannot really be destroyed, because its destruction leads to silence, must be revisited: but with irony not innocently. . . . Irony, metalinguistic play, enunciation squared. Thus, with the modern, anyone who does not understand the game can only reject it, but with the postmodern, it is possible not to understand the game and yet to take it seriously. Which is, after all, the quality (the risk) of irony. There is always someone who takes ironic discourse seriously. . . . I believe that postmodernism is not a trend to be chronologically defined, but rather an ideal category or, better still, a *kunstwollen,* a way of operating. (pp. 73–74)

Eco creates an image of time and space that is very different from the irreversible linear arrow and progressive sequence of modernity. Time is not an irreversible line on a trajectory in which new and modern understandings are better than the outdated past. Modern conveniences that save us nanoseconds perpetuate a linear notion of time that is ultimately destructive of our psyche. The violence of our contemporary world is exacerbated, in part, through the fragmentation of our lives in modern society. In addressing this problem, postmodern theorists and contemporary philosophers reconceptualize time as duration, eternal recurrence, or proleptic experience. On the one hand, time is a duration in which the past is embedded in the present, as Henri Bergson (1997) contends. On the other hand, for Nietzsche (1968), nothing abides, but all returns to be destroyed again and again. The *process* of becoming endures, but nothing in that process endures, except as repeated enduring states. Modern notions of being, Nietzsche contends, have arisen from discontent with becoming. We would argue that many ethical dilemmas result from the unwillingness of human beings to engage in the difficult and messy process of becoming. In order for us to engage in the process, we must learn to be attentive and value every experience. We must learn to be fully present in every moment. Eternal recurrence is more than "mere" becoming; it reveals the eternal value of every moment. In both duration and eternal return, Bergson and Nietzsche reject modern notions of linear time in favor of the process of becoming, which is so integral to this notion of proleptic eschatology.

Another important philosopher who helps us understand the notion of prolepsis and ethics is Thich Nhat Hahn, a Vietnamese Buddhist monk who is influential in the movement known as "engaged Buddhism." Hanh believes that when a person is not focused on the present moment, she or he is not actually living in the present, but rather suffers from delusion through attachment to either perceptions of the past or the construction of a desired future. Hahn (1995) contends that in Buddhism the effort is to practice mindfulness in each moment. To this end, it is essential to maintain constant awareness of all thought processes and practice conscious breathing and contemplation to become aware of the steady stream of thoughts bombarding our minds. In modern society, in which material accumulation and consumption are considered signs of success, it becomes essential to transcend the cultural pressures to segment time and distance ourselves from mindfulness. Hahn is one among many philosophers in both Eastern and Western traditions who contend that contemplation and meditation are needed to provide an atmosphere in which proleptic experiences can occur.

Without such contemplation, the crises of modern life are amplified, precisely because history and time are conceived of as linear and thus capable of being broken. If the present can be broken, it can also be conceived of as degraded and meaningless. Then the modern pathos is projected backward and forward, infusing this vision on every moment: past, present, and future. A proleptic sense of hope reconnects space-time with individuals and society in order to transcend this modern embedded pathos. James Macdonald (1988) writes, "The impetus for choosing and becoming in us is not something that need be externally imposed; but it is rather a process of helping others see possibilities and helping them free themselves from going beyond this present state of embedded existence" (p. 113). Postmodern ethics must reconnect artificial bifurcations: students and teachers, space and time, meaning and context, knowing and the known, humanities and sciences, and especially past, present, and future. What modernity has rent asunder, proleptic eschatology reevaluates as holistic by embracing the fragmented beauty. It celebrates the process of becoming and the interdependence of eternal becoming by reuniting ethics and aesthetics, theology and the arts. The following narratives explain our journey toward understanding this concept of becoming, a concept integral to our understanding of ethics and education.

Complexity of Identity Formation

In order to move toward our aesthetic understanding of life experiences, we must continue to explore the complexity of the identity we create for ourselves and the identities imposed on us by family, government, religion, social convention, and schools. We all tend to categorize ourselves in various ways: married Irish Catholic politician, single white male graduate student, black lesbian feminist historian, Greenpeace environmental activist, African American southern writer, white conservative Republican talk show host, fundamentalist southern Christian preacher, Polish Jewish Holocaust survivor, and so on. Images may come to mind as you read these familiar identity categories. However, sometimes the stereotypes do not fit every individual, especially when complex and contradictory identities emerge. What happens when people identify themselves as the following: gay conservative Republican Marine, millionaire land developer environmental activist, pro-choice Irish Catholic politician, divorced fundamentalist Christian preacher, Hispanic grandmother corporate lawyer, and so on? The more we explore our identities, the more contradictions and complexities we will uncover.

   Consider the case of Father Romuald Weksler, a Roman Catholic priest from Poland, who discovered in the 1990s that he was born to Jewish parents in 1943 in the town of Stare Swieciany. His father was a well-known tailor. His mother was trapped in a Jewish ghetto and destined to be murdered and cremated at the Nazi concentration camp at Majdanek. In desperation, his mother begged a Catholic woman, Emilia Waszkinel, to take her infant son to save him from certain death. When Emilia hesitated, the Jewish woman argued that as a devout Catholic who believed in Jesus, Emilia should save the baby for the Jew in whom she believed. The mother then predicted that the boy would grow up to be a priest. Emilia took the child as her own and named him Romuald. For fear of reprisal from the Nazis, Emilia Waszkinel never revealed these events and raised the boy as a Catholic. In his twenties, and after unexplained protests from his parents, Romuald entered a seminary and was ordained a Roman Catholic priest. After the collapse of the Soviet Union, Romuald, who had grown curious and skeptical about his genealogy, gained access to records that revealed the long-held secret. He changed his name to Father Romuald-Jakob Weksler-Waszkinel, a combination of his adopted Catholic name and his Jewish birth name. In interviews (Cohen, 1999), Father Weksler-Waszkinel explains some of the complexity of his double identity. In Israel, where many people want him to reject his priesthood and return to his Jewish heritage (something he does not want to do), Weksler-Waszkinel feels like an outsider. And in his Catholic Polish community, he complains that prejudice against Jews persists. He wears a Star of David with a cross on the inside and laments, "I am in the middle, and I know that what is needed is contact, understanding, and love" (Cohen, 1999).

Father Weksler-Waszkinel's story is not an isolated incident. As information technologies and democratic openness in formerly closed countries become more and more accessible, people are discovering misplaced paternity, unreported adoptions, and family secrets. We particularly like the Oscar-nominated British movie for best film in 1996, *Secrets and Lies,* which explored these issues provocatively, and the 1995 U.S. film *Lone Star,* which explored intermingled bloodlines on the Texas–Mexico border. My (Patrick) own grandmother's grandfather was Jewish. However, because of the intense hatred and persecution of Jews and the unfolding events in Nazi Germany, my grandmother hid her genealogy from the family. Madeleine Albright, secretary of state for the United States under President Clinton, discovered that some of her grandparents were Jews killed during the Holocaust. This information had been hidden from her, and she grew up thinking she was a Catholic and later a convert to the Episcopalian church until journalists discovered her heritage when she was nominated for secretary of state.

The complexity of double identity or multiple identities can sometimes be hidden: a gay man or lesbian woman might date the opposite sex, marry, or "act straight" in order to avoid harassment or emotional disequilibrium; a light-skinned African American individual might claim to be Italian or some other nationality in order to "pass" in white society; a Jew might claim to be a Christian in order to avoid persecution (as in the excellent film *Europa, Europa*); a young person might profess a religious doctrine that she or he does not believe in order to please a parent, relative, or pastor; or a bored student might pretend to be studious and engaged in a lesson in order to impress a teacher and win a grade. People go to great lengths to hide any part of their identity they may be ashamed of or uncomfortable exposing. However, hiding one's identity, either overtly by denial or unconsciously by repression, is not always possible.

Consider the case of social construction of race in U.S. society. An analogy we often use for our students may be instructive. The analogy centers on the idea of "black" and "white" from two different perspectives: physics and pigment. In physics, black is the absence of all light and thus the absence of color, as in the void of total darkness. On the other hand, white light is the fullness of the entire spectrum of color, as in the refraction of white light entering a prism to form a rainbow. In pigment, black and white take on the opposite values. Black is the fullness of all colors mixed together, while white is the absence of all color. Thus, depending on the context, black and white may represent similar or opposite perspectives. It is especially important to note that black and white are dependent on the other for their very definition and existence.

We use this analogy to suggest that objectifying and condemning persons based on color is not only immoral but also illogical. The objectification of "blackness" or "redness" or "yellowness" or "whiteness," and by extrapolation "masculinity" and "femininity," all result from socially constructed norms. There are numerous historical examples of the absurdity of our socially constructed racial and gender values. In the state of Louisiana, a birth certificate was required to list a child as "Negro" if the child had as little as one thirty-second non-Caucasian, African ancestry. This practice was not challenged until the 1970s (Diamond & Cottrol, 1983). Films such as *Eve's Bayou* or Anne Rice's book and film *All Saints* explore the complexity of racial identification in the nineteenth and early twentieth centuries in New Orleans, where labels such as mulatto, quadroon, and octoroon categorized people by the percentage of African American blood.

Another example involving race was widely reported in March 1994 when a high school principal in Alabama threatened to cancel the prom when he heard that a black student and a white student planned to attend the dance as a couple. The principal's ban on interracial dating caused an avalanche of both protest and support. Pertinent here is the comment of one student who asked, "Who am I to date since I am biracial: my mother is white and my father is black?" The principal, she reported, chastised her parents for making a mistake, noting that she was evidence of the damaging result of tolerance of interracial dating. This principal had a history of controversial social positions, and this case drew considerable national attention. There is also some opposition to interracial dating from African American leaders as well. Khalid Muhammad (1994) warns black men, "You want to wear your 'X' hat, but you want to have a white girl on your arm. . . . Now don't get me wrong. A white girl is alright for a white boy, but I'm talking about rebuilding the black family" (p. 2). Racial purity has proponents in all ethnic groups. The legislation of racial purity leads to the social construction of identity and attempts to circumvent laws and practices by individuals.

As a white kid growing up in the Deep South of the United States, race and multiculturalism were topics associated with "Blacks" or "Cubans" or "Asians." My (Patrick) first memory of contemplating the notion of "whiteness" occurred during a family discussion about the use of the name Emmie Slattery for the "white trash riffraff" character created by Margaret Mitchell in her 1936 novel *Gone with the Wind.* Let me introduce Emmie briefly.

> It would be interesting to know who was the father of Emmie Slattery's baby, but Scarlett knew she would never learn the truth of the matter if she waited to hear it from her mother. Scarlett suspected Jonas Wilkerson, for she had frequently seen him walking down the road with Emmie at nightfall. Jonas was a Yankee and a bachelor, and the fact that he was an overseer forever barred him from any contact with the County social life.

There was no family of any standing into which he could marry, no people with whom he could associate except the Slatterys and riffraff like them. As he was several cuts above the Slatterys in education, it was only natural that he should not want to marry Emmie, no matter how often he might walk with her in the twilight. (Mitchell, 1936, pp. 44–45)

Scarlett O'Hara eventually concluded that Jonas Wilkerson was the father of Emmie Slattery's baby. When Scarlett was persuaded to dismiss Jonas as overseer at Tara, she lamented, "Oh well. What else can you expect from a Yankee man and a white-trash girl?" (Mitchell, 1936, p. 49).

This scene from *Gone with the Wind* is emblazoned in my memory. Before I could even read, I knew all about Emmie Slattery. As a young boy in the 1950s in Shreveport, Louisiana, I would eavesdrop as my great-aunt Nell talked about Emmie to the adults in the parlor of her stately Victorian home—now a bed-and-breakfast tourist attraction—constructed at the turn of the century by her father, the revered family patriarch John Bernard Slattery. The history of Shreveport is intimately tied to the fortunes and failures of John Slattery. In the 1920s, he constructed an office building that was the tallest structure between Dallas and Atlanta at the time of completion. Slattery Boulevard, located at the heart of the old family farm, which was sold to keep other investments solvent during the Great Depression, is an oak-shaded and azalea-lined residential neighborhood today.

In a letter written in 1937 that was discussed again and again for years, Aunt Nell passionately denounced Margaret Mitchell and her "poor white-trash girl, Emmie Slattery." Aunt Nell was determined to protect the venerable Slattery name and thus preserve her dignity, identity, and social status in the Shreveport community. Some of my relatives believed then—and a few may even continue to believe today—that the honor, tradition, and southern heritage of the family was tarnished irreparably by Margaret Mitchell. As the oldest living member of the family, Aunt Nell probably thought it her duty to be particularly outraged, and her protestations ignited my own childhood imagination. How could Margaret Mitchell defame our family name and threaten our venerable southern identity by assigning the name "Slattery" to the riffraff and poor white trash in her novel?

By the 1950s, *Gone with the Wind* had become more than a novel; it was the mythical history of the southern way of life. Margaret Mitchell had not simply written an obscure narrative or fictional biography; she was recounting a grand narrative of the "war of northern aggression." For the Slatterys, Mitchell was telling our story—and we had been miscast in the role of white trash riffraff! In this atmosphere, it was only natural for my Aunt Nell to accuse Margaret Mitchell of historical distortion, genealogical slander, and personal vilification.

Aunt Nell was not the only outraged Slattery. President Franklin D. Roosevelt's influential undersecretary of the interior in Washington, D.C., Harry Slattery, also took great offense that the character Emmie Slattery had been cast as the "white-trash girl." The *Washington Post* on September 29, 1936, reported that Harry Slattery had threatened to sue Mitchell. Anne Edwards (1983) in *The Road to Tara* contends that Margaret Mitchell had never heard of Harry Slattery prior to the *Post* article, and that "she was appalled at the ridiculous untruth of his statement" (p. 240). Further, the article included this unsubstantiated claim:

> The world might know her as Margaret Mitchell but she is first and foremost the wife of John Marsh. She still cooks breakfast in that little flat in Atlanta, and he keeps working at his job, in spite of the fact that they suddenly came into a fortune. Atlantans have tried to fete and exploit them—*they wrote the book in collaboration over a period of seven years*—but they keep their heads and decline all interviews. (1983, p. 240; emphasis added)

Although Harry Slattery eventually withdrew his threat to sue Margaret Mitchell after she assured him in a lengthy and self-effacing letter dated October 3, 1936, that the choice of names in her novel was made only after extensive research to ensure that no connection could be made to actual people, the accusation of collaboration with John Marsh lingered (Harwell, 1976). The Slattery protest was quickly forgotten by the news media; the joint authorship speculation in the *Post* article by Slattery haunted Mitchell for the rest of her life (Edwards, 1983).

I too was haunted by childhood memories of Emmie Slattery, Margaret Mitchell, *Gone with the Wind,* and the protest surrounding the use of our family name in the novel. As I eavesdropped in the family parlor during one of Aunt Nell's recountings of both her letter and Margaret Mitchell's response, I remember feeling the shame so passionately expressed by my adult relatives. Were we really white trash? What will happen if others begin to believe that the Slatterys are really riffraff? I fantasized that I would join the protest all the way to Washington, D.C., to assure the world that we were not white trash.

This was the first of many occasions when I was influenced to believe that my racial and social identity were more a factor of who I was *not* than who I *was*. Beginning with Emmie Slattery, I learned to construct my identity by negation rather than by affirmation. Racial and cultural identity, for me and many other white relatives and friends, meant "not black," "not riffraff," and certainly "not white trash." However, it was many decades later before I asked the question, "So what does it mean to be 'white' anyway?" In 1950 the civil rights battles had not yet been waged in earnest, and multiculturalism was nowhere on the U.S. radar screen.

Our positionality in the erratic vagrancies of family heritage, social hierarchy, culture, race, ethnicity, language, geographical and psychological place, gender, and sexuality all contribute to our identity constructions and the emergence of racist or antiracist practices. To assume an antiracist position, we must first interrupt and problematize notions of race and ethnicity that have become deeply entrenched in our way of being in the world. Otherwise, the ongoing tragedy of racism will continue to infect and deform many global societies. As an adult, I am now thankful for the fictional life of Emmie Slattery; I hope she will continue to force readers to evaluate the complexity of racial identities, dangerous sexualities, gender bias, and social class hierarchies. Reread *Gone with the Wind* through the eyes of the poor white trash riffraff girl, Emmie Slattery—a woman virtually erased by Scarlett O'Hara—and ponder the meaning of racial and class identities. Likewise, recognize the complexity and diversity of subject positions and social experiences that create categories such as "black and white" or "aristocracy and white trash." Note how they are all socially produced and discursively sustained as you consider the ethical ramifications of racism.

Reflecting on the vagrancies of identity construction leads to an analysis of two important postmodern concepts: "The Death of the Author" (Derrida, 1981, 1982) and "The Death of the Subject" (Foucault, 1972a, 1977). These concepts foreground self-deception and the limitations and contradictions of truth statements by individuals, thus revealing a "fictional self" capable of many complex meanings rather than an "authentic self" capable—in the Enlightenment sense—of being wholly knowable and rational. In other words, we never fully "know" ourselves because we are always in the process of learning about our heritage, beliefs, and values, and we are continually influenced by many complicated factors we are not even consciously aware of. Sometimes we wear masks; sometimes we repress feelings and experiences. Sometimes our unconscious influences us. Sometimes the voices of our deceased relatives shade our judgment or inspire our imagination. And, recalling the case of Father Weksler-Waszkinel, our identity may be hidden from us by parents, religious leaders, teachers, or governments. Or, in the case of my great-aunt Nell, our identity may be formed as we absorb the prejudices of the social and cultural heritage of our family.

The death of the subject is a difficult concept to grasp. It implies that the cohesive, unified identity of an individual that is fully capable of self-presence is an illusion of modern rational thinking and the scientism of modern psychology. Philosopher Rene Descartés's *Cogito* ("I think, therefore I am") continues to be undermined as postmodern psychology investigates the nature of language and human existence. Sarup (1989) contends that the autonomous subject has been dispersed into a range of plural, polymorphous, subject positions inscribed in language, thus emphasizing diverse forms of individual and social identity. Bakhtin (1993) locates "self" within the dialogue between self and others, creating a relationship of simultaneity in difference. Hongyu Wang (1997) explains, "The self, while distinguishable to itself, is always seen in relation to others and to the world of lived experience. At the same time, for Bakhtin, the sense of self is not only relational, but unfixable. The self is engaged in its continuous becoming and transforming" (p. 20). Robin Usher and Richard Edwards (1994) present the postmodern case when they contend that the idea of self-presence as perfect representation is replaced by the "decentered subject, where the subject of consciousness, the reasoning, thinking, transparent subject, is displaced by the opaque subject of the unconscious" (p. 57). We find it helpful to explore Usher and Edwards's concern on the biological level first and then move to the psychological.

An article in the *Cleveland Plain Dealer* titled "Is the Child Yours? DNA Testing Uncovers Surprising Number of Dads Who Aren't the Father" (Torassa, 1997) is illustrative. Genetic research at University Hospitals of Cleveland, the article reports, requires up to 10 percent additional volunteer subjects in order to account for "misidentified paternity." Unreported adoptions, children switched at birth, sperm donors, secret affairs, and the like all contribute to the growing awareness that biological heritage is more opaque than certain. What is the ethical responsibility of a hospital or researcher when misplaced paternity is discovered? Recent stories of children switched at birth, only to discover the misplaced identity years later, cause hospitals to shutter. Legal and moral questions abound. Should people's lives be disrupted when false identities are uncovered? Should hospitals and researchers remain silent? When and how should parents tell their children they were adopted? Born out of wedlock? Conceived by artificial insemination? While legal and medical ethicists struggle to address these complex questions and help us negotiate the difficult human concerns, it is important to remember in the process that identities are complex and evolving rather than static. Literally, some of us are not who we think we are. Gregory Howard Williams (1995) in *Life on the Color Line* reminds us of the uncertainty of racial identity. He grew up in Virginia thinking he was a white Italian boy. But as an early teen, he was sent to live with relatives in Indiana. These relatives were black, and the young Gregory literally had to change his identity overnight. James McBride (1996), author of *The Color of Water,* writes about his light-skinned mother who hid the fact that she was a Polish Jewish immigrant to the United States. His mother told the family that she was a light-skinned black woman in order to hide her rejection by her Jewish family when she married a black man.

We are reminded here of the philosopher Hans-Georg Gadamer's critique of consciousness in which he undermines the notion of a self-transparent consciousness that believes it is fully itself, the center of being, completely in control, and immune to influences outside or inside itself. Gadamer teaches us that subjects are prejudiced. The horizon, and thus identity, is always shifting. In the same light, meaning is shifting, ambiguous, and uncertain. If the self is transparent, why should we expect literature, math, science, art, or even ethics to be fixed? Yet modern positivism demands linear logic, unalterable truth, and fixed meaning. Postmodernism forces us to take a posture of incredulity toward such metanarratives in our work and in our lives. We believe that the previously cited examples challenge us to begin with the assumption of ambiguity rather than the modern belief that linear progress and sequential development can lead to certainty and completion.

What might this mean for educational ethics and classroom practices in the university and in K–12 schooling? Usher and Edwards (1994) offer this insight:

> [I]t is impossible to be a teacher without also being a learner, that in order to be a teacher it is first necessary to abandon the position of the "one who knows," recognising both one's own lack of knowledge and of self-transparence and mastery and that one's own learning is never, and never will be, complete. (p. 80)

It follows here that the distinction between teachers and students is never so clear-cut as it is conventionally assumed, particularly in schools. Postmodern theorists such as

Usher and Edwards contend that psychoanalysis provides the means to reconceptualize this aspect of authority in the teacher–student relationship. However, this deconstruction does not imply an advocacy of chaos in the classroom, without any structure or a move to destruction. On the contrary, it means the discovery of negotiated limits, ambiguity, contrasts, multiplicity, irony, layers of interpretation, uncertainty, and shades of difference. Teachers and students must therefore continue the learning process indefinitely and defer final explanations. Usher and Edwards (1994) explain:

> It is important to stress that what we are talking about here is not the humanistic conception of "lifelong learning" as the continual adaptation to the needs of the existing socio-economic order. Nor is it merely a restatement of the notion of learner centeredness. . . . Rather it is an argument for teachers to continually question the ground upon which they stand, to question their own ready implication in the discourse of mastery. For this, teachers need to be trained to analyse what is repressed in order to foreground the affects, release the emotions [and imagination], and broaden the sense of fulfillment. The pupils would then be allowed to extend their analysis to their environment. To create the space they live in rather than just fit in with the set rules. Literally. To paint. To build. To co-operate. To participate. The limit then would be the analysis of the transference. (p. 80)

Usher and Edwards admit that postmodern theories resonate with certain strands of progressive education but without its teleology of emancipated free expression and its containment within the overall framework of modernist educational theory and practice. They write that psychoanalysis in the Lacanian mode, then, is itself radically self-subversive and a process that does not simply examine its own ground but systematically cuts the ground away from itself. What we propose is that the very concept of expertise be vigorously challenged. We must begin by asking questions, challenging authorities, deconstructing metanarratives, and problematizing even the notion of our self-identity. This is not done to lead us to despair or nihilism. Rather, the goal is to set a tone for open and scholarly investigation of notions of "truth," a process we begin in the next section.

An Arts-Based Installation Exploring Religion and Sexuality

I (Patrick) presented one of my arts-based autoethnographic educational research projects at the Reclaiming Voice II conference in Los Angeles in June 1999 with professors Linda Skrla of Texas A&M and James Koschoreck of the University of Cincinnati, and at the Arts-Based Educational Research Association conference in Albuquerque in February 2000. The title of the presentation was "Knowledge (De)Constructed and (Re)Embodied: An Art Installation That Disrupts Regulation of the Body in Classroom Practices." This arts-based research project, done in collaboration with Craig Richard Johanns, an independent artist in Austin, Texas, seeks to deconstruct notions of the body and practices of sexual regulation in schools and classrooms through an art installation of actual artifacts and other symbolic representations of my conscious and unconscious memories of my elementary classrooms in a Catholic school in the 1960s. The work recalls the methodology of assemblage tableaus by Edward Kienholz and Nancy Kienholz described earlier (Hopps, 1996). This art installation includes two canvases, two freestanding 1960s-style wooden school desks with textbooks and personal memorabilia arranged on top of and under the desk, and a wooden classroom bench converted into a makeshift altar forming a tableau. The installation includes contemporary protest music by Rage Against the Machine titled "Take the Power Back" and religious chants by the Monks of Taize titled "The Spirit Is Willing but the Flesh Is Weak" playing in the background. Candles and incense burn, purposely creating a monastic milieu. The viewer is invited to experience the tableau while kneeling on an antique confessional prie-dieu. (These images can be seen at www.coe.tamu.edu/~pslattery.)

Viewers of the installation are warned in advance that religious, violent, and sexual images are juxtaposed with educational material and classroom furniture in the tableau. Some viewers find this evocative and illuminating; others find it provocative and unsettling. Although this arts-based research installation may be didactic in the way it evokes multiple reactions and insights, like the work of Jackson Pollock discussed in Chapter 1, it initially emerged from my unconscious without a specific didactic intent other than to probe my memories of the body and sexuality in my schooling experience. The installation tableau seeks understanding about regulation of my body in the Catholic school classrooms of my youth. However, once my inner work becomes an aesthetic representation in a public space, the piece is available for others to experience, evaluate, critique, and apply to other contexts. In effect, it becomes a piece of interactive research in an ongoing process of deconstruction and recreation.

When I started this tableau installation, I began by working within, turning to the unconscious for direction and inspiration. Like Pollock, "when I am engaged in the process, I am not aware of what I am doing" (Chipps, 1971, p. 548). Only after the tableau was completed could others respond to it and possibly construct a didactic purpose. Because regulation of the body continues to affect students in schools today, it is imperative that teachers and researchers investigate regulation of the body and experiences of sexuality. One way to do this is through traditional social science projects that quantify and codify such experiences for the purpose of exposing generalizations about sexuality in schools and curricular material. Another approach is to provide thick descriptions in case studies of individual students. However, in this arts-based installation, I take another approach by using the lessons of Pollock, Jung, and autoethnographers to work within in order to research bodily regulation in schools and classrooms. The unconscious is the place of my research, but expanded discourse about spirituality, sexuality, social justice, and school curricula are also my goals. Foucault's notion of governmentality informs my work as I come to understand the ways in which my body was regulated by catechisms, priests, and nuns that bombarded my consciousness with notions of celibacy, purity, heteronormativity, virginity, and chastity.

Foucault on Regulation and Governmentality

Theoretical support for this work comes from Foucault's notion of regulation and governmentality (1972a, 1972b, 1977, 1979). Foucault (1983) writes that power works through language and that language not only describes and defines human beings but also creates institutions to regulate and govern them. Literally, power is inscribed in our bodies, and language governs our mentality. (As we investigate later, the images in my autoethnography installation tableau emerge from the unconscious and evoke such an understanding of bodily regulation in classrooms.) Because the social sciences categorize people into "normal" and "abnormal," Foucault was interested in finding out historically what constituted madness, criminality, perverted sexuality, and illness. Many modern philosophers from Kant to the present have assumed that "normal" and "ethical" are universal concepts that have remained static over time. Foucault disagreed. As we discussed in Chapter 1, he examined historical documents in order to deconstruct this assumption. He found that definitions of normal and the treatment of abnormal persons have varied over time and place. The abnormal was understood historically only through the ideas of the normal. In other words, "normal" people became obsessed with studying and controlling the "abnormal" people and eventually began to regulate and govern the abnormal people using their power to control.

In studying Foucault, I began to recognize the ways in which I had been constructed as an object of such regulation and governmentality in my adolescent classrooms, especially concerning issues of sexuality. Although the exploration of the effects of such regulation might be effectively explicated using quantitative statistical methodologies, qualitative case studies, or traditional ethnographies, the researcher as artist working within explores the autobiographical context of her or his lived experience first and then allows the unconscious to direct the creation of an aesthetic text that represents symbolically these experiences. Autoethnography is an attempt to disrupt notions of normalcy in research. I agree with Linda Brodkey's conclusion, "To the extent that poststructural theory narrates a story, it tells a complex story about the power of discourse(s) over the human imagination" (1996, 24). The recovery of imagination through the complex narrative of autoethnography offers a poststructural alternative to continued regulation and governmentality of human bodies in schools and society.

As discussed earlier, in Foucault's philosophy, persons considered abnormal are silenced because they do not have the knowledge of the truth. In *Discipline and Punish,* Foucault explores power relations and oppression, contending that discourse has a role in power relations and that the seeming abstractions of discourse do have material effects on people's bodies because language is inscribed in our bodies. This is the primary notion I explore in my tableau installation. What are the material effects on my body that have resulted from memorizing the Baltimore Catechism texts and performing Catholic rituals in my elementary classrooms in the 1960s? How might others be informed by my display of these memories in a psychoanalytic art tableau?

Foucault documents the movement toward punishment as regulation in prisons of the early nineteenth century. We presented in Chapter 1 the six ways this is accomplished: spatialization, minute control of activities, repetition, detailed hierarchies, normalizing judgments, and the panopticon. Remember that Foucault contends that this results in a docile worker who becomes reformed in prison and an automaton for a capitalist factory. When schools function like prisons, students become passive receptors of inert information and react like docile automatons in a system of educational or religious proselytization and indoctrination. My autoethnography explores such reactions to the regulation of my Catholic education. Those who do not accept the prevailing ideology imposed in the panopticon remain "abnormal" and can be kept away from the normal indefinitely in the prison system.

Although Foucault's analysis of discipline and punishment in society deals specifically with prisons, the analysis can be applied to any institution that seeks to control those judged to be abnormal. In my autoethnographic tableau, I apply these notions to regulation of the body, mandatory chastity, the preference for celibacy in the priesthood or religious community, and unquestioned heteronormativity in my Catholic school classrooms. The artwork itself is a construction of a tableau with the juxtaposition of symbols that flow from my unconscious. Some symbols are carefully and purposely incorporated into the tableau, but only after they resonate with the unconscious. However, they can be understood only in the context of the multiple layers of meaning in the entire work of art (Foucault, 1983).

Jackson Pollock used this process as he incorporated symbols from mythology, Native American spirituality, and Mexican muralism in his psychoanalytic drawings. Pollock lived in Arizona in his youth and traveled in Mexico on several occasions. He was highly influenced by Native American arts; he admired and collaborated with the Mexican artists José Clemente Orozco, David Alfaro Siqueiros, and Diego Rivera. The context of Pollock's drawings can be understood only if the conscious and unconscious influences of these artists and styles are considered. This is an essential feature of the artist working within to explore ethical and educational issues.

The Installation: Aesthetic Representations

In the art installation, I look specifically at the normalization and regulation of sexuality in a Catholic school classroom of the 1960s (Foucault, 1979, 1986a, 1990). Images from my Catholic catechism are included in the tableau, which is titled *10,000 Ejaculations,* as well as the canvases titled *(De)Evolution of the Marathon Runner* and

Hopelessness by Craig Johanns. The Catholic nuns who taught in my elementary school spent a great deal of time instructing the students to say prayers in Latin and English (e.g., Hail Mary/Ave Maria, Our Father/Pater Noster). One type of prayer was called the ejaculation. Ejaculations were short and spontaneous prayerful outbursts such as "Jesus I love you" or "Jesus, Mary, and Joseph protect me." Ejaculations were particularly recommended by the nuns in times of temptation. The gravest temptations were "impure thoughts," which could lead to the deadly sins of touching one's body, masturbation, orgasm, or sexual intercourse.

The Catechism displayed in the tableau pictures angelic celibate priests and nuns with the word *best* inscribed under the drawing. A devout and pure married couple is identified as *better.* A single eunuch is labeled *good.* Good, better, and best represented holy lifestyles. However, the unmistakable message was that a sexless celibate life was clearly superior, preferred by God and the nuns. Of course, same-sex relationships and homosexuality were not even options open for discussion. The Baltimore Catechism, still in use today in some Catholic schools, outlines the prescription: "The doctrine of the excellence of virginity and of celibacy, and of their superiority over the married state, was revealed by our Holy Redeemer, so too was it defined as a dogma of divine faith by the holy council of Trent" (Confraternity of Christian Doctrine, 1962, p. 103). A copy of a 1962 sixth-grade Baltimore Catechism can be seen in the tableau representing not only pre–Vatican II Catholic theology, but also the pervasive hidden curriculum and subliminal messages found in all school textbooks.

Students in Catholic elementary schools in the pre–Vatican II 1950s and 1960s were often required to make *Spiritual Bouquets.* The spiritual bouquet was a decorated greeting card with space provided to list prayer offerings for a special person, often the student's mother. One such card that I made in school on April 11, 1961, and saved by my mother in a scrapbook, can be seen in the tableau. The spiritual bouquet contained a numerical listing of prayers to be offered for the recipient. The greater the quantity of prayers offered, the greater the implied religious fervor of the student. My classmates and I always felt compelled—both in the overt religious instruction and the subliminal suggestions of our conscience—to offer as many prayers as possible. This would not only demonstrate holiness and piety, but also our efforts to save the souls in purgatory who needed our prayers to escape to heaven. Each prayer was assigned a numerical indulgence that reduced time spent in purgatory by deceased souls.

The most highly recommended prayers were rosaries and communions at Mass, which provided maximum indulgences for the recipient of the spiritual bouquet and/or "the poor souls in purgatory." However, these prayers were time consuming and laborious. Although I often felt compelled to include a few rosaries and communions on the spiritual bouquet, I usually preferred to pad the prayer offerings with lots of ejaculations. One of my spiritual bouquets with an offering of ten thousand ejaculations for my mother is seen in front of a replica of Michelangelo's *Pietà.* I enthusiastically presented a spiritual bouquet to my mother every year along with a ragged bouquet of assorted flowers and weeds from our yard. Adding thousands of ejaculations to a spiritual bouquet provided an appearance of religious fervor and spiritual gratitude. Offering to recite ten thousand ejaculations for Jesus, Mary, the nuns, and my mother became a passionate religious mantra—although I do not remember actually keeping an exact count of the prayers, I just rattled them off in my head until I got distracted. The ironic juxtaposition of spiritual ejaculations and celibate, heteronormative sexuality is deconstructed in this tableau.

The Religious Sisters of Mercy were my teachers in New Orleans. I was never physically or verbally reprimanded by the nuns, probably because I was a compliant student with an angelic attitude. However, underneath my facade of purity, perfection, and piety were adolescent confusion and guilt, which began during puberty. I find many interesting parallels with Jackson Pollock's inner demons and the manifestation of his complex and at times conflicted sexuality in his sketches and paintings. A comprehensive, controversial, and, in conservative art circles, blasphemous look at Jackson Pollock's ambiguous sexuality is found in the biography by Naifeh and Smith (1989). The authors present a disturbing view of Pollock as an infantile, insecure mama's boy, an exaggerator of sexual conquests, and an abusive husband who may have been attracted to men. One passage implies that Pollock associated his drip technique with boyhood memories of watching his alcoholic father urinate on rocks. I am particularly struck by the accounts in the book related to Lee Krasner that examine Pollock's inner turmoil over his sexuality (e.g., pp. 272–275). I suspect that Pollock's ambiguous and complex sexuality will continue to inspire debates and discussions. For me, the best way to understand Pollock's sexuality is to meditate before his sketches and paintings, beginning with *Male and Female* and *Stenographic Figure* (Naifeh & Smith, 1989, pp. 432–433).

Although sexuality was never overtly discussed in my school or home, the hidden message that governed my thinking was that sex was sinful. My Baltimore Catechism again:

> The sixth commandment of God is Thou shalt not commit adultery. The sixth commandment forbids all impurity and immodesty in words, looks, and actions whether alone or with others. Examples of this would be touching one's own body or that of another without necessity simply to satisfy sinful curiosity, impure conversations, dirty jokes, looking at bad pictures, undue familiarity with the opposite sex. (Confraternity, 1962, p. 125).

Along with classmates, I began to privately explore my sexuality as a junior high school student. I wonder today how the catechism lesson about familiarity with the opposite sex may have contributed to the experimental encounters between male classmates.

Occasionally in seventh grade, and without my parents' knowledge, I rode the St. Charles streetcar to the French Quarter with friends after school on Fridays to see sexy peep shows at a penny arcade on Bourbon Street. This installation creates a "peep show" in which only a few glimpses into the adolescent experience can be seen, possibly eliciting some of the same emotions: curiosity, discomfort, arousal, guilt, disgust, or passion. The religious and sexual emotions are juxtaposed to reinforce adolescent confusion. For example, the faces of naked men and women, juxtaposed next to Bernini's *Estasi Di Santa Teresa* (*The Ecstacy of St. Theresa*), all display similar expressions. With the body of Jesus on their tongues, are these men and women experiencing the ecstasy of Christian mysticism or of sexual orgasm—or both? The painting of a woman mystic in spiritual ecstasy is remarkably similar to the expressions of sexual ecstasy in the erotica photographs. Juxtaposing sexual and religious symbols invites the viewer to reexperience the confusion and guilt of adolescence.

The impression that sex was evil and touching the body sinful was reinforced by the fact that the body was always covered in my Catholic school; the nuns exposed only their faces and hands, girls covered their heads with veils, and modest dress was demanded at all times. In the classroom, we were taught to avoid "impure thoughts" by praying ejaculations. However, I often fantasized about bodies and sex as I sat at my junior high school desk. The images from erotic magazines in the tableau foreground my fantasies of the human body as an adolescent student, albeit covered with white hosts—the body of Jesus—to protect me from my impure thoughts. The pubescent male is constantly aware of his body through spontaneous erections and sexual fantasies. Efforts to control and regulate the body through prayer may have sublimated sexual arousal temporarily, but the religious manta was seldom successful.

In this tableau installation I have covered the genitals and explicit eroticism of the photographs with the symbolic body of Jesus: communion wafers. There are layers of meaning: the unconsecrated nonbody of Jesus covers the impure erotic body images in the photographs; the body-less memory of the student who once sat in this now empty desk remembers suppressed erotic bodily experiences; the bodily remembering is done under the watchful eye of the Virgin Mary, who is holding the limp body of Jesus; Mary, whose body was taken into heaven as celebrated on the Assumption, models virginity and purity as she watches over the school desk like the nuns of my 1960s Catholic schooling.

In this autoethnography tableau, the viewer enters the bodily experience as voyeur in a way similar to viewers of *Jane Doe* by the Kienholzes, discussed earlier. The viewer may be tempted to move the communion wafers from the photograph of the naked male and female bodies—either physically or in fantasy—to view the genitals. This may even cause the viewer to experience some level of arousal. However, like the adolescent student, this arousal must be quickly suppressed in the public space of the art gallery. This parallels the experience of students who sit at desks trying to control fantasies for fear that an erection or flushed face will be publicly noticed. Many adolescent males hide their uncontrollable erection by covering it with a book, shirttail, or sweater. When I was in school and an unexpected fantasy or erection occurred, in an effort to suppress images of sexual ejaculations I would attempt to regulate my body with the prayerful ejaculations taught by the virgin nuns. If the voyeur attempts to remove the symbolic body of Jesus from the sexual images in my art tableau, she or he will find that the communion hosts are glued to the photographs. The body of Jesus literally represses the impure thoughts and prevents them from being manifested.

When I first discovered masturbation in junior high, I was overcome with religious guilt. I kept a secret calendar under my mattress—along with any erotica or pornography that my friends at school would share—and I would draw a circle around the date each day that I masturbated. A calendar and photograph of a young man masturbating are placed under my desk in the tableau, hidden, in a sense, like my calendar and erotica under my mattress. The calendar served several functions. First, it recorded the number of times I masturbated so that I would have an accurate count for Friday confession before Mass, which was required by the priest and taught by the nuns from the catechism. Communion was not allowed unless the soul had first been washed clean by the priest's absolution. Because a missed communion was a public admission of mortal sin, and because my catechism and religion lessons instructed me that the worst mortal sin was sex or touching one's body, the calendar protected me from a public admission of masturbation—or worse, the suspicion of sexual intercourse. Second, I thought that by keeping a count of my evil transgressions I could gradually wean myself off this sinful act. Third, the calendar provided me with hope that during the next month I could reduce the number of times I masturbated and thus minimize the risk of a scolding from the priest at the next Friday confession.

The final element of the installation is a cardboard artwork in the bottom corner of the desk, an art therapy project completed by my father in the psychiatric hospital on the morning of his death by suicide. After finishing the art project, my father left the hospital with a twenty-four-hour pass, bought a pistol, called me in Santa Fe, and told me he was going to shoot himself. As we remember from Chapter 2, I tried to dissuade him and asked if he had seen a priest, said his prayers, or gone to communion to eat the body of Jesus. As I listened frantically and helplessly on the other end of the phone, his final words to me were, "Only God can help me now." He shot himself in the heart and died two hours later. My active imagining of these dramatic events creates a parallel between my father's limp body, the limp body of Jesus in the *Pieta* in the tableau, and the limp body of those who were taught to recite ten thousand ejaculations to suppress impure thoughts, erections, and orgasms. Thus, my desk and the floor beneath the desk are littered with ten thousand white communion hosts, reminiscent of Jesus' body as well as globs of white semen staining my linen and the floor beneath my seat. My elementary education was regulated by thousands of ejaculations, literally and spiritually. A complex sexuality curriculum of governmentality is exposed in the tableau.

This installation is a construction and reconstruction of memories of my body in junior high classrooms. I collected artifacts from scrapbooks, yearbooks, and family closets. I also imagined furniture and icons, which I searched for in antique stores and junkyards. I worked within to reconstruct images from my unconscious, while remembering Jackson Pollock's admonition that the creative process also involves consciousness of the overall effect of the piece. Although the symbols are particular to my Catholic school experience, I believe that the issues I raise in this installation are applicable to many students. Repression of the body, sexual fantasies, uncontrollable sexual responses, and guilt and anxiety about sexuality are all a part of the educational experience of students who sit at school desks. Because there is no student seated in the desk in this installation—only the reminder of my presence in the plaster casts of my hands and my actual handprints from a first-grade art project—the viewer is reminded of the absence of the body and the attempt to repress sexuality in the school curriculum.

The hidden curriculum of the body has a powerful impact on the lived experience of students. These early life experiences, according to Jungian and other psychologies, emerge from the unconscious and affect our relationships and our education in multiple ways for our entire life. I have worked as an adult to (re)member my body with my spirit, my sexuality with my spirituality, and my fantasies with my imagination. I have concluded that the only way to avoid the hopelessness of my father's suicide and Jackson Pollock's alcoholism and depression is to remember wholistically, to live with my whole body, and to take the power of my body back from those who regulated it, including the governmentality of my own conscious and unconscious actions (Foucault, 1979, 1986a, 1986b). This autoethnographic arts-based research tableau is an ongoing project to (re)member teaching and learning with the whole body. Autoethnography has the power to evoke memories and elicit insights that contribute to our understanding of students and classrooms and to the reintegration of ethics and aesthetics that we propose in this chapter.

The Vision of Jackson Pollock

Modern art, before its lofty ambitions were trivialized by American pop art, was searching for excellence and transcendence, partly in response to the hopelessness and destruction first identified in the surrealist manifesto. Jackson Pollock and many of his contemporaries sacrificed everything, including sometimes their lives and their sanity, in a glorious attempt to make sense of a century that makes little sense in its horrific embrace of totalitarianism, materialism, and destruction. The regulation and governmentality of the body is another moral tragedy of modern life, particularly in the schooling process. The excavation of autoethnographic narratives will hopefully contribute to understanding and ameliorating this tragedy. James F. Cooper (1999) offers, perhaps, a fitting conclusion and tribute to Pollock and all artists working from the unconscious: "Jackson Pollock took more with him than a tortured life when he fatally crashed his automobile against a tree on Fireplace Road in East Hampton, New York. His death signaled the end of an era of courageous experimentation that made American culture alive and relevant" (1999, p. 7). We encourage educators and artists to pick up Pollock's aesthetic torch and renew such courageous experimentation in their work. In the next section, we relate several situations in which action was needed to address horrific injustices that exist in our world today. We respond in the spirit of the surrealist manifesto and the transcendent work of Jackson Pollock.

Aesthetics and Justice

I (Dana) found out how elusive and distancing the language of war and patriotism can be recently in Wooster, Ohio. On my drive to work, I pass an East of Chicago Pizza restaurant with a fairly large sign that reads "U.S., love it or leave it." I am offended by the sign because it communicates a bifurcated illusion of democracy, freedom, and war. This became especially clear to me when I discussed the language with Jane, the manager of East of Chicago Pizza. "What are you buddy, a commie, a red?" the manager's husband asked me as I discussed my displeasure with the sign. To the manager's credit, she reminded her husband that I, like her and her employees at East of Chicago Pizza, had a right to freedom of speech. "But," she continued, "the sign is meant to say to the terrorists amongst us, hey, if you don't like it here in this country, and the freedoms we enjoy, get out." My response to Jane was, "I understand what the message means to you. However, I also know what it means to people who have historically and presently experienced racial profiling, lynchings, bombings, and internment camps—like African Americans, Muslims, and Native Americans—as they have tried to fight abuses of freedom." Jane sought to remind me, "It's not like the Confederate flag. And blacks actually have more rights than whites do now." I mentioned to Jane that I appreciated her taking the time to hear my opinion, even though we disagreed. I also informed her that I would be writing an editorial to the local paper and her corporate headquarters outlining my disdain for the message she is posting and why I find it so offensive.

Jane's husband was obviously offended by my message and once again poked his head out of the door to say, "You're a commie, and you are welcome to write dumb-ass editorials to the newspaper if you want. That is what makes this country great." I tried to communicate to Jane's husband that I was a strong supporter of democracy, freedom, and justice, and I recognize that in some countries freedom of speech is a luxury, not a given. I also argued that certain people and groups have more freedom and rights than others because of their gender, race, economic class, and sexual orientation. Moreover, I think the sign may communicate to local people that if you refuse to recognize and fit into this unjust and discriminating structure, you become labeled and a potential target. I asked Jane and her husband to consider how working families feel when they have to work three jobs to pay the bills and put food on the table. I told Jane, "I know that many of the people who work with you at East of Chicago Pizza, as well as yourselves, are good, decent, hardworking people who are trying to do best by their families. I am also aware that there are few jobs in this area that provide health benefits and livable, not minimum wages. Sadly, many of these people are being labeled as lazy, uncaring, and a drain on the United States economy. The truth is that half the new jobs produced are at minimum wage. It is a structure that refuses to pay a living wage and permits, legitimatizes, and reproduces poverty that is 'Un-American.' Anyone who objects to this unjust system is labeled a commie and told to leave when in reality these people are often the greatest supporters of democracy. The same is true with racism and racial profiling, which I think you are contributing to with your sign." Jane thanked me for my opinion but said that her team of forty employees had voted thirty-nine to one to keep the sign, and it was going to stay.

This experience with signs and language is a common aesthetic experience in the daily landscape of modern life. We believe that one of the important dimensions of ethics and aesthetics is the deconstruction of the signs and symbols that constantly assault our visual and auditory landscapes. Two episodes at my university further illustrate this point. When I arrived at Ashland University three years ago, I immediately placed a *Safe Place* sticker on my office door. It was meant to convey my willingness to support gay, lesbian, bisexual, and transgendered people in the community and on campus. Within two weeks of the first semester, my sign had been ripped down. I replaced it right away, only to find that three days later someone had used a marker to scribble over "A safe place to discuss gay, lesbian, bi, and transgender issues" with "A safe place to discuss disease." I was outraged as I began to understand more fully how discussions of the issues I was supporting with my sign were not only rare on campus, but also formally and informally thwarted. This sad scenario became clearer in early October when a colleague invited me into his office to ask if I knew what my *Safe Place* sign was communicating to the campus community. He said, "People could take it the wrong way. You wouldn't want that because you would be risking your career here." Again, I was shocked as much by the request to remove the sign as by the professor's apparent sincerity. I refused to honor his suggestion, and the *Safe Place* sign remained on my office door.

On several occasions over the past few years, undergraduates have taken advantage of the sign on my door to share their stories of coming out, telling parents, and facing hateful reactions in the community from both students and professors. Two doctoral students have approached me because of the sign as well. Mike, a doctoral student in educational leadership, confessed to me in my office that he had been hiding his gay identity because he feared being ostracized and condemned by some of the more conservative students and faculty. He was at dissertation stage, however, and he was enthusiastic about studying how gay teens in rural communities established support networks. I remember him saying, "I've done everything that professors have asked of me in this program and now I am doing something for me. Something important." I was the first person Mike informed at Ashland, and he knew that he had my complete support. Unfortunately, this was not the case with others, as Mike was to find out. His proposal and passion were dismissed immediately on the grounds that the university did not have the professional expertise to support Mike in his dissertation. Mike was crushed, and I think he may even have dropped out of the program.

Elsa, a lesbian doctoral student, is much more open about her sexual orientation. In fact, she came out to her doctoral cohort in my class. Elsa is determined to cross borders at Ashland as she uses queer theory as a basis for studying the experiences of gay and lesbian administrators in the Columbus, Ohio, school district. Again, like Mike, Elsa has a passion for gay and lesbian issues, and I worry that she will receive little support from others besides me and one other faculty member. This is made clear to her in various ways. For example, Elsa stopped by my office recently to ask me to peruse a section of a research article she was required to read for one of her doctoral leadership courses. In a section titled "Family Discord and Distress," Marc Robert (1982) writes,

> Traditionally, the family has been the one institution we could count on. It was a refuge—the glue that held our social fiber together. However, for a variety of reasons, the glue has lost some of its strength. Divorce, serial marriages, non-connubial life styles, and *gay rights* are producing conflict where there used to be harmony and accord. No longer are disorganization and delinquency limited to minorities and the poor. (p. 5; author's emphasis)

I was shocked and outraged that such blatant prejudice is being perpetuated by a professor in our doctoral program. Elsa struggled with appropriate ways to address this issue in class, especially because her professor was prominent in a local church and a leader in the school community. What will the African American and working-class doctoral students do when they read this passage? What consequences will Elsa face if she speaks out against such hatred? Will her "leadership" students support her? Will faculty members stand up for her? The answers to these questions are not known. What is certain is that there are many Elsas and Mikes who are formally and informally being encouraged to become desensitized through various signs, languages, and texts.

Marginalization extends beyond sexual orientation to gender, class, religions, ability, and race. This was clearly evident when a cohort of doctoral students presented their mentoring projects. One of the presentations focused on how a middle school principal was attempting to increase the passing rates of African American and Hispanic students on state proficiency tests. The presenter discussed how her school was doing everything it could to "raise the level of success" of minority children. I asked Denise, a principal and friend, two questions. First, how can you explain that African American and Hispanic children score 200 points lower on average than Caucasian children on SATs and other standardized tests even when other factors are the same: family income, college degrees, technology at home, and parental involvement? Denise replied that the discrepancy had to do with minority children's lack of exposure and experience. I then asked her to describe the experiences, opportunities, and literature she has been exposed to in her doctoral program that have allowed her to view "success" from the perspectives of African American and Hispanic students. There was a deafening silence among the thirty-five people in the room, including Denise, who finally spoke and said, "Well, there haven't been any."

We believe that whether it is the color line, the sexual identity code, the class structure, or the glass ceiling, tensions simmer below the surface of many social and educational practices, policies, and programs. Educators from historically marginalized groups remind us that white privilege, heterosexism, economic inequity, and patriarchy are life or death issues that go unexamined in teacher training and doctoral programs. The logics, skills, and language of the status quo are manifest in codes of silence, lies, and secrets whereby people from underrepresented groups must deculturize, defeminize, and desensitize themselves in order to "successfully" complete their degrees. The ability to desensitize, disobey one's history, and remain silent may be as essential for advancement for some graduate students as it is for African American, Hispanic, and Muslim customers at East of Chicago Pizza when it comes to employment. If there is little or no support for students to pursue these issues in their training, we believe there is a much greater possibility that they will never be addressed in the institutions or communities in which they will eventually make decisions.

One way in which I have tried to support my gay and lesbian friends lately is by attempting to feel the hatred directed their way. To this end, I have placed an earring in my right ear. Within a week, the same colleague who had warned me about my *Safe Place* sign asked me, "Aren't you afraid of what people will think and say about you?" Actually, I am not afraid; I want to confront prejudice. I do find it a bit awkward, however, when I walk around campus and some of the men see my stud, give me a slight frown, and turn away in disapproval. I experience the same reaction when I go to some campus meetings. Several faculty have tried to convince me that I should wait until after tenure to "push the limit" by wearing an earring in my right ear. I have heard "look at that fag" muttered once under someone's breath. But the saddest aspect of this scenario is that the person who has exerted the strongest pressure for me to remove my *Safe Place* sign and take out my earring is also the man who made a pass at me two years ago.

Liberation Theology and Aesthetic Inspiration

We have found liberation theology to be helpful in confronting the injustices described in this chapter, especially when liberation theology offers a renewed sense of hope. A central tenet of the Latin American liberation theology movement is the "preferential option for the poor." In other words, working for economic justice, land reform, health care, education, and decent housing for the neglected masses of people in impoverished countries was the foremost concern of the Catholic religious leaders and theologians who began this movement. This notion also permeates our philosophy of ethics and education, and, as should be clear from the preceding narrative, we include in our "preferential option" any student or citizen who is marginalized, ostracized, excluded, or hated. Throughout this chapter, we insist that aesthetics and theology must direct our ethical stance toward a passion for justice. We now explore liberation theology not simply for religious inspiration but also for aesthetic insights that may inspire work for justice in multiple ways in schools and society.

In an effort to create an aesthetic experience of liberation theology and its potential to inspire a new approach to educational ethics, we view the film *Romero* with our undergraduate and graduate classes. This powerful film tells the story of Oscar Romero, the Roman Catholic archbishop of El Salvador who was assassinated in 1980 at the hands of the military junta backed by the U.S. government. Romero sacrificed his life in a passionate stand against social injustice and oppression in his country. Before his death, he said, "If they kill me, I shall rise in the Salvadoran people," and his life does continue to inspire many people in El Salvador and beyond. Romero was murdered while celebrating the Catholic mass in a convent chapel. Oscar Romero was inspired to speak out for the poor at a time when such a posture was unpopular with the landowners and military leaders of El Salvador. Although the focus of the film is on liberation theology within the Catholic church, we use the film to investigate liberation as a metaphor for thinking about education, justice, and ethics. We study liberation theology not to promote any one particular religious worldview, but to launch our imaginations to consider various alternatives to the injustices that exist in schools and society.

In many ways, liberation theology is also an educational movement indebted to Paulo Freire and other critical educators. It emerged as a response to the massive poverty in South and Central America, oppression of indigenous populations during colonial periods, and socioeconomic repression of poor and marginalized peoples in modern times. Liberation theology addresses social issues that affect the poor within the tradition of social justice as promulgated in Vatican documents such as *Gaudium et Spes* (Flannery, 1975), in the general conferences of Latin American bishops from Medellin, Colombia, in 1968 to those in Santo Domingo, Dominican Republic, in 1992, and in the biblical imperatives of the prophets. Theological studies by scholars such as Uruguayan Jesuit Juan Luis Segundo (1973), Brazilian Franciscan Leonardo Boff (1979), Basque Jesuit Jon Sobrino (1985) of El Salvador, and the most prominent liberation theologian, Peruvian Gustavo Gutierrez (1973), author of *A Theology of Liberation: History, Politics, and Salvation,* have all contributed to the development of liberation theology. The work of Gutierrez and other theologians was challenged and condemned by many within the Roman curia and by right-wing governments and wealthy landowners in Latin America. As has been the case historically when new theological developments challenge the *Sitz im Laben* (worldview) of institutional churches, several liberation theologians have also been "silenced." The attempts to silence the liberation movement, whether with papal bulls or army bullets, has only strengthened the resolve of the *communautes de base* (basic ecclesial communities). The intense debate over the theological and social foundations of liberation theology is evident in the numerous publications from the left and the right. The scholarship of Gustavo Gutierrez and the response of the Vatican congregation reveal many parallels with the current debate between critical scholars and those entrenched in modern bureaucratic or "banking" (Freire, 1970) models of education.

Five essential frames of reference permeate liberation theology and liberation pedagogy. First, liberation theology emerged within the context of one hundred years of Roman Catholic social encyclicals, beginning with *Rerum Novarum* in 1891, which legitimated theological reflection on social justice issues. Liberation theology must not be mistaken as simply a political or social ideology; rather, it is rooted in an overwhelming religious experience of justice. The encyclicals of the twentieth century have challenged the global community to explore the question of justice and freedom in society. Pope Leo XIII's 1891 letter *Rerum Novarum* addressed the condition of human labor and the political implications of human dignity. It also addressed the pressing problems of industrialization and the oppression of workers. However, the most influential encyclical on liberation theology was the Vatican II document *Gaudium et Spes* of 1965, which described the church in its relationship to the world. This document defined human existence socially and referred to the social dimension of sin, a most significant theological articulation.

Some would contend that the social encyclicals emerged out of the guilt of institutional religion for its complicity in centuries of oppression of indigenous cultures, silence in the face of the murder of Jews during the Holocaust, and sanctioning of brutal inquisitions and crusades. Even recent Guatemalan bishops' pastoral letters contend that the Catholic church committed grave errors and sins when Christianization was confused with Westernization. Others argue that the encyclicals express an authentic commitment to social justice. Of course, the encyclicals alone do not explain the entire history of social justice positions of the Roman Catholic church in the twentieth century. For example, the relationship between the papacy and Mussolini, the Lateran Treaty of 1929, the Concordat of 1931, the condemnation of *Action Francaise* by Pius XI in 1914 (but published in 1926!), the rise of the Catholic Worker Movement by Dorothy Day and others, the reaction of the church to Hitler during World War II, Pope John Paul II's criticisms of liberation theology and silencing of theologian Leonardo Boff, and the forced removal of clerics from political office around the world, all offer additional perspectives on the complex and sometimes contradictory impulses of the churches on social justice issues.

Despite the influence of European theologians such as German Jesuit Karl Rahner and German Lutheran Jurgen Moltmann, especially in the renewal of eschatology discussed in Chapter 2, it is important to understand that the Latin American context is ultimately most significant in the development of liberation theology. Rahner contends that there have been two important transformations in the history of Christianity: first, when the church ceased to be a Jewish sect in the second century and began developing a European identity, and second, when theology ceased to be Eurocentric following the Second Vatican Council's recognition of a "world church" in the 1960s and began developing a global consciousness. The emergence of the global church gave birth to liberation theology.

The commitment to a "preferential option for the poor" by liberation theologians is intimately related to Paulo Freire's critical pedagogy, particularly in his text "Conscientizing as a Way of Liberating" (1971). This relationship between theology and pedagogy has informed critical postmodern scholars and helped offset egocentric ideological struggles for intellectual dominance. Thus, ideological entrapment is avoided with authentic deference to the theological rootedness of the human experience within unique sociohistorical and cultural milieus. There are two ways in which dominant theories and theologies can become destructively ideological, according to Rosemary Radford Ruether in her article "Christology and the Latin American Liberation Theology":

> One [destructive approach] is by directly identifying Christ and the church with the social hierarchies of [the status quo] system and by making God the author and vindicator of it. The second way is indirect through divorcing religion from life, body from soul, Christian hope from human hope. In this way the message of liberation is alienated and directed to a never-never-land beyond the stars which has no concrete implications for the world. (1983, pp. 25–26)

The preferential option for the poor that is the foundation of liberation theology and critical pedagogy must not, according to Ruether and other theologians, be sacrificed on the altar of any ideology.

The Vatican reaction to liberation theology offers an opportunity for critical postmodern scholars to reflect on the resistance of educational bureaucrats, right-wing politicians, and liberal philanthropists. This analysis can lead to refinements and advancements in critical pedagogy that allow for the inclusion of theology in postmodern educational proposals. It also creates a broader base of acceptance in the educational and political communities and thus raises the hope for democratic reform.

It is noteworthy that curricularist James Macdonald has concluded similarly that "the act of theorizing is an act of faith, a religious act. Curriculum theory is a prayerful act" (qtd. in Schubert, 1992, p. 60). Alfred North Whitehead (1929) has also insisted that "the essence of education is that it be religious" (p. 14). This commitment to a spirituality and a practice of liberation is integral to liberatory theology and critical postmodern theory in the effort to truly effect a preferential option for the poor in society, in the churches, and in schooling.

The ongoing discourses on liberation theology and the dialogues between Gustavo Gutierrez and the Vatican raise the following questions: Is liberation theology a political project? Is it a religious enterprise? A social-historical revisionary critique? An ideological construct challenging economic boundaries? A campaign for social and religious literacy? Is liberation theology a compassionate plea for justice indebted to the social sciences, including Marxism, or is it a dangerous revolutionary ideology for Latin America? Is liberation theology an existential project disconnected from religious salvation, or does it engender an eschatological sense of the eternal in the present struggle for justice? Is liberation theology, in a Bergsonian sense, durational, or is it a passing fad, a pop theology? Can liberation theology inform critical ethical theories and enrich contemporary pedagogy, or is it empty denominational religious rhetoric destined to disappoint critical scholars as well as the poor?

Contemporary scholarship concludes that liberation theology can inform and enrich our critical pedagogy if it develops a comprehensive and global worldview in the development of a liberatory praxis. Ultimately, the theology of liberation is a commitment to a hope that leads to praxis. Likewise, critical postmodern pedagogy is also committed to hope—a hope rooted in democratic reform, social justice, and praxis. Henry Giroux (1988) has been an outspoken proponent of this position: "We must develop a social vision and commitment to make the liberal arts supportive of a democratic public sphere in which despair will become unconvincing and hope a practice for students and teachers alike, regardless of race, class, religion, gender, or age" (p. 243). Likewise, Richard Shaull (1990) writes, "There is no such thing as a neutral educational process. Education either functions as an instrument which is used to facilitate the integration of the younger generation into the logic of the present system and bring about conformity to it, or it becomes the practice of freedom, the means by which men and women deal critically and creatively with reality and discover how to participate in the transformation of their world" (p. 15). Jonathan Kozol (1995) echoes our sentiments as well when he writes, "Things that are wrong, are wrong in such obvious ways. We lack the moral and theological will to act on what we already know" (p. 4). For we know that in the United States every day, 15 children are killed by firearms, 2,600 babies are born into poverty, 2,833 children drop out of school, 8,493 children are reported abused or neglected, and 13 million U.S. children under age twelve are hungry or at risk of hunger (Remson & Carm, 1996). And though we know that millions of American youth come to our schools pained by poverty, dysfunctional and dangerous family circumstances, and psychological, physical, and mental stress, we continue to delineate our task and education reform in terms of enhanced teaching methods in math and science, technological advancement, accountability test scores, and other disciplines of study. Although these areas can be one small component of educational evaluation, we must have the courage to reexamine our priorities in education (Kirylo, 2001).

James Kirylo (2001) provides an appropriate conclusion to this discussion of liberation theology and critical pedagogy as he integrates theology and ethics with a passionate vision for justice:

> Within the midst of finding solutions to poverty in the United States, the terminology used to identify the affected population multiplies and builds. Consider some of the language identifying the affected population: the "urban underclass," the "deprived," the "disadvantaged," the "underprivileged," the "homeless," "street people," the "underemployed," "welfare queens," the "at-risk," the "underachievers," "those people," and the "have-nots." The danger of these labels is that they blind us to the complex lives lived out in the classroom. To be sure, the effects of poverty impact physical and mental growth, cognitive progression, academic achievement, socioemotional functioning, and production in later life. When entering into a discussion about Liberation Theology, one discovers that history plays an important role in three ways. First, the colonial heritage of Latin America and how it affects current conditions needs to be understood. Though the parties involved are no longer called "Indians" and "conquerors," they are now called

"the majority poor" and the "wealthy landowners" respectively. For example, in Brazil, 10 percent of the population owns 65 percent of the wealth, while the poorest 40 percent have just 12 percent. Latin America remains largely economically depressed, suffers from widespread social and economic inequality, extreme poverty, and authoritarian traditions; and continues under foreign economic control and political influence. Thus, Liberation Theology views history from the perspective of the marginalized and poor, that is a "history from the reverse side, the underside—the side of the poor" (Cleary, 1985, 86). (Kirylo, 2001, p. 85–86)

Like Kirylo, we seek to look at ethics and aesthetics from the "underside" of history and culture to "release the imagination" (Greene, 1995), become attentive to "invisible children in society and its schools" (Books, 1998), and develop a passion for justice in schools and society that will ameliorate the "savage inequalities" (Kozol, 1991) that exist. In the next chapter, we continue to explore this theme as it is understood in the context of ecology and sustainable communities.

4 Diversity and Human Nature: The Urgency of Ecological Sustainability

The Ecological Moment

The 2001 attacks on New York City and Washington, D.C., bring tears to our eyes for many reasons. We feel the pain and anguish of the victims and their families, and we lament the tragedy of thousands of lives shattered by these senseless and evil acts. In addition, we are sad witnesses to the destruction of offices, plazas, trees, and other urban landscapes in New York City where we once lived and visited as children. We lament as well the suffering of millions of Afghani people who are living through decades of war, starvation, ethnic violence, Taliban oppression of women, and deplorable misogyny. We join the global community in trying to comprehend the implications of these tragic events and determine how to respond appropriately.

The international response to the countless tragedies of the late twentieth century and early twenty-first century will shape the course of civilization in the years ahead. In this chapter, we explore the ethical imperative to work for ecological sustainability in the context of war and terrorism. We believe that the human and natural worlds must forge a new relationship in this ecological moment, a relationship based on mutual interdependence. When citizens understand the urgency of ecological sustainability, they will recognize that hunger, poverty, resource distribution, pollution, racism, terrorism, and war are all inextricably linked.

Unfortunately, many women and men throughout the world refuse to accept responsibility for ecological sustainability. This too is part of the ecological moment. Consider recent reports about global warming:

> The Earth's temperature in 2001 is expected to be the second highest in the 140 years that meteorologists have been keeping records according to the United Nations weather agency. Temperatures are getting hotter, and they are getting hotter faster than at any time in the past. Nine of the ten warmest years since 1860 have occurred since 1990, and temperatures are rising three times as fast as in the early 1900s. As it has in the past the [United Nations] organization attributed much of the warming to the greenhouse effect from burning fossil fuels. There are always skeptics on everything, but certainly the evidence we have today shows we do have global warming, and that most of this is due to human action. ("This year," 2001)

Despite clear and convincing data, many people respond like Pito Robles of New York in this news report about warm winter temperatures in December 2001:

> In the natural world, daffodils bloomed, and the grass at the New York Botanical Garden was a lush green the week before Christmas. In Pennsylvania, a baby killdeer hatched in December instead of April. And in Massachusetts, Bill Davis, a state wildlife biologist, came home from a deer station one recent day with a sunburn. "It's global warming, dude," said Pito Robles, 28, an auto mechanic who on Thursday was dangling his fishing line into the Hudson River near West 66th Street in Manhattan. "I don't care if the whole planet burns up in a hundred years. If I can get me a fish today, it's cool by me." (Belluck & Revkin, 2001)

Pito expresses the sentiments of too many citizens who do not care about the earth and the next generation as long as they can have pleasure today. We report to the millions of Pitos of the world that ecological destruction is not cool—it is immoral. The effects are not a hundred years away; they smolder before our eyes. Skin cancer, coastal flooding, dramatic weather disturbances, drought, crop failures, rising sea levels, and melting polar ice caps should be enough to convince us to take action for change and sustainability on our beautiful planet, which is our only source of life.

We recall another image of ecological destruction in New York City that has also convinced us to address environmental degradation: a Native American overlooking Manhattan with a tear crawling down his cheek in a 1970s commercial deploring the pollution of the North American continent. In the introduction to *Deep Ecology for the 21st Century,* George Sessions (1995) speaks to the forces that contribute to our growing uneasiness with escalating war and environmental degradation:

> Government leaders and economic elites in Industrial Growth Societies continue to push for endless economic growth and development. Consumerism in the industrial world is now both a way of life and an addiction. New Age visions promote mega-technology solutions to economic and environmental ills, and propose massive high-tech global management and development schemes for the biosphere. Third World countries are now trying to become First World countries by destroying their ecosystems and wild species as they emulate the industrial and consumer patterns of the ecologically destructive unsustainable First World. (p. xx)

We have become mired in a continually expanding global economic ideology that willingly sacrifices the divinity and diversity of our natural environment on the altar of consumerism and corporate profit. In our view, ecological destruction is not unrelated to war, genocide, patriarchy, racism, and feelings of alienation. It is no coincidence that the United States has been involved in the most wars and was the greatest contributor to ecological destruction in the twentieth century; it also leads the industrialized world in teen suicides, murders, and incarcerations. We painfully ask ourselves the question that Bill McGibbon, author and environmentalist, posed in

The End of Nature: "How should I cope with the sadness of watching nature end in our lifetimes, and with the guilt of knowing that each of us is in some measure responsible?" (1999, p. xxv). More important, how can educators encourage a society that is "absolutely awash in a sea of addictions: romantic lies, sex, shopping, television, legal drugs, alcohol, self-destruction, fast cars, abuse of other people, and so on" (Glendinning, 1995, p. 39) to direct its imagination and energy to ecological sustainability?

Most media pundits, policy analysts, politicians, and educators, ourselves included, did not dream of the terror experienced on September 11. But was this tragedy really so unpredictable? What would lead the wealthiest nation in the world, the most technologically advanced superpower, to miss or dismiss the warning signs of terrorism? Is it possible that something so amazingly horrible as September 11 could also be happening to our natural environment right before our eyes? In this chapter, we present evidence that convinces us this is the case. We believe that North Americans—indeed, most global citizens—do not comprehend the depth of the escalating ecological crisis. We concur with Wendell Berry: "The order and magnitude of the present catastrophic situation is . . . so enormous, so widespread, and we don't know what we are doing. The violence already done to the earth is on a scale beyond all understanding" (qtd. in Sessions, 1995, p. xx).

We argue that teachers, professors, school leaders, parents, students—indeed, all citizens—must do more than recognize the manifestation and the gravity of racial, class, gendered, and ecological crises in our communities; we must accept responsibility to work to eradicate them. Several conceptual frameworks underlie our analysis of ecological destruction, diversity, and sustainability in this chapter. First, we share with Herbert Kohl the belief that educators for social justice are "enraged at the prospect of any of his or her students dying young, being hungry and living meaningless and despairing lives" (1998, p. 286). We support Peter McLaren's conception of revolutionary pedagogy as "a socialist-feminist multiculturalism that challenges those historically sedimented processes through which race, class, and gender identities are produced within capitalist society" (1997, p. 287). Educators concerned with social justice, according to McLaren, are "dedicated to reconstituting the deep structures of political economy, culture, and power" (p. 287).

The neo-Marxist, radical democratic, and social reconstructive philosophies of Michael Apple (1996), bell hooks (1994), Robert Young (1990), and George Counts (1932), as well as the questions posed about the prophetic roles of educators by David Purpel (1989, 1999) and Maxine Greene (1995), inspire our teaching convictions and political activism. The political dissidence of intellectuals such as Noam Chomsky (2000), Angela Davis (1998), and Edward Said (1997) and the work of artists such as Adrienne Rich, Diego Rivera, Judy Chicago, Paul Robeson, Eve Ensler, Robert Mapplethorpe, and Stephen Chapman Crane frame and embolden our criticism as well. Like Thomas Merton, philosopher and theologian, we are worried that westernized nations are proceeding on a rudderless voyage directed by the madness of economic growth in the name of progress. We share the concern that educators are increasingly forced to manufacture consent for global capitalism and the ravaging of the environment that it requires, as well as domesticating possible sites, passions, and imaginations of resistance. We do hold out hope, however, that educators will more forcefully fight injustice from platforms of constitutional authority and civic and spiritual responsibility in locations around and outside of schools. Our support for extending critical pedagogy beyond schools to broader social movements such as ecology has its birth in the work of Kenneth Mostern (1994), Franz Fanon (1963), Paulo Freire (1998), and Carolyn Merchant (1992). Merchant's clear and thorough discussion of revolutionary thought and social movements in *Radical Ecology: The Search for a Livable World* reaffirms our convictions as they relate to ecological crises:

> Radicals refuse to blame homelessness and starvation, the rape of women and abuse of children, the theft of labor and land, hope and self-respect on divine providence or unchangeable human nature. [And] responses to people's pain, if they are to be truly and lastingly effective, must be aimed at the system: at capitalism, sexism, racism, imperialism, homophobia, the bureaucratic state, and the domination of nature. (1992, pp. xi, xii)

Along with Merchant, our definition of radical implies not only the importance of an inward autobiographical journey and discovery—the type we shared with you in the first three chapters of this book—but also the transference of this reflection into an agenda for justice and ecological action.

Ecology, Open Systems, and the Mississippi River

The moral disaster of ecological destruction is in many ways related to our inability to understand that nature is a complex open system relying on diversity, decay, and reconstruction and not a closed system that is doomed to entropy. We propose a process view of the natural environment to ameliorate the problem of wasteful destruction and enhance the possibility of ecological sustainability. Paul Davies (1990) explains this concept:

> There is no claim that the Second Law of Thermodynamics is invalid, only that it is inadequate. The second law only applies to closed systems . . . which are isolated from their environment. When a system is open to its environment and there can be an exchange of matter, energy, and entropy across its boundaries, then it is possible to simultaneously satisfy the insatiable desire of nature to generate more entropy and yet have an increase in complexity and organization at the same time. The universe as a whole can be considered as a closed system, but as far as any subsystem of the universe is concerned, it is open to its environment. (p. 10)

Embracing nature, and by correlation all life processes, as open systems in which creative growth emerges from disequilibrium and decay is an essential first step in educational efforts to promote an ethical vision of ecology and sustainability. After observing open and closed systems and their environments, the French Jesuit paleontologist Pierre Teilhard de Chardin wrote in *The Phenomenon of Man* (1959), "We are now inclined to admit that at each further degree of combination something which is irreducible to isolated elements emerges in a new order. . . . Something in the cosmos escapes from entropy, and does so more and more" (qtd. in Davies 1990, p. 10).

Let us consider the Mississippi River as an example of our open system process cosmology, as well as a metaphor for thinking about all natural and educational processes. I (Patrick) grew up in New Orleans a short distance from the Mississippi River. I have fond memories of riding my bicycle to Audubon Park to sit on the levee for hours watching the cargo vessels and listening to the tugboat horns. I imagined distant lands and exotic destinations as I watched huge ships glide past me on the river. However, at other times the Mississippi became my feared enemy. When the water rose to flood stage, I would stand on top of the levee and look down in amazement at the houses behind the levee that were lower than the water level. The levees protected us, but on September 9, 1965, during Hurricane Betsy the levee broke and drowned hundreds of New Orleanians. I vividly remember that night; it was my twelfth birthday and my family was huddled in the center closet of our home as the roaring winds blew out the windows, tore off the roof, and disintegrated the garage. We even relit my birthday candles when the electricity went out so that we could see in the dark. Certainly, the most precious gift I received that terrible night was the survival of my family and friends.

Louisiana is a place where the environment is entwined with the lives of the people who live along the bayous, marshes, and, most prominently, the Mississippi. For millions of years, there has been a building up and tearing down of the land in Louisiana. The Choctaw people first named the Mississippi the "old-big-strong river," the *Missah Sippa* in their native dialect. In contemporary times, the Mississippi has been called The Great River by native people, Old Man River in American fiction, and the Father of Waters or Big Muddy by ship captains. It has also been called the Mother of Lands (Bradshaw, p. 1991).

Geologists believe that the Mississippi once extended northward to the southern tip of Illinois. For millions of years, this shallow extension of the Gulf, called the Mississippi embayment, received the waters and sediment of the Missouri, the Ohio, the Red, the Arkansas, and other tributaries. Over time the sediment filled the embayment and built the delta. This alluvial soil created the vast wetlands along the Gulf of Mexico that are an immense resource and vital link in the ecological system of the entire northern hemisphere (Mancuso, 1991). In our ecological vision, we must constantly remember that everything is interconnected in the web of life, from the smallest quantum elements to the largest constellations in the universe. Educators must orchestrate school environments in which the interconnectedness of subject matter, human beings, and the natural environment is constantly and consciously foregrounded. Without such awareness, students will not take the next step of ethical action for ecological sustainability.

As the river meandered unabated for centuries, its natural course was not predetermined; rather, the river gradually searched for new directions to the sea. Over thousands of years, the river has been free to move and meander to form new lands and destroy others. As the river moved, subsidence occurred, returning some of the land to the sea. New land was formed when spring floods poured fresh water and mud to replace what was lost to subsidence. Floods and erosion, subsidence and deposits, oxbows and deltas: These are the elements of the history of the natural turmoil of the Mississippi River. The film *Old Man River* (Mancuso, 1991) visually documents this process, and we often use this film to help our students understand our metaphor. The film also demonstrates how human intervention destroys the natural processes and threatens the entire North American ecosystem.

Attempts have been made to stop the river's process of creation and destruction. The river has been trapped in a levee system constructed by a modern corps of engineers. Massive steel locks in Pointe Coupee and Feliciana parishes in Louisiana now prevent the river from shifting west to the Atchafalaya Basin, the old Acadiana home to which it longs to return. Locks and canals have been built to divert the flow of the Mississippi to more economically productive routes through Baton Rouge and New Orleans for commerce and industry. And in the process, the irreplaceable mud deposits drop off the continental shelf and into the Gulf of Mexico. The natural environment in Louisiana, like the rest of the planet, is in crisis: The marshes are disappearing, animal and plant species are dying, and the water is polluted. The ecological system is in disarray. Many recent reports warn that the river is unfit for animal life and dangerous to humans. The manipulation of the river over past centuries (including attempts by the U.S. military to divert the river at Vicksburg for strategic advantage during the Civil War) has brought the river to the brink of annihilation. The mighty Mississippi is no longer free to meander and build new deltas. It has been forced to conform to modern demands for productivity and commerce, rather than searching to create new places and support species of fish and wildlife.

Our process orientation to ethics, education, and ecology respects the interconnectedness of reality while refusing to succumb to the modern mechanistic paradigm just described. We propose instead a nonlinear and open system cosmology. Process thinkers Donald Oliver and Kathleen Gershman (1989) explain:

> We suggest that healthy societies are those whose symbolic roots allow them to cope economically while maintaining an intimate, even warm, sense of organic connectedness *to* and transcendent unity *with* their natural environment. . . . Our critique of modernity refers essentially to its culture (and) to its meaning system. We understand that meaning (culture), the temperament, strength and diversity of a people, social structures, technology, and the natural environment are all inextricably tied together. (p. 4)

Like Oliver and Gershman, we constantly connect the dilemmas of modern society with the natural environment. Our environmental and psychological sustainability depend on it. In Walker Percy's novel *The Message in the Bottle,* it is clear that poets and novelists have an insight very different from modern scientists and humanists:

> The modern age began to come to an end when people discovered that they could no longer understand themselves by the theory professed by the age. They . . . lived by reason during the day and at night dream bad dreams. The scientists were saying that by science [people] were learning more and more about the world as an environment and that accordingly the world could be changed and [people] made to feel more and more at home. The humanists were saying that through education man's lot was certain to improve. But poets and novelists and artists were saying something else: that at a time when, according to the theory of the age, people should feel most at home they felt most homeless. Someone was wrong. (1982, p. 25)

Why do people feel so disconnected from the earth and alienated from one another? We contend that the poets and artists are correct; they expose the anguish of homelessness and "place-less-ness" of contemporary women and men. Our challenge is to discover the capacity to envision ecological sustainability and actively work for environmental causes. But we get ahead of our metaphor.

In 1993 the world watched in horror as the Mississippi River flowed over her banks and the human-made levees in the Midwest, absorbing farmland and dislocating thousands of people from their land and homes. The river that drew these people to her banks and had accommodated their lives on many diverse levels reclaimed her right to meander. The once negotiated and adaptive relationship, established through years of toil between these people and the river, was irrevocably altered. The floods indelibly marked this trauma on the people and the land along the banks of the Mississippi. This five-hundred-year flood, while certainly a part of one's understanding of the cycle of the river and a motivation for constructing levees in order to stave off the ultimate confrontation with the forces of nature, can be rationally explained but nonetheless still emotionally devastating. We contend that we place too much confidence in the modern structures we build in an effort to control these forces. Our structures create a sense of security. After all, we have apparently been successful in our efforts to manipulate nature and impose on her for our convenience in the past. What occurred in 1993 was a radical collapse, not only of the physical constructs—the levees—but also of our psychological constructs—our confidence that nature's power could be controlled by our levees. Ironically, it became clear that the vast damage and dislocation caused by the river's flow was exacerbated by the presence of the levees themselves, which prevented the rising waters from filling the natural floodplains. In the wake of the 1993 disaster, some engineers began to recognize that the practice of constructing levees to block floodplains must be reevaluated. In some cases, levees were removed to provide land for meandering and spring overflow. In our metaphor, closed systems and levees cause parallel damage in schools and social institutions and must be reevaluated and in many cases removed.

Using the Arts for Reflection on Sustainability

In order to explain our ecological vision to students, we incorporate several films and works of literature into our syllabi. The novels include *The Autobiography of Miss Jane Pittman* by Ernest J. Gaines and *The Thanatos Syndrome* by Walker Percy, and the films are *Old Man River* and *Green* (an account of environmental racism along the stretch of the Mississippi below Baton Rouge known as Cancer Alley). These novels and films are all set in Louisiana and relate in some way to the Mississippi River. We present below a synopsis of one of the novels. Later in this chapter, we connect the novels and films to our metaphor of the river and our theme of ecological sustainability.

In the opening scene of Walker Percy's *The Thanatos Syndrome,* Tom More, the protagonist and a psychiatrist, begins to arrive at the conclusion "that something strange is occurring in my region [of Louisiana]" (Percy, 1987, p. 3). He notes that the strangeness "began with little things, certain small clinical changes which I observed" (p. 3). Tom concludes that these "little" things are important and that "even more important is the ability—call it knack, hunch, providence, good luck, whatever—to know what you are looking for and to put two and two together" (p. 3). We are told by Tom that this process "consists not in making great discoveries but in seeing the connection between small discoveries" (p. 3). In all of these statements by his narrator, Percy is setting the scene for the process through which Tom More comes to discover the horror of the Blue Boy project, an attempt by some to flood the water supply in the Mississippi River with heavy sodium in order to control unwanted defects in the population of Feliciana, the setting for the novel, and to increase certain brain functions that would contribute to an increase in, if not perfection of, the intelligence of those persons.

The most striking example of the strangeness of which Tom More takes note is the inability of some of the infected persons to have self-reflection and context. These individuals can respond to questions with the accuracy and precision of a savant and yet display no sense of self-reflection or no sense of the context in which the language is being used. In the opening chapter of the novel, Tom More notes of a patient:

> For some reason—perhaps it is her disconnectedness—she reminds me of my daughter as a four-year-old. It is the age when children have caught on to language, do not stick to one subject, are open to any subject, would as soon be asked any question as long as one keeps playing the language game. A child does not need a context like you and me. Mickey LaFaye, like four-year-old Meg, is out of context. (Percy, 1987, p. 8)

Tom's reflection here is important to our overall reflection on ethics and education because it is precisely this inability to provide connection and context to a given place and person that inevitably leads to indifference about other people and destruction of the environment. Furthermore, such effects eradicate in individuals the important quality of self-reflection, which is essential for autobiographical analysis and imagination, two pivotal ingredients in the development of ethics and activism for justice.

It seems clear, then, that Tom More's observation that those infected by the heavy sodium additive lack context and self-reflective abilities can go far toward defining this necessary sense of ethical meaning. For without a context and the ability to reflect on that context in terms of significance and place, no true human experience can be lived. No dialectic will result between the subjectivities of humans and the objective world. In such a situation, only violence and destruction can occur.

The tragedy in *The Thanatos Syndrome* is an apt metaphor for the moral tragedy looming before us in schools and society. Bob Comeaux, Max Gotlieb, and Van Dorn are school administrators and the perpetrators of the Blue Boy project. Tom More calls them brain engineers and neuropharmacologists. They have discovered a chemical that delivers haunted souls from mental suffering. Comeaux outlines the reason for Blue Boy, stating, "Tom, get this, a one hundred percent improvement in ACT scores in computation and memory recall in these very subjects" (Percy, 1987, p. 197). Comeaux also gloats that he can do more than increase intellect. He claims that the effects of another additive, progesterone, in the drinking water can produce a reduction in sexual activity. As he says, "Goodbye hassles, goodbye pills, rubbers, your friendly abortionist. Goodbye promiscuity, goodbye sex ed—who needs it? Mom and Dad love it, the kids love it, and the state saves millions. Family life is improved, Tom" (p. 197).

As we read Comeaux's words, we are appalled at the cynicism in such a belief. For embedded in these ideas is the desire to control the way human beings conduct themselves by stripping them of the very thing that makes them human, which is conscious awareness of their context and their reflective powers through language. Again Comeaux says to Tom, "The hypothesis, Tom . . . is that at least a segment of the human neocortex and of consciousness itself is not only an aberration of evolution but is also the scourge and curse of life on this earth, the source of wars, insanities, perversions—in short, those very pathologies which are peculiar to homo sapiens" (Percy, 1987, p. 195). The irony of Comeaux's words lies in the fact that the thing he desires to suppress through the intervention of the heavy sodium—namely, consciousness—is the quality that makes us human: a combination of spirituality, compassion, commitment, and mystery. By removing consciousness, Comeaux hopes to control the pathologies faced by the human community—but at what cost? By removing the pathologies through chemical intervention, one also removes the possibility for self-reflection and the triumphs of the human spirit that spring from that mystery and turmoil. This establishes a context in which people are disconnected not only from themselves but also from their natural environment. Let's examine what happens in the novel as a result of the Blue Boy Project.

As Percy's tale continues to unfold to its conclusion, we are struck by even more ironies. Comeaux continues to rattle off the advantages of the heavy sodium by responding to Tom's questions about the use of language, about "reading and writing. . . . Like reading a book. . . . Like writing a sentence" (1987, p. 197), in a manner that reveals the tragedy of such actions, and thus by means of our metaphor, the abuse and dysfunction in schools:

> We're in a different age of communication—out of McGuffey Readers and writing a theme on what I did last summer. Tom, these kids are way past comic books and star wars. They're into graphic and binary communication—which after all is a lot more accurate than once upon a time there lived a wicked queen. [Tom responds:] You mean they use two-word sentences. [Comeaux continues:] You got it. And using a two-word sentence, you know what you can get out of them? They can rattle off the total exports and imports of the port of Baton Rouge—like a spread sheet—or give 'em a pencil and paper and they'll give you a graphic of the tributaries of the Red River. Tom, would you laugh at me if I told you what we've done is restore the best of the Southern Way of Life? (Percy, 1987, p. 197)

We think the irony is clear; individuals subjected to the heavy sodium have an increase in intelligence, just as Comeaux points out, but it is an increase without any contextual, spiritual, or autobiographical meaning. This parallels projects by educators who create and deliver a curriculum that is disconnected from environmental, cultural, and personal interests. That modern accountability movements in education attempt to produce students equipped with a large amount of data and the ability to perform well on a test is a given, but the students are, all too often, stripped of any kind of meaningful understanding of that data. For example, a frustration experienced by many teachers occurs when students are unable to write a critical analysis because they cannot navigate through the complexity of subjective thought. Although school systems may promote critical thinking skills in the published curriculum guides of the district, the effect of the emphasis on rote memorization, predetermined solutions to complex problems, canonical hegemony, rigid structural analysis, and standardized testing all contribute to the impairment of a student's ability to meander, like the river, and to create, discover, and respond from a self-reflective perspective.

How do we move out of the horrors of the Blue Boy Project? We do as Tom More and immerse ourselves in the local community, noticing connections and working for justice. It is not surprising to witness Tom's reaction to this tragedy. He too has experienced trauma in his life. Tom was cut off from his family and culture while serving a two-year prison sentence for selling narcotics. This gave Tom the understanding necessary to guide him through the muddy waters of this horror. Because of his personal tragedy, Tom came to operate out of sensitivity to what Carl Jung called synchronicity, to see in the disconnected, the connected (Jung, 1977). As mentioned earlier, Tom came to the insight that "living a small life gave me leave to notice small things. . . . Small disconnected facts, if you take note of them, have a way of becoming connected" (Percy, 1987, p. 68). From such a perspective, Tom discovers Blue Boy and is empowered to put a stop to it. In this ability to experience synchronicity and connectedness, Tom can become a moral agent for change. This is what we also hope to accomplish with our students. Once students begin noticing connections, asking critical questions, and rejecting compartmentalization, they become empowered to uncover and dismantle ecologically destructive practices, just as Tom More in the novel discovered and exposed the Blue Boy Project.

There is one more tragic dimension of the Blue Boy Project. Tom More discovers that without context and a sense of self-reflection, even given the high brain functions of those infected, a more primitive, dark, and ominous behavior results. In the local school, Belle Ame Academy, Tom uncovers rampant sexual abuse of children by the administrators. The most appalling aspect of the sexual abuse, however, is that the children are responding to the abuse as if it were normal and expected. The additive has stripped them of their reflective power and context to such an extent that even in the face of abuse they are lost and powerless to break free from the horror. Instead, as Tom notes, "the children [are] above all: simpering, prudish, but, most of all, pleased. It is the proper pleased children" (Percy, 1987, p. 330).

In schools and society, the marginalized suffer most. By stripping persons of the ability to function within the parameters of language and reflective thought, any imposition becomes acceptable. They become, in essence, like lower primates, willing to submit to any kind of training as long as that training is pleasurable to them—like Pito Robles in our opening example about global warming. The implications of this scene in terms of ethics and education are quite disturbing. We do admit that it offers an extreme example, but the point it makes is important. When we opt for rigid conformity, we must not be persuaded into an attitude of denial at the possibility of abuse. But denial is difficult to fight. Within such a system, the value of diverse human stories is nullified because all are absorbed into the story of the power brokers. Language is reduced to binary utterances because mystery and nuance are replaced by the established and proper response to the objective world. Blind obedience to political or religious authorities trumps dissent and activism. Subjectivity, diversity, and difference disappear; and ecological destruction, economic graft, sexual abuse, terrorism, war, and other moral catastrophes flourish. We love *The Thanatos Syndrome* because it clearly makes the connection between reflection and action, what Paulo Freire and other critical theorists call *praxis*.

As discussed in the preceding section, the Army Corps of Engineers has structured, enclosed, and diverted the Mississippi River in order to prevent a natural meandering of the water. Likewise, the brain engineers of Percy's novel have also tampered with the water supply from the Mississippi River in order to suppress consciousness, reduce resistance to sexual abuse, and increase intelligence. Both engineers are committed to proactive manipulation of the water for specific predetermined purposes. The result has been an ecological imbalance in nature and, for Percy, sexual and psychological deviance in the people of Feliciana. In a similar vein, educational engineers today believe their curricular structures will promote order, harmony, homogeneous sociopolitical structures, and shared Western values in society. The irony, as we have seen, is that what they actually produce are individuals who have lost the ability to approach experiences in life with a self-reflective sense of context or consent. Critical thinking evaporates and resistance is nearly impossible. Moreover, like the children drugged with sodium at Belle Ame Academy, it becomes impossible to motivate citizens to take action for justice and ecological sustainability. Self-reflexive individuals are sacrificed for economic or educational efficiency and productivity.

As Percy pointed out, the students at Belle Ame Academy could speak in binary sentences, rattle off import and export figures with computerlike precision, and dramatically improve their ACT scores. However, there was no context of meaning, no rootedness in the particularity of their place, no understanding of the earth and water, and no sense of self or wonder. Without these qualities, education is reduced to sterile standardization. And like the marshes of Louisiana that are dying for lack of sustenance from a river that has been cut off and polluted, so too are students perishing in classrooms dominated by the ideology of the brain engineers of education. Students, like the river, must be allowed to meander, explore, create, and become rooted in the earth that gives birth to the creative and imaginative reservoirs of knowledge within individuals. The fictional character Tom More becomes a courageous model of this challenge for meaningful and substantive reform, which is the lifeblood of any democratic society. It is this natural process that leads to personal, societal, cultural, and critical literacy, not the artificial structures of the modern reform engineers of the educational or political landscape.

Once we have established a theoretical framework for thinking about connectedness, rootedness, self-reflection, and critical literacy, we are then ready to challenge our students to consider ecological activism. Before we explore the ecological issues in more detail, we pause to consider the story of one of our students who faced many of the same traumas as the children in Belle Ame Academy.

A Classroom Story of Rape, Domination, and Ecological Sensitivity

Two years ago a twenty-four-year-old undergraduate student came to my (Dana) seminar in tears. When it appeared that her friends' attempts to soothe her were not having a nurturing effect, she blurted out to the class, "What a fucking asshole that man is. He makes me feel so small. He owns me." Those of us who were not friends with Katy wondered whether she was angry with a relative, a lover, a spouse, or the world. But as Katy revealed to us that day, she was upset that none of the administrators at her community college where she was taking courses would recognize, much less address, the verbal, physical, and sexual advances of one of her professors. The thirty-five-year-old professor was the instructor for the last course she needed to be eligible for student teaching. Katy told us that this professor had cornered her in his office to convince her to go out with him. When Katy rebuffed him, he threatened her with lower grades and public humiliation if anyone found out about his advances.

On more than one occasion, according to other students, Katy was singled out in his course to answer the hardest questions. "He was out to get her for blowing him off," one student commented in class. Neither the department head nor the human resources director at the community college committed to doing more than sympathizing with Katy, and she was frustrated and worried that her professor might even resort to flunking her as payback for her rebuke. As a straight A student, and heavily in debt with college loans, Katy could not afford to fail the class.

We decided with Katy that her work in our Social and Political Issues in Education course could be dedicated to building positions of power from which to contest and dismantle the realities of patriarchy, discrimination, and exploitation as they exist in classrooms. Once articulated, twelve other students—women of all ages—enthusiastically joined the project. Although I met with the group for many hours outside of class to discuss their research, it was not until the day they presented their work that I recognized the deeply ingrained secrets, lies, and silences of patriarchy. Katy began the hour-long presentation with her story and her proposal for providing safe places for young women to discuss their fears, inhibitions, and experiences with gender discrimination and intimidation. Shortly thereafter, a shift in the posture of the other women occurred. There was a group huddle, a cathartic sigh of relief, and then one by one all of the women stepped to the podium and told their personal stories of incest, guilt, molestation, sexual abuse, and emotional trauma. Some unleashed stories about ministers, family members, and coaches sexually abusing them at age ten or eleven. One woman recalled how the eighth-grade cheerleaders were required to sit in the front row in class so that the male math teacher could drop a pencil from his desk to the floor and look up their skirts. The link between all of these stories was repressed silence, loss of identity, and feelings of powerlessness. Women of all ages recalled incidents in which they were encouraged to remain silent about their priests, ministers, and teachers who had sexually abused them because the men were well-respected in the community. Others were persuaded to avoid counseling because uncles or grandfathers might be arrested and convicted of rape.

The most striking aspect of these autobiographies, besides the residual self-blame, was that several of the other women knew the male teacher who had seated the cheerleaders in the front row of the classroom. "I had him in class twenty-two years ago. You mean he is still there? I hated his class because he made me feel so awkward. I was scared, but my mother encouraged me to think nothing of it," said Janie. Another woman spoke up to say that she had gone with her parents to the principal's office to address the patting and touching by the same teacher several years ago. What they heard from the principal was that "Mr. Smith has a family—a wife and children—that you must consider." Nothing happened. Finally, Janie admitted that her own daughter, twenty-two years after her own experience, had asked to be switched out of Mr. Smith's class because she felt "creepy and uncomfortable" around him. "I didn't want to believe it. I wanted to block out of my mind my own trauma with Mr. Smith and my minister who molested me. And now my daughter, who is a cheerleader, is feeling the same way I did as a girl and now as a woman. Nothing has changed."

Our class extended ninety minutes longer than scheduled as we discussed a range of issues including the pitfalls of erasing memories, protecting abusers, and annihilating history. About half the women in the class openly confessed their traumas and, more important, expressed relief in knowing that others were experiencing the same fears and pressures in their lives. We also discussed the fact that half of all women are either physically or sexually assaulted in their lifetimes and that schools often reinforce behaviors of exploitation. Consider this story of these women, as well as the saga of Lot's wife and her refusal to erase memories that we discussed in Chapter 3, as you read another compelling history of one of our students.

When I was almost 15, I was raped by my sister's husband. This sister had two kids by this man. When my sister found out what had happened, she did not believe me. She stayed with him and acted as if I had never told her. I was so devastated that my own flesh and blood could ever do this that I tried to kill myself on more than one occasion. I slit both my wrists and could have died. My sister soon came to her senses and left him, but she never told me that she was on my side. Now that my sister was a part of my life, I still had to look at two innocent children and see the man that raped me. This was a very hard concept for me to grasp because I knew that these children had nothing to do with what had happened in the past, but the feeling of fear that they were like him was still there. My nephews went without their Aunt Abby for some years to come. I have realized that I have let these children down because I was not there for them as an Aunt should be. I have however tried to make up for lost times by having them over to my house or spending the weekend with me and my two children. However, I still have a great mistrust at times, or fear for my own children when they are alone. My nephews still see their father on occasion, but they will probably never know what happened to their Aunt Abby because I love them and do not want to see them hurt by this man. I am 28 years old and my life has been through hell and back. I probably have not seen the last of what is in store for me, but I say, "bring it on" because some way and some how I will survive and make the best out of any situation. I have found that songs help a wounded heart, and also being stubborn is a good character trait to have because I will never give up. (Morgan, 2002)

Think back to our discussions of Anselm Kiefer's painting. Remember that Lot's wife could not walk forward if it meant erasing the memory of her loved ones. It is essential that our discussions in class do not end with powerful confessions of abuse and despair. These stories convince us that ecological sustainability is related to our work as educators and our senses of our eschatological self and place. We constantly encourage students to make connections between the raping of women, the beating of gay and lesbian students, the sexual abuse of children, and the exploitation of the environment with platforms of personal hope and social transformation.

This is exactly what Eve Ensler is accomplishing with her V-Day festivals and performances of her plays *The Vagina Monologues* and *Necessary Targets*. V-Day is an antiviolence charity with worldwide affiliates that seeks an end to the oppression of women under slogans such as "Afghanistan Is Everywhere." Ensler draws connections between women terrorized by the Taliban and American housewives beaten to death in their own homes. She seeks to end violence against women by the year 2005, and her plays provide an international audience energized to accomplish this goal. Whether in Afghanistan, West Africa, India, Serbia, or a community college in Ohio, women routinely experience torture, mutilation, sexual abuse, and exploitation by sexist men and patriarchal power structures. The rape of mother Earth and the rape of women are deeply related pathologies that must end—and 2005 is not soon enough.

When I (Dana) wrote about the events with the women students in my classroom for my university third-year teaching evaluation, a few members of the committee viewed my course experience negatively, claiming that education is not supposed to be therapeutic. One member stated, "Since you are not a psychologist, you should not be discussing issues that could traumatize the women in the class." Although the committee was made up of thoughtful and caring people who were probably looking after the best interest of the institution and my career, I believe they underestimate the prevalence and horrors of rape, sexual abuse, and physical violence. Moreover, in addition to supporting my claim that education can be therapeutic, I referred to situations in which gay and lesbian students, African Americans, Latinos, Native Americans, working-class people, physically challenged individuals, depressed or suicidal students, HIV positive or AIDS patients, students with dyslexia or learning differences, or recently divorced individuals could all be traumatized by the emotional impact of our discussions. But does that mean that teachers should refrain from exploring topics and stories related to these people? Victims of discrimination, violence, and disease do not desire silence and ignorance, for silence certainly will not end racism, bigotry, misogyny, rape, educational malpractice, suicide, gay bashing, or ecological destruction.

The committee members were certainly worried about the legal ramifications for the university, as well as the way the tenure and promotion committee would view my file, if the story of the project by my women students remained in my evaluation. Nonetheless, the committee chose to report their concern about my raising "potentially sensitive topics in the classroom." I was disappointed and saddened. However, in my letter of appeal to the committee, I articulated my justification for addressing sensitive issues in classrooms with compassion, always with the understanding that people who have experienced rape, sexual abuse, and racism can excuse themselves. After my appeal, the committee rescinded their critical statement and removed the passage from their letter. I remain committed to using the personal secrets, lies, and silences that haunt the lives of students, as well as my own, as a basis for easing pain and making broader, empathetic connections to other aspects of our lives, especially ecological degradation.

War, Ecological Destruction, and the "Power Over"

The ecological crisis is here! The war is being waged in our hearts, our souls, and our backyards. Right outside our windows, our communities have excessive levels of arsenic in the water and sulfur dioxide in the air. Schools have extremely dangerous levels of mercury in the walls, asbestos in the pipes, carcinogens in the ventilation systems, and lead in the paint. Pesticides and herbicides cover playground equipment. Vinyl siding emits petrochemicals around our homes and lawns, while gypsy moth and mosquito spray residues stain doorways and window panes. Kitchens and cars are covered with poisonous cleaning agents. Pest control chemicals that are only now beginning to be thoroughly studied for carcinogenic effects cover our baseboards. Even our food is laden with herbicides, pesticides, steroids, antibiotics, and growth hormones (Gelbspan, 1995; McGibbon, 1999).

Pollution is not limited to our homes, schools, or offices. When we step outside between 8:00 A.M. and 9:00 P.M. most days of the year, it sounds like a war zone. Gas-powered lawnmowers and tractors not only emit toxic fumes into the air, but also poison our souls with a constant, warlike clamor. Leaf blowers, edgers, weed whackers, and snowblowers without mufflers prevent the possibility of peaceful pleasure for children who dare to explore the mysteries of their yards. Entire afternoons, sometimes entire weekends, are spent with machines that no longer work for us, but we for them. Our lawn technology has come to define success, productivity, sexuality, and libido in ways that are particularly enticing to adults, especially men. This technology also reveals people's desire for control, power, and perversion that contributes to war and ecological destruction.

In many homes in our neighborhoods, the lawns and leaves receive more energy and attention than the children. On any given day, a variety of lawn care companies will spend up to three hours on each property mowing, edging, trimming, blowing, pruning, and spraying chemicals. Several retired folks on my (Dana) block spend an enormous amount of time on their John Deere and Cub Cadet tractors. One man in particular, perhaps in his late sixties, has produced a yard that is, according to community standards, perfect. Four shrubs surround his tan, vinyled home, and several newly planted trees are growing in his front yard. More impressive to his neighbors is that he "cares enough" to mow his yard twice a week to ensure perfection. Each time he rides his new, two-thousand-dollar John Deere tractor, he rotates mowing directions. One day he will mow diagonally from front to back, and the next perpendicularly. His precision and dedication do not stop with his lawn. I often watch as he adds Scotts Turf Builder and a variety of chemicals to kill "weeds," "pests," and other "evildoers" in his yard. Chem-Lawn comes once a week to assure him of his prowess, position, and "victory" over nature. I do not mean to demean this man whose behavior, like that of many of the middle-aged men in my neighborhood, resembles that of my friends and relatives, but I do find his efforts fascinating and disturbing. I want to understand why he has chosen this addiction. Why does he feel that his yard must resemble the gardens of an English estate or a golf course putting green? Does he feel he is being a productive citizen if he keeps his yard neat and trim? How has he come to believe that a golf course lawn is beautiful? What did the back-yards of his childhood look like? Does he feel a loss of control in his own life that propels him to need to control and kill nonhuman species? Does he abuse a spouse or a dog like he beats his lawn? And does he even consider the irony of the sign placed on his lawn by the chemical company that reads "Caution. Harmful Chemicals. Keep Off the Lawn"?

We could ask many questions about this condition, but we are particularly interested in the ramifications of this man's behavior on the environment. Specifically, is he aware that a few lawn applicants are developed with some of the chemicals that produced Agent Orange, the defoliation spray that caused cancer in Vietnam vets? Does he consider where the chemicals that he sprays on the beetles, wasps, ants, and weeds will eventually run off to? Does he care? Does he believe that Buddhism, pantheism, Judaism, or Christianity support his behavior? Did he read *Silent Spring* in school? In other words, how can he justify the extermination and contamination of hundreds of life's creatures, including his own grandchildren, in the name of having a manicured yard? Maybe Rousseau was right; modern people have "left home" and lost spontaneity and freedom, including perhaps even morals and virtues, because we have become too civilized and too corporate. Ecophilosopher Jerry Mander (1995) explains:

> Our society really "left home" when we placed boundaries between ourselves and the earth, when we moved en masse inside totally artificial, reconstructed, "mediated" worlds—huge concrete cities and suburbs—and we aggressively ripped up and re-designed the natural world. By now, nature has literally receded from our view and diminished in size. We have lost contact with our roots. As a culture, we don't know where we came from; we're not aware we are a part of something larger than ourselves. Nor can we easily find places that reveal natural processes still at work. As a corporate culture, we have begun to feel that one place is as good as the next; that it's okay to sacrifice this place for that one, even when the new place is not even on Earth. In the end, this leaves us all in a position similar to the millions of homeless people on our streets. In truth, we are all homeless, though we long to return. (p. 313)

Mander's analogy of homelessness to describe our relation with our natural world is most compelling. Several of our neighbors immerse themselves in their yards as a means of escaping the banality and isolation of their work as sales and marketing executives. They appear to be as detached and homeless regarding their interest and allegiance to their jobs as they are unaware of the beauty beneath their manicured lawns. Our neighbors will decry the sterile soullessness of their corporate work, yet they bring the same corporate illusions and landscapes to their own backyards, infecting and polluting the entire neighborhood. We wonder how our neighbors balance the noise and fumes of their machines with the rights of others to enjoy clean air and tranquility? We all become homeless and unrooted in our own yards as our neighbors' machinery turns family picnics, gardening, and play into screaming sessions. Do we think of each other? Do we consider the birds, the squirrels, and the chipmunks and their homes? Several of our friends also enjoy jet skiing and snowmobiling, but we don't believe they have thoroughly considered the destructiveness of their hobbies and the impact on beavers, fish, eels, and waterfowl. Even minimal efforts to limit such vehicles in a place of natural beauty such as Yellowstone Park have met with angry resistance, and in 2002 George W. Bush reversed Bill Clinton's ban on these vehicles in the park. Because nature is considered a recreational commodity and not a life-sustaining habitat, citizens revolt when any land is set aside for preservation and animal life.

Each day I (Dana) walk for an hour around my neighborhood in Wooster for exercise and meditation. I study the landscapes of my neighbors' homes and notice many of the environmentally destructive practices—and no doubt my friends consider my zero-scaping and push mowing absurd. I am also fascinated by the signs that periodically pop up on lawns. For instance, I noticed that most people whose yards were manicured like golf courses tended to display "George Bush for President" signs in 2000. I also witnessed, with a few exceptions, that the same houses now display U.S. flags and patriotic slogans such as "United We Stand" or "God Bless America" posted next to Chem-Lawn and TruGreen warning signs. These are also the homes with garages that shelter the largest sport-utility vehicles. We believe there are connections to be made here. Automobile largesse, toxic control, and acts of war do not stop at the fence line of people's yards. Think back to our previous discussions of self-reflection, semiotics, hermeneutics, and human nature as we explore this proposition.

We believe that in most cases exuberance for sport-utility vehicles, war, Chem-Lawn, and patriotism are very much interrelated. After all, "the rage to conquer is a sign of madness, and madness is rarely limited to one dimension of our lives" (Glendinning, 1995, p. 38). Chevrolet and Ford advertisements for Suburbans, Explorers, and Excursions not only interpose huge sport utilities onto natural landscapes, often around mountains, but they also surround listeners and viewers with a language of comfort, prestige, strength, and domination over nature, highways, and less competitive drivers. Lawn mowers, weed whackers, leaf blowers, and applications of chemical lawn treatments, all of which were nonexistent seventy-five years ago, provide a phallic illusion of self-absorbed control, domination, and aggressive competition in landscapes and relationships. The modern isolationist view that nature is separate from humanity rather than an integral dimension of existence and growth also sheds light on why many citizens have only myopic lenses through which to understand the terror of September 11 and the graft of the Enron debacle.

In an unpredictable world, we desire to be comfortably in control of our environment in order to climb mountains in our Bravadas, forge huge puddles in our Expeditions, and outperform the enemy weeds with Roundup and Ortho. The disposition to conquer reminds us of the "Stomp the Comp" slogan used by midlevel managers at Wal-Mart. Once it has entered a community, Wal-Mart lowers prices by a few cents below those of local businesses on all their products, runs advertisements promoting the lowest prices in town, puts mom and pop out of business, and then without competition to worry about, raises prices. Within ten years of Wal-Mart moving into a community, fifty local businesses close down, on average (Quinn, 2000, p. 4).

We don't believe that this approach to business is any different from the way many of us approach our yards and our planet. At least fifty varieties of worms, ants, beetles, and plant life are probably uprooted once Scotts, Ortho, or Monsanto move into a neighborhood's lawns. A competitive struggle of the survival of the fittest ensues, and the way to win the struggle in an unpredictable and dangerous world is to have the most gigantic of sport utilities, the most powerful lawn equipment and chemicals, and the largest stockpile of weapons of mass annihilation. Unfortunately, our self-absorbed destruction is not unrelated to a ravaging of nonhuman life and a blatant ecological crisis, and eventually to the psychological dysfunction and sexual abuse discussed earlier.

Perhaps this explanation can also illuminate why so many U.S. citizens disdain peace and reconciliation and support the use of force to conquer countries and cultures that seek to retain their self-determination, biodiversity, and regional sustainability. Witness many of the U.S. government's policies in Central America, Africa, and at home. We have a history of waging war as a basis for not only maintaining our wealth and economic domination, but also for reinforcing the ideology of our rugged uprootedness.

Perhaps there is also a connection between the feelings of people who need to be rooted in positions of power and expressions of control, winning, and isolationist patriotism. If the presidential election of 2000 is any indication, the American public appears less concerned about the integrity of the electoral process than in maintaining that process. Whether George W. Bush or Al Gore was actually elected president seemed a minor concern; the public demanded finality rather than quality and any decision rather than electoral chaos. Perhaps many of our reactions to September 11 are an expression of our inability to control the events and circumstances that led to the attacks; they also reflect a society that feels a loss of place, context, and roots. We were caught off guard, and our power was threatened on September 11. Our superiority was challenged; our God-like global, political, and economic prowess was infiltrated. Simply, it appears to us that many citizens are unable to understand or commit to invigorating a plurality of worldviews and lifestyles, human and animal, because they have lost touch with their own. This aggressive and isolationist tendency is obvious in our relationship with our lawns when we begin to demonize and fear our eight-legged friends who are essential to sustaining life on this planet. This is evident when we destroy the natural beauty of our yards: the dandelions, the worms, the bugs, and the snails. And it is evident when we assume that we have been ordained and anointed with permission to pick and choose which creatures we will annihilate in the name of our market-driven libidos. Let us abruptly shift our thoughts from yards to schools for a moment. As we continue, consider the infiltration of toxins, chemicals, and machines into our natural world and how environmental degradation may carry over to the rest our lives.

Sara's Story

Look no further than high school classrooms to see how distorted potentials of human nature and lack of place have crept into our psyches. Recently I (Dana) met a fifteen-year-old student who was distraught about school and life. Besides being an A and B student, Sara was deeply interested in and committed to social justice in her community. Since she was twelve, Sara had spent two nights a week working at a homeless shelter because she was outraged at the conditions that propel women and children into lives of poverty if a spouse or partner is lost. Sara also worked at a food bank on Saturdays. She actively participated in boycotting and picketing two large grocery store chains that refused to provide health benefits to its employees, who were allowed to work only thirty-four hours a week. Most recently, Sara had been involved in a letter-writing campaign to state senators regarding their lack of support for campaign finance reform. Mike, on the other hand, was a ninth grader with As and Bs, but his heart was dedicated to different impulses. Mike was not committed to or involved in civic causes in or out of school. In fact, he often labeled student activists as "dorks" and "fags." Mike liked hanging out with his buddies, cruising Main Street in our town, and crashing parties with his new stereo system blaring loudly. He intended to be extremely wealthy, and it didn't matter how he achieved this goal. Neither Mike nor Sara ever got in trouble and, to the best of our knowledge, both avoided drugs and alcohol.

In order to prepare Mike for the state achievement tests, Mike's parents purchased a video, CD, and workbook packet to help him study. They linked monetary rewards to a study schedule and his performance on the tests. Sara, on the other hand, was too involved in the community to worry about state tests. She loved giving time and energy to poor children and elderly folk whom she encountered at the shelters. Sara had little time to take practice tests, fill out repetitive worksheets, or look over the study guides suggested by her teachers. As it turns out, both Mike and Sara passed every section of the state tests, with one exception. Mike aced the citizenship section, whereas Sara's score fell below the acceptable norm. Mike received a new bike from the school principal in addition to a five-hundred-dollar scholarship from the state for his outstanding achievement. Sara was labeled deficient in citizenship. Some teachers openly questioned her academic ability and commitment to her studies. Sara was also required to take remedial courses to improve her citizenship score in the summer.

Something is inherently wrong and distorted in a society in which the Saras are looked on as failures in need of citizenship remediation while the pseudo-citizens like Mike are rewarded and put on pedestals. As it turns out, Sara's self-esteem and commitment to school and social causes have plummeted. She no longer trusts or respects the adults in her school who encourage her to put aside her convictions and volunteer activities until after college. She questions the integrity of a system and society in which care, compassion, connection, and interdependence are dwarfed by distorted illusions of citizenship. She fears she is being encouraged to constantly disobey her heart.

Sara's story illuminates the extent to which our vision of justice, democracy, and a healthy planet are constantly manipulated by forces that paint distorted notions of citizenship, success, and natural beauty in our hearts. Many people in our society view the natural world and students like Sara simply as resources that can be turned into commodities for trade. According to Carolyn Merchant (1996),

> The notion of resources as commodity or free goods forms an inexhaustible tap whose waters go into an inexhaustible sink. Following the model of a factory, nature is conceptualized as a dead machine, isolated from its environment, whose parts are manipulated for assembly line production. Resource depletion (the tap) and environmental pollution (the sink) are not part of the profit-less accounts, hence there is no accountability to or for nature. Because the individual, or individual corporation, is free to profit, there are no ethical restraints on nature's "free" goods or free trade. The result is a Hobbsean Good Society and an egocentric ethic. (p. 213)

Nature is not just "free" goods for the raping, and Sara is not just a human resource to be developed. Neither deserves to be broken down, ripped from their roots, and rebuilt in the image of a marketable commodity that is ready for unbridled competition in the New World Order. We argue that without some deeper interrogation of the forces that have shaped our egocentric ethics, we become blind to how those same forces may guide us away from the qualities of people and our ecological selves that make for a healthier and less toxic world. Consider Enron, Watergate, Iran-Contra, Chernobyl, and global warming. Like the Union Carbide disaster in Bhopal, India, each disaster is another reminder of how profits become more important than people. If our concept of a beautiful yard has been formed by advertising, peer pressure, and corporate agendas rather than by our souls, then a vision of a just society and ecological sustainability remain dormant. As you digest these last few passages, consider what forces are driving us to spend our lives adding toxins to the soil, plants, rivers, our homes, and our children. Who benefits when our patterns of life are no longer sustainable for the creatures in the woods, streams, bogs, valleys, plains, mountains, air, and schools? And who is behind the push to have citizens define their patriotism through shopping instead of addressing the destruction of cultural and ecological diversity that hyperconsumerism demands?

The toxicity in our schools, neighborhoods, and egos is a symptom of a deeper global ecological trauma. Spring comes a week earlier than it did two decades ago in the northern hemisphere. The United States pours 15 percent more carbon dioxide into the air than it did ten years ago. Glaciers are melting and sea levels are rising. The planet is warming at a faster rate than it has in the previous ten thousand years. Entire forests are defoliated because of industrial air pollutants and acid rain, and greenhouse gases are contributing to dangerous holes in the ozone layer. The water we drink often has unhealthy levels of industrial waste, chemical runoff from our beautifully manicured laws, toxic fertilizers from agribusiness and hog farms, chemicals from the nuclear industry, oil dumped in drainage systems by homeowners and businesses, and plastic resin. The soils in which our food grows are devastated by excessive pesticide and herbicide spraying. Tropical forests are disappearing at a rate of one hundred acres a day. Why? For consumption such as the creation of grazing land for cattle that will provide hamburgers for McDonald's and other fast-food restaurants. We have witnessed an incredible loss of wild species around the world, with extinction estimates around ten thousand species a year (Gelbspan, 1995; McGibbon, 1999; Naess, 1995).

    We have known this information for years but have failed to act. When I (Patrick) first studied ecology in the early 1970s, I became outraged by these facts. I decided to take action, and I began by refusing to eat beef and pork. I did not want to contribute to the proliferation of cattle grazing and hog farms, and I also wanted to do my part to help save the rain forests. I think I was also appalled by the condition of the sickly cows my uncle sold to the fast-food industry—the healthy cows commanded a higher price on the market. At a young age, I understood the direct connection between food consumption and environmental degradation. I have never demanded that others adopt my vegetarian diet, but I have challenged friends and students to eat as low on the food chain as possible in order to preserve the land and forests. I always point out the complexity and difficulty of making ethical dietary decisions. For example, although I do not eat meat and have gradually become a vegetarian over the years, I still eat seafood in my Louisiana gumbo. It is almost impossible to live in the modern world and eat an ethical diet that avoids all ecological destruction. The challenge is to begin reducing our consumption and wastefulness. This will only happen once we recognize the connections between each small act and the larger ecological milieu.

    Many people choose a vegetarian diet—vegetables and no meat—or vegan diet—same as vegetarian but also no milk, cheese, eggs, or animal products of any kind—for health reasons only or for a combination of ethical living and healthy living. Some followers of organic and raw food movements avoid all processed foods. Some will argue that vegetarianism and veganism are potentially dangerous because the body needs proteins, fats, and other animal products. Joanne Stepaniak (1998) provides an excellent response to this myth and supplies detailed information about the healthy benefits of a vegan diet. The irony of specious attacks on vegetarianism is that the daily consumption of fried foods, sweets, hamburgers, milk shakes, processed preservatives, and carbonated drinks by North Americans make us the most overfed and undernourished people on the planet. The food we eat is causing incredible damage to our blood, arteries, intestines, skin, hearts, and stomachs. An ethical diet can actually save our lives and reduce our medical expenses. Joanne Stepaniak writes:

> Embracing veganism compels practitioners to live moral and compassionate lives while minimizing their impact on the Earth and its resources. The American Vegan Society's tenet of "dynamic harmlessness," doing the least harm and the most good, encourages vegans to search for options that will protect and improve the lives of all living beings as well as eliminate suffering, bring about the responsible use of natural resources, and inspire peace and harmony among people. Consequently, veganism is not passive self-denial. On the contrary, it instills active and vibrant responsibility for initiating positive social change by presenting a constant challenge to consistently seek out the highest ideal. (1998, p. 129)

One of the most radiant women I (Patrick) have ever met is an eighty-year-old Carmelite nun who lived in a cloistered monastery from her eighteenth birthday. In her later years, she served as the convent extern, the only nun who could talk to visitors. As a young teacher, I often brought my students to her monastery for a visit. On one occasion during a question-and-answer session with the extern nun, a high school girl remarked, "Your skin is so remarkably clear and beautiful. What makeup do you use?" The nun responded, "I have never used makeup in my life. My skin shines like this because I have never eaten meat and only consumed the food we grow organically in our garden behind the chapel." It is ironic that women and men use plastic surgery and poisonous injections of Botex to remove wrinkles in an effort to look radiant and beautiful—and as an interesting side effect deaden their facial muscles and their ability to visibly express human emotions. (Recall our discussion earlier of loss of consciousness in Percy's novel.) We would offer this Carmelite nun as a challenge for considering natural methods of skin care that do not produce harmful side effects, either physically or psychologically.

The agricultural poisoning of our soil, wind, water, food, and bodies is a worldwide environmental health threat. Remember that although public outcry led to the banning of DDT in the United States, companies continue to sell it abroad, and its use is increasing (Stauber & Rampton, 1995). All told, "from Chernobyl radiation to the Gulf War oil spill; from tropical rainforest destruction to polar ozone holes; from Alar in apples to toxins in water, the earth and all its life are in trouble" (Merchant, 1992, p. 18).

Some of our more skeptical friends write off as alarmist the overwhelming body of research that links increased rates of cancer and disease to ozone depletion, pesticides, herbicides, and other toxins introduced into our environment. They dismiss the fact that the fossil fuel industry, chemical companies, mining conglomerates, and the Big-3 automakers spend close to one billion dollars a year to convince U.S. citizens that toxic sludge is good for them and that the environmental crisis is a hoax propagated by leftist whackos and junk science. Citizens are bombarded with advertising images meant to convince them that Exxon, Dupont, and Cargill are protecting the environment (Gelbspan, 1995; Naess, 1995a). "Green washing" has become an essential component to counter the growing sentiment of U.S. citizens that corporations are not protecting natural environments and to convince them that "environmental activists who criticize and attack industry are eco-terrorists, fear mongers, and the latest incarnation of the communist menace" (Stauber & Rampton, 1995, p. 126).

The influences of major polluters became especially clear to me (Dana) as I fought to prevent the fluoridation of our local water supply. Ninety-nine percent of European and Scandinavian countries have refrained from adding fluoride to the water because of links to various cancers, osteoporosis, and fluorosis. Yet the phosphate fertilizer industry has a lot of money to gain if they can convince dentists, doctors, legislators, and citizens that fluoride is necessary in drinking water. Although a local fluoridation referendum in my community was defeated, a phosphate fertilizer company probably influenced a local congressman in Ohio to push for state legislation that would put the decision to add fluoride in drinking water in the hands of local city councils, not citizens. In other words, companies are promoting the idea that it was "unnatural" *not* to add fluoride to the water, and citizens had only the right to have it removed.

The research is extremely mixed on adding fluoride to drinking water, especially in light of the fact that the water fluoridation campaign evolved out of the need by the military-industrial complex to find renewable ways to dispose of nuclear waste from the development of weapons of mass destruction. Moreover, the precautionary principle has not been thrown out; it has been turned on its head and is being used against citizens. Corporations such as Monsanto, Archers Daniels Midland, and Cargill now tamper with our food and water supplies with the philosophy that something is safe until proven otherwise. Shouldn't it be the other way around? Consider the North American Free Trade Agreement, General Agreement on Tariffs and Trade, and the policies of the World Trade Organization that were written by multinational corporations for multinational corporations. Today, companies can collect damages from other countries that enact environmental or occupational safety legislation if it affects their bottom line. Thus, Monsanto will be able to sue El Salvador if the people decide they deserve company retirement plans or no longer want to grow tomatoes infused with pork or flounder genes to make them more frost resistant. We ask the most skeptical of our friends and family if they really think that Monsanto would be unwilling to sacrifice the safety of its genetically engineered food and the people who eat it if it meant greater profits. Do we truly believe that Ford Motor Company and Exxon would be unwilling to sacrifice the health of our planet and our children if it meant more Explorers were sold? And do we really believe that the same corporate forces that are dictating educational policy will seek to create imaginative and socially conscious citizens (like Sara) who will contest unhealthy human and planetary agendas?

We ask these questions at a time when George W. Bush is seriously undermining many environmental protections, including the marginalization of environmental reports on global warming from within his own administration in May of 2002. Since taking office in 2001, Bush has (1) gone against the overwhelming evidence of climatologists and the wishes of people in 180 countries by refusing to sign the Kyoto Agreement on global warming; (2) reduced protections against arsenic in water; (3) reversed legislation that would block mining companies from causing "substantial irreparable harm" to water quality and natural resources; (4) retreated from conserving sixty million acres of untouched national forest; (5) rolled back protection for diminishing wetlands; (6) significantly eased field-testing controls of genetically engineered crops; (7) cut by 50 percent the funding for research into renewable energy sources; (8) took steps to abolish the White House Council on Environmental Quality; (9) proposed to eliminate new marine protections for the Channel Islands and the coral reefs of northwest Hawaii; (10) cut funding by 28 percent for research into cleaner, more efficient cars and trucks; (11) suspended rules that would have strengthened the government's ability to deny contracts to companies that violate workplace safety, environmental, and other federal laws; (12) okayed Interior Department Secretary appointee Gale Norton to send out letters to state officials soliciting suggestions for opening up national monuments for oil and gas drilling, coal mining, and foresting; (13) abandoned a campaign pledge to invest $100 million for rain forest conservation; (14) rescinded a proposal to increase public access to information about the potential consequences of chemical plant accidents; (15) suspended rules that would require hard-rock miners to clean up sites on western public land; (16) eliminated funding for the Wetlands Reserve Program, which encourages farmers to maintain wetlands habitat on their property; (17) cut the Environmental Protection Agency budget by $500 million; (18) proposed to curtail the ability of groups to sue in order to get an animal placed on the Endangered Species List; (19) rescinded the rule that mandated increased energy-saving efficiency regulations for central air conditioners and heat pumps; (20) abandoned his campaign pledge to regulate carbon dioxide, the waste gas that contributes to global warming; (21) nominated David Lauriski, ex–mining company executive, to the post of assistant secretary of labor for mine safety and health; (22) okayed Interior Department Secretary Gale Norton to go forth with a controversial plan to auction oil and gas development tracts off the coast of eastern Florida; (23) announced his intention to open up Montana's Lewis and Clark National Forest to oil and gas drilling; (24) proposes to redraw boundaries of national's monuments, which would technically allow oil and gas drilling "outside" of national monuments; (25) allowed Interior Department Secretary Gale Norton to shelve a citizen-led grizzly bear reintroduction plan scheduled for Idaho and Montana wilderness; (26) refused to fund continued cleanup of a uranium slag heap in Utah; (27) appointed a vice president quoted as saying, "If you want to do something about carbon dioxide emissions, then you ought to build nuclear power plants" (Vice President Dick Cheney on *Meet the Press*); (28) proposes to reverse regulation protecting sixty million acres of national forest from logging and road building; (29) nominated Linda Fisher, a Monsanto executive, for the number-two job at the EPA; (30) nominated J. Steven Giles, an oil and coal lobbyist, for deputy secretary of the interior; (31) nominated Bennett Raley, who advocates repealing the Endangered Species Act, for assistant secretary for water and science; (32) proposes to ease the permit process, including environmental considerations, for refinery, nuclear power plant, and hydroelectric dam construction; (33) proposes to give government the authority to appropriate private property through eminent domain for power lines; (34) proposes that $1.2 billion in funding for alternative renewable energy come from selling oil and gas lease tracts in the Alaska National Wildlife Reserve; (35) plans on serving genetically engineered foods at all official government functions; (36) forced out Forest Service Chief Mike Dombeck and appointed a timber industry lobbyist; and (37) is making it harder for citizens to sue corporations that commit ecological crimes.

If George W. Bush truly cared about U.S. families and restoring integrity to the White House, he would immediately wage war on the criminals who exploit natural environments for their own profit, including members of his own family. Instead of crusading for corporate welfare kickbacks for the insurance, airlines, weapons, and fossil fuel industries, perhaps Bush could support renewable forms of life and sense of place.

More than any other modern American, author Rachel Carson is credited with "giving birth to populist ecological awareness. She refused to accept the party line! *Silent Spring,* her bombshell best-seller, gave a dramatic, prophetic, and factual account of massive agricultural poisoning from the chemical industry's sales ($300 million a year in 1962) of DDT" (Rampton & Stauber, 2001, p. 124). Her work led to a broadening of consciousness, as well as the practical development of such events as Earth Day, which began in 1970. The big chemical companies were more worried that *Silent Spring* would dampen their profits then they were about what their chemicals were doing to the environment. Therefore, they put together a smear campaign even before the book was published. In addition to trying to intimidate the publisher into canceling the publication, the National Agricultural Chemical Association doubled its public relations in an attempt to discredit Carson and the damaging evidence she was providing. The spirit of Carson's prophetic call prevailed, however. With an even greater ecological crisis before us today, the chemical industry has intensified efforts to deflect criticism and accountability for its environmental and economic abuses. Dow, Dupont, and Monsanto are waging a war of public relations as much as they are waging a war on the environment and the future of our children. The aim is to prevent people around the world from realizing what has been lost and what is being destroyed. It is our responsibility as informed and committed educators to remember and honor Gandhi's idea that democracy and freedom "become unholy when their hands become dyed red with innocent blood [either human or nonhuman]" (qtd. in Merton, 1965, p. 55).

Deep Ecology and Its Relevance to Education and Ethics

Deep ecologists remind us about the overwhelming and absurd economic, political, social, and spiritual crises facing us. As a conceptual framework, a philosophy, and a movement, deep ecology seeks to move beyond superficial environmental activism, which is often limited to recycling. Deep ecologists ask more probing questions about diversity, religion, human nature, and ecological justice, such as: How have we been socialized? What effect has the society in which we were born had on our dietary patterns, our sexuality, our lifestyles, or our transportation patterns? What historical forces—such as immigration, urbanization, social mobility, educational opportunities, or religious traditions—have helped to create the economic patterns that dictate our lifestyle and material consumption? How have the values, politics, and economics of the schools affected our children and society? What environmental values have we formed as a result? What expectations do we hold for our children and their children? How might the values of the next generation differ from our own? How can we help bring about a world that will provide human life with a high quality of subsistence? (see Merchant, 1992, pp. 4–6). These questions reveal that deep ecology moves beyond programs to promote clean air and water to call for overhauling the human spirit in order to develop the potential to act for justice. Arne Naess, one of the most influential deep ecologists, argues for the special role that deep ecology could play in our lives:

> For one, it rejects the monopoly of narrowly human and short-term argumentation patterns in favor of life-centered long-term arguments. It also rejects the human-in-environment metaphor in favor of a more realistic human-in-ecosystems and politics-in-ecosystems one. It generalizes most ecopolitical issues: from "resources" to "resources for"; from "life quality" to "life quality for"; from "consumption" to "consumption for"; . . . where "for" is, we insert "not only humans, but other living beings." (1995b, p. 452)

Naess's conception of ethics "for" nonhuman life is related to and stretches Zygmut Bauman's insightful work in developing a constructive postmodern system of ethics that extends beyond being "with the other" to a position of being "for the other," which we discussed in earlier chapters. An ethics "for" humans and nonhumans is politically, socially, and ecologically edgy in that it challenges the status quo and challenges people to reconsider and redesign their relationships "for" diversity, caring, and progress. Caroline Merchant (1992) echoes this sentiment:

> [Deep ecology] pushes social and ecological systems toward new patterns of production, reproduction, and consciousness that will improve the quality of human life and the natural environment. It challenges those aspects of the political and economic order that prevent the fulfillment of basic human needs. It offers theories that explain the social causes of environmental problems and alternative ways to resolve them. (p. 9)

The essence of the movement, according to Naess, is to not only ask deeper questions about the ingrained values of societies, but also to develop newer and more unifying worldviews (1995). These views emphasize differences within a conception of similarity of creation, situatedness, and unification. Philosopher, theologian, and educator Fritjof Capra expresses the unifying potential of deep ecology this way:

> Deep ecology does not separate humans from the natural environment, nor does it separate anything else from it. It does not see the world as a collection of isolated objects but rather as a network of phenomenon that are fundamentally interconnected and interdependent. Deep ecology recognizes the intrinsic values of all living beings and views humans as just one particular strand in the web of life. (1995, p. 20)

What is proposed is not a shift away from caring for humans to nonhumans, but a general and overall commitment to caring for all life forms, human and nonhuman alike (Naess, 1995a).

One of the important contributions deep ecology can make to ethics and education is its potential to advance holistic perspectives and embolden action for justice. In this sense, deep ecology extends the responsibilities of its adherents beyond the potentially narrow confines of the environmental movement to a broader and more prophetic role:

> Supporters of the Deep Ecology movement do not consider the ecological crisis to be the only global crisis; there are also crises of social justice, and of war and organized violence. And there are, of course, political problems, which are distantly related to ecology. Nevertheless, the supporters of the Deep Ecology movement have something important to contribute to the solution of these crises: they provide an example of the non-violent activism needed in the years to come. (Naess, 1995b, p. 453)

Gandhi's philosophies and practices of nonviolence and political liberation, for example, resemble the philosophies expressed by deep ecologists in that they extend beyond the diversity of humans to all living creatures. Nature conservation and ecological sustainability are nonviolent at their cores. Gandhi suggested: "I believe in advaita (non-duality). I believe in the essential unity of man [all humans] and, for that matter, all that lives. Therefore I believe that if one man gains spirituality, the whole gains with him and, if one man fails, the whole world fails to that extent" (quoted in Naess, 1995a, p. 235). Gandhi condemned violence in the form of poverty, political repression, caste systems, and terror as much as he opposed the violence against animals in his native India. On many of his pilgrimages, Gandhi brought his own goat as a way to communicate his opposition to the cruelty of the milking process. He also refused to have scorpions, spiders, and snakes removed from his bedrooms based on his principle that the species can satisfactorily coexist without violence. If one were thoughtful, one could look in one's shoes before stepping on a scorpion and avoid a bite. Likewise, if men and women were attuned to walking on the floor in the pitch-blackness of their bedroom without trampling nonhuman life, they might be able to avoid trampling on other humans in their daily relationships. According to Thomas Merton, the "spirit of non-violence sprang from an inner realization of spiritual unity in himself. The whole Gandhian concept of non-violent action and satyagraha is incomprehensible if it is thought to be a means of achieving unity rather than as the fruit of inner unity already achieved" (1965, p. 6). Gandhi' philosophies on ecology have sometimes been referred to as biosophical egalitarianism because they are based on a respect for the sacredness of all life and a belief that love is the law of our existence.

Discussions of deep ecology can also be found in theology, literary criticism, social justice movements, and the ecological revolution of the 1960s. Some persons associated with the movement include Rachel Carson, Wendell Berry, Albert Schweitzer,

David Brower, Aldo Leopold, Arne Naess, Alan Watts, Henry David Thoreau, John Muir, Robinson Jeffers, Aldous Huxley, George Orwell, Lewis Mumford, Black Elk, Luther Standing Bear, and George Santayana. Inspiration is also derived from the ways of living and religious values of native peoples from around the world including Zen Buddhism, Native American mythologies, Taoism, and nature-centered movements of the Catholic church in the nineteenth century (Sessions, 1995). We now ask you to consider the concepts of biosophical egalitarianism and deep ecology as they relate to your lives.

Let us return to our discussion of veganism. "How many of you have eaten roadkill, euthanized cats and dogs, or diseased chicken, cattle, and pork," I (Dana) ask my students each semester. "That's disgusting," students respond. "It may be disgusting, but if you have eaten chicken, pork, or beef in the last five years, then you have probably eaten roadkill, euthanized cats and dogs, and diseased chicken, cattle, and pork." I ask my students to imagine a huge, open-bedded, eighteen wheeler pulling up to the community collection center for the dead deer, dogs, rabbits, bear, raccoons, and squirrels recovered from roadsides. These carcasses are then loaded onto the truck, which moves on to the processing plant, where all of these animal carcasses will be ground up and sold back to beef, chicken, and pork farmers as feed.

Cows, pigs, and chickens ingest their diseased relatives up until the time they are slaughtered for our consumption. The point of this foray into the feed and meat-packing industry is that both the process and the end result are violent and despicable. Animals are mistreated, misfed, tortured, exploited, and sentenced to lives of misery for the sole purpose of increasing profits for the beef and chicken industries. What goes around, comes around, however. This is how mad cow disease is born, with its gestation period of up to ten years.

Also consider what is happening in the dairy industry. Local farmers tell us that in order to compete with corporate milk farms, much less feed their families, they must sacrifice the vitality, health, and well-being of their cows in order to increase milk production. One way to do this is by pumping them full of hormones, steroids, and antibiotics. What you have, according to Jeremy Rifkin (1993), is a situation in which castrated, drugged, and docile cattle are exploited horrendously in the name of profit (see also Lyman, 1998). The drawback is that many cows are living shorter, less healthy lives. It takes only sixty days to bring a chicken from egg to dinner plate thanks to hormones, antibiotics, and steroids. The chicken industry has increased processing efficiency by 33 percent (it used to take ninety days), and it has done so with an understanding that more birds will either die or arrive diseased on the way to the butcher.

Many educators either promote or contribute to the marketing of milk, which is not only inhumane to the animals involved, but also possibly unhealthy for children and the environment. Our friends in the dairy industry—fourth-generation farmers—will no longer drink cow's milk because the process has become too contaminated with bovine growth hormones, antibiotics, and steroids that move directly from cow to child. Add the pesticides that are sprayed on the cows and you a have toxic cocktail of contaminants that are increasingly linked to earlier onset of menstrual cycles, acne, ear infections, viral infections, Guillain-Barré syndrome, multiple sclerosis, and cancer in humans (see Oski, 1996). It never ceases to amaze us how many of our students either have multiple sclerosis or have relatives with MS. When we discuss the politics of milk, inevitably one or two people in the class will comment on their association of milk consumption with the onset and aggravation of MS symptoms. They also describe how their relative's MS goes into remission when they stop drinking cow's milk. The extent to which this is true is still vigorously debated in the scientific community, but the dairy industry conceals so many hideous secrets about milk that we must remain skeptical.

Milk is definitely not "natural" for large numbers of African American kids who are lactose intolerant. This means that milk consumption can create or intensify stomachaches, diarrhea, and general malaise. Consider this situation in the context of free and reduced-cost lunch programs, in which most of the meals are laden with milk products. Is this a racist policy? Also consider that milk has more than twenty-five proteins that can lead to allergies. If your child has diarrhea, asthma, sinus congestion, or a constantly runny nose, take her or him off milk for a week and you will be amazed at how many of these symptoms disappear. We must also get over the myth that we should drink milk for its calcium content. Milk actually has elevated levels of phosphoric acid that prevent the absorption of calcium to a significant degree. Also remember phosphoric acid the next time your school becomes a Pepsi or Coke campus. When our children drink Pepsi, the phosphoric acid works to deplete the calcium stored in their growing bodies (Marcus, 1998).

It is easy to understand why our friends on the dairy farm decided to stop drinking cow's milk and turned instead to soy-based nutritional substitutes. But getting the facts on milk is not easy because the American Dairy Association has friends and lobbyists in high places. Along with the beef industry, the American Dairy Association has opposed the development of a food pyramid that eliminates the consumption of milk and beef because it will mean reduced profits. In other words, the food pyramid our sons and daughters are studying in class is actually less healthy than the one recommended by doctors on the panel who oversee the guidelines (see Marcus, 1998). Industry executives such as Phil Angell of Monsanto are also brazen enough to acknowledge their lack of concern for food and diet safety: "Monsanto should not have to vouchsafe the safety of biotech food [or any food]. Our interest is in selling as much of it as possible. Assuring its safety is the FDA's job" (Teitel & Wilson, 1999, p. 19). Unfortunately, as noted earlier, Monsanto writes much of the legislation regarding Round-Up soybeans, bovine growth hormones, and genetically modified foods, in addition to securing high-powered government positions.

If the toll on human health is not enough to convince us that consuming beef and milk is unhealthy and possibly unethical, the environmental cost from cattle grazing is enormous. According to Jeremy Rifkin (1993), the 1.28 billion cattle populating the earth graze on about one-fourth of the planet's landmass and consume enough food to feed hundreds of millions of people. Remember that 36,000 people die every day from starvation—that is one person every three seconds—and fifty people could avoid starvation with the grains it takes to feed one cow or pig:

> Domesticated cattle are responsible for much of the soil erosion in the temperate regions of the world. Cattle grazing is a primary cause of the spreading desertification process that is now enveloping whole continents. Cattle ranching is responsible for the destruction of much of the earth's remaining tropical rain forests. Cattle raising is also partially responsible for the rapid depletion of fresh water on the planet. . . . Cattle are also a chief source of organic pollution; cow dung is poisoning the freshwater lakes, rivers, and streams of the world. (1993, p. 187)

Today, our consumption of milk and beef products poses major cultural, political, economic, and ecological hardships for people around the world. Thirty-three percent of the world's total grain harvest goes to feed cattle and other livestock at a time when as many as a billion people suffer from chronic hunger and malnutrition. Moreover, millions of indigenous peoples are being forced off their ancestral lands by huge multinational corporations to make room for commercial feed grain production. "And while millions of human beings go hungry for lack of adequate grain, millions more in the industrial world die from diseases caused by an excess of grain-fed animal flesh gorging on grain-fed beef and dying from the diseases of affluence" (Rifkin, 1993, p. 2). Remember this information the next time you order fast food. McDonald's may whet your children's appetites with ads for Happy Meals, but the process of getting the hamburger to your child's tray probably produced excessive levels of pain and suffering for the cows, rivers, forests, birds, and uprooted trees and will produce excessive health and nutritional problems for your child and the children of the world. Remember this information as you watch school lunch lines in cafeterias. What products are included in the meals? Who benefits from the sale of these products? What negative health consequences result from continual exposure to lunchroom diets and vending machine products in the hallway? And, finally, why is there so much waste and indifference as huge amounts of food are thrown away daily? There is definitely something rotten in the food-processing and food-service industries, especially in our schools. In fact, it is an ethical nightmare.

Ecofeminism and Centralizing Marginalized Voices

Ecofeminism is committed to interrogating and transforming domination that has historically been linked to sexism, racism, classism, heterosexism, ageism, and religious intolerance and extends the commitment to justice to the unjustified human domination of nature as well. Ecofeminism's roots in critical feminism, liberal feminism, radical and socialist feminisims, and black and Third World feminisims are unified in their critique of forces of domination. Karen Warren (1997) articulates the ecofeminist agenda:

> [Ecofeminism] not only recognizes the multiple voices of women; located differently by race, class, age [and] ethnic considerations, it centralizes those voices. Ecofeminism builds on the multiple perspectives of those whose perspectives are typically omitted or undervalued in dominate discourses, for example Chipko women, in developing a global perspective on the role of male domination in the exploitation of women and nature. An Ecofeminism perspective is thereby structurally pluralistic, inclusivist, and contextualist, emphasizing through concrete example the crucial role context plays in understanding sexist and naturalist practice. (p. 7)

The motivation to bring marginalized voices to the center of our educational discussions has been a major project of this book and our work as teachers. So it only makes sense to include the prophetic and multivariant voices of ecofeminists and their criticism of environmental racism, colonialism, and the dualisms and hidden values of modern science and positivism in our current discussion of ecological destruction.

As discussed in earlier chapters, there are grave dangers in articulating our beliefs and interpretations as if they are objective, neutral, and value-free. The preponderance of binaries such as Western/Eastern, American/Un-American, patriotic/unpatriotic, New World/Old World, civilized/uncivilized, democratic/undemocratic, and advanced/Third World rationalizes and hides hierarchies and hegemonies of power. Ecofeminists are adamant that Western and male versions of positivism and progress serve to limit the development of less exploitative relationships to science, culture, and nature (Warren, 1997).

Ecofeminism extends this critique further by insisting, "Western civilization isn't working for most people—women and men . . . and it certainly isn't benefitting nonhumans" (Plant, 1997, p. 129). Theologian Rosemary Redford Ruether is even more specific in her criticism of advanced consumerist societies:

> We have acquired a highly developed sense of our individuality, of our superiority or inferiority, but have relatively little sense of our collective nature, of the way in which our communion with everything else assures our survival and shared happiness. . . . We exalt the individual and regard the most powerful, wealthy, or brilliant individuals as absolutes, quasi-divinities to be protected against all the ebbs and flows of history. . . . In an age of nuclear power and biotechnology, the limitations and outright dangers of a dissecting, invasive and compartmentalized method of knowing as promoted by Western science and technology have become much more manifest. (1996, pp. 20, 83)

Most of us live in well-heated houses that have adequate ventilation and cooling systems so that we have very little idea what deforestation means to women who have to gather wood for fires. "Drought means women walk twice as far each day seeking water. Pollution means a struggle for clean water largely unavailable to most of one's people, it means children in shanty towns dying of dehydration from unclean water" (Ruether, 1996, p. 6). We must constantly remember that the top 20 percent of the world's human population owns 82 percent of the wealth, while the other 80 percent scrapes along with 18 percent of the wealth. In addition, over a billion people, disproportionately women and children, starve and die prematurely from the poisoned waters, soil, and air generated by the industrialized world's vision of progress and civilization (Ruether, 1996, p. 5). Ecofeminists encourage us to remember that we all have a responsibility to care for the human and nonhuman labor that produces the products and food we consume. Gladys Parentelli explains:

> Making ethical decisions implies having a deep respect for all that is living and for everything that directly or indirectly affects life, whether it be persons or other forms of life—animals, plants, forests, water, land—or objects that in various ways impinge upon life, such as tools, machinery, etc. Ethics presupposes an all-encompassing respect for life. It demands a continual reflection with regard to the consequences of my love or my aggression, my responsibility or my irresponsibility, my respect or lack of respect, my options, my decisions, my words, my actions, my omissions, what I consume, what I save, what I spend, what I throw away, what I preserve. (1996, p. 32)

We ask you to compare the similarities of deep ecology, ecofeminism, and our ensuing discussion of ecological postmodernism, environmental racism, and the ecological self. Consider the consequences, responsibilities, connections, and possibilities of your relationships to others and the natural world.

Ecological Postmodernism and the Ecological Self

One of the most memorable and important experiences of my (Patrick) teaching career occurred when I was a visiting professor at the University of Manitoba in the summer of 2000. I presented several lectures on curriculum theory and taught a graduate seminar on critical theory, education, and postmodernism. At the invitation of my friend and colleague Dr. Roy Graham, I traveled to Winnipeg prior to the seminar to meet with the students, present an initial lecture, and begin planning the summer program. As I do in all of my courses, I arrange for as many community field experiences as possible. The Canadian students in Manitoba were particularly enthused by my suggested format, and we decided to include field experiences every afternoon for the entire two-week seminar. The program included visits to the Winnipeg Harvest food bank for a tour, discussion, and several hours of volunteer labor with the staff; a former Trappist monastery for prayer, art making, and discussion with visiting Tibetan monks; and the Winnipeg Fringe Fest to attend a memorable play titled *Father I Femme for Myself,* written by and starring a young drama director from a local high school who was gay and a talented male-to-female entertainer. The other character in the play was the young man's father, a rugged macho rancher who was trying to come to terms with his son's sexual orientation and cross-dressing. The actual father and son starred together on stage in this powerful and insightful play. We also visited a local art gallery's opening reception for a series of installations on various social issues, and we spent an afternoon with Mike Calder, an aboriginal teacher who led the group in a sweat lodge experience.

All of these field experiences were informative and inspirational, but the sweat lodge ceremony is the one that changed my life. It also dramatically affected the students, as evidenced by this comment on the final course evaluation:

> The most distinctive experience in this course for me was the sweat lodge ceremony, as it helped in stripping each of us of our traditional educational roles as teachers and students to being people sharing a cultural and spiritual experience. As we learned in the sweat lodge, the bear is courage. After two weeks of complex conversations and group dynamics, it was refreshingly simple to sweat, to touch the earth, and to reflect on universal themes. (Higgins & Wilson-Baptist, 2001, p. 24)

When we arrived at the First Nations Center south of Winnipeg, Mike warmly welcomed us, gave us a tour of the property, and then invited us to enter the changing hut to remove our clothing and jewelry. Some of us were a bit uncomfortable because it was the first time we had undressed as part of a graduate seminar. The women put on light flowing gowns and the men wore loose gym shorts. After an opening ceremony that incorporated tobacco and hot "grandfather" stones at the entrance to the sweat lodge, we crawled one at a time through the small entrance to begin the ceremony. We sat on the cool, dank earth in a circle around the white-hot rocks with the canvas roof close to our heads. As the layers of heavy canvas were closed over the opening by Mike's assistant on the outside of the sweat lodge, we found ourselves enveloped in total darkness in a confined space. Mike taught us that the sweat lodge was like the womb of Mother Earth, and we were on a journey of healing and rebirth.

Mike began the ceremony by pouring a cup of cool water over the stones, and hot steam immediately filled the small lodge. He gently pounded a drum, intoned ancient chants, and taught indigenous lessons that had been passed down for generations. We were mesmerized, and we started to sweat. Mike encouraged us to move closer to the ground as the heat intensified. The searing heat was like nothing I had experienced in my life, not even in a sauna. After about thirty minutes, I found myself prostrate on the ground rubbing shoulders with sweaty students on either side of me. We were told in advance that the door would be opened if anyone needed to leave, and I was worried that I might not last the entire three hours, despite the fact that we were given water breaks outside of the lodge every half hour.

As I became more desperate in the heat and sweat, something miraculous happened. I bent forward and put my nose into the ground and discovered that I could inhale cool air out of the earth and refresh the inside of my body. Suddenly I was able to endure the searing heat on my skin. My breathing slowed, and I entered a prayerful meditative state, listening to Mike's chants and lessons with one ear and dwelling on my own rebirth with the other. I wrote the following reflection in my journal the next day: "The sweat lodge will linger in my memory forever. I felt connected to the Earth in ways that I never have before. The cool air from the ground was sucked up through my nostrils and refreshed my burning body. What an incredible ecological lesson!" The sweat lodge experience provided an important understanding of my ecological self.

In this section, we challenge you to reflect on the theme of ecological postmodernism and the ecological self. Charlene Spretnak seeks to extend ecofeminism beyond "minimalist" conceptualizations of interdependence to a "radical nonduality of unitive dimensions of being, a gestalt of a subtle, unitary field of form, motion, space, and time" (1997, p. 425). Spretnak is suspicious of certain forms and expressions of deep ecology and their potential for posing gender-neutral conceptions of the self as they relate to the natural world. As an alternative, she proposes a framework of ecological postmodernism that "acknowledges both the enormous role of social construction in human experience and our constitutive embeddedness in subtle biological, ecological, cosmological, and quantum processes" (1997, pp. 432–433). Spretnak asks us to "break out of the conceptual box that keeps modern society self-identified apart from nature and to reconnect with a fuller, richer awareness of the human as an integral and dynamic manifestation of the subjectivity of the universe" (p. 433). Let us use another teaching moment as the basis for a better understanding of ecological postmodernism and its connection to our work as educators.

Some of the most memorable and spiritually moving experiences in my (Dana) courses occur on community farms. Recently, I led a group of twenty-five principals and teachers to the Caretaker Farm, a thirty-five-acre organic farm with a mission that is social, spiritual, and environmental more than economic. Sam Smith, the sixty-eight-year-old "caretaker" who has a reputation in the community for being an activist, visionary, and teacher, met with us for several hours to discuss a variety of trends such as globalization, land ethics, alienation, ecological imperatives, sustainable agriculture, and organic farming. We had focused on these issues in class, but it wasn't until we actually were among the rows of lettuce, beets, cabbage, and soil that most students began to remake and reconnect the importance of the natural world to their own existence. Some people were visibly moved by more than Mr. Smith's words. People from small villages, large cities, and suburban towns described how their fondest memories of childhood involve peaceful moments amidst nature. As we knelt down to feel how every square inch of earth houses a community of more than a thousand different living organisms, one or two students were moved to tears as they recalled their rootedness in the rivers, plant life, and animals on their families' farms. A woman who had lived in Latin America for most of her life shared how she associated her family and spirituality, especially her grandmother, with the land and animals that cared for her as a child. "When I vacated the mountains and streams of our village farm and came to the United States, I felt like I left behind more than my family. I left my sense of purpose and being."

All of us came away from Caretaker Farm with a greater appreciation for the social, political, and economic contexts of our work but also with a reinvigorated understanding of our ecological selves. Even students who had been skeptical of my reasons for visiting Caretaker Farm discussed several days later how it was one of the most moving educational experiences they had ever had. "No offense, Dana, but we learned more in five minutes of kneeling in the earth and feeling the energy of the life in the soil than we have in our three years of graduate studies." We share this story to reinforce the potential of alternative educational experiences as much as to impress on you the importance of grounding our humanness in the nonhuman "natural" subjectivity that engulfs us. As we move to a discussion of environmental racism, and eventually to a discussion of September 11 and the Enron debacle in Chapter 5, we ask you to reflect on the "influences of landscape, weather, and other dynamics of one's bioregion on imagination and mood; the self-regulating dynamics of the body-mind; the effect of daily exposures to strong and weak electromagnetic fields; and the subtle manifestations of nonlocal causality and other relational dynamics that lace the universe that have shaped your ecological and postmodern selves" (Spretnak, 1997, p. 433).

Environmental Racism

The protagonist in Ernest J. Gaines's novel *The Autobiography of Miss Jane Pittman* is a former enslaved woman living in the fictional Louisiana city of Bayonne. Like most of Gaines's novels, the setting is suggestive of the author's childhood home in Pointe Coupee, Louisiana. In the novel, Jane Pittman reminisces about her life as an enslaved child on a Louisiana antebellum plantation, as a free woman during Reconstruction in the South, and as a black woman during the Civil Rights movement. As she approaches the age of 108, Jane reflects on the significance of rivers:

> Before the high water we didn't have school here. The children went to school in the Bottom or at Ned's school up the road. [Huey] Long came in after the high water. The damage from that high water was caused by man, because man wanted to control the rivers, and you cannot control water. The Indians used to worship the rivers till the white people came here and conquered them and tried to conquer the rivers, too. . . . And that's when the trouble really started. (Gaines, 1972, pp. 147–148)

Ernest Gaines—like Langston Hughes, who writes in his poem "The Negro Speaks of Rivers" that he has known rivers ancient as the world and older than the flow of human blood in human veins (Hughes, 1973)—creates images of rivers running deep with ancient powers, worshiped and respected as a source of life for the soul. We are warned that attempts to control and conquer rivers is not only futile but also the beginning of disaster. The environmental devastation resulting from control and pollution is inextricably linked to the personal and cultural disaster resulting from slavery and racism. In this section, we examine this link between environmental degradation and racism as a part of the broader project to address ecological justice. We introduce this topic with our students by reading and viewing the novel and film *The Autobiography of Miss Jane Pittman*. This literary account allows us to examine the history of racism in a particular place—south Louisiana—and draw connections to natural phenomena—flooding and rivers. Following from our earlier discussion of the Mississippi River, the character Jane Pittman offers insights into ways we can further understand the impact of ecological degradation on an entire society. We must begin our investigation of environmental racism with the moral catastrophe of slavery and racism.

Pointe Coupee means "a place cut off." It is surrounded by water: the Mississippi to the east and north, the Atchafalaya to the west and south. Pointe Coupee is immersed in Louisiana culture—rural and racist; Catholic, Creole, and Cajun; black, white, and mulatto; catfish, cotton, and crawfish; and an abundance of water. Jane Pittman reflects on rivers and water in Pointe Coupee:

> I don't know when the first levee was built; but from what I heard from the old people the water destroyed the levee as soon as it was put there. Now, if the white man had taken heed to what the river was trying to say to him then, it would have saved a lot of pain later. They tell me he said, "This here water got to be confined. . . . We got to get the water to running where it's suppose to run. Suppose to run in the river, and we got to keep it there." Like you can tell a river where to go. (Gaines, 1972, pp. 148–149)

Like the river, people have been confined and leveed in their movements through societal institutions. Pointe Coupee has a long history of such confinement and environmental disasters. Defined by rivers, built by delta silt, and destroyed by spring floods and subsidence, communities like Pointe Coupee reflect ecological rhythms. However, since the floods of the 1920s, the U.S. Army Corps of Engineers has spent billions of dollars on projects to control the Mississippi, and the river has been confined by levees and dams. Jane Pittman warns us that these efforts are futile:

> Now he's [the white man] built his concrete spillways to control the water. But one day the water will break down his spillways just like it broke through the levee . . . ; the water will never die. That same water the Indians used to believe in will run free again. You just wait and see. (Gaines, 1972, p. 150)

Likewise, U.S. society and U.S. education have erected control structures that often prevent the free flow of creative analysis and the free flow of individuals through institutions. We believe that these futile efforts must be challenged, just as the attempts to control the Mississippi River must be reevaluated in light of the ecological destruction of the wetlands and the devastation of communities following the 1993 floods.

Jane Pittman, a determined young woman who struggled to anchor her life in the midst of post–Civil War bigotry and social upheaval, delights in her emancipation and sets out on foot for Ohio, the place of hope promised by a northern soldier during the war. Jane witnesses terrible tragedy, murder, and starvation as she wanders for weeks through the marshes and forests near Pointe Coupee on the way to freedom in Ohio. On the verge of exhaustion, she arrives at a clearing, which opens to a bend in the river. Jane discovers that she has been walking in circles and is trapped by the Mississippi. She is still in Louisiana, a place that will be her home for the next one hundred years. Jane does not despair; her soul grows deep like the river in the anguish of her childhood home.

In the end of the novel, Jane Pittman is the only person in the city of Bayonne who has the moral authority to confront the evils of racism and proclaim liberation for her people. Preparing for her triumphant march into the city, she reflects,

> Today I felt something funny in the air. My heart was jumping too much. I wasn't scared I might get hurt—when you get to be a hundred and eight you forget what scared is: I felt something funny in the air, but I didn't know what it was. I just sat there looking at the grass, and I could remember the times when I used to bend over and run my hands through the dew. (Gaines, 1972, p. 41)

Jane Pittman's moral authority derives from her connectedness to the earth—a connection nurtured in ways similar to our sweat lodge and Caretaker Farm experiences. Jane Pittman drew strength from the land, as does the aforementioned student from Latin America, and she slowly uncovered the meaning of liberation in the anguish of Pointe Coupee. Like an enslaved girl searching for freedom in a promised land, and like a river meandering and searching for its course to the sea, we breathe deeply in the struggle in the place of our journey—as I (Patrick) had to do in the sweat lodge. Novelists such as Ernest Gaines invite us into these places where our roots can absorb that chthonian moisture, the subterranean primeval ecological energy, which gives us sustenance. We are nourished and energized for activism when, like Jane Pittman, we choose to bend toward the earth, touch the dew, and imbibe.

We suggest that teachers and students must reconceive the context of their places of learning—no matter how hostile the environment—as fertile ground for meandering and self-reflection and not as a polluted landfill that poisons and suffocates creative growth. As we have insisted throughout this book, we must use field experiences to help people break free of the mundane. Unfortunately, the mundane is all too often pervasive. Jonathan Kozol dramatically documents the devastation caused by institutional barriers in schools of the inner cities in the text *Savage Inequalities: Children in America's Schools* (1991). Chapter 1, "Life on the Mississippi," is pertinent to our discussion here. Kozol describes the anguish of the children who live in East St. Louis, Illinois, a city that lies in the heart of the Mississippi embayment known as the Bottoms. The Bottoms is located on the east side of the Mississippi River opposite St. Louis and is surrounded by embankments called the Bluffs. Kozol explains:

Towns on the Bluffs are predominantly white and do not welcome visitors from East St. Louis. . . . The two tiers, Bluffs and Bottoms, . . . have long represented different worlds. Their physical separation helps rationalize the psychological and cultural distance that those on the Bluffs have clearly tried to maintain. People on the Bluffs overwhelmingly want this separation to continue. . . . The pattern of concentrating black communities in easily flooded lowland areas is not unusual in the United States. Farther down the river . . . in the Delta town of Tunica, Mississippi, people in the black community of Sugar Ditch live in shacks by open sewers. . . . Metaphors of caste like these are everywhere in the United States. Sadly, although dirt and water flow downhill, money and services do not. (1991, pp. 9–10)

Kozol documents the ways in which the people of East St. Louis have been poisoned by industrial pollution and imprisoned by economic fraud and neglect. The hopes and dreams of a generation of children have been stifled, and the school system continues to deteriorate. The people of the Bottoms in the Mississippi Delta, long recognized as being some of the most impoverished of all Americans, are being subjected to the same abuse as the river itself: restricted, polluted, and harnessed for economic gain.

Kozol documents how barriers are erected to prevent the people of East St. Louis from meandering out of their place:

Two years ago, the one pedestrian bridge across the Mississippi River to St. Louis was closed off to East St. Louis residents. [The bridge] puts you right into downtown St. Louis, quite close to the arch. The closing of the bridge was ordered on the day before a street fair that takes place each summer during the July Fourth celebration. . . . For the people in East St. Louis it's an opportunity to bring their children to the city to relax. Mothers walk their kids across the bridge. (1991, pp. 18–19)

Kozol investigates the reasons for the closing and speculates that fear of crime at the fair was at the heart of the decision. Regardless of the reason, he concludes, it was a decision that denied the people of East St. Louis access to the fair and an opportunity to look back across the river for a moment of self-reflection. The president of the NAACP in East St. Louis is quoted as saying, "We seem to have been *isolated*" (Kozol, 1991, p. 19; emphasis added). The savage inequality that plagues children in U.S. schools, especially in the Mississippi Bottoms, leads Kozol to write that "in Calcutta this would be explicable, perhaps. I keep thinking to myself, 'My God! This is the United States!' " (p. 17). Kozol's image of deep poverty in the Mississippi embayment transforms our metaphor of the river into a frightening reality of anguish and despair for children in U.S. schools and a vivid example of environmental racism.

Gaines's novel is a healing story. It is a story of turmoil and triumph. Like the children of East St. Louis, Jane is cut off. Her geographic location is bounded by the river, and her desire to flee to Ohio after her freedom from slavery is thwarted by the great expanse of the river. The river prevents her escape. Although Jane's life in Pointe Coupee is riveted with pain and suffering, she is guided by the ancient forces of her heritage that course through her veins, just as the waters of the Mississippi River course through the regions of Louisiana. She responds the only way she knows how—out of the wisdom gained from suffering, a wisdom that connects her to the earth and releases in her patience and waiting. This is not to say she is inactive in her desire for justice. Instead of the mechanistic, chemical solution to social ills described in Walker Percy's novel *The Thanatos Syndrome,* Jane longs for another solution, one based on an authentic sense of place. Her solution includes the voices of the earth, the river, and the grand oak trees. Jane's sense of justice will not allow her to forget these most important voices. "Once interrelationships are established, the distortions internalized and expressed by individuals can be understood [as] social actors themselves, and human agency in the making of history can be enhanced" (Kincheloe & Pinar, 1991, p. 2). It is precisely through the process of creating interrelationships with the forces of her place that Jane must live out justice.

In her narrative, Jane refers to a sermon preached at the river by her foster son Ned that gives readers a clearer understanding of Jane's psychology—or should we say, her spirituality. Although she cannot remember everything Ned said, what she does remember is profound. She quotes from Ned's sermon:

> This earth is yours and don't let that man out there take it from you. . . . It's yours because your people's bones lays in it; it's yours because their sweat and their blood done drenched this earth. . . . I'm not telling y'all men own the earth. . . . Man is just a little bitty part of this earth. When we die he go back in the earth just like a tree go back in the earth when it fall. . . . These same people is now buried in this earth, and their bones' fertilizing this earth. (Gaines, 1972, p. 107–108)

With these words indelibly etched on Jane's soul, it is not surprising, then, to witness her response to years of slavery, racism, lynchings, and civil rights struggles. Her response is inclusive, for she takes in all that she experiences as a way to find significance in her place. Thus, we see Jane incorporating her surroundings into a liberating cosmology that is simple, yet profound and rooted in the earth. Her conversations with the oak tree illustrate this:

> That tree has been here, I'm sure, since this place been here, and it has seen much much much, and it knows much much. And I'm not ashamed to say I have talked to it, and I'm not crazy either. It's not craziness when you talk to trees and rivers . . . when you talk to the Oak tree that's been here all these years, and knows more than you'll ever know, it's not craziness; it's just the nobility you respect. (pp. 147–148)

The oak tree is Jane's *axis mundi* (that is, roughly, "anchor in the world") to which she clings in the midst of turmoil. The tree stands tall and strong and becomes a symbol of the enduring human spirit, a symbol of eternity. The language it teaches Jane is the literacy of the cosmos, which becomes, then, a literacy of empowerment for those who listen to its wisdom.

Jane has found her way to freedom through learning the ways of the earth, the oak, and the river. We too must follow the ways of the earth and become grounded in the significance of place. Only by so doing can we hope to be less victimized by the structures that dehumanize us. And yet how can this be accomplished? Jane does not come to her ecological and cosmological understanding haphazardly. Rather, she comes to it in process, taking in all of the particulars of the anguish of her environment. It is Jane's connection to place that empowers her to triumph in her quest for freedom.

Jane's passionate beliefs do endure and she does act on them. By the end of Gaines's novel, Jane has lost her husband in a ranching accident, her foster son Ned is killed because of his teaching, and now she must endure the murder of another son, Jimmy. Again the forces of the established structures of society seem to consume Jane's community, and Jimmy is killed because he challenged the entrenched structures of prejudice and injustice: the exclusion of people of color from using a drinking fountain. In all of this, Jane has not been weakened. She listens and acts on her passionately held beliefs and the wisdom of the ancient oak and the Mississippi River. At the age of 108, she travels to the city of Bayonne, where Jimmy was killed, to carry on his work. Her poignant words reveal her ardently held beliefs: "I'm going to Bayonne. . . . Just a little piece of [Jimmy] is dead. . . . The rest of him is waiting for us in Bayonne. And I will go" (Gaines, 1972, p. 245). Gaines ends the novel with Jane headed for Bayonne, her resounding words of conviction "I will go" ringing in our ears.

A significant addition to the final scene of the novel is the film adaptation's version of the Bayonne trip and confrontation (Korty, 1973). In the movie, we witness Jane's triumphant walk to the fountain. The nobility and respect she so long gave to the oak is now given to her. She is out of time in this scene, and no one can touch her; they must let her pass and allow her to drink. What is the significance of such an action? Jane engages in the deconstruction of societal structures. She deconstructs racism by her action, which defies the sign "Whites Only," and as she drinks she transforms her place in time into an integrative experience. There, as the cool, clear arch of the water touches her mouth, she is refreshed and so is everyone around her. She drinks in the memory of Jimmy, the prejudice of the white social and economic structures, and the alienation of her people. She drinks in the turmoil of her place, the turmoil of the river, for the cool arch that touches her lips was born from the Mississippi, and, in a sense, she drinks in all who suffer. Jane has transcended her place, her fictive boundaries, and creates in all of us a reconceptualized paradigm of understanding, one that leads to liberation because it is attached to the notion of totality. In her transcendent totality, Jane embodies for all of us the words of the Langston Hughes's poem "The Negro Speaks of Rivers" (Hughes, 1973). Jane's soul, too, has grown deep like rivers.

Jane Pittman is a fictive character who inspires hope. Her story is an important beginning of discussions about environmental racism for our students. Next we turn to documentary films such as *Green* (Dunn, 2000), which investigates the lives of real people struggling with cancer, poverty, asthma, and pollution along the Mississippi River. Laura Dunn documents the environmental disaster of the one hundred miles between Baton Rouge and New Orleans, home to over 150 petrochemical plants that are responsible for producing 25 percent of the nation's petrochemicals. Imagine 1.5 major plants per mile. This area reports the highest concentration of toxic emissions to the air, land, and water in North America. The residents of this area, who are predominantly African American, Cajun, and poor, suffer from astronomical rates of cancer, asthma, and other debilitating medical ailments. Laura Dunn, like the producers of the film *Toxic Racism,* tells the story of the people of color along the river and challenges all who watch her film to take action against environmental racism. Bill Moyers has also dramatically addressed these issues in another film we view with our students titled *Trade Secrets* (Moyers, 2001).

It has taken a while for environmentalists, like feminists, to recognize the unique environmental perils that face communities and peoples of color and/or poverty. African American, Native American, and Latino peoples face environmental threats to a much greater degree than do whites. This is especially true for women and children. Dorcetta Taylor (1997) insightfully points out that although *Silent Spring* ushered in movements to clean up rivers such as the Potomac for tourism, many rivers— such as the Anacostia in Washington, D.C., which runs through an African American community—were not cleaned up. As evidence, Taylor (1997) refers to studies that demonstrate the discriminatory effect of the Clean Air Act; to work documenting the lack of regulations that protect the health and safety of migrant workers; to research demonstrating how waste dumps and incinerators are located in predominantly African American, Latino, and Native American communities; and to studies that pinpoint higher levels of lead poisoning in children of color (pp. 44–45; see also Merchant, 1992, 1996; Warren, 1997).

In 1991 the First National People of Color Environmental Leadership Summit was held to draw attention to both the distributive and corrective justice needed to address environmental racism. The delegates agreed on the following seventeen principles to guide ecology. The group

- Affirms the sacredness of Mother Earth, ecological unity, and the interdependence of all species, and the right to be free from ecological destruction
- Demands that public policy be based on mutual respect and justice for all peoples, free from any form of discrimination or bias
- Mandates the right to ethical, balanced, and responsible uses of land and renewable resources in the interest of a sustainable planet for humans and other living things
- Calls for universal protection from nuclear testing and the extraction, production, and disposal of toxic/hazardous wastes and poisons that threaten the fundamental right to clean air, land, water, and food
- Affirms the fundamental right to political, economic, cultural, and environmental self-determination of all peoples
- Demands the cessation of the production of all toxins, hazardous wastes, and radioactive materials and that all past and current producers be held strictly ac-

countable to the people for detoxification and the containment at the point of production

- Demands the right to participate as equal partners at every level of decision making, including needs assessment, planning, implementation, enforcement, and evaluation
- Affirms the right of all workers to a safe and healthy work environment, without being forced to choose between an unsafe livelihood and unemployment. It also affirms the right of those who work at home to be free from environmental hazards
- Protects the right of victims of environmental injustice to receive full compensation and reparations for damages as well as quality health care
- Considers governmental acts of environmental injustice a violation of international law, the Universal Declaration of Human Rights, and the United Nations Convention on Genocide
- Must recognize a special legal and natural relationship of Native peoples and the U.S. government through treaties, agreements, compacts, and covenants affirming sovereignty and self-determination
- Affirms the need for urban and rural ecological policies to clean up and rebuild our cities and rural areas in balance with Nature, honoring the cultural integrity of all communities and providing fair access for all to the full range of resources
- Calls for the strict enforcement of principles of informed consent and a halt to the testing of experimental reproductive and medical procedures and vaccinations on people of color
- Opposes the destructive operations of multinational corporations
- Opposes military occupation, repression, and exploitation of lands, peoples, and cultures and other life forms
- Calls for the education of present and future generations to emphasize social and environmental issues, based in our experience and an appreciation of diverse cultural perspectives
- Requires that we, as individuals, make personal choices to consume as little of Mother Earth's resources and to produce as little waste as possible, and that we make conscious decisions to challenge and reprioritize our lifestyles to ensure the health of the natural world for present and future generations. (Taylor, 1997, pp. 42–44)

Because people of color have experienced centuries of colonialism, imperialism, slavery, genocide, and discrimination, they are uniquely qualified to speak to the limitations and possibilities of environmental activism. Supporters of deep ecology and ecofeminism, for instance, are themselves restricted by many of the perspectives and injustices they claim to abhor, such as racism, classism, and ethnocentrism. We must never forget that whiteness continues to accrue extensive economic, legal, educational, social, political, medical, and environmental privileges for white people. We believe the platforms and movements, like the one just articulated, are important in that they arise out of the experiences of people and groups who continue to bare the brunt of environmental injustice. At the same time, we respect the efforts of activists to connect with and link to the diverse values, situations, and spirituality of all·people interested in justice.

Ecological Futures

When Rachel Carson published her scathing commentary on the pesticide industry, *Silent Spring* ushered in many new trends. Foremost, it became obvious to all activists that "very powerful pressure groups would not only vote against necessary changes in the direction of responsible ecological policies, but they also had the power and influence to monopolize the mass media with counter information" (Naess, 1995b, p. 446). Carson ushered in a wave of activism on behalf of the environment and our relationship to it. It was clear that an ethics of dualism and ego was no longer adequate to deal with some of the major ethical problems of the day. With the possibilities and uncertainties of nuclear proliferation, racism, global warming, psychic alienation, and war at even greater levels today, an ethics of inclusiveness, rootedness, care, connection, and unity through difference is essential. Our visions and convictions are born out of movements such as the Norwegian Green Party and their attempts to root sustainability, ecological justice, and human and nonhuman rights in realities of economic growth and technological advances:

> Social development can proceed only at the cost of the quality of life, which after all, is a basic value; social and global solidarity implies reversing the trend towards the growing differences between rich and poor; the material standards in the rich countries must be reversed; and bureaucracy and the power of capital must also be reduced. [This program] includes a technology adapted to nature and humans, cultural diversity, viable local communities, and a respect for nature and life. Other key issues included an increase in the minimum wage; redistribution of wealth; decentralization and the support of small organizations; the participation of children and the young in productive work; ecological architecture that gives children access to free nature, not just parks; transfer of military resources to environmental tasks; global cooperation and security; and the support of groups who work for alternative kinds of societies. (Sessions, 1995, p. 252)

We believe that progress can be justified only if it prevents the mass destruction of indigenous cultures and the earth's natural beauty and ecosystems. Profit is acceptable if it does not come at the cost of spiritual, environmental, gendered, or racial dislocation and its symptoms. Simply, our profit, products, and progress, as well as our spirits, must be balanced and rooted "with" and "for" the quality of life deserved by all human and nonhuman life forms.

We approach the postmodern ecological crisis with fear and despair but also with profound hope. Studies of deep ecology, ecofeminism, environmental racism, and postmodern ethics are inspirational points of departure because they are more politically lively, courageous, aesthetic, probing, personal, and risky than conventional ethical wisdom. Each "offers an alternative vision of the world in which race, class, gender, and age barriers have been eliminated and basic human needs have been fulfilled" (Merchant, 1992, p. 236). We see educators as healers and caretakers of complexity, spirituality, chaos, primal urges, and difference in this "self-educating universe" (Sessions, 1995). Much of our inspiration derives from the possibility that teachers will extend an awareness of the human experience to what George Sessions describes as "those profound communications made by the universe about us, by the sun and moon and stars, the clouds and rain, the contours of the earth and all its living forms . . . [that draw] us back into itself to experience the deepest of all mysteries" (1995, p. 15).

We recognize that many of the issues in this chapter, and in this book, may seem overwhelming to a majority of students when they enter our courses. That is why we occasionally reference a variety of manifestos and lists as a means of redirecting our commitments. We have found that documents such as the ones provided below have proven beneficial for students as they reenvision their personal choices, professional aims, and teaching convictions. We end this chapter by combining some helpful hints from Arne Naess and Carolyn Merchant. These are just a few of the items we use with our students as they begin to ask "what can we do?"

- The dangers of radioactive, toxic, and hazardous wastes to human health and reproduction have been exposed by citizen activists, and regulations concerning disposal have been tightened.
- The rapid clear-cutting of tropical rain forests and northern hemisphere old-growth forests by corporations on both public and private lands and the associated decimation of rare and endangered species have been brought to public awareness, and cutting in some areas has been curtailed.
- The dangers of pesticides and herbicides on foods and in water supplies and the availability of alternative systems of agriculture have been made visible.
- Direct, nonviolent action has become an acceptable and highly visible means of political protest.
- Alternative, nonpatriarchal forms of spirituality and alternative pathways within mainstream religions that view people as caretakers and/or equal parts of nature rather than dominators are being adopted by more and more people.
- Ecological education and individual commitment to alternative lifestyles that reduce conspicuous consumption and recycle resources has begun in many schools and communities.
- Resources should be replenished, environments restored, and biodiversity maintained by all industries and businesses, especially transnational corporations.
- Reproductive health care and family planning should be available to all women.
- Use simple means. Avoid unnecessary complicated means to reach a goal or end.

- Endeavor to maintain and increase the sensitivity and appreciation of goods of which there is enough for all to enjoy.
- Appreciate ethnic and cultural difference among people.
- Promote concern about the situation of the Third and Fourth Worlds and attempt to avoid a material standard of living too much different and higher than that of the needy.
- Appreciate and choose meaningful work rather than work to make a living.
- Attempt to satisfy vital needs rather than desires and reduce the number of possessions.
- Try to act resolutely and without cowardice in conflicts, but remain nonviolent in word and deeds.
- Move toward vegetarianism and veganism, total or partial. (Naess, 1995, pp. 259–61; Merchant, 1992, pp. 236–237; 1996; p. 219)

5 Prophetic Voices and Proleptic Hope: Teaching Convictions after Enron and 911

September 11, 2001

We find ourselves writing this last chapter in the weeks and months following the September 11, 2001, attacks on Washington, D.C. and New York City. Our emotional paralysis and existential angst are palpable. We struggle to integrate these events into our daily lives, our scholarship, and our teaching, and we also recognize the enormous responsibility to deepen our understanding of important theological, historical, economic, cultural, and political phenomena. We believe that the global community is on the threshold of an opportunity to heal divisions and nurture peace, but we are also mired in the rhetoric and reality of escalating conflict, cycles of vengeance and retaliation, and potential global annihilation. We scour the media, religious publications, university bulletin boards, Internet sites, and political institutions for prophetic voices, an enlightened vision, or even a temporary sensible solution. Conflict, condemnation, fear, and militarism dominate the airwaves; prophetic voices are silenced and meaningful notions of hope are muted. We live in dangerous times, and we also live at a moment of incredible opportunity. As our Chinese students often remind us, danger and opportunity are inseparably linked in a mysterious yin and yang dance. In this final chapter, we explore our ethical vision and enunciate our proleptic hope for humanity as we add our voices to those who search for wisdom and ethics in schools and society in our post–September 11 global community.

Rather than accepting differences and affirming diversity, most human societies have taken two other approaches to dealing with conflict and opposition. First, individuals and institutions often divide all of reality into dueling opposites: black or white, quantitative or qualitative, Western or Eastern, male or female, straight or gay, body or soul, dream or reality, Democrat or Republican, Catholic or Protestant, Muslim or Christian, reason or emotion, capitalist or socialist, Christian or Jew, liberal or conservative, moderate or radical, "for us" or "against us," and so on ad nauseam, with each opposite pole fighting the other for supremacy. The group with the most power dominates, subjugates, enslaves, colonizes, castigates, and seeks either to destroy the opposite pole or force it to conform to their values, religion, politics, and culture in a process of assimilation. This philosophical perspective, deeply ingrained in the global political consciousness, has contributed to an endless litany of moral catastrophes such as the Crusades, inquisitions, Salem witch burnings, McCarthyism, Nazism and the Holocaust, enslavement, genocide, ethnic cleansing, the Trail of Tears, gay bashing, violence by Hindu Tamils in Sri Lanka, Hutu and Tutsi genocide in central Africa, ethnic cleansing in the Balkans, apartheid in South Africa, cycles of violence between Palestinian Muslims and Israeli Jews, Japanese American imprisonment, war and nuclear confrontation between Pakistan and India, "comfort women" in World War II, the rape of Nanking, the bombing of Hiroshima and Nagasaki, and now the post–September 11 cycle of terrorism, censorship, and violence.

Bifurcation and domination infect schools as various groups vie for prestige, power, and control: academics versus athletics, major sports versus minor sports; men's athletics versus women's athletics; teachers versus students; administrators versus faculty; popular kids versus social outcasts; gifted versus remedial; rich versus poor; ethnic majority versus ethnic minorities; teacher unions versus school boards. We believe that schools and society do not have to be reduced to antagonistic bifurcations and conflicting divisions. Mutually beneficial cooperation is not only possible but also essential in a nuclear age, and schools must model peaceful, nonviolent, and democratic practices.

Second, some societies and institutions consider themselves enlightened because they deal with oppositional perspectives dialectically, with each extreme of the bifurcated pole presenting its values, one as a "thesis" and the other as the "antithesis." Through the use of Hegel's philosophical dialectic of logic, reason, dialogue, and compromise, the community then arrives at a "synthesis." This synthesis becomes the new thesis to which one can present a new antithesis. Reasonable people can then exist in harmony in a "melting pot" of community consensus. However, many people insist that this process erases uniqueness and diversity and perpetuates injustice as individuals are assimilated into the synthesis of conformity and forced to surrender their heritage. Others resist the mandatory suppression of their culture and values in the name of synthesis, consensus, or standards.

These traditional philosophical solutions to diversity and conflict through annihilation, assimilation, or synthesis have produced horrific injustices. Prophetic leaders search for alternatives in contemporary postmodern society that is open to diverse perspectives and transcends the need to eradicate, enculturate, colonize, or convert persons of different races, cultures, economic classes, linguistic patterns, genders, physical features, abilities, sexual orientations, religions, or cosmologies. North Americans and others privileged by their socioeconomic and ethnic status must remember that the world is far more diverse and complex when viewed through a holistic prism. Consider this analysis. If we could shrink the earth's population to a village of precisely one hundred people, with all the existing human ratios remaining the same, there would be eight Africans; twenty-one Europeans; fifty-seven Asians, Middle Easterners, Pacific Islanders, and Australians; and fourteen from the western hemisphere, with nine of these from South and Central America and five from North America; fifty-two would be female and forty-eight would be male; thirty would be white and seventy would be persons of color; thirty would be Christians with the majority being Catholic, and seventy would not be Christians with the majority being Muslim, Hindu, or Buddhist; approximately ninety would be heterosexual and ten would be homosexual, with some from each group identifying as bisexual, transgendered, or intersexual; six people would possess 60 percent of the world's wealth and most would be from the United States; eighty would live in substandard housing; seventy would be unable to read; fifty would suffer from malnutrition; one would be near death and one would be near childbirth; and only one would have a college education and own a computer. These numbers must convince the privileged to change the way they live and the way they relate to other people. These numbers must also be at the forefront of any discussion of ethics. The world is incredibly diverse, and the imbalance of resources and opportunity is a staggering injustice. This must change. This is the ethical imperative of the postmodern era, an imperative still ignored in the complacency and greed of post-911 and post-Enron United States.

When we consider our world from such a compressed perspective, the need for acceptance, understanding, and education becomes glaringly apparent. Moreover, the acceptance and affirmation of differences with respect for each individual person must become the goal of education and ethics. Schools and society must find a way to affirm all people in their diversity and differences (Nieto, 1996). We must encourage and support the development of a shared prophetic and democratic vision for a just and compassionate human community. Unfortunately, the fear of diversity and antagonism against minority persons is rampant. Consider the comments made to *Sports Illustrated* in 1999 by Major League Baseball pitcher John Rocker:

> Imagine having to take the 7 train to the ballpark looking like you're riding through Beirut next to some kid with purple hair next to some queer with AIDS right next to some dude who just got out of jail for the fourth time right next to some twenty-year-old mom with four kids. The biggest thing I don't like about New York are the foreigners. I'm not a very big fan of foreigners. You can walk an entire block in Times Square and not hear anybody speaking English. Asians and Koreans and Vietnamese and Indians and Russians and Spanish people and everything up there. How the hell did they get in this country? (Lum, 2001, p. 2)

Rocker's appalling attitude is not "an isolated aberration," as some claim in their effort to minimize the problem and deflect attention from racism, homophobia, and xenophobia. We must come to terms with the fact that John Rocker reflects the deeply entrenched bigotry and hatred that permeates our society, even if only a few like Rocker verbalize it publicly. His statement is especially repugnant because young people emulate athletes and often mimic their insensitive and ignorant attitudes. These comments earned Rocker—a multimillion dollar athlete—a two-week suspension and a two-thousand-dollar fine.

Patriots, Prophets, and Enemies of the State: Voices from Our Communities

Few voices speak to the events of September 11, 2001, in ways that are comforting to us. Most U.S. citizens appear to support the "war against terrorism" and George W. Bush as a basis for maintaining undefined "freedoms." Recent editorials in the *Akron Beacon Journal* illuminate this situation. According to Mary Thornburg, "History reveals that our flag and patriotic songs embody the ideals of a great and courageous nation" (Thornburg, 2001, p. A12). Virginia Druckenbrod wrote that people who wave flags in the faces of Arab Americans and demand that they return to "their country" are really freedom fighters. Ronald Neal comments that terrorists "will never succeed because U.S. gun sales are up 20% [and] doesn't this say something about how we as Americans view our individual freedoms" (Druckenbrod, 2001, p. A15). A few weeks later, Joseph R. Bennett wrote a scathing response to a suggestion that the United States follow the rule of law with terrorists and those who harbor them. Bennett began by referring to the earlier letter as "the most sickening example of anti-Americanism I have read" and then adds:

> The World Trade Center still smolders atop countless corpses. Osama Bin Laden fanatics poured into Afghanistan vowing a "holy jihad" to the death of the United States. Government buildings have been shut down and American citizens killed as a result of the mailing of Anthrax. Only an enemy of our country would not have his eyes opened to our justification in undertaking, by any available measures, a strategy to punish the culprits of these acts and to ensure against their repetition. (Bennett, 2001, p. A15)

Craig Parrish of Uniontown, Ohio, was also irate at what he viewed as anti-Americanism exhibited by some U.S. citizens:

> I, for one, am tired of this nation worrying about whether or not we are offending some individual or their culture. . . . There are a few things that those who have recently come to our country—and apparently some Native Americans—need to understand: First of all it is not our responsibility to continually try not to offend you in any way. The idea of America being a multicultural community has served only to dilute our sovereignty and national identity. As Americans we have our own culture, our own society, our own language, and our own lifestyle. This culture called the American way has been developed over centuries of struggle by millions of men and women who have sought freedom. . . . We are proud of our heritage and those who have defended our freedoms. We celebrate

Independence Day, Memorial Day, and Veterans Day with parades and proudly wave our flag. . . . But once you are done complaining, whining and griping about our flag, our pledge, our national motto or our way of life, I highly encourage you to take advantage of another great American freedom: the right to leave. (Parrish, 2001, p. A12)

Citizens are also quite passionate in their discussions of George W. Bush. When asked by the *Akron Beacon Journal* "How has George W. Bush performed as president so far?"opinions were dramatically polarized. Several people such as Donna Copeland wrote that "Bush exemplifies the best of what a leader can be." She continues, "He has restored our faith in the office. It was so badly degraded by our former president, no one thought it possible. People once again are proud of our country and our president" (Copeland, 2002, p. A9). Patricia Claar writes that Bush "brings dignity and leadership that we as a country so desperately need. . . . More than 6 million people of many faiths have joined the presidential Prayer Team organized by the Rev. Franklin Graham [Billy Graham's son who, it should be noted, was widely criticized for his reckless comments about Islam as an evil and wicked religion], promising to remember Bush and our government in daily prayer. . . . We thank President Bush. He is in our prayers and is doing a wonderful job" (Claar, 2002, p. A9). Elizabeth M. Saxer writes on the same day that "we couldn't ask for a better president at this time. I am sure that most people regardless of their political party, believe this. . . . Faith in our president and country is very important at this time" (Saxer, 2002, p. A9). And even after the Enron debacle was exposed, Annie Dill wrote on February 6 that "a president serves as a father figure, and Bush has been one we can look up to, rather than down on" (Dill, 2002, A9).

Not every citizen trusts or has confidence in the Bush administration and U.S. military operations in Afghanistan, however. Aurea Dumas suggests that although Bush may "look good," there is nothing "there":

Like Ronald Reagan before him, Bush is doing a good job of exactly what he was hired to do: give a performance. . . . Good grief, it's almost an embarrassment to listen to the man try to give an off-the-cuff answer to a reporter. It's painful to watch him search for a word and finally fall back on a few key phrases and cliches he's memorized for use on a few subjects. Like Reagan, Bush appears simply to be a photogenic front man for the little core group actually running the presidency, making the decisions and then having him make the public announcements as his own. (2002, p. A9)

Will Franz echos this doubtful disdain in his editorial on the same day:

If the question were whether he's using his phony-baloney war on terrorism to its best advantage in a sincere effort to divest us of our rights, I'd say definitely [he is performing well]. If the question were whether he's using the war to draw our attention away from important internal matters such as health care, the steel industry and jobs, I'd have to say yes, he's moving right along. When the dust has cleared, the people who proudly voted for George W. Bush will finally see that the scandal and corruption going on now in his administration make Clinton's dalliances look like what they actually were—personal and private indiscretions. . . . I hope that news of the Republican-controlled Carlyle Group, one of the world's largest private equity firms with more than $12 billion under management, eventually comes to light, and both Bushes, along with a litany of former high-ranking Republicans, are investors and board members. I hope it finally becomes obvious to the American people that the Carlyle Group makes its money from military conflicts and weapons spending. You don't think that would factor in as having anything to do with Bush's promise to send our soldiers anywhere in the world, for as along as it takes to fight terrorism, would it? (Franz, 2002, p. A9)

And, in one of the most compelling editorials we have read, Walter E. Davis discusses the assumptions that underlie many of our perceptions about war, George W. Bush, and freedom:

One set of assumptions about the United States is that it is a great democracy and fights for freedom and democracy at home and around the globe. Its wars are defined as "good." Its interventions and acts of atrocities are justified, simply mistakes or did not happen. The war in Afghanistan is primarily a struggle to the death with terrorists, who despise our freedoms, and will replace the repressive Taliban regime with a democratic one. Another is that the United States is the premier empire competing with lesser empires and nation-states for the world wealth (sometimes cooperating with or coercing cooperation from them). It intervenes around the globe and commits and supports atrocities consistent with imperialism. Its immediate goals in Afghanistan are to establish a pro-capitalist government, repressive or otherwise, and to establish more long-term military bases to further strengthen its hegemony in the region, in order to protect its own interests. Over the past several months, we have witnessed one of the most aggressive displays of nationalism ever seen, with the call for vengeance and war followed by unprecedented flag displays. There is no other nation-state or empire in which war and violence are more glorified than in America, and pro sports make a significant contribution to this. The recent cry for war and vengeance by the only "superpower" with the largest military system ever known confirms that militarism is a prominent characteristic of the United States. . . . One action has been to display the flag. Another has been to be openly critical of the U.S. government. (Davis, 2002, p. A9)

These editorials are a small sampling of public opinion in a midwestern city. They reveal how passionate opinions have become, as well as how the majority of Americans are exhibiting an enthusiasm for retaliation, nationalism, and flag waving that might make John Rocker proud. They also illuminate how the eternal vigilance of government that Thomas Jefferson called the price of liberty is frequently viewed as unpatriotic by the U.S. government and many U.S. citizens. We lament this tragic situation.

A particularly disconcerting event occurred at the commencement ceremony of California State University in December 2001. Janis Besler Heaphy, president and publisher of the *Sacramento Bee,* was the commencement speaker for the crowd of over ten thousand graduates and guests. About five minutes into her nine-minute address, she began to raise questions about civil liberties violations. When she urged that citizens safeguard the rights to free speech, against unlawful detainment, and for a fair trial, she was loudly booed. When she wondered what would happen if racial profiling became routine, the audience cheered. Ms. Heaphy tried to finish, but when she argued that the Constitution makes it our right to challenge government policies, a clapping chant and heckling forced her off the stage. Romona Ripston, executive director of the American Civil Liberties Union chapter in Los Angeles, comments, "We've always known that if you took the Bill of Rights to the street and asked people to sign it, you would be unable to get a majority of Americans to do so" (Egan, 2001, p. B1).

This incident gives us an indication why Japanese Americans were interned during World War II and why Leonard Peltier, a leader of the American Indian Movement in the 1970s, is still behind bars today. In the latter case, U.S. political elites were becoming concerned that Native American freedom fighters were organizing to reclaim some of their ancestral land that had been stolen by the U.S. government. To counter this "radical" movement, the FBI propped up a pro-government Lakota leader on the Pine Ridge Reservation in South Dakota in ways and for reasons similar to U.S. support for Latin American dictators. Slush funds, goon squads, and weapons were brought onto the reservation to quell the growing despair and unrest directed at the U.S. government. As it turns out, two undercover agents entered the Pine Ridge Reservation and engaged in a shootout with AIM members under circumstances that have never been fully explained. The U.S. government was determined to destroy AIM at all costs, even if it meant lying to imprison one of its leaders. In what has been called by many civil rights leaders and lawyers one of the greatest travesties of justice in U.S. history, Leonard Peltier was sentenced to two consecutive life terms for murdering two special agents. Despite a valid argument of self-defense, no proof that Peltier's gun could fire the bullets that killed the agents, obvious intimidation and coercion of witnesses by the government, and a confession of murder some years later by a non-AIM member, Peltier was convicted by an all-white jury and sentenced to two consecutive life terms.

Some said it could never happen again, but now we understand the emotions that propel the public to antidemocratic hysteria. Look at our willingness to accept the imprisonment of Muslims such as Pastor Rabih Haddad in a cell at the Metropolitan Correctional Center in downtown Chicago as we write. Haddad has been locked up in solitary confinement since December 14 without criminal charges being filed, denied bond, and without the government releasing any of the alleged "evidence" against him. Haddad, along with thousands of Muslims, has been racially profiled by the U.S. government for being Arab and Muslim. Educators cannot teach about historical events in isolation from current realities of racial profiling or Native American oppression or we risk perpetuating and repeating grave injustices that lead to the demise of democratic freedoms.

Perhaps we underestimate the antidemocratic urges of U.S. citizens. Perhaps we are too optimistic and too utopian to relate to contemptuous calls for vengeance by our relatives and neighbors who sport U.S. flags on their cars or who are trying to imitate the fashions of the Afghani freedom fighters. We do not find humor in the fashionable jokes such as the bumper sticker that reads, "Osama Bin Laden and al-Qaeda—Endangered Feces." We are disturbed by what we see and hear in many public places. I (Dana) came across a flier stapled above a urinal in a local restaurant that juxtaposed a few lines of italicized writing with a Boeing 767 and a variety of tanks, missiles, war planes, and attack helicopters. The message read, "Dear Mr. Bin Laden, We appreciate you taking such a strong interest in the American Airline Industry. Now that you are familiar with Boeing's line of commercial aircraft, we would like to get you acquainted with Boeing's other fine products. We look forward to demonstrating their capabilities to you in person in the very near future. Sincerely, America." We believe these jokes are made in misplaced anger, hatred, and nationalism and serve only to postpone understanding and prevent sustainable futures.

Even before September 11, we heard few voices that resonated with love, compassion, empathy, and introspection. We recall a newspaper editorial by Deborah Maurer from Medina, Ohio, two years ago. Her words portray what many white, middle-class, patriotic Americans and educators may believe, but are afraid to say, about children living in poverty:

> The only "intended pain" that I see was inflicted on these "suffering children" [was] by the two people who brought them into the world without regard to how they would be financially supported. Perhaps if the parents had thought of their children's futures as they were conceiving them, there would be no "suffering." Perhaps if these children learn that sitting home, waiting for the welfare check as a non-productive member of society doesn't pay off, they will then have the incentive to not follow in their parents' chosen way of life. I feel that a way to reinforce the values of work vs. welfare in the children of recipients would be mandatory field trips in which children are given bus tours of the suburbs to see how we, the working people, live. This would be especially useful to the younger children, perhaps second and third generation welfare recipients. Perhaps when these children see that if you get a job you can buy a home, cars, boats and take family vacations to places like Disneyworld, they will confront their parents and ask why: Why don't you want to work? Why do we get food stamps? Why don't we have warm clothes? Why do we live in subsidized apartments? And, finally, why don't you want to give us a better life? (Maurer, 1999, p. B7)

We wonder how Deborah Maurer is explaining the events of September 11 to her neighbors. When it comes to the thousands of deaths of children due to massive starvation and Allied bombing, will Deborah Maurer argue—like so many others—that the children's parents are to blame? Why don't the parents of the starving children leave the country, find a job, and provide for their families? Don't the Afghani people understand? If they would only adopt the values of U.S. working people, they too could spend their money on Disneyland, SUVs, boats, luxury goods, and junk food. Perhaps we could fly everyone around the world to Medina, Ohio, to see what they are missing. Maybe this is the type of compassionate conservatism to which George W. Bush referred in his campaign for president.

We also encounter many educators who denigrate parents for taking drugs, not attending school conferences, committing nonviolent crimes, and collecting welfare. "Since these parents don't care and aren't providing for their children, they shouldn't be allowed to be parents," some say. We respond by asking why the "caring parents" allow one country to consume 50 percent of the world's food and 80 percent of the world's resources at a time when one person dies of starvation every three seconds. What do "caring parents" do when one-fourth of children under age fourteen in underdeveloped countries are working seventy hours a week in factories owned by Nike, JC Penny, Gap, J.Crew, Mattell, and Hasbro and earning barely enough to eat? What would "caring people" do if they knew that the lives of 21 million children could be saved if U.S. banks released them from the hostage of their debts (Madeley, 1999, p. 21)? How do "caring people" respond to a situation in the United States in which there are 268 billionaires, 35 million people living below the poverty level, 40 million people without health insurance, and one in five children going to school hungry? Sadly, our challenging questions are seldom addressed. Disinterest, disconnection, and dislocation are too prevalent today. Many global problems were considered overwhelming or impossible to understand even before September 11. If this is the case, then we have an even greater responsibility to inspire our students with a variety of explanations and alternatives in a millennium that has been ushered in with terrorism, war, hatred, and nationalism. This must be the focus of educational ethics in the twenty-first century.

Educators are working to uncover the contexts of September 11 in a culture in which the mainstream media celebrate retaliation with a theatrical roar of triumph:

Michael Kelly of the *Washington Post* wrote, "American pacifists are on the side of future mass murders of Americans, they are objectively pro-terrorist, evil, and liars." Jonathan Alter of *Newsweek* wonders whether torture would "jump-start the stalled investigation into the greatest crime in American history" while he urges pacifists to shut up because "it's kill or be killed." Bill O'Reilly on Fox TV, Dallas, stated "the US should bomb the Afghan infrastructure to rubble—the airport, the power plants, their water facilities, the roads. The Afghans are responsible for the Taliban. We should not target civilians, but if they don't rise up against this criminal government, they starve, period." A. M. Rosenthal of the *Washington Times* wants the US to bomb Iraq, Libya, Sudan, Iran, and Syria in addition to Afghanistan. Ann Coulter, formerly of the *National Review*, responds to terrorism by stating that the US should "invade their countries, kill their leaders, and convert them to Christianity." Steve Dunleavy of the *New York Post* writes, "The response to this unimaginable 21st-century Pearl Harbor should be as simple as it is swift—kill the bastards. A gunshot between the eyes, blow them to smithereens, poison them if you have to. As for cities or countries that host these worms, bomb them into basketball courts." Rich Lowry of the *National Review* suggests, "If we flatten part of Damascus or Tehran or whatever it takes, that is part of the solution." Charles Krauthammer of the *Washington Post* writes, "We are fighting because the bastards killed 5,000 of our people, and if we do not kill them, they are going to kill us again." Thomas Friedman of the *New York Times* is quick to declare, "We have to fight the terrorists as if there were no rules" and only the perverted "give peace a chance." And George Will of the *Washing-ton Post* notes, "The Bush administration is telling the country that there is some dying to be done. The goal is not to 'bring terrorists to justice,' which suggests bringing them into sedate judicial settings—lawyers, courtrooms, due process, all preceded by punctilious readings of Miranda rights. Rather, the goal is destruction of enemies." (Mokhiber & Weissman, 2001) President Bush has even escalated the belligerence by calling Iraq, Iran, and North Korea an "Axis of Evil" in his State of the Union address in January 2002. Bush's lack of recognition of negotiations in process during the Clinton administration with North Korea (however tentative and strained) and his lack of insight into the growing urge toward democracy among young people in Iran is a tragic oversight. The preferred rhetoric is retaliate, isolate, intimidate, kill, flatten, starve, poison, and bomb: Is this an agenda of democracy, freedom, and justice, or a rhetoric exposing deeper societal support of violence, brutality, and imperialism?

This is the same "patriotic" language that flared up amongst the media, government officials, and citizens as groups of Japanese Americans were stripped of their liberties and their property and placed in degrading internment camps during World War II, and when African Americans were jailed, beaten, and lynched as they tried to integrate "whites only" schools and restaurants and secure the right to vote. It is the same language used when the U.S. military bombed Kosovo, Iraq, Libya, Somalia, and Panama, and when Native Americans were repeatedly forced off their ancestral lands. Today the language of revenge and the message of the "war against terrorism" in presidential speeches and mass media direct our anger toward an external "enemy" and an "axis of evil" while numbing us to historical injustices and genocide perpetrated against peoples in our own country. Ohio resident Teresa M. Shimp makes this point in her recent editorial (Shimp, 2001):

> Most Americans believe Sioux Indians should own clear title and power over the Black Hills once and for all time. The Indians are a clear part of the American heritage and deserve our respect and benefits. Our oldest authentic Sioux habitat, the Black Hills, is being desecrated like no other time in history. . . . This cannot go on—not if we as a people have any real integrity for history or antiquity forthcoming. The Indians are given no such respect in this age, even though they have been forced to live in deplorable conditions as they hang on to the integrity of a treaty that gave them the rights to something they already owned. They have been cheated repeatedly throughout history. We travel thousands of miles over seas, spending millions on recognizing foreign peoples' rights to their proper homelands, their suffering children and families along with sufferings from all kinds of illness. But our native Indians live worse than those seen suffering overseas in concentration camps. We even build memorials to the foreign sufferers, but our own Indians should get our attention first by title to their own promised lands. (p. A12)

African Americans as well have much to shudder about when it comes to the waging of war and the "routing out" of enemies. A passage from the Black Radical Congress on September 13, 2001, makes this chilling point:

The Black Radical Congress (BRC) strongly condemns the horrific terror attacks that occurred on September 11, 2001. As a people that has survived over 400 years of genocidal oppression on these shores, we are all too familiar with the human suffering caused by both terrorism and racial hatred. From the amputations, beatings, and rapes of Chattel Slavery, to the New York City Draft Riots of 1863, to the post-Reconstruction terrorism of the Ku Klux Klan, to the Tulsa Race Riots of 1921, to the government sponsored Counter-Intelligence Program (COINTELPRO) of the 1960s, to the contemporary state-sanctioned police murder and brutality we are fighting today, we as Black people have lots of experience with the horrors of terrorism in the U.S., as it has too frequently been directed against us. That is why we must show our full and unqualified support and compassion for all those suffering as a result of this horrible tragedy, most of whom have come to experience terrorism for the first time, as *we continue our 400+ year struggle to rid ourselves of this evil, both domestically and around the world.* (BRC, 2001, p. 1; emphasis added)

My (Dana) seven-month-old son was recently given a shirt emblazoned with fire trucks, police cars, and tanks. On the pocket was written, "To the rescue." We believe it is essential to celebrate the heroic efforts of the people who responded to the carnage of September 11. We also believe that taking appropriate action to protect and defend ourselves from terrorist attacks is necessary—in accord with time-honored traditions of human rights, protection of civilians, prisoner of war conventions, good faith negotiations, repudiation of collateral damage, and the like. At the same time, we must remain vigilant to ensure that our rush to "rescue" and "free" people and lands is not overwrought with ethnocentric, imperialistic, and corporate fervor or with a lack of historical analysis. George W. Bush is neither our father nor our savior. He has been effective in striking fear into the hearts and minds of U.S. citizens, but it remains unclear whether he has the ability to understand the conditions of democracy, human rights, Geneva convention protocols for treatment of prisoners, compassion, or peace.

Our news anchormen and anchorwomen also appear "anchored" more to supporting war and George W. Bush than to practicing investigative journalism, as evidenced by the scant attention being paid to the "collateral damage"—the death of civilians. The *London Guardian* has run stories and headlines that graphically describe how U.S. helicopters have chased down and killed women and children in addition to bombing farming villages such as Niazi Kala. U.S. newspapers have shied away from these stories. Dan Rather, who has a major influence on what many citizens believe, announced that when his president speaks of war, he will get in line to support him. But what if George W. Bush is more interested in securing the fortunes of his family and friends in the military, defense, and oil industries than he is in retaliating for September 11 or securing democracy? Is it our role as educators, citizens, and journalists to get involved only in the ways the power elite demands? What dangers lie before us if we agree to get in the patriotic line like obedient sons and daughters and refuse to discuss alternatives? What are the long-term results of indiscriminate retaliation and destruction? Will we breed more terrorists in the process?

I (Dana) can speak to the power and scope of manufactured consent from personal experience with print and television media. In almost every interview I have granted to the press about my research on high-stakes testing, my condemnation of corporate influence on educational and political reform has been edited out. This occurred in my interviews with the *Cleveland Plain Dealer, Cleveland Fox News,* and even editorials I have had published in newspapers around the state. Is it surprising that many of the corporations I chose to implicate such as MBNA and British Petroleum were major advertisers in the newspapers? I can also speak to the extent to which state, federal, and local governments dictate and direct public opinion as opposed to engaging it. This became especially obvious to me when my testimony on poverty, hunger, and economic disparity before the Governor's Commission for Student Success (a group of CEOs, bureaucrats, politicians, and a handpicked teacher and administrator chosen by Ohio Governor Taft to stem the tide of growing opposition to high-stakes testing) was completely dismissed as unimportant. It is obvious that the "public forums" the commission hosted were developed in partnership with the Ohio Department of Education as a public relations stunt to convince citizens of the need for—their consent for—high-stakes testing and greater state control (see Rapp, in press). Not only was public debate discouraged, but it was also thwarted on almost every occasion. When I take groups of students to these forums, an overwhelming number describe the community forums as "directed," "predetermined," "autocratic," "insulting," and "Stalinistic." One commission decision maker was brazen enough to declare that his commission and business leaders knew what was best for students more than local people and communities. The mass media in Ohio, with one exception, chose not to expose the undemocratic and manipulative impulses behind the commission's cover, thereby furthering the manufacturing of consent. Unfortunately, the public has bought in.

As these examples suggest, we live and teach in a time when making ethical decisions demands that we research, investigate, and expose the multiple perspectives surrounding these issues, even those that are not flattering to U.S. authorities. In short, we must teach with conviction within a sea of misinformation, propaganda, advertising, and hidden agendas.

We are always amazed at the number of students, parents, and teachers who do not know they have the right to opt their children out of state tests. This is disturbing because many of us know how standardized tests demoralize and de-skill teachers and students, as well as destabilize local control of educational curricula. In Ohio, some of the forces behind "higher standards" and yearly testing are the same as those that represent for-profit prisons and stiffer sentences for younger juvenile offenders. So when representatives from groups such as FairTest discuss with our students the procedures for opting out of tests, teachers become outraged that they have been misled by the state, the mass media, and their administrators. "We were never told that we had an alternative," they say. Their reaction is similar when they read Howard Zinn's *People's History of the United States* (1995) or James Loewen's *Lies My Teacher Told Me* (1995) for the first time. Keep this context in mind as we recall the following story.

In August 2001, I (Dana) telephoned each of the elementary schools in a local town to ask about my rights to opt my child out of Ohio proficiency tests. In all seven cases, the principal conveyed clearly that according to state law, students are required to take the tests. "You have no options," I was told. I didn't challenge the principals directly, but I did call the superintendent of Pupil Services to express my dismay at how I was being misled. Our conversation was not pleasant. I was told that "I was looking to inflame and damage the district" by raising these issues publicly and that the district would like to work with me. The superintendent confessed to some degree that the tests were not in the best interests of all students and that curricula had suffered significantly in spirit and diversity. She stated that because the tests were "required" by state law, parents could not opt children out. Without addressing the deeper complexities of students rights, I responded that the state often uses the word *require* instead of *recommend* to mislead parents and assert its agenda. "It's like immunization. The state tells me that immunizations are 'required,' but in reality, they are recommended, and I can opt my child out for philosophical, religious, or medical reasons in every U.S. state." I referred her to Ohio Statute 3313.67.1 to make my point. In the case of proficiency tests, my daughter is not "required" to take any of the Ohio tests. "You know it and the district knows it," I said. The most disconcerting point in the conversation came when the superintendent of Pupil Services communicated that if parents found out about their rights, there would be outrage and distrust directed toward the district. Moreover, the district would lose funding from the state of Ohio for each child who did not take the test. My final question to the superintendent was, "How many children will have to be sacrificed on the alter of high-stakes testing, lies, and deceit before adults say enough is enough?"

The overuse and abuse of high-stakes testing is an issue that affects all educators. Every teacher has horror stories. Consider the story told to us by a student teacher in a fourth-grade classroom. On one of the first days of testing, a young girl looked pale and sickly. Like many students on testing days, she was stressed out and had caught a cold as a result. Barbara, the student teacher, noticed the child throw up in an airplane vomit bag that she hid in her sweater. Barbara grabbed the child and rushed her to the nurse's office. The child's mother was gravely concerned as she arrived. "These damn tests. Leslie is an A student and she used to love school. But now she can't sleep before test days, and several friends have encouraged us to put her on anti-anxiety medication during testing periods." Barbara blurted out, "You know that Leslie doesn't have to take the tests. They are optional. I'll grab some information for you." Both mother and child were greatly relieved.

The next day Barbara and Mrs. Jones, her mentor teacher, were called into the principal's office and chastised for giving the parent information about opting out. Barbara's supervising teacher was unaware of what Barbara had done the day before, and she was worried about how she would be received by her principal and coworkers. The principal informed Mrs. Jones that Barbara had "misled" Leslie's mother. He denounced the move as "unprofessional" and asked, "What would happen if we let the parents of all the good test takers know they had the option to opt their children out?

Not only would we lose money from the state, but we would look terrible in the eyes of the community because our scores would go down. We don't want that! I want you to call Leslie's mother and let her know that her child must take the tests. No options. Now get in line and don't create any more havoc!" Barbara was quietly outraged at the principal's callousness and deceit. Her mentor teacher detested high-stakes tests but worried more about being seen as a "fink" or "traitor" by her principal and other faculty in the school.

Leslie was informed by phone that night that she was required to take the tests. She was back in school the next day. Although Leslie retched periodically throughout the two-hour testing period, she held in her vomit. Two other children were not so fortunate. They could not control their retching. As Barbara tells it, they rushed to Mrs. Jones's desk and asked to go to the bathroom to vomit. "No! You will have to use the garbage can in the corner if you want to throw up, and you cannot leave until everyone is finished taking the test." Apparently the principal had informed teachers that they were not to allow "good test takers" to leave the room to throw up because, according to state law, their scores would be discounted. All twenty-four students continued taking their tests in a room stinking of vomit and lies.

What should Barbara and her mentor teacher have done in this situation? What other lies, myths, and misinformation are fed to kids and parents in school, by the state, or by the mass media? Should we write off the episodes of vomiting, stress, and emotional drain like we write off "collateral damage" in wars? And who benefits when teachers who speak out against exploitation, manipulation, and lies are labeled "traitor" and "unprofessional"? We encourage you to keep these questions in mind as you reflect on your reactions to school shootings such as the Columbine massacre and why they occurred. We argue that if children are disrespected to the point of being lied to, forced to vomit, intimidated, dehumanized, and terrorized, then they will seek revenge in any way they can—even if it means suicide and slaughter. The same may hold true for many cases of terrorism. If people like Mrs. Jones, Barbara, and Leslie are placed in perpetual states of fear until they are willing to overlook deception and exploitation, they may be more able and willing to blindly accept and follow the advice of governmental leaders when it comes to the internment of Japanese citizens, the imprisonment of Leonard Peltier, and the profiling of Arabs and Muslims. "A population blinded by fear will ultimately turn to 'Big Brother' to protect them from nonexistent and/or wholly manufactured threats both in the U.S. and abroad" (McGowan, 2001, p. 127). For example, constant government warnings of terrorist attacks and predictions that the "war on terrorism" may last indefinitely mire citizens in fear, thus extinguishing possibilities for dissent. Powerful elites in the U.S. government, business, media, and the military create these situations of entrenched fear in order to solidify their power and advance their privileged agenda. This is true in education and in war.

Do you remember the image of the Palestinian children waving flags and supposedly cheering the deaths of the U.S. citizens who died in the World Trade Center? How did it make you feel? Were you disturbed? Disgusted? Angry? If your reaction to this image was anything like ours when we first witnessed it, you were outraged. How could anyone celebrate the death and destruction of September 11? Now consider that the image of the children cheering was probably taken in 1991 as a Palestinian crowd was celebrating the death of Israeli soldiers whom they believed to be terrorists. Are you angry now? Do you feel betrayed? Why did the mass media run this clip without fully checking its source? To what extent has mass media inflamed our vengeful reactions and manufactured our consent for war and retaliation? Is this any different from the false stories run by the mass media about Iraqi soldiers ripping Kuwaiti children from their incubators when the United States invaded Iraq in 1991? What other stories are false? We have friends who work for major media companies who tell us that this type of incident is quite common in a market in which ratings trump commitments to quality assurance, reliability, and equal treatment of different voices.

Historian and social activist Howard Zinn (1995, 1997) writes that the tendency of many people with power is to lie to maintain that power. Remember Bill Clinton's lies about Monica Lewinsky, Ronald Reagan's deception about Iran-Contra, and Richard Nixon's lies about Watergate? Remember the lies we were told about the sinking of the *Maine*, the Bay of Pigs, and the Gulf of Tonkin? Now consider the mixed support offered for war and George W. Bush's leadership by citizens discussed earlier in the chapter. What other wars should Dan Rather have supported? The war on women's right to vote? The Civil War to protect states' rights for slavery? Would Dan Rather and other journalists have stood in line with the experts and governmental leaders who approved of the genocide of Native Americans? The internment of Japanese Americans? The lynchings in early twentieth century United States? The hate crimes against gay men and African Americans? Would he have stood in line with experts such as former U.S. Secretary of State Henry Kissinger and former Secretary of Defense Robert McNamara, who masterminded the deaths of fifty thousand U.S. citizens and two million Vietnamese people? (McNamara, Blight, & Brigham, 1999)

In a popular "Kids with Character" series run by the *Akron Beacon Journal,* elementary students are considered stellar citizens and their pictures can appear in the paper if they "always listen when someone else is speaking, follow rules and instructions, and always remember to say thank you." Former U.S. Secretary of Education and drug czar William Bennet preaches this same principal in his hugely popular *Book of Virtues* in which he retells children's stories to inculcate passive submission to parental authority. Recall the child abuse artwork of Edward Kienholz and Nancy Kienholz in Chapter 3, the series of installations that depict child abandonment, incest, rape, and abuse. Recall also the stories in Chapter 2 of Father Gilbert Gauthier in Louisiana and Father John Geoghan in Massachusetts, both convicted pedophile priests. Silence is not always a virtue; it can be abusive and deadly.

Now consider what has happened to Enron, one of the most emulated and profitable corporations in United States. Enron, headquartered in Houston, with influential board members such as Wendy Graham, the spouse of Senator Phil Graham of Texas, was lauded by business theorists as the "quintessential 21st-century corporation" (Krugman, 2001a). Economist Paul Krugman writes the following about Enron's bankruptcy (the largest in U.S. history) at the end of November 2001, which was barely noticed because of the media attention to the war in Afghanistan: "The [Enron] case shows how adept corporate executives have become at shifting risk away from themselves and onto others, in particular onto their employees. Enron's leaders have walked away from the debacle chastened but very, very rich. Many of the employees have lost their life savings" (p. A23).

Enron employees, like many other workers in corporations, had their retirement money invested in Enron. The corporation's now-famous "lockdown" forced employees to remain invested in the company's stock during the firm's death spiral. Some may argue that the workers accepted the risk of the market when they invested in Enron stock, and their loss should only be counted in the amount of the original investment. However, deceit by Enron leaders and their inside collaborators, many of whom made millions of dollars, explains the bigger picture of manipulation and greed. Workers lost everything: their jobs, 401K retirement, and security vanished in a few short weeks in the fall of 2001. Corporate leaders left "very, very rich." It is also interesting that Enron, a major financial contributor to George W. Bush and other politicians, was one of the first corporations to receive millions of dollars in federal support immediately following the September 11 attacks: $1.4 billion for IBM; $833 million for General Motors; $671 million for General Electric; $572 million for Chevron Texaco; $254 million for Enron. What happened to the needs of small business owners and displaced workers in New York City? Where was the protection for investors and workers? Paul Krugman (2001b) concludes:

> The Enron experiment was, in essence, about doing away with regulation—regulation of prices, regulation of financial trading. [Do you remember the savings and loan scandal of the 1980s?] Most of these regulations had their origin in fear that consumers, workers and investors would be exploited by those whom Theodore Roosevelt called "malefactors of great wealth." The great economic lesson of the 20th century was that to work, a market system needs a little help from the government: regulations to prevent abuses, active monetary policy to fight recessions. The debacle in Houston demonstrates that this great lesson has lost its relevance. (p. A-27)

The lesson is clear. Students, workers, and ordinary citizens can become expendable pawns in a cycle of corporate greed, graft, and political maneuvering if we relinquish oversight, independent audits, and ethical standards. Krugman (2002) even concludes, "Unlike the terrorist attack . . . the Enron scandal clearly *was* about us. It told us things about ourselves that we probably should have known, but had managed not to see. I predict that in the years ahead Enron, not September 11, will come to be seen as the greater turning point in U.S. society" (p. A27; author's emphasis).

Despite what we see and hear on CNN, FOX, MSNBC, NBC, ABC, and CBS and through the public relations of our government, dissenters' voices are being offered in nonmainstream media venues. We encourage readers to visit various alternative sources for untangling the one-sided polemics used to spike ratings on most mass media outlets and hearing the wisdom. For insight and inspiration, explore magazines, websites, newspapers, and radio stations that cite *The Progressive, UTNE, Mother Jones, Sojourners,* the Institute for Alternative Journalism, Media Watchdog, Media Foundation, FAIR (Fairness and Accuracy in reporting), Alliance for Community Media, Alliance for Cultural Democracy, Greenpeace, Human Rights Watch, Amnesty International, *The Advocate, YES, The Sun, Souls, Substance, Rethinking Schools, The Rouge Forum, Radical Teacher, Adbusters, AFSCOLE@aol.com, portsideMod@netscape.net, PeaceNet, Corporate Crime Reporter, The Nation, In These Times, Covert Action Quarterly, Essential Information,* and the *Oregon Peace Worker.* Don Angelo, writer for the *Peace Worker,* offered a context and explanation for the war on Afghanistan that is all but missing from the reports of Peter Jennings and Dan Rather:

> The U.S. has a long history of capitalistic imperialism, supporting dictators rather than democracies, toppling governments such as the Sandinistas in Nicaragua, invading countries such as Cuba (Bay of Pigs), Granada, or Panama, murdering heads of state such as Salvador Allende in Chile, installing or protecting our own stooges such as the Shah of Iran, the ruling family of Saudi Arabia, and the various presidents of South Vietnam. We don't care if Union Carbide accidentally kills 20,000 in Bhopal [India] and maims 50,000 more. We don't care if the CIA sponsored contras murdered 30,000 civilians in Nicaragua, we don't care if . . . we support 26 of the 35 [undemocratic countries around the world. We don't care] if the President's son [George W. Bush] calls up the trade minister of Argentina and says it would be in Argentina's best interest to award the natural gas contract to the Enron bid. Yes, our own Dubya did that. Enron built the pipeline to Chile, and donated $100,000 to Dubya's gubernatorial campaign. (2001, p. 6)

Political elites in the United States have as much to gain from protecting Enron as they do in the war in Afghanistan, according to one of journalism's loudest dissenters, George Monbiot of the London-based *Guardian.* In 1998, Dick Cheney, now U.S. vice president but then chief executive of a major oil services company, was quite clear about why he would be in Afghanistan: "I cannot think of a time when we have had a region emerge as suddenly to become as strategically significant as the Caspian. But the oil and gas there is worthless until it is moved. The only route which makes both political and economic sense is through Afghanistan" (Monbiot, 2001, p. 1). How many students will read accounts in the media or their textbooks about Cheney's ties to the oil and gas industry and how these connections are related to the war in Afghanistan? How many children will read this excerpt from a speech delivered in 1933 by Major General Smedley Butler of the U.S. Marine Corps who identified many U.S. war efforts as economic in origin?

> War is just a racket. A racket is best described, I believe, as something that is not what it seems to the majority of people. Only a small inside group knows what it is about. It is conducted for the benefit of the very few at the expense of the masses. I helped make

Mexico, especially Tampico, safe for American oil interests in 1914. I helped make Haiti and Cuba a decent place for the National City Bank boys to collect revenues in. I helped in the raping of half a dozen Central American republics for the benefits of Wall Street. The record of racketeering is long. I helped purify Nicaragua for the international banking house of Brown Brothers in 1909–1912. I brought light to the Dominican Republic for American sugar interests in 1916. In China I helped to see to it that Standard Oil went its way unmolested. (Mokhiber & Weissman, 2001, p. 1)

Unlike Dan Rather, actor and activist Peter Ustinov did not stand in line to support "leaders." Ustinov argued that there can be experts in little things, but never experts in moral things. As a child, Ustinov probably heard an adult speak up in church to say that ministers are human like everyone else. He recognized that his calling was not to shut up and follow the orders of his boss, mayor, governor, state department of education superintendent, ministers, bankers, doctors, and president. So does our getting in line on the war on terrorism exhibit patriotism, character, and religious conviction, or a refusal to support those who are "leading" us? Would we get in line if President Bush were to declare that in these trying times U.S. citizens need to band together to shift 99 percent of the resources to 1 percent of the population by slashing health care coverage, ending social security, and eliminating all environmental protections? What would have happened if Helen Keller, Dorothy Day, Rosa Parks, Martin Luther King Jr., Aung San Suu Kyi, Chief Seattle, Jesus, and the Dalai Lama had got in line? Each of these prophets was considered an enemy of the state at the time of his or her activism. We raise these questions not to denigrate our nation nor to be unpatriotic, but to engage our colleagues and students in a broader debate about the complexities of war and the convictions demanded at this dangerous time.

When we look beneath the assorted responses to the horror of September 11 and the deceit of Enron, whether on CNN or in our classrooms, we wonder who is speaking to the hopes and fears of the next generations. Who has the prophetic strength of Wendell Berry to ask if the Bush administration's $500 billion ten-year arms contract with Lockheed Martin will actually breed more violence to justify its existence? We agree with Maxine Greene: "Where oppression or exploitation or pollution or even pestilence is perceived as natural, as a given, there can be no freedom. Where people cannot name alternatives or imagine a better state of things they are likely to remain anchored or submerged" (1995, p. 50). Educating for justice, responsibility, and peace must become a priority in schools and society. We concur with Herman E. Daly and John B. Cobb Jr. (1994) in their book *For the Common Good: Redirecting the Economy toward Community, the Environment, and a Sustainable Future* that we must have a paradigm shift in the way we think:

Yes there is hope. On a hotter planet, with lost deltas and shrunken coastlines, under a more dangerous sun, with less arable land, more people, fewer species of living things, a legacy of poisonous wastes, and much beauty irrevocably lost, there will still be the possibility that our children's children will learn at last to live as a community among communities. Perhaps they will also learn to forgive this generation its blind commitment to ever-greater consumption. Perhaps they will even appreciate its belated efforts to leave them a planet still capable of supporting life in community. (1994, p. 400)

As we documented in Chapter 4, the ecological degradation of the planet is actually intensifying. The urgency of a new vision of ecological sustainability is obvious, and clearly the environmental issues are directly related to economic policies, corporate greed, the gluttonous consumption by a few, and the manufactured consent by most that supports the violence, terrorism, and war that plague the human community. These conditions are now *the* ethical imperative for education. Let us turn for a moment to see how various people are using religious and spiritual views to shape their reaction to the crises before us.

Death Penalties and War: Revelations from the Pulpit

When we see "God Bless America" attached to almost every storefront, automobile, and church, in addition to an increasing number of television commercials, we wonder where people are turning for inspiration and insight. Do citizens feel they need their God's support, strength, and help in order for the United States to make it through trying times? Do they believe, like Jerry Falwell and Pat Robertson, that the events of September 11 are a sign that God is punishing the United States because of our tolerance of civil liberties, homosexuals, feminists, multiculturalists, and others? Do some actually believe that the United States is the chosen nation and George W. Bush is an imperial intermediary between a Christian godhead and the world? Why do some of our neighbors place bumper stickers on their cars that read, "It's time to kick some terrorist ass" next to others that read "What Would Jesus Do?" and "Real Men Love Jesus"? We share these questions with you as we seek ecumenical inspiration in the midst of terrorism, war, greed, and economic bankruptcy. Exploring the issue of capital punishment might help us gain some insight into these phenomena.

I (Patrick) have always felt uncomfortable with capital punishment. As a young high school teacher in south Louisiana, I often spoke out forcefully against state-sanctioned murder. I cited statistics on the expense of implementing the death penalty, the unbalanced application of the death penalty on racial minorities and the poor, the ability of the wealthy to buy their way out of sentencing, and the hundreds of well-documented cases of innocent people on death row and a few even being put to death—a phenomenon that led the Republican governor of Illinois to place a moratorium on capital punishment in his state in the late 1990s. The fact that the United States is one of the only industrialized democracies to impose capital punishment should cause us to ponder our politics. However, support for the death penalty remains strong in the United States, and my students have always been no exception. Why are vengeance, retribution, and hatred so deeply rooted in some societies?

On November 5, 1977, I was decorating the Rice Festival building in New Iberia, Louisiana, with a group of my students in preparation for the homecoming dance. I was a young teacher at Catholic High School, and I very much enjoyed the extracurricular activities. One of my favorite students was David LeBlanc, a strapping young man with an infectious smile. David was in my English class, and he volunteered to help me with projects after school on numerous occasions. I had not noticed that David and his girlfriend Loretta Bourque were missing at the dance, and it was not until early the next morning that the terrible news of David and Loretta's murder was confirmed when a sheriff's deputy brought a senior ring to the school where the principal and several teachers had gathered. David's ring was the only identifying artifact at the crime scene, and we were asked to confirm the initials "DAL"on the ring: David Augustin LeBlanc, December 21, 1960–November 5, 1977. The senior class offered the following tribute to David in the class yearbook: "David pursued a very active life. He enjoyed his friends and loved his school. His memory lightens up our lives with the thought that we too can live as fully and purely as he did." Whenever I discuss capital punishment, I always begin by recalling the memory of David LeBlanc and Loretta Bourque and the terrible tragedy inflicted on them, their families, and their friends by their ruthless murderers—brothers Elmo and Patrick Sonnier.

Many people will recognize the story of David and Loretta because their murder was made famous in a film titled *Dead Man Walking* in 1996. Susan Sarandon won the Academy Award for best actress for her portrayal of Sr. Helen Prejean, a Catholic nun who worked in Hope House for the poor in New Orleans and was inspired to visit the Sonnier brothers in Angola Prison in Louisiana. I was reluctant to see this film when it came out because of my lingering pain over David and Loretta's violent murder, but I eventually took one of my classes to view it in Mansfield, Ohio, and discuss capital punishment over coffee afterward. I was pleasantly surprised by this film, for it accurately portrayed the multiplicity of complex emotions surrounding the events in Louisiana in the late 1970s. *Dead Man Walking* forces viewers to recognize the layers of emotions that contribute to our reactions to the death penalty today.

Immediately after it was known in the community that David and Loretta had been murdered, talk of retribution and violent retaliation became rampant. The white community quickly concluded that they must have been killed by black men, and a few began discussing a vigilante response against the black community. I remember seeing cars of black youths circling the funeral home in St. Martinville, Louisiana, at David's wake, apparently aware they were being targeted. Emotions escalated as whites accused blacks and blacks taunted whites. The pastor tried to calm the tension, even orchestrating an emotional rendition of "Let There Be Peace on Earth and Let It Begin with Me" at the funeral Mass. Tears flowed in a steady stream of despair.

It was not long before the murderers were apprehended, and much to the shock of the white community—but not a surprise in the black community—Elmo and Eddie Sonnier were young white oil field-workers. If vigilante justice had been applied, innocent black men would have been killed, as so often happened with lynchings in the South in previous times and as so often happens in capital punishment cases today when death is erroneously applied to innocent people. I witnessed firsthand the wave of emotions that led irrational and racists citizens to strike out in revenge. Capital punishment must end because innocent people are regularly caught up in the cycles of fear, vengeance, and racism.

The opening scene of the film *A Lesson before Dying* should convince anyone of the unjust power structures that routinely convict innocent poor and minority people and condemn them to death. The closing scene of the play *The Laramie Project* should also give us pause. In this play, Matthew Shepard's father asks the court to spare his son's killer in order to stop the cycle of violence. Capital punishment is one of the most important ethical issues of our time, and all educators must view these films and plays, as well as read many historical and legal texts, so they will be prepared to lead our students and citizens to deeper understandings of appropriate justice that avoids retribution, revenge, and error. We are all diminished when we get trapped in cycles of violence and injustice.

Sr. Helen Prejean continues to speak out against capital punishment but always with a deep compassion for victims of crime. She urges us to reject a barbaric practice that does not deter crime, reduce violence, save money, or impart justice—and it most certainly does not equate with insensitivity for victims of crime. There are many high-profile cases in which parents insist that the death penalty not be applied to the murderers of their children, and the parents of Matthew Shepard in Wyoming are one recent example. These parents know that capital punishment only perpetuates cycles of violence. Instead, they argue for life sentences without the option of parole. This certainly reflects our beliefs as well. Removing violent criminals and murderers from society with life sentences is an alternative available to us, and many religious leaders such as Pope John Paul II have consistently used this argument in an attempt to persuade those countries that still use the death penalty to change their practices. We are not safer or more secure in a society that sponsors murder in any form. Bob Hebert (2002) provides the most recent studies that clarify this ethical issue:

> In the spring of 2000 a team of lawyers and criminologists at Columbia University released the first phase of the most far-reaching study of the death penalty in the United States. It showed that the system of capital punishment was riddled with unfairness and incompetence, with serious errors erupting with alarming frequency at every stage of the process. The study showed that of every three capital sentences reviewed, two were overturned on appeal. Those were cases in which at least some of the mistakes were caught. No one knows what percentage of the remaining cases were tainted. Today [February 11, 2002] the team is releasing a massive second phase of the study, which focuses on why there are so many mistakes in death penalty cases, and what can be done about them. The study [directed by law professor James S. Liebman] describes the capital punishment system as "broken." (p. A29)

Read this chilling report and ask yourself how a civilized democracy can continue to allow such a barbaric practice and why the United States is willing to accept a high level of error that routinely executes innocent people. Then listen to the supporters of the death penalty, and we think you will agree that they are driven by retribution, fear, and hatred.

Baptist Pastor Dallas Billingham of Akron, Ohio, supports the death penalty for terrorists and murderers. He even demands, "Those who are responsible [for the September 11 events] must pay with their lives. . . . They have no regard for human life. We believe in capital punishment, in paying for a life with a life, and the bible supports that. If we have to go to war to get these guys, then we are justified to do it" (Pluto, 2001, p. A7). Pastor Billingham's warmongering tone is not unlike many of the media pundits quoted earlier. On what grounds does Billingham understand the hearts, minds, and souls of Muslims, Arabs, Hindus, Buddhists, and pantheists around the world? How many people like Timothy McVeigh, Osama bin Laden, and starving people in Iraq and Pakistan have become terrorists because they have not been shown a model of compassion and democracy? If you have not read Mark Twain's *War Prayer,* (see Zwick, 1992) we encourage you to do so. It is a stunning rejection of both warmongering and the ushering off to war of young men to massacre the enemy in the name of a compassionate God. Twain was outraged that the U.S. government—particularly Theodore Roosevelt—was willing to sacrifice the lives of hundreds of thousands of Muslim men, women, and children in the Philippines in order to protect U.S. business interests. Twain condemned the many ministers who used their pulpits to blindly support a war against the "evildoers" of the time. Although Twain was labeled unpatriotic by legislators, ministers, and citizens for his antiwar *War Prayer* in 1906, we suggest that he was honoring a prophetic responsibility for justice.

Twain's perspective, unlike Billingham's, derives from what we see as a Gnostic potential. Elaine Pagels (1979) explains, "Like circles of artists today, Gnostics considered original creative invention to be the mark of anyone who becomes spiritually alive. Each one, like students of a painter or writer, expected to express his own preconceptions by revising and transforming what he was taught. Whoever merely repeated his teacher's words was considered immature" (p. 19). Instead of simply repeating the verses of church or political elders, Twain painted a bleaker picture of U.S. war on indigenous peoples. Catholic priest Father Paul Schindler, like Twain, countered the barrage of pro-military and eye-for-an-eye justifications by local clergy such as Billingham. He asked this poignant question in a recent editorial: "We should ask why so many people in the world hate us [the U.S. government]? . . . You can talk about the Bay of Pigs, about the Contras, about sweat shops in Third World countries. . . . [We bombed the Iraqi] people to hell. That's why some people danced in the streets when they saw what happened to us" (Pluto, 2001, p. A7). Three thousand miles away Muslim novelist Orhan Pamuk writes with a similar eye for understanding the social milieu in the September 29 edition of the *Guardian:*

What prompts the old man in Istanbul to condone the terror in New York in a moment of anger, or a Palestinian youth fed up with Israeli oppression to admire the Taliban who throw nitric acid in women's faces, is not Islam, nor the idiocy described as the clash between east and west, nor poverty itself, but the feeling of impotence deriving from degradation and the failure to be heard and understood. (Pamuk, 2001, p. 1)

And Ken Sehested, executive director of the Baptist Peace Fellowship of North America, issued this prophetic challenge with Kyle Childress to U.S. citizens in light of September 11 and the national address that George W. Bush delivered soon thereafter. It is entitled "Walking through the Valley of Death."

> The Body of Christ must remain alert when Caesar quotes Scripture. The text of Holy Writ is forever threatened with being co-opted, is always in danger of being robed in the garments of empire, of being mobilized to endorse injustice, of being segregated from intended conclusion. . . . The Body of Christ is called to ask the questions currently being disguised by newspaper headlines. For instance: Not so long ago, following the bombing of the Murrah federal building in Oklahoma City, state authorities, news media and common mobs alike began harassing people of Arab descent living in the U.S., only to discover that responsibility actually lay with one of our own decorated war veterans of European lineage. . . . It was the U.S. who originally recruited, trained and supplied bin Laden and his colleagues for guerilla warfare. Back then, his services were as a "hot" proxy agent in our "cold" war with the Soviet Union. He has since found a more lucrative offer on the "free market" of global political violence. And of course there's the recent demonization of Saddam Hussein, whose original chemical weapons arsenal was supplied by the United States back when he was still our ally against the Iranian Ayatollah. To our shame, and our peril, we have little knowledge of a millennium of Western meddling in Arab affairs, deposing this ruler, propping up that one, with no criteria other than cost/benefit calculations. Few in the United States realize that our nation, aided by Great Britian, has waged the longest bombing campaign in human history against Iraq. Since the formal end of the Gulf War—and without even the semblance of United Nations' authority—we have over the past decade, on a weekly, sometimes daily basis, continued to rain death from the skies. UNICEF, the United Nation's own child-welfare agency, has indicated that at least a half-million Iraqi children have died since the end of Desert Storm from causes directly related to the international economic sanctions. The competition of loyalty is that stark. Choose this day whom you will serve. In the valley of the shadow. (Sehested, 2001, p. 1)

Although I (Dana) do not refer to myself as a Christian, the Jesus I imagine is an intellectual dissident and social activist. I agree with theologian and peace activist John Dear (2000), who says, "[Jesus is] trouble for the establishment, trouble for the religious elite, trouble for rulers, and trouble for the war-making empire. Jesus was a rebel—but with a difference—he was the revolutionary face of nonviolence" (p. xv) In *Jesus the Rebel,* Dear reinforces the seditious spirit of Jesus in his own response to war:

> Our country prides itself on being "number one" in the world. As the world's police force and economic tyrant, we attempt to possess and control all the kingdoms of the world— from Iraq and Yugoslavia to Nicaragua and El Salvador. As we do this, however, we also

find ourselves worshiping the false gods of violence. . . . As our militarism insures our economic domination over the poor, we gain the world and lose our souls to the forces of death. (2000, p. 6)

Before his death, Father James Guadalupe Carney, a Catholic priest, also spoke prophetically to the links between Christian consumerism, militarism, and cultural imperialism. He reportedly was hunted down and assassinated in Honduras by the CIA and mercenaries trained by the U.S. taxpayer–funded School of the Americas. In 1985 Carney wrote:

> I've a deep conviction that most middle-class Catholics are phony Christians, just as materialistic and self-serving, and as liable to go along with others, as any non-Christian, and often more so. . . . [Christ] tore into the system and those that held the masses in the bondage of ignorance and poverty. He cursed them, and said, "Woe to you hypocrites, you priests, and to you rich, and to you who are honored and accepted by the world." . . . I hate the way blacks, Indians, dark skinned foreigners are treated and kept marginalized. I hate the way the United States tries to control other countries of the world, and world trade, for its own benefit, trying to export our materialistic way of life to other countries. I hate and resent the way the rich and middle-class Americans and Hondurans can live in big, comfortable houses, have cars, land, and education, while my brothers and sisters, the poor, are forced to live as they do. (pp. xvi, xvii)

Unfortunately Carney's reading of the world, like Jesus, Gandhi, Martin Luther King Jr., Malcolm X, Marcus Garvey, Oscar Romero, and Medger Evers before him, resulted in his death. We would like to think that we live in a time when we will not be killed for publicly dissenting. But can we be sure?

Dr. Chung Hyun Kyung, professor of theology and Buddhism, prophesied in the 1995 video *Arms for the Poor* that the doubling of sales of conventional weapons since the end of the cold war would come back to haunt U.S. citizens. She contends that in order to ban land mines in the war, we have to take them out of our hearts first. "If you [the United States] inflict so much pain and violence to the people in other parts of the world eventually it will come back to your family. I can see it happening in USA. So I ask, what is the spiritual ground of USA? You talk about democracy and freedom—number one country in the world—what is your spirituality?" (Kyung, 1995). Although most of us condemn the Taliban for their narrow and fanatical views, who among us will interrogate our frenzied flag waving? Would we recognize ourselves in our enemy: overzealous and willing to use violence in the name of our own gods, be they Christian or consumerist? We must reflect on the story of Bigger Thomas in the novel *Native Son* (Wright, 1940) and the events in the *Autobiography of Miss Jane Pittman* by Ernest J. Gaines (1972) in relation to these prophetic messages. In each case, a majority of citizens was unable or unwilling to act or speak against a massive wave of injustice, and those who did were shunned. Now consider that we live in a time when calls for nonviolence have largely been dismissed as pacifism run amok, even by many religious figures such as Pastor Billingham who claim to be defenders of economic and social justice. We turn again to José Comblin (2000), who asks us who will be willing to fulfill a deeper religious and human desire by acting for ethics and justice. Which citizens or educators are willing to investigate the origin of the land mines in their own hearts, as well as in the fields of Afghanistan?

Our Response to the September 11 Attacks

Thus far we have presented multiple voices of reflection on September 11 from the vantage point of several weeks and months later. We now consider the ways we initially responded with our students. Perhaps one of the most frequently asked questions by my (Patrick) students and colleagues in the days immediately following the attacks on September 11 was, "Why do they hate us so much?" This question, of course, reveals not only genuine shock and sincere puzzlement, but also varying degrees of naiveté and historical amnesia. Renowned and respected theologian John B. Cobb Jr. offered perhaps one of the best responses to this question in *Process Perspective:*

> The first response to the September 11 tragedy must be one of shock, anger, horror, and, especially, deepest sympathy for those who have lost friends and family. We grieve with them. We respect and admire the courage of the many who work to find the bodies of the dead. . . . We rejoice in the solidarity with the sufferers that has been shown across the nation. The attack has been a wake-up call to our whole nation. . . . For some, the response is one of aggrieved innocence and the need for vengeance. We have been led to believe that our global actions have been basically for the sake of all humanity, so that anyone who hates us must be ignorant or evil. Our president has encouraged this interpretation by telling us that "America was targeted for attack because we're the brightest beacon for freedom and opportunity in the world." This self-righteous interpretation justifies us in trying to exterminate our enemies. The excessive rationalization will not only escalate violence but also intensify the anger against us and provoke more attacks in the future. Down that path there is no security. (2001, p. 3)

Next, Cobb outlines the many grievances, not in order to justify violence but to understand the complexity of U.S. involvement in global events. These grievances against the United States include cold war exploitation, economic policies that have led to widespread misery and the death of children, and lack of attention to the plight of displaced Palestinians, to name just a few. Like us, Cobb is very clear in his denunciation of terrorism and his call to bring to justice those who are specifically responsible. He concludes, "The history of the Near East has not left us innocent . . . [and] for us to respond to the death of innocent Americans [on September 11] by inflicting death on equally innocent Arabs, may temporarily reduce the ability of our enemies to injure us. It will not reduce their hatred" (2001, p. 3). Sooner or later, that hatred will find another expression in other destructive acts that will lead to escalating cycles of violence.

The absurdity of escalating cycles of violence, especially in an age of nuclear, chemical, and biological weapons of mass destruction, causes us to agree with Cobb when he insists there must be a better way to deal with global conflicts. I (Patrick) have always taught with this conviction, and that is why I show the film *Vukovar* and meet with people from the former Yugoslavia in my classes. My students always recognize the absurdity of the cycles of violence in Serbia, Bosnia, Kosovo, and Croatia, and following the film and field experiences they insist that alternatives must be found. Following September 11, the United States is now caught in the web of such violence. Our military attacks must be targeted to perpetrators only, and our values of human rights and democracy must be integral to all that we do. To do any less would destroy not only our credibility, but also any moral authority we possess.

I have found that my graduate students generally share this philosophy. However, it is important to note that 48 percent of the graduate students in my department at Texas A&M are international students, African Americans, or Hispanics. On the evening after the attacks, my students were prepared to explore the historical, cultural, political, and religious complexity of the September 11 events, and we did so in the context of a documentary film titled *Killing the Dream,* which traces the history of colonialization, military imposition, and U.S. cultural hegemony that has dominated Haiti for over two hundred years. This history is totally distorted in textbooks. When Russian diplomat Oleg Chernov visited Stanford University in August 2001, he was discussing the great revolutions of modern times and offered this comment, "Lenin was second" (Clymer, 2001), and then he corrected himself to give credit to the French Revolution of 1789. Although Chernov eventually named the American Revolution, the French Revolution, and the Russian Revolution, he reflected the cultural bias and the widespread historical disregard of the Haitian Revolution begun in 1791. Democracy in Haiti has consistently been thwarted for over two hundred years, and the Haitian Revolution is not even included in most textbooks. Could this be because enslaved blacks overthrew the white plantation owners? The film *Killing the Dream* certainly believes this to be true. And my students, especially those from the Caribbean, were passionate in their condemnation of the domination of Haiti and the distorted views of history perpetuated in textbooks today. This film provided my graduate students with an entré into a discussion of the complexities of U.S. foreign policy globally. This is an essential first step in our vision for a different kind of response to September 11. We must deconstruct ourselves and our own faults and failures as we respond to terrorism.

Although my diverse class of graduate students embraced the opportunity to connect the events of September 11 to the broader historical context, my undergraduates were generally hostile to this idea. These are middle-class, white, Bible Belt teenagers from Texas, and the rhetoric of the media and President Bush was reflected in their unquestioned support for bombings and, for some, the total annihilation of wide expanses of the Middle East. Their rhetoric was militaristic and their anger was palpable. As a professor, I want to introduce my students to critical thinking in historical analysis, but I had to work with them in their own context by allowing a few minority voices to slowly emerge in the discussion in the weeks following September 11. This is the approach I took with undergraduate students on September 12, and many were willing to consider, however tentatively, the possibility of alternative readings of the situation. Teaching convictions requires patience and multiple approaches.

I (Dana) first heard about the bombings at 10:23 A.M. as I was taking a break from teaching a three-and-a-half-hour undergraduate seminar. It had been an amazing morning. Many of the people involved in Social and Professional Issues—the final course that undergraduate teacher education students are required to take before beginning student teaching—were actually beginning to share their personal stories of fear, joy, pain, and triumph. I welcomed this process in light of the fact that our first eight classes together were marked by hesitancy, politeness, defensiveness, and fear. Some students had even became withdrawn. More than a few called or e-mailed me to communicate that discussions of child abuse, domestic violence, gay bashing, and underemployment were too real, too painful, and too recent. Some students even went so far as to say that they "hated" the intensity of the topics in our class as much as the lack of structure. A few were bold enough to question "Why don't we stick to 'real' educational issues like standards, testing, and getting along with our principals? Why do we need to talk about racism, ecological destruction, and hatred?"

Our two most recent meetings had been dramatically different. We were awakening, opening up, and announcing our joys and pains in uninhibited, freeing, and spontaneous ways. By 9:45 A.M., on September 11, more than a handful of students had erupted with their life stories of overcoming poverty, physical abuse, bulimia, and deaths of loved ones. Tears flowed, laughter resonated, students danced. Then, at 9:45 A.M., an hour and fifteen minutes into our class, Laura, a senior majoring in the fine arts, became an indelible part of our memories. Laura had never added a word to any of our class discussions. I was worried because she hadn't returned my e-mail requests for her interpretations and reactions to the issues we were raising. None of us, especially me, knew what to expect from her presentation. I had strongly encouraged students to use the arts as a means of engaging, reflecting, expressing, and evoking what they were feeling and thinking, and I had hoped that Laura would appreciate this opportunity to exhibit and describe her artistic passion as much as anyone. Yet I wasn't sure whether Laura was in step with the directions in which we were heading. "I want you to tell me how my three paintings speak to you, knowing that there is no correct answer; then I'll tell you what I see," Laura said as she placed three 3' × 2' paintings in the chalk tray under the blackboard.

Complete silence. Laura had created three separate but connected paintings with wide, black brush strokes on a white backdrop. Intermixed on two were assorted images and small crosses drawn with a pencil. The abstractness of the art led me to worry that Laura's efforts would go unappreciated by many students who feared and disliked offering their interpretations of art publicly (perhaps I was doubting myself more than the students). As it turned out, several students, especially the quieter ones, related personal images of the apocalypse, of murder, and of the crucifixion of Jesus. They spoke of how the different forms and figures of Laura's art provoked visions of hope, redemption, and healing. After fifteen minutes and a wonderfully rich and intense discussion, Laura spoke up to say, "I have never told anyone this story, and rarely do I share my art with strangers. You are still strangers. The images before you are meant"—a tear, then two, then Laura reached for a handkerchief—"to depict my coming to terms with death, actually the suicide, of a friend last year in my dorm. I didn't predict it. I simply can't explain it. It haunts me every day." One or two students rushed to embrace Laura with open minds and hearts. A few others, slowly gaining their emotional and public fortitude, readied themselves to relive and embrace individual and collective stories of family suicide. "Get the Kleenex ready," Carol announced.

I was shocked to realize that more than a third of the people in the class had experience with suicide in one way or another. It wasn't long before Kari stood up and announced, "I hate to interrupt you, Laura, but I have to quickly unravel my inquiry project because I am choking on it. I contemplated suicide," Kari began. "I wanted to kill myself because I was so depressed and hopeless for myself and my world. I am telling you this story because there are so many children and teens that need our help and aren't getting it. I got help, support from a teacher, and I love living more than I ever expected." After several minutes and more embracing, Laura and Kari sat down next to each other. Talk of hope and healing began to fill the room. I knew it was time to take a break. "After our break," I said, "let's discuss how more lasting platforms of hope can be generated out of deeper discussions of suffering. Moreover, I leave you with this question: How can we and will we relate to what we just experienced, discussions of suicide and terror, and what we will face in the next few days, months, and years in our lives and when we work with children in schools? OK, let's come back at 10:35."

We never returned to our discussion of hope and eschatology because as I was walking out of the classroom, Sandy Gallagher, a colleague, escorted me aside to report that the World Trade Centers and Pentagon had been bombed by "suicidal terrorists," and it was possible that several more airplanes had been hijacked. The plane that eventually crashed in Pennsylvania was changing directions directly over our heads around the time that Sandy and I were talking.

It's been months since hijacked planes were driven into the symbols of world trade and military might, as well as into our souls. Our daily routines cannot hide the trauma that each of us—young, middle-aged, old, yellow, brown, white, gay, bi, straight, fundamentalist, atheist—is feeling. Although there are still rush hour traffic jams, lines in supermarket checkout aisles, fans at sporting spectacles, sexual encounters, and people mowing their lawns, there is also hesitation that our daily rituals cannot hide. As U.S. citizens begin to reflect on our vulnerability and our lack of predictive imagination, I have many questions: Who among us is working to prevent nuclear proliferation? Who is working to enlist, hear, and protect the voices of people, communities, and countries that are politically and economically marginalized? Who will protect my Muslim friend Mohammad who is afraid to e-mail me with his reactions to war? Who will be willing to admit that Osama bin Laden is a former CIA employee, ally, and benefactor of U.S. tax dollars? Who will investigate whether the war on terrorism is a cover-up for a war for oil and greater arms sales? How are teachers defining and discussing freedom, patriotism, and terrorism to and with children? What ethical visions and acts by parents, activists, citizens, and educators do the events of September 11 warrant? And what prophets will we look to for inspiration and strength?

I feel as though I understand as little about how the horrific events of September 11 occurred as I do about the contexts that led up to them. It is unimaginable that three thousand people came to such hideous and unnecessary deaths. The caretaker in me sees no justification for this act, no matter how desperate the perpetrators may feel. My dovish side cries for my children, the people of Afghanistan, and the families who lost loved ones on September 11. And the trickster in me continues to question whether I have the emotional, spiritual, and imagintive potential and patient skepticism to understand and act for what may be right and what may be needed, whatever that may be. I am asking these questions to myself in a coffee shop in Westlake, Ohio, as I overhear two women discuss how they would like to see their eighth-grade daughters' teachers focus more on verb conjugation than on war, hatred, and anthrax. "Discussions of the terrorism, genocide, and world peace will not get my daughter into an Ivy League school," one of the women complains.

Like many of my students, I am driven to turn on the television only when my morbid fascination with war, destruction, and violence are peaking. Most of the time, however, I try to refrain from watching or listening to media images because I know they will never become unglued from my memory, my person. Each time a friend mentions airplanes and images of the World Trade Center, the second plane's explosive crash into the South Tower rushes through my mind. Combined with the visual images, some real, some fantasy, of people having to make the choice between jumping off a one-hundred-story burning building or being seared alive is too much to handle. I also have apocalyptic thoughts—thoughts of further destruction, nuclear escalation, conventional holocaust, and biological warfare—of what will happen if the United States cannot—uncharacteristically—refrain from matching violence with violence. I know I am not alone in these fears.

I find it disconcerting that many of the angry and militant protestations for revenge and war are coming from U.S. citizens whose families' health, income, leisure time, and job security have been jeopardized dramatically in the last ten years as a result of corporate domination and greed. These conditions have rapidly intensified under the Bush administration. Sadly, many of the working-class whites who have lost and are losing the most in the "new world order" and the "global economy" are those who are caught up in the greatest anti-Muslim and xenophobic frenzy. I continue to wonder whether the U.S. government's sudden fixation on an external enemy is in any way related to their fears of growing unrest about economic injustice within our own borders. Foreign enemies have a convenient way of surfacing when the dissatisfaction of the masses appears to be growing. We always have war in the United States. We have wars on drugs, cold wars, wars on crime, wars on terrorists, wars against communist spies, and wars on education, but never wars for ecological sustainability, wars for universal health coverage, wars for livable wages, or wars against racism. In fact, we seriously question whether U.S. citizens truly understand what peace means.

A tradition of U.S. and corporate imperialism supports the inscription chiseled in granite on the U.S. Department of Commerce Building that reads, "Commerce defies every wind, overrides every tempest, invades every zone." We also recognize that we live in a time when citizens are becoming outraged at their longer work hours, their smaller paychecks, and the reality that one-third of us will be laid off each year. Could it be that the war on terrorism is being fought for reasons that have little to do with protecting an idealized American way of life or supporting justice around the globe? Could it be that this war, like the Gulf War, is about greed and accumulation for a few? Could it have anything to do with these ideas articulated by historian Michael Parenti?

> Throughout history there has been only one thing that ruling interests have ever wanted—and that is everything: all the choice lands, forest, game, wealth, riches, and profitable returns; all the productive facilities, gainful inventories, and technologies; all the control positions of the state and other major institutions; all public supports and subsidies, privileges and immunities; all the protections of the law with none of its constraints; all the services, comforts, luxuries, and advantages of civil society with none of the taxes and costs. Every ruling class has wanted only this: all the rewards and none of the burdens. The operational code is: we have a lot; we can get more; we want it all. (1996, p. 5)

It us not only disturbing to consider that the events of September 11 could have been prevented, but also maddening to believe that a frenzy of trading in the airline, defense, and insurance industries may have occurred in the days leading up to the attacks. Is this a sign that Wall Street, political elites, CIA directors, and the military-industrial complex were in some way informed about potential attacks? How many representatives and senators bought or sold stock in the defense and airlines industries on September 8, 9, and 10? Moreover, why has the United States been so quick to raise the issue of oil reserves in Uzbekistan and Siberia with President Putin of Russia? Is it too conspiracy-minded to consider that the terrorist acts of September 11, and the lack of government attention to terrorist threats received leading up to them, were part of a larger plan, the kind of plan Michael Parenti writes about? These are the questions that increasingly haunt us.

Several working-class friends of ours, some of whom are veterans of various wars, also raise a brow when they hear that certain U.S. politicians and CEOs desire to protect "our" way of life. They note that 5 percent of the U.S. population has 95 percent of the wealth; 90 percent of the stock market's returns are accumulated by the richest 10 percent; U.S. citizens have three to six weeks less vacation than people in other industrialized countries; the salaries of Fortune 500 CEOs go up 25 percent on average when they oversee company layoffs; the buying power of most U.S. families has shrunk considerably; and the U.S. military budget is equal to the amount of the next six largest military budgets combined (Zepezauer & Naiman, 1996). Our friends want to know why $13 billion dollars of U.S. taxpayers' money is going to bail out the airlines industry alone, and why $100 billion is going to prop up Fortune 500 companies such as Enron, with no caps on executive pay attached. Our friends know that $500 billion has been given to Lockheed Martin by U.S. taxpayers and much of it will go toward excessive CEO salaries and production facilities overseas. They recognize that the U.S. government has not been as open with its checkbook when it comes to supporting U.S. families with health care, safer school buildings, clean air and water, family leave, affordable medication, airport security, and longer vacations. So, when I hear veterans of foreign wars asking who benefits when U.S. elites pull away from international treaties to ban weapons sales and when some mention that the war in Iraq had more to do with U.S. oil interests and defense contracts than freedom, I take notice.

Perhaps Patrick and I are being patriotically sacrilegious by raising these questions at this time. Some say that we need to unite, not divide. Although we hear the call of "we are one nation together," we wonder how people, including ourselves, can forget recent history—a history during which the government has systematically violated the Constitution and stolen Native American and Mexican land, refused to allow women to vote, refused to grant Chinese Americans the ability to attain citizenship until 1957, imprisoned Japanese Americans, and enslaved African Americans, and it continues today to deny human rights to many of these same people and others. I constantly ask myself to consider how "the most violent nation on earth, the heir of Indian and African genocide, the only nation ever to drop an atomic bomb on a civilian population, the world's biggest arms dealer, the country that napalmed over ten million people in Vietnam (to 'save' it from communism), the world's biggest jailer can be waving the flag for freedom" (Abu-Jamal, 1996, p. 116).

Images and dreams continue to abound as we write. I (Dana) reflect on my days in Paris in 1983 when I was a university student studying French at the Alliance Française. This was a time when Paris metros and bus stations were sites of periodical bombings by Palestinian and Iranian groups who condemned what they believed to be colonial policies by the United States and France. Students from thirty-five different countries were represented at Alliance Française, and I remember being told by a professor that we were not allowed to discuss politics because the climate was too volatile. I didn't understand the motivation for his comments until I heard a student from Germany innocently mention Ronald Reagan by name. As if trained for this exact moment, four Iranian students arose and shouted, "Viva Khomeini, Viva Khomeini!" The ferocity and passion in their eyes and the strength and quickness in their movement made it obvious that Ronald Reagan was anything but a hero to them. Sadly, the moment ended abruptly as the professor stepped in. But I would never be the same. Within five seconds, I had almost completely broken my affiliation with William F. Buckley, the *American Spectator,* George Will, and the Disneyesque veneer of my high school history books. I knew that these students were serious in their determination to live lives according to their standards, not the Shah's, not Reagan's, not mine. As I think of Bush's "Axis of Evil" pronouncement lately, I wonder what the reactions of Iranians will be? Who are the radicals? Who are the fundamentalists? Who lives in countries with recent histories marked by assassinations of civil rights leaders, legal apartheid, the genocide of native peoples, the stockpiling of weapons of mass destruction, and the military occupation of countries against the will of people throughout Latin America?

I also have some recent images of George W. Bush and Madeline Albright on two separate occasions. The first occurred when Bernard Shaw was interviewing Bush during the 2000 presidential elections. Shaw asked Gore first, then Bush, "What, if anything, would you do differently in terms of U.S. policy in Rwanda in light of the 500,000 lives that have been lost?" After Gore muttered something about requesting troops sooner to end the killing, Bush said that he would have called troops home right away. Shaw followed up by asking Bush about the possibility of further bloodshed. Bush responded that this was the price that had to be paid to protect U.S. interests. I wonder if Bush believed that the mother of the children who needed medical supplies were hacked by machete-wielding soldiers was supporting U.S. "interests"? Would Bush have responded the same way if 500,000 people were dying in Switzerland? I wonder if our current president learned this approach from his father, who had a history of negotiating arms deals for such "democratic" leaders as Noriega, Hussein, Pinochet, and bin Laden.

Madeline Albright, former ambassador to the United Nations under President Clinton, was also callous and narcissistic in her approach to foreign policy rhetoric. When Albright was asked in 1996 on national television for her reaction to the fact that 500,000 Iraqi children had died in the last five years because of the U.S. embargo on food and medical supplies, she replied, "we think the price is worth it" (qtd. in Chomsky, 2000, p. 31). Each time I reflect on the U.S. "humanitarian" bombings of Kosovo, our napalming of Vietnamese civilians, and our dropping of the atomic bomb on Japanese civilians, I can't help but become angry. I agree wholeheartedly with human rights activist Noam Chomsky when he writes, "Saddam Hussein's invasion of Kuwait was brutal, cruel, and unforgivable. But it was certainly no less brutal than the U.S. invasion of Grenada, the U.S. invasion of Panama, or the Turkish invasion of northern Cyprus—not to mention U.S. support for the right-wing totalitarianism and death squads in Chile, El Salvador, and Guatemala, among others" (2000, p. 7).

I wonder how we would feel if we lived in a country whose land had been ravaged by U.S. mining companies; whose mineral wealth had been raped, with the profits going to financiers and bankers outside the country; whose military was trained in the United States and by the CIA to kill farmers, civil rights leaders, Jesuit priests, and indigenous peoples who opposed dictatorships; and whose loans and interest rates from the World Bank depended on a show of austere cutbacks in social services. When I (Dana) watch television or view newspaper images of U.S. politicians, clergy, and business executives proselytizing that the United States is the "city on the hill," "the land of freedom," and "the greatest nation in the world," I wonder how I would feel knowing that the United States has higher levels of poverty, suicide, hunger, crime, and ecological destruction and greater disparity of wealth, than most other industrialized countries. Like a growing number of working-class Americans and many people around the world, Muslim and non-Muslim, I wonder if I would grow to despise the triumphalism, isolationism, material excessiveness, and spiritually corrupt choices of U.S. economic and political elites. I wonder if I would be tormented by the fear that globalization means that Monsanto will control my ancestors' land, seeds, and food chain (as in Brazil), that McDonald's will put mom-and-pop coffeehouses out of business (as in Vienna), that MTV will invade my children's psyches (as in Mali), that Ford Motor Company will poison my air and water (as in Mexico), that Disney, Gap, JC Penny, Wrangler, J.Crew, Eddie Bauer, and Banana Republic will exploit my thirteen-year-old in their tax-free factories (as in Honduras). I wonder what I would think if I knew that the U.S. defense industry's profits and sales have doubled since the cold war (the U.S. now provides 67 percent of the world's arms and weapons) and that Saddam Hussein's arsenal of chemical and biological weapons, technology, and intelligence was mostly supplied by the CIA and U.S. arms companies. If I lived in Latin America, would I have grounds to worry that the United States would train and oversee thugs who would protect the interests of multinational corporations and brutal military regimes in the name of freedom and justice?

Many people in the world love U.S. citizens and some of the freedoms we enjoy. They also recognize, however, that U.S. society and policies are laden with contradictions, polarizations, complexity, pitfalls, and possibilities. This point was made by Kent State students in early October at a local discussion of terrorism, peace, and war held by the American Friends Action Committee and the Ohio Committee on Corporations, Law, and Democracy. I (Dana) was struck by their passion and insight. The older folks in the group—those who have spent their lives in organizations fighting for nonconscription laws and world peace—were especially inspiring. In one of the conversations, an older peacenik linked the events of September 11 and the resultant commitment to vengeance to the failure of public schools. In one respect, I agreed with her, especially in light of my belief that schools are dedicating an irrational amount of time to technical skills and vocational preparation above care, connection, critical thinking, and interdependence. Yet I gave into the urge to playfully say, "U.S. schools are doing their job well. Too well." "What the heck do you mean?" she demanded. Fortunately, I had a copy of Father Carney's autobiography in my book bag, and I was able to read a short passage to the group:

> Americans learn from their childhood how to be good, efficient, docile, obedient employees or workers. It becomes very natural for them to enter into the capitalist system of competition and of seeking personal gain, because in school and in sports children learn to compete with each other to see who wins the prize or the highest marks. Those who win are praised and honored, and those who lose or lag behind are often looked down on. This prepares them for competing later on in the economic world of capitalism. It is a very deep and penetrating teaching of violence, to live according to the law of the strongest. Instead of teaching children to share things with others, to seek equality and brotherhood, to serve the community, they are taught to seek their own advancement, their own development and betterment. (1985, p. 4)

I reiterated that U.S. institutions, in my perspective, often command the language of freedom, liberty, care, connection, compassion, character, and citizenship (remember Kids with Character) in order to extinguish their very possibility. The role of schooling, as opposed to education, is to convince students and the public that by using this language and attributing it to the status quo, democratic values are in place throughout U.S. society. I went on to say that in reality schools are assigned the role of domesticating visions of freedom, democracy, and citizenship for many groups. No wonder U.S. citizens reacted with such an outpouring of anger, I argued; they were expressing an outward rage at their institutions, including schools, that neuter their imaginations and manipulate their passions in the name of liberty and progress. Several people in the group, however, were willing to explain the events of September 11, as well as the Gulf War, in terms of economic imperialism and corporate greed, while believing that the U.S. educational system somehow remained unaffected by these same forces.

Like Enron stock, the activities of students and educators are increasingly governed by the irrational criteria of efficiency, profit, and quick returns rather than being inspired by a vision for a just society. Skilled and paid performance, or competence, is the overwhelming aim of U.S. educational agendas and the most important and valued outcome of educational processes (Usher & Edwards, 1994; Young, 1990). Students and teachers are manipulated in a system that regards them more as "administered subjects" and "resources to be developed rather than human beings who are valued in themselves and who are encouraged to choose and shape their own future" (Morgan, 1997, p. 70; see also Adorno, 1991; Bauman, 1993). We cannot forget that many state, corporate, and educational agendas have not been crafted to dismantle deeper structural injustices; they could be developed to legitimate and refine the interests of a ruling class (Chomsky, 2000; McLaren 1991, 1994, 1997). More than ever, educators appear to be trained, hired, and rewarded for being the "wards of the state" and "clerks of the empire" that Parenti describes. They are charged not only with overseeing and safeguarding the U.S. ideological doctrines and global interests of Enron and Dick Cheney, but also with "creating educational structures that anesthetize students' critical abilities" to recognize the complexities of injustice (Chomsky, 2000 p. 4).

We believe that the most formidable issues for educators concerned about ethics (e.g., race, gender, sexuality, culture, religion, poverty, health, war, hatred, and class) are continually overshadowed by a telescopic focus on performance and effectiveness, while millions of children and adults in the United States and abroad despair, and hopeless gurus of school change drum on about the need for "high-performing schools," "new sciences of leadership," and "continuous improvement." If every teacher promoted the qualities that would make professors of school change proud, if every teacher tutored for three hours after school, if every parent worked with his or her child each evening, and if every student aced high-stakes tests and received A grades, would there be more peace, higher wages, less hatred, more leisure time, greater voter turnout, less crime (including corporate), fewer terrorist attacks, and more social justice? Absolutely not. The frenetic explosion of systems-oriented accountability, standards, and accreditation agendas is only serving to mask unjust social conditions with amplified languages of autonomy (see Chomsky, 2000; Giroux, 1992; Greene, 1995; Kincheloe, Slattery, & Steinberg, 2000; Miller, 1990).

José Comblin, Smedley Butler, Aung San Suu Kyi, Wendell Berry, the Black Radical Congress, John Deare, Father Carney, and Barbara my student teacher are dangerous to the status quo because they refuse to accept injustice and toe the line drawn by people in positions of power. But then, neither did Gandhi, Jesus, Nelson Mandela, Sojourner Truth, and Casar Chavez when they were fighting abusive economic and political power. Instead, they prophetically unmask oppressive realities to present different ways of living through loving. This is the space in which we find ourselves at the moment. As discussed in Chapter 3, artists are equally subversive and dangerous when they seek to transcend the status quo. Let us now turn to some of these artists who have not been blinded by fear and violence and have chosen to speak out as a source of inspiration.

Dead Awakening and the Artist's Response

One of the wisest men I (Dana) have ever met, I'll call him Mohammad, will not return my e-mail or phone calls. Mohammad speaks several languages and has lived throughout the world. He has experienced severe poverty and famine as well as moderate material success. Although I was listed as the instructor for the fifty-four-year-old Mohammad in the summer of 2001 at the Leadership Academy in Massachusetts, it was he who was my teacher and prophet, much as Dr. Smith was for Candida, as we saw in Chapter 2. One comment Mohammad made sticks in my mind in particular. I remember him saying, "Dana, you speak publicly of the truth about the lies, hatred, racism, class biases, and hegemony that many U.S. citizens have come to internalize. You are aware that people do not want to hear the truth and they will try to harm you and your family. Beware. Develop strong friendships and know that the last thing your bosses, police, legislators, neighbors, and even family members want to hear is the truth. You must continue to speak the truth in the years to come!" Was Mohammad trying to warn me? Did he have a premonition of the events to come?

Mohammad and I remained in touch by e-mail up until September 11. We were planning to rent and share a summer cottage in Vermont together. Since September 11, however, Mohammad has not returned my numerous messages. I know it is he—a Muslim, a black man, a father, a husband, a teacher, a prophet—who must be heard but is afraid to speak. Has someone spit on his dark-skinned children as Bull Connor, police chief in Birmingham, Alabama, did when young students protested racial segregation? Are Mohammad's sons called "sand niggers" in school? Do drunken patriots drive cars through the front doors of his mosque? Does Mohammad worry that his phone messages are being tapped, his e-mail messages traced, and his public conversations monitored? Does he fear that Attorney General John Ashcroft and the Bush administration could falsely arrest him at any moment? Maybe they have. We share Amiri Baraka's long poem *Somebody Blew Up America* (2001) for its analysis and prophetic insight into what African Americans have been experiencing for centuries. We also offer it as a tribute to Mohammad and many Muslims for what they are facing in the Unites States now.

> *They say it's some terrorist, some barbaric A Rab, in Afghanistan*
> *It wasn't our American terrorists*
> *It wasn't the Klan or the Skin heads*
> *Or the them that blows up nigger*
> *Churches, or reincarnates us on Death Row*
> *It wasn't Trent Lott*
> *Or David Duke or Giuliani*
> *Or Schundler, Helms retiring*
>
> *It wasn't*
> *The gonorrhea in costume*
> *The white sheet diseases*
> *That have murdered black people*
> *Terrorized reason and sanity*
> *Most of humanity, as they pleases*
>
> *They say (who say?)*
> *Who do the saying*
> *Who is them paying*
> *Who tell the lies*
> *Who in disguise*
> *Who had the slaves*
> *Who got the bux out the Bucks*
>
> *Who got fat from plantations*
> *Who genocided Indians*
> *Tried to waste the Black nation*
>
> *Who live on Wall Street*
> *The first plantation*
> *Who cut your nuts off*
> *Who rape your ma*
> *Who lynched your pa*
>
> *Who got the tar, who got the feathers*
> *Who had the match, who set the fires*
> *Who killed and hired*
> *Who say they God & still be the Devil*
> *Who the biggest only*
> *Who the most goodest*
> *Who do Jesus resemble*

Who created everything
Who the smartest
Who the greatest
Who the richest
Who say you ugly and they the goodlookingest

Who define art
Who define science
Who made the bombs
Who made the guns
Who bought the slaves, who sold them

Who called you them names
Who say Dahmer wasn't insane

Who? Who? Who?

Who stole Puerto Rico
Who stole the Indies, the Philippines, Manhattan
Australia & The Hebrides
Who forced opium on the Chinese

Who own them buildings
Who got the money
Who think you funny
Who locked you up
Who own the papers

Who owned the slave ship
Who run the army
Who the fake president
Who the ruler
Who the banker

Who? Who? Who?

Who own the mine
Who twist your mind
Who got bread
Who need peace
Who you think need war

Who own the oil
Who do no toil
Who own the soil
Who is not a nigger
Who is so great ain't nobody bigger

Who own this city
Who own the air
Who own the water

Who own your crib
Who rob and steal and cheat and murder and make lies the truth
Who call you uncouth

Who live in the biggest house
Who do the biggest crime
Who go on vacation anytime
Who killed the most niggers
Who killed the most Jews
Who killed the most Italians
Who killed the most Irish
Who killed the most Africans
Who killed the most Japanese
Who killed the most Latinos

Who? Who? Who?

Who own the ocean
Who own the airplanes
Who own the malls
Who own television
Who own radio

Who own what ain't even known to be owned
Who own the owners that ain't the real owners

Who own the suburbs
Who suck the cities
Who make the laws

Who made Bush president
Who believe the confederate flag need to be flying
Who talk about democracy and be lying

Who the Beast in Revelations
Who 666
Who know who decide
Jesus get crucified
Who the Devil on the real side
Who got rich from Armenian genocide

Who the biggest terrorist
Who change the bible
Who killed the most people
Who do the most evil
Who don't worry about survival

Who have the colonies
Who stole the most land
Who rule the world

Who say they good but only do evil
Who the biggest executioner

Who? Who? Who?

Who own the oil
Who want more oil
Who told you what you think that later you find out a lie

Who? Who? Who?

Who found Bin Laden, maybe they Satan
Who pay the CIA,
Who knew the bomb was gonna blow
Who know why the terrorists
Learned to fly in Florida, San Diego

Who know why Five Israelis was filming the explosion
And cracking they sides at the notion
Who need fossil fuel when the sun ain't goin' nowhere

Who make the credit cards
Who get the biggest tax cut
Who walked out of the Conference
Against Racism
Who killed Malcolm, Kennedy & his Brother
Who killed Dr King, Who would want such a thing?
Are they linked to the murder of Lincoln?

Who invaded Grenada
Who made money from apartheid
Who keep the Irish a colony
Who overthrow Chile and Nicaragua later

Who killed David Sibeko, Chris Hani,
the same ones who killed Biko, Cabral,
Neruda, Allende, Che Guevara, Sandino,
Who killed Kabila, the ones who wasted Lumumba, Mondlane,
Betty Shabazz, Die Princess Di, Ralph Featherstone,
Little Bobby

Who locked up Mandela, Dhoruba, Geronimo,
Assata, Mumia, Garvey, Dashiell Hammett, Alphaeus Hutton

Who killed Huey Newton, Fred Hampton,
Medgar Evers, Mikey Smith, Walter Rodney,
Was it the ones who tried to poison Fidel
Who tried to keep the Vietnamese Oppressed
Who put a price on Lenin's head

Who put the Jews in ovens,
and who helped them do it
Who said "America First" and ok'd the yellow stars

Who killed Rosa Luxembourg, Liebneckt
Who murdered the Rosenbergs
And all the good people iced, tortured, assassinated, vanished
Who got rich from Algeria, Libya, Haiti, Iran, Iraq, Saudi, Kuwait, Lebanon, Syria,
    Egypt, Jordan, Palestine,

Who cut off peoples' hands in the Congo
Who invented Aids
Who put the germs
In the Indians' blankets
Who thought up "The Trail of Tears"

Who blew up the Maine & started the Spanish American War
Who got Sharon back in Power
Who backed Batista, Hitler, Bilbo, Chiang kai Chek

Who decided Affirmative Action had to go
Reconstruction, The New Deal,
The New Frontier, The Great Society,

Who do Tom Ass Clarence Work for
Who doo doo come out the Colon's mouth
Who know what kind of Skeeza is a Condoleeza
Who pay Connelly to be a wooden Negro
Who give Genius Awards to Homo Locus
Subsidere

Who overthrew Nkrumah, Bishop,
Who poison Robeson, who try to put DuBois in Jail
Who frame Rap Jamil al Amin, Who frame the Rosenbergs, Garvey,
    The Scottsboro Boys,
The Hollywood Ten
Who set the Reichstag Fire

Who knew the World Trade Center was gonna get bombed
Who told 4000 Israeli workers at the Twin Towers
To stay home that day
Why did Sharon stay away?

Who? Who? Who?

Explosion of Owl the newspaper say
The devil face cd be seen
Who make money from war
Who make dough from fear and lies
Who want the world like it is

Who want the world to be ruled by imperialism and national oppression and terror
violence, and hunger and poverty.

Who is the ruler of Hell?
Who is the most powerful
Who you know ever Seen God?
But everybody seen The Devil

Like an Owl exploding
In your life in your brain in your self
Like an Owl who know the devil
All night, all day if you listen, Like an Owl
Exploding in fire. We hear the questions rise
In terrible flame like the whistle of a crazy dog

Like the acid vomit of the fire of Hell
Who and Who and WHO who who
Whoooo and Whooooooooooooooooooooooo!
(Baraka, October 13, 2001)

José Comblin asks us to consider the stance that people of conscience and people of faith should take toward situations of injustice when diverse and just perspectives are not profitable or patriotic. Recalling our discussion of theology in Chapter 3, consider this question in light of Mohammad's story and Comblin's analysis in *Called for Freedom: The Changing Context of Liberation Theology* (2000):

> Freedom of expression has been nullified in practice. All the media have fallen into the hands of groups identified with the economic model that some are seeking to establish. There is no more dialogue because there are no more interlocutors. Critics are, in practice, isolated from the lines of communication [and] . . . we have arrived at a totalitarian society in which there is only a single type of thinking and criticism vanishes. (p. 114)

Doublespeak, propaganda, censorship, intimidation, and popularity polls are trumping democratic engagement. If prophetic voices such as Mohammad's are being silenced and shunned, what can we do? Where do we turn for wisdom and prophetic strength? Comblin calls on people of faith to denounce the destruction of the human being and all of creation, as well as those who profit from it. He also calls for prophets to reestablish ethics in their public lives.

As we said in Chapter 3, we believe that our understandings of social justice and ethics can be influenced and inspired by repeated and varied exposure to the arts. Artists offer explanations that can serve as windows into the haunting nature of unfulfilled promises and destinies that affect each one of us. Kandinsky's book *Concerning the Spiritual in Art* (1977), for example, is at once an opportunity to understand materialism in art as well as the reformatory nature of conventional wisdom. Kandinsky's criticism provides us with opportunities to reflect on the extent to which the "tyranny of the materialistic philosophy divides our soul sharply." As we mine Kandinsky's philosophies and criticism further, we notice larger and larger cracks in the "false wisdom" and "blind spots" that increasingly dot our landscapes and attach us to socially anemic ends. Yet we also begin to resurrect and reconstruct glimpses of another art, according to Kandinsky, "that which is capable of educating further" (p. 2). At a time of escalating disparity of wealth, homelessness, environmental destruction, and war, we look for inspiration and hope to the "powerful prophetic strength" of art to "educate further," and to the spirit of Nietzsche's maxim that "no artist tolerates reality."

We have found Richard Wright's work to be particularly prophetic to our understanding of September 11. We see similarities between the reactions of U.S. citizens to September 11 and the reactions of whites to the murders committed by Bigger Thomas in Wright's novel *Native Son* (1940). Many white people like the Daltons fancied themselves as benevolently progressive for donating food and pool tables to blacks living in ghettos. Yet few whites had the wherewithal to recognize the insidiousness of their privilege and the stage it set for black rage. After all, it was Mr. Dalton who charged blacks higher rents than whites to live in unsafe tenements. He was also responsible for preventing blacks from moving into white communities. In other words, Mr. Dalton's excessive privilege and his social status were directly related to Bigger Thomas's misery.

We know that the Unites States can erect tall towers that pay tribute to economic accumulation. But we are uncertain whether people can imagine the forces that can prevent us from understanding what would propel a Bigger Thomas, a Dylan Klebold, or an Osama bin Laden to want to destroy the towers, other people, and themselves in fits of anger and hatred. Wright's message was clear: at some level, white America recognized its own culpability and guilt in not dismantling racial genocide when it reacted so violently in killing Bigger Thomas. As you read the following passage from *Native Son,* ask yourself how the plight of Bigger Thomas is related to our reactions to September 11 and what Richard Wright was trying to tell us about oppression, hatred, racism, and vengeance:

> How can law contradict the lives of millions of people and hope to be administered successfully? Do you believe in magic? Do you believe in burning a cross [or raising a flag]? You can frighten a multitude, paralyze their will and impulses. Do you think that white daughters in the homes of America will be any safer if you kill this boy? No! I tell you in all solemnity that they won't! The surest way to make certain that there will be more such murders is to kill this boy. In your rage and guilt, make thousands of other black men and women feel that the barriers are tighter and higher! Kill him and swell the tide of pent-up lava that will break loose, not in a single, blundering, accidental, individual crime, but in a wild cataract of emotion that will brook no control. (1940, p. 361)

Wright's prophetic warning can extend beyond race relations to the ramifications of class warfare, capital punishment, record numbers of prisoners, and the American crusade to rid the world of "terrorists." Most whites ignored Wright's message for decades, and the emotional, psychological, and social genocide of African Americans continues. Today, close to 90 percent of whites live in neighborhoods that are less than 1 percent black, and, according to Cornell West (1993), despair, hopelessness, and up-rootedness are growing for many blacks in the United States. West argues, like Wright fifty-three years earlier, that we are at "crucial crossroads in the history of this na-tion—and we either hang together by combating these forces that divide and degrade us or we hang separately. Do we have the intelligence, humor, imagination, courage, tolerance, love, respect, and will to meet the challenge?" (1993, p. 159). We believe there will be an even greater backlash if we ignore the more complex realities of Sep-tember 11, as well as the work of artists who portray them.

We are moved by the prophetic prose and poetry of Adrienne Rich (2001) when she speaks to the importance of an "oppositional imagination." Although Rich often addresses her calls for revisioning to women specifically, her analysis and insights are also opportunities for discovery by a cross section of people. Rich explores the con-cept of "Dead Awakening," an idea she borrows from Henrik Ibsen's play of the same title, as a means for encouraging us to "awaken . . . and understand the assumptions in which we are drenched." Like Maxine Greene's conception of "wide-awakeness" addressed in Chapter 2, "dead-awakening" or "revision" implies "the act of looking back, of seeing with fresh eyes. Of entering an old text from a new critical direction" (Rich, 2001, p. 11). It is intimately associated with the development of an oppositional imagination in that it necessitates deeper, more prophetic understandings and com-mitments. The probing critique, rebellious analysis, and insightful condemnation of the status quo by artists such as Rich are as essential now at a time of war as they ever were. If our main sources of information such as textbooks and television media con-tinue to live "under the naming and image-making power of a dominant culture," Rich insists that we need "an art to resist it" and hopefully contribute to what Peter McLaren (1991) refers to as the destruction of the obviousness of our lives.

We have included in this section poems, stories, and passages developed by some artists whose names you will recognize and some of whose you will not. Mr. Nathaniel Ruffin, an eighty-year-old African American man with whom we have worked on understanding children's responses to exposure to stress, violence, and beauty in Lorain, Ohio, provides detailed accounts of the racist forces (including ac-tions by "well-meaning" educators) that channeled him into a career in the merchant marines instead of as a medical doctor. Mr. Ruffin's life history also shocks us into fathoming how Nazi prisoners of war were sometimes more welcome than African American soldiers at roadside restaurants when they traveled together to prisoner-of-war camps in Ohio and Pennsylvania. Mr. Ruffin's understanding of the underlying guilt of white administrators and of African American children's legitimate rejection of suburban standards and logic is vibrant, and his three catalogs of African American teachers, scientists, military officers, inventors, and artists who are not included in the public school curriculum (a curriculum his grandson is currently being tested on) are as telling as his words: "It isn't so much that it is intentional, for racism today is very

subtle, . . . it's hard to break and, after you do things and after your mind gets pro-
grammed a certain way, in time . . . you really don't have any real thoughts on it"
(Rapp, 2001a, p. 14). Mr. Ruffin's profound sadness reminds us that the United States
developed a constitutional framework for equality but has never fully committed itself to achieving it.

Poverty, racism, and genocide compel alternative visions of justice and freedom
in the world. How do we accomplish this in our classrooms? I (Patrick) use many
films, including *Vukovar,* which has elicited some of the most vocal responses from
students. *Vukovar* is a disturbing film that exposes cycles of violence, ethnic hatred,
rape, the absurdity of war, and cultural division or "Balkanization" (a common term,
but one that is offensive to those who live in the Balkan Peninsula and cherish their
homeland). The film, shot on location in the city of Vukovar, Croatia, during a lull in
the Bosnian conflict in 1992, tells the story of two young lovers who marry just before the 1989 collapse of the Berlin Wall in Germany and the eventual breakup of
many communist countries, including Yugoslavia. The young man is a Serbian Orthodox Christian who is drafted and eventually required to fight against his home-
town. The young woman is a Croatian Byzantine Catholic whose home is destroyed,
parents are killed, and body is violated in a vicious rape. From the end of World War
II up through 1992, the families of both young people lived together in an ethnically
mixed neighborhood, never believing that the atrocities of the past could ever revisit
them again. Vukovar had become a large cosmopolitan city with striking vistas overlooking the Danube River. It is a historic and ancient city separating Croatia and Serbia, two countries that suddenly reignite old hatreds and return to war. Many places
of violence in the world today are inhabited by rival communities that must find a way
to share the land despite a fractured and violent past: Israelis and Palestinians,
Catholics and Protestants in Northern Ireland, and Croatians and Serbs in Vukovar.

This film traces events leading up to the 1992 war and then documents the total
destruction of Vukovar. The ethnic hatred of the two countries is contrasted with the
love of the two young people. We are left with the haunting question of why cycles of
violence destroy families, countries, and lovers. The final scene in the film is a stunning visually aerial tour of the desolate city of Vukovar. Every home is destroyed and
every landmark lies in ruins, but the young woman has given birth to a child. Does the
child represent hope for peace or the beginning of the next generation of violence? In
the film, as in the post–September 11 global community, it is up to us to decide.

After viewing this film, I take my students to visit former Yugoslavians who
now live among us in our own community. I arrange in advance meetings with
refugees and immigrants from the various countries that make up the former Yugoslavia. The last time I conducted this tour was in Cleveland in the summer of 2001.
We visited with Serbs at St. Sava's Orthodox Catholic church, Bosnian Muslims at the
mosque in Parma, Ohio (a mosque that was, coincidentally, in the news when it was
damaged in a retaliatory automobile assault following September 11), Slovenian and
Croatian Byzantine Catholics at their downtown Cleveland community center, and international students and business leaders from Sarajevo (home of the Olympics in the

1980s and a beautiful cosmopolitan and ethnically diverse city) at the Dom social center in East Lake, Ohio.

I spent an entire Saturday with my students visiting these various people. Although most of them are now U.S. citizens, they all still have family, business, or friends in the former Yugoslavia. At the end of the day, my students have intense headaches. At each stop on our tour, we are convinced by the story we heard: The Muslims are the victims; no, the Croatians are the victims. The U.S. media have maligned the Serbs; no, the Serbs are evil and the Muslims in Kosovo deserve the support of the U.S. military and the United Nations peacekeepers. The Croatians are to blame; no, the Serbs started it. Look at what they did in World War II; no, consider the Ottoman Empire hundreds of years ago. What about the schism between the churches in 1000 CE? And so forth.

Recall that the United States had just bombed Serbia and forced Slobodan Milosevic out of the country and into a war crimes tribunal in the Hague shortly before the summer of 2001, and that the Serbs were furious with the United States siding with their enemy. Others, however, were furious with the United States and other global powers for allowing genocide, rape, and destruction to continue for so long before they intervened.

Everyone we spoke to had a story. Many elderly woman wept as they spoke of the rapes, the executions of their relatives, and the torching of their homes and villages. Even in the churches, we heard impassioned calls for vengeance and retribution. At every stop, we gently prodded for suggestions and solutions. Again and again we were told, "It will take generations to solve this problem. We were just beginning to heal the division from World War II, and now this war!" The most optimistic speaker was a young woman from Sarajevo who had lived through bombings in 1992 and the destruction of 1999. She had just arrived in the United States in the summer of 2001, and she reported that the young people do not want to perpetuate the ethnic hatred; they want their city to return to the ethnically diverse cosmopolitan community they knew as children. We hope she speaks for many others.

The purpose of this field experience, like all of the field experiences we conduct with our students, is not only to provide an in-depth study of a specific issue such as the political and religious history of the conflict in the former Yugoslavia, but also to use this experience as a metaphor for exploring cycles of violence, ethnic hatred, the absurdity of war, and ethnic divisions around the world and throughout history. In addition, we urge our students to use this experience to examine Balkanization and cycles of violence in their own communities, schools, and churches with an eye toward alternative solutions to hatred, violence, war, rape, genocide, and terrorism. My students present political solutions to the ethnic violence in Serbia, Kosovo, Bosnia-Herzegovina, Slovenia, Albania, Montenegro, and Croatia (all parts of the former Yugoslavia that they now understand on an intimate personal level after our tour), as well as ecumenical solutions to the division between the various religions. Removed from the Yugoslav context, solutions appear possible. However, once my students begin to express their initial proposals for resolution, the complexity of historical, emotional, religious, economic, and political realities explode. Even so, I hope to inspire in my students a commitment to study and understand these complexities, listen to all parties involved, search out minority voices that are not even present in the discussions for further insights (i.e., Bosnian Jews, Roma, mixed-race children, immigrant workers), and apply the lessons of the former Yugoslavia to the division and Balkanization in their own communities. This is one of a series of field experiences I use with students to explicate educational ethics. Films and narratives are an integral part of the process to frame our discussions and activities.

If you have viewed the beautiful and provocative Spanish movie *I, the Worst of All,* you are aware that art is nonconformist at heart and that people with power fear it. Juana Inez de la Cruz was recognized around the world as a passionate, ironic, and intelligent poet. Many labeled her the tenth Muse because of her limitless daring for interpreting Descartes, Gassendi, and Christian Scripture. Unfortunately, Sister Juana was living during the Spanish Inquisition and many in the Catholic Church condemned her as a heretic, a disobedient woman, and a lascivious nun. What did Sister Juana know that so upset and scared the religious hierarchy? Did intelligence extend beyond gender? Could Platonic love exist between a veiled nun and crowned vicarate? Were her "perverse attentions" really a stab at the Savior, as the Church insisted? Eventually, the archbishop of New Spain (in seventeenth-century Mexico) confiscated her books, burned them, and made reading her poetry a crime. But he could not fully manufacture her consent, because her divinely orchestrated imagination and memories could not be erased.

In *Art and Alienation,* Herbert Read makes the point that art is "eternally disturbing, permanently revolutionary," and writes, "It is so because the artist, in the degree of his greatness, always confronts the unknown, and what he brings back from that confrontation is a novelty, a new symbol, a new vision of life, the outer image of inward things. . . . The artist is what the Germans call *ein Rutter,* an upsetter of the established order" (qtd. in Zinn, 1997, p. 653).

Herbert Read took part in a mass protest against nuclear warfare and the addictive "reason" of the times in 1961. He argued that "an act of disobedience is or should be collectively instinctive, a revolt of the instincts of man against the threat of mass destruction. . . . We must release the imagination of the people so that they become fully conscious of the fate that is threatening them" (qtd. in Zinn, 1997, p. 654). This is exactly what Sister Juana was attempting to do in her work as scientist, theologian, philosopher, and teacher. We must reseize the potential of releasing the imagination for our work as citizens and educators.

Art can engage the imagination of the artist as much as the audience's imagination. I (Dana) say this in the context of recently being involved with a group of teachers who were outraged both at the extent to which standardized tests were dictating their work and at how policymakers and administrators refused to invite or honor their perspectives on the issue. As a group, we interwove a variety of objects, images, poems, and songs into an art installation that depicted our disgust at how high-stakes testing was destroying the imagination of children, how drugs were used to medicate students into ideological submission, and how racial, class, and gender injustices were being masked by state policy. While I was attending an antitest rally at a Cincinnati school, several elementary school students began to pick up the empty Ritalin bottles, the skulls, and the hammers laid out on the base of this installation. "This is exactly how we feel about these tests," one young child said as he held up part of a skeleton. Parents and journalists overheard the children and began to ask them questions. Many appeared shocked when the students relayed stories of hating school, sadness, and constant feelings of inadequacy. I am certain that without our art installation, the abuses of high-stakes testing would never have captured the imaginations of students, parents, legislators, and journalists in Cincinnati that day to the degree it did. Within three days, we had interviews and photo opportunities with print and television media around the state, even *TIME Magazine,* as well as numerous calls from parents around the state asking about their rights to opt their children out of tests.

Educators can engage the arts and artists as a means for extending "beyond the same elites and voices that recycle the older frameworks to leaders . . . who can situate themselves within a larger historical narrative [and] who are attuned to the frightening obstacles that now perplex us" (West, 1993, p. 7). David Purpel speaks to the importance of this role for educators:

> As educators we must confront ourselves and the public with the harsh reality of the basic ignorance and intellectual failures of those who by conventional standards have had the very best education. . . . Educators must confront our moral failure by seriously considering the relationship between the realities of hunger, poverty, and misery and the nature of existing educational programs. . . . The profession must begin with the perspective of hunger, war, poverty, or starvation as its starting point, rather than from the perspective of problems of textbook selection, teacher certification requirements, or discipline policies. (1993, pp. 350, 360)

We agree with David Purpel. What is needed is a concerted commitment to politics and struggle at a time when there appears to be a strengthening of power exhibited by some of the people who call themselves leaders and a warning of conviction and creative action by those of us who oversee the landscapes of education and democracy.

Aung San Suu Kyi, the Burmese civil rights leader who has led a brilliant campaign against the ruthless state of martial law in Burma, has answered an ethical and spiritual call through nonviolence and civil disobedience. Like Martin Luther King Jr. and Mahatma Gandhi, Abdul Gaffar Khan, Aung San Suu Kyi (another Nobel Peace Prize winner) argues for peace as a moral and spiritual principle more than a political tactic. She argues that we must not encourage and perpetuate the tradition of bringing about change through violence, because even if we achieve democracy in this way, we will never rid ourselves of the notion that change necessitates violence. Whether the issue is bringing about democracy through the heightened militarism of "enduring freedom" or raising performance with high-stakes testing and homogenized curricula, we ask that you consider Aung San Suu Kyi's response as a means to inform your reactions. We also ask you to consider your greatest sources of inspiration. Whose bold actions have you found to be prophetic and inspiring? Ultimately, what cosmological images inform your thinking, where did these images originate, and how could they inform the *ein Rutter* in you?

Teaching Convictions

I (Dana) think back to the powerful impact that a series of images of poverty, racial hatred, hunger, gay bashing, and ecological destruction had on an audience of two hundred students and professors at the Leadership Academy in Massachusetts in July 2001. Most of the audience was moved to tears by the real and gut-wrenching displays of injustice and hope. In fact, many people left the audience to approach and encourage the men and women (principals and teachers) who had taken the risk of condemning injustice in the world and speaking of alternative futures. I'll always remember, however, the professor next to me who, not knowing that this presentation came from one of the groups of students with whom I worked, turned and asked, "Why don't they lighten up a little? Is the world really that bad? Why don't they focus on issues that educators will face in schools?" I responded to Professor Jones as I respond to students, family, friends, and colleagues. Maybe we have lightened up too much. Maybe we are willing to lock ourselves in our university offices and our school classrooms to the point of becoming comfortably numb to unacceptable levels of suffering, dehumanization, and injustice to others and to the planet. I honestly believe that Professor Jones recognizes the need to address race, war, poverty, patriarchy, and homophobia despite his cold reaction. I say this after watching him move to a corner of the auditorium, place his head in his hands, and begin crying uncontrollably fifteen minutes after our discussion. The events of September 11, as it turns out, have only solidified my convictions.

We don't know where the tragic events of September 11, 2001, and the collapsed of Enron two months later will eventually lead, but there is reason for hope. College students; Quaker organizations; Muslim leaders; human rights campaigners; gay rights groups; theologians; United Nations leaders such as Kofi Annan, who was awarded the Nobel Peace Prize shortly after the tragedy; Amnesty International; and even some politicians from around the country and around the globe are organizing and marching for peace and antiracism, not only in our hometowns of Austin, Texas, and Cleveland, Ohio, but also in Washington, D.C.; Eugene, Oregon; San Francisco, California; and New York City. Farmers, small business owners, factory workers, child labor fighters, environmental activists, and human rights advocates are also taking part in antiglobalization protests in places such as in Seattle, Genoa, and Quebec. Many high school students and their parents in New York, Massachusetts, and Ohio are refusing to take part in high-stakes testing. Ralph Nader is inspiring audiences around the country at the new democracyrising.com rallies. And citizens seem to be voicing opinions with a greater commitment to complexity and justice. Hank Rossiter of Dalton, Ohio, for example, provides a lucid analysis and alternative to war and militarism (Rossiter, 2002):

> President Bush in his State of the Union speech, voted to continue the "war" on terrorism and suggests markedly increasing the military budget as one means of accomplishing this end. My fear is that we in the United States are developing a siege mentality that drives us, as individuals and as a nation, to pursue questionable policies and behaviors; and that brands dissent as un-American. May I offer some alternative measures in this "war" that might prove more effective, if we, as a nation, have the political and moral will to pursue them? (1) We must eliminate the root causes of terrorism by changing our foreign policy from one of supporting our chosen authoritarian regimes to one of investing in basic and democratic rights of all peoples. (2) We must end the arms trade. The U.S. remains the largest arms merchant. (3) We must consistently condemn all terrorism, whether carried out by U.S. "Enemies" or allies. (4) We must isolate the criminals by exposing the lies terrorists spread and by putting them in open and fair trails. It is highly hypocritical of the U.S. to say we are fighting for justice while refusing to join the world's International Court. (5) We must promote alternative energy sources and conservation, thereby reducing our dependence on foreign oil products which are often at the center of misguided Middle East policies. (6) We must end the "Star Wars" missile defense program. It will not work and is not needed. Such a program will literally waste billions of dollars that could be spent on basic development needs both here and abroad. There is no simple or quick way to end terrorism. If the U.S. is actually the causes of terrorism, then we must join the world community, rather than acting like a rogue state, intent on imposing our will militarily. We must stop putting our economic well-being above our ethics. For if we *invest* in war, with our dollars and our psyches, war will *surely* come. (A4)

Citizens appear to be waking up to the urgency of activism and action on a multitude of issues. This gives us a deep sense of hope.

We believe that professors and K–12 educators should continually seek to understand the complexities of the post-Enron and post-911 moment while working with individuals and groups to more forcefully demand peace, tolerance, acceptance, justice, equal economic privilege, and ecological sustainability. We can also affirm the work of people in, outside, and around our groups who will "blow our minds," unsettle our convictions, and demand that we proclaim our love of freedom loudly (Camus, 1960; Hillman & Ventura, 1992). We can nurture our emotional, theoretical, theatrical, artistic, empirical, spiritual, and prophetic ties with people who are acting on the margins of counterhegemonic movements, such as the WTO protestors in Seattle and the campaign to end the death penalty in Austin.

Our collective impulses can begin to publicly address some aspects of these situations if we practice it (*praxis* it) with and for those we love. Tolstoy's acquaintances often commented that as a teacher he was able to "fire minds to white heat" in which "electric sparks were striking into the depths of souls and setting in motion all kinds of thoughts and plans and decisions (Troyat, 1967, p. 309). Perhaps this is our calling as educators. After all,

> What kind of person can we admire, can we ask young people of the next generation to emulate—the strict follower of law or the dissident who struggles, sometimes within, sometimes outside, sometimes against the law, but always for justice? What life is best worth living—the life of the proper obedient, dutiful follower of law and order or the life of the independent thinker, the rebel? (Zinn, 1997, p. 402)

If educators are serious about peace, ecological justice, erasing racism, reversing hatred, and ending starvation, then we must migrate to people who will inspire, challenge, and propel us to act through their language, art, and theories and, above all, their radical democratic energy. We need to surround ourselves with radical democrats whose commitments to social justice are part of an unfinished praxis out of which more spirits, visions, actions, and movements have come/are coming/are about to come. We must not go quietly into the night.

Individual teachers make a huge difference in this process. We think of Jane Haggard, an instructor in a rural college in south central Texas who has developed a speech course based on her commitment to social advocacy issues. Her Power of Positive Speaking: Speech Methods and Practices course takes students on a mindful journey of self-reflection by way of research, writing, and speaking assignments. Throughout the semester, students are challenged to review the contributions of family, friends, or community/national/world figures who have made positive impacts on society. Based on their review of these notable figures throughout the semester, a foundation for advocacy is built. The final course assignment challenges students to determine and promote their own social advocacy. The biographies of people from the student's personal life who advocate for social change and who displace hegemonic status quo mentalities become role models and mentors for the final speaking assignment. The speech class becomes a laboratory for social justice.

Occasionally, a service-learning methodology emerges from the students' self-reflective odyssey. Among the experiences that illustrate this component of the course is that of the team who visited a children's hospital and ultimately became actively involved in the lives of these children, many of whom were in long-term care. This team developed an activity by which to care for the children's emotional well-being as a diversion from illness and a reprieve from boredom and loneliness. The students and young patients developed friendships as they visited and laughed together. Another example of the service-learning methodology emerging from an advocacy-based classroom is a team of students who worked at a mission house for the homeless and displaced families within the community. This experience not only taught the students the principles of research, a course goal, but also, and more important, provided transformative insights into how they can make a positive impact in their community through social action.

Dr. Haggard is guided by a philosophy that provides students with an opportunity for transformation of their own design in order to develop a vision of justice in their community, nation, and world. Her course Voices of Advocacy: Vision and Action offers total immersion in social advocacy issues from the beginning to the end of the semester. The development of this course illustrates the instructor's own transformation as she takes the hidden agenda of the curriculum—social conscience and agency—into the forefront of the speech classroom design.

It is our hope that other educators will provide examples of critical theories translated into constructive actions for social justice, like Jane Haggard and the many other teachers and students highlighted throughout this book. It is also our hope that we can begin by dealing with "the raw stuff of life, emotions and impulses and attitudes as a means for overcoming the traps of false moral fervor" (Wright, 1940, p. 357). These are our teaching convictions. This is the spirit that underpins this book. And here is the strength that propels us to continue teaching convictions, compassion, and justice in our classrooms and communities in the dangerous days ahead: In danger lies an opportunity. *Carpe diem!*

Teaching Convictions in a Postmodern World

The journey of writing this book has been one small part of our lives for the past three years: Dana and Kathy's son Heron was born on May 22, 2001; Patrick's daughter Kayty married Gannon Lamson, and their son Kaiser Isaac—Patrick's first grandchild—was born on February 15, 2001; Dana traveled to Scotland with his stepfather, Bill Rapp; Patrick sent his oldest daughter Michelle off to college at the University of Texas to study architecture; Dana's daughter Madeline began using words to express her passionate side; Patrick's son Josh turned sixteen and played in the Texas Cup High School Hockey Championship Tournament; Patrick and Josh were in a rollover accident on I-35 in Waco on the way to Dallas on December 16, 2000; Dana began exploring plans for new career options, resulting in a new position at Massachusetts College of Liberal Arts; and Patrick and Craig held two gallery shows of their artwork in Austin in 2001–2002.

We have both experienced births and deaths, successes and failures, harmony and conflict, exhilaration and despair, and certainly doubt over the past three years. We live in the challenging and difficult postmodern era—a time when familiar patterns of relating to the world have been interrupted, comfortable ways of living in community have been problematized, traditional institutions in society have been troubled and reordered, socioeconomic structures have been disrupted, theological beliefs and spiritualities have been transformed, global relations have been agitated, categories of race, class, gender, sexuality, family, ethnicity, ability, and theology have been deconstructed and reconstituted, and theories of ethics and morality have been exploded. These developments cause some citizens to retreat into the security of old patterns and behaviors. Sociopolitical and philosophical upheaval cause others to reevaluate their lives in relation to the emerging global context. Postmodern changes inspire a few to speak prophetically for justice in the midst of poststructural pastiche and uncertainty. Although we encourage this last impulse and challenge ourselves to work for justice, we realize how difficult it is to break free of prejudices, or even recognize our biases, in order to nurture a sense of possibilities and hope.

As we come to the end of this book, we realize that we have been convinced to interrupt and problematize our own privileged positionality in the world. Although we certainly contribute to racism, environmental degradation, heterosexism, gender bias, religious intolerance, and poverty, either by our silence, our lifestyle, or our privilege, we also seek to dismantle the structures that perpetuate these injustices. We encourage you to do the same. As we review this text before publication in the summer of

2002, we wonder what 2003 holds for us and for the world. But in the proleptic spirit discussed in Chapter 2, we do not pause to wonder for long. We ground ourselves in the present moment and commit ourselves to the task of ethical living in a democratic and just society.

We wanted to explore many other topics in this book, but we ran out of space and time—or maybe we could have organized our priorities in other ways. In either case, our files are full of additional research materials. Like the phenomenologists who foreground what is experienced but seemingly absent, we strive to notice what is ambiguous, uncertain, or neglected. We wanted to include more poetry, art, narratives, and lyrics. We wanted to add an entire chapter on intersexuality based on the work of William Stanley, dean of education at Redlands University in California, and Anne Fausto-Sterling, professor and feminist biologist at Brown University. We wanted to explore classroom tracking as it relates to race and ethnicity in the spirit of the work of Michelle Fine, professor of psychology at the City University of New York, and Lois Weis, professor of education at the State University of New York at Buffalo. The work of Jeanne Brady, director of the doctoral program in educational leadership at St. Joseph's University in Philadelphia inspires our thinking about public pedagogy and aesthetics, and we wanted to explore further ethical issues in relation to public activism. We realize that our commitment to teaching convictions on critical ethical issues and education is continually beginning anew.

As we ponder the things that were not included in our book, we are reminded that education never ends. Poets and philosophers teach us that the journey of life is a process and not a final destination. As we said in the prelude, ethics is a way of living and being in the world and not a static set of rules and regulations. Thus, in the postmodern global community, teaching convictions is the only possible curriculum we can imagine. When we work to dismantle racism and patriarchy, deconstruct heterosexism and classism, work for equity and equality, teach tolerance and acceptance, respect the earth and all living things, comfort the afflicted and afflict the comfortable, and live simply so that others can simply live, then we understand a deeper and compelling vision and agenda of educational ethics. Let us commit ourselves to addressing critical ethical issues in our schools and society and living for justice, compassion, and ecological sustainability in the postmodern global milieu.

REFERENCES

Abu-Jamal, M. (1996). *Live from death row.* New York: Avon Books.

Abunimah, A. (2001). The truth about terrorism. In Russ Kick (Ed.), *You are being lied to: The disinformation guide to media distortion, historical whitewashes, and cultural myths* (pp. 114–117). New York: The Disinformation Company.

Adorno, T. W. (1991). How to look at television. In D. Ingram & S. J. Ingram (Eds.), *Critical theory: The essential readings* (pp. 69–82). New York: Paragon.

Aichele, G., et al. (1995). *The postmodern bible: The Bible and culture collective.* New Haven, CT: Yale University Press.

al-Faruqi, I. R. (1979). *Islam.* Niles, IL: Argus Communications.

Alinsky, S. (1969). *Reveille for radicals.* New York: Vintage.

Angelo, D. (2001, October). Why did they do it? *Oregon Peace Worker,* p. 6.

Apple, M. W. (1992). The text and cultural politics. *Educational Researcher, 21*(7), 4–11.

Apple, M. W. (1996). *Cultural politics and education.* New York: Teachers College Press.

Apple, M. W., & Christian-Smith, L. (Eds.). (1991). *The politics of the textbook.* New York: Routledge & Kegan Paul.

Arons, S. (1983). *Compelling belief: The culture of American schooling.* New York: McGraw Hill.

Aston, J. (2001a, July). Autopsy of hate: Ten years later. *Outsmart 8*(6), 64–69.

Aston, J. (2001b). Deconstructing heterosexism and homophobia in schools: Case study of a hate crime by an adolescent offender. *Dissertation Abstracts International* (UMI No. 3011676).

Bakhtin, M. (1993). *Toward a philosophy of the act* (Michael Holquist & Vadim Liapunov, Eds.). Austin: University of Texas Press.

Banks, J., & Banks, C. M. (Eds.). (1997). *Multicultural education: Issues and perspectives.* Boston: Allyn & Bacon.

Baraka, A. (2001, October 13). *Somebody blew up America.* Archived from www.pipeline.com/blewupamerica.

Barndt, J. R. (1991). *Dismantling racism: The continuing challenge to white America.* Minneapolis: Augsburg.

Barthes, R. (1975). *Roland Barthes by Roland Barthes* (R. Howard, Trans.). London: Macmillan.

Bateson, M. C. (1994). *Peripheral visions: Learning along the way.* New York: HarperCollins.

Bauman, Z. (1993). *Postmodern ethics.* Oxford, England: Blackwell.

Bell, D. A. (1992). *Faces at the bottom of the well: The permanence of racism.* New York: Basic Books.

Belluck, P., & Revkin, A. C. (2001, December 23). A mittenless autumn, for better and worse. *New York Times,* pp. A1, A18.

Bennett, J. R. (2001, December 12). Bush restoring integrity? *Akron Beacon Journal,* p. A15.

Bennett, W. (1986). *What works: Research about teaching and learning.* Washington, DC: U.S. Department of Education.

Bennett, W. (1987). *James Madison High School: A curriculum for American students.* Washington, DC: U.S. Department of Education.

Bennett, W. (1988). *James Madison elementary: A curriculum for American students.* Washington, DC: U.S. Department of Education.

Bennett, W. (1993). *The book of virtues: A treasury of great moral stories.* New York: Simon & Schuster.

Benson, S. (2001, November 4). *Benson's view.* [Editorial Cartoon]. *Arizona Republic.* Available: steve.benson@arizonarepublic.com

Bergson, H. (1997). *The creative mind: An introduction to metaphysics.* Sacremento, CA: Citadel Press.

Boff, L. (1979). *Jesus Christ liberator: A critical christology for our time* (P. Hughes, Trans.). Maryknoll, NY: Orbis Books.

Bonhoeffer, D. (1966). *The cost of discipleship.* New York: Macmillan.

Books, S. (Ed.). (1998). *Invisible children in the society and its schools.* New York: Lawrence Erlbaum.

Bowers, C. A. (2001). *Educating for eco-justice.* Athens: University of Georgia Press.

Bradshaw, J. (1991, July 14). The mother of lands. *The Lafayette Sunday Advertiser,* p. D.

BRC. (2001, September 13). Terror attacks of September 11, 2001. Message posted to electronic mailing list, archived at http://groups.yahoo.com/messages/brc_press

Britzman, D. P. (1995). Is there a queer pedagogy? Or, stop reading straight. *Educational Theory, 45*(2), 151–165.

Brodkey, L. (1996). *Writing permitted in designated areas only.* Minneapolis: University of Minnesota Press.

Buksbazen, J. D. (1977). *To forget the self.* Los Angeles: Zen Center of Los Angeles.

Burg, D., & Feiffer, G. (1972). *Solzhenitsyn.* New York: Stein & Day.

Burke, P. (1992). *The death and return of the author.* Edinburgh, Scotland: Edinburgh University Press.

Burke, P. (1995). *Collected poems.* Unpublished manuscript. Scottsdale, AZ.

Burke, P. (1998). *Georgia O'Keeffe at Ghost Ranch.* Unpublished poem.

Burns, J. F. (2002, January 27). Bin Laden stirs struggle on meaning of jihad. *New York Times,* p. 1.

Campbell, J., with Moyers, B. (1988). *The power of myth.* New York: Doubleday.

Camus, A. (1960). *Resistance, rebellion, and death: Essays.* New York: Vintage.

Capra, C. (1995). Deep ecology: A new paradigm. In G. Sessions (Ed.), *Deep ecology for the 21st century: Readings on the philosophy and practice of the new environmentalism* (pp. 19–25). Boston: Shambhala.

Carney, J. G. (1985). *To be a revolutionary: An autobiography.* San Francisco: Harper & Row.

Carson, R. (1962). *Silent spring.* Greenwich, CT: Fawcett.

Catholics speak out. (2000, October 23). [An open letter to candidates for office from Roman Catholic voters.] *New York Times,* p. A7. Also available: www.quixote.org/cso

Center for a Postmodern World. (1990). *Position paper on postmodernism* [John B. Cobb Jr., Ed.). Claremont, CA: Claremont Graduate School of Theology.

Cernuschi, C. (1992). *Jackson Pollock: "Psychoanalytic" drawings.* Durham, NC: Duke University Press.

Cheney, L. V. (1994, October 20). The end of history. *The Wall Street Journal,* p. A22.

Chipps, H. B. (Ed.). (1971). *Theories of modern art: A source book of artists and critics.* Berkeley: University of California Press.

Chomsky, N. (2000). *Miseducation.* New York: Rowman & Littlefield.

Claar, P. (2002, January 9). How is President Bush performing? *Akron Beacon Journal*, p. A9.

Clandinin, J. D., & Connelly, M. F. (2000). *Narrative inquiry: Experience and story in qualitative research.* San Francisco: Jossey Bass.

Cleary, E. L. (1985). *Crises and change: The church in Latin America today.* Maryknoll, NY: Orbis Books.

Clymer, A. (2001, August 4). Russian tries to pierce missile shield with charm. *New York Times,* p. A3.

Cobb, J. B. (2001). Introduction. *Processed Thoughts, 15*(4), pp. 1–4.

Cockburn, A., & St. Clair, J. (2000). *Five days that shook the world: Seattle and beyond.* New York: Verso.

Cohen, R. (1996). Moving beyond name games: The conservative attack on the U.S. history standards. *Social Education, 60*(1), 49–54.

Cohen, R. (1999, October 10). For a priest and for Poland, a tangled identity. *New York Times,* pp. A1, A6.

Cohn, R. (2002, January/February). Editor's note. *Mother Jones,* p. 4.

Comblin, J. (2000). *Called for freedom: The changing context of liberation theology* (P. Berryman, Trans.). Maryknoll, NY: Orbis Books.

Confraternity of Christian Doctrine. (1962). *The new St. Joseph Baltimore catechism.* (Official Rev. Ed. No. 2). New York: Catholic Book Publishing.

Cooper, J. F. (1999, Winter). Jackson Pollock: The right stuff. *American Arts Quarterly,* pp. 3–7.

Copeland, D. (2002, January 9). How is President Bush performing? *Akron Beacon Journal,* p. A9.

Counts, G. S. (1932). *Dare the schools build a new social order?* New York: John Day.

Culclasure, S. P. (1999). *The past as liberation from the present.* New York: Peter Lang.

Curran, C. (1986). *Faithful dissent.* Kansas City, MO: Sheed & Ward.

Daly, H. E., & Cobb, J. B., Jr. (1994). *For the common good: Redirecting the economy toward community, the environment, and a sustainable future* (3rd ed.). Boston: Beacon Press.

Davies, P. (1990). Cosmogenesis. *Creation, 6*(3), 10–13.

Davis, A. (1998). *Blues legacies and black feminism: Gertrude "Ma" Rainey, Bessie Smith and Billie Holiday.* New York: Vintage Books.

Davis, W. E. (2002, January 9). How is President Bush performing? *Akron Beacon Journal,* p. A9.

Dear, J. (2000). *Jesus: The bearer of God's peace and justice.* Franklin, WI: Sheed & Ward.

de Beauvoir, S. (1948a). *The ethics of ambiguity* (B. Frenchman, Trans.). New York: Philosophical Library.

de Beavuoir, S. (1948b). *The second sex.* New York: Vintage.

DeFranco, A., & Phillips, U. (1999). Stupid's pledge. *On Fellow workers* [CD]. Ellicott Station, Buffalo, NY: Righteous Babe Records.

Derrida, J. (1972). Discussion: Structure, sign and play in the discourse of the human sciences. In R. Macksey & E. Donato (Eds.), *The structuralist controversy* (pp. 247–272). Baltimore: Johns Hopkins University Press.

Derrida, J. (1981). *Positions.* Chicago: University of Chicago Press.

Derrida, J. (1982). *Margins of philosophy* (A. Bass, Trans.). Chicago: University of Chicago Press.

Dewey, J. (1934a). *Art as experience.* New York: Minton Balch.

Dewey, J. (1934b). *A common faith.* New Haven, CT: Yale University Press.

Dewey, J. (1938). *Experience and education.* New York: Macmillan.

Diamond, R. T., & Cottrol, R. J. (1983). Codifying caste: Louisiana's racial classification scheme and the Fourteenth Amendment. *Loyola Law Review, 29*(1), p. 255.

Dill, A. (2002, January 9). How is President Bush performing? *Akron Beacon Journal,* p. A9.

Doll, W. E. Jr. (1993). *A post-modern perspective on curriculum.* New York: Teachers College Press.

Druckenbrod, V. M. (2001, October 31). Because U.S. will win, we will be more secure. *Akron Beacon Journal,* p. A12.

Dumas, A. (2002, January 9). How is President Bush performing? *Akron Beacon Journal,* p. A9.

Dunn, L. (Director). (2000). *Green* [Film]. Austin, TX: Two Birds Films.

Eco, U. (1991). Postscript to *The name of the rose.* In Charles Jencks (Ed.), *The post-modern reader* (pp. 73–75). New York: St. Martin's Press.

Edwards, A. (1983). *Road to Tara: The life of Margaret Mitchell.* New Haven, CT: Ticknor & Fields.

Egan, T. (2001, December 21). In Sacramento, a publisher's questions draw the wrath of the crowd. *New York Times,* pp. B1, B5.

Ellis, C. (1997). Evocative autoethnography: Writing emotionally about our lives. In W. G. Tierney & Y. S. Lincoln (Eds.), *Representation and the text* (pp. 115–142). Albany: State University of New York Press.

Ellsworth, E. (1997). *Teaching positions: Difference, pedagogy, and the power of address.* New York: Teachers College Press.

Fanon, F. (1963). *The wretched of the earth.* New York: Grove Press.

Fausto-Sterling, A. (2000). *Sexing the body: Gender politics and the construction of sexuality.* New York: Basic Books.

Fitzgerald, B. (2001). *Locked away minds of rainbow flags.* Unpublished poem.

Flannery, A. (Ed.). (1975). Gaudium et Spes: Pastoral constitution on the church in the modern world, 1965. In *Vatican Council II: The counciliar and post counciliar documents* (study ed., pp. 903–1001). New York: Costello.

Foucault, M. (1972a). *The archaeology of knowledge.* New York: Pantheon.

Foucault, M. (1972b). *Power/Knowledge.* New York: Pantheon.

Foucault, M. (1977). *Language, counter-memory, practice.* Ithaca, NY: Cornell University Press.

Foucault, M. (1979). *Discipline and punish: The birth of the prison.* New York: Vintage Books.

Foucault, M. (1983). *This is not a pipe* (J. Harkness, Trans.). Berkeley: University of California Press.

Foucault, M. (1986a). *The history of sexuality, Vol. 2: The use of pleasure.* (R. Hurley, Trans.). New York: Pantheon.

Foucault, M. (1986b). *The history of sexuality, Vol. 3. The care of the self.* (R. Hurley, Trans.) New York: Pantheon.

Foucault, M. (1990). *The history of sexuality, Vol. 1: An introduction* (R. Hurley, Trans.). New York: Vintage Books.

Foucault, M. (1993). About the beginnings of the hermeneutics of the self. *Political Theory, 21*(3), 198–227.

Fox, M. (1990). *Original blessings.* San Francisco: Harper.

Franklin, K. (1997). Hate crimes or rites of passage? Assailant motivation in antigay violence. *Dissertation Abstracts International* (UMI No. 9715571). Available: http://www.lib.umi.com/dxweb

Franz, W. (2002, January 9). How is President Bush performing? *Akron Beacon Journal*, p. A9.

Freire, P. (1970). *Pedagogy of the oppressed.* New York: Continuum Press.

Freire, P. (1971, March). Conscientizing as a way of liberating. *Contacto*, pp. 5–13.

Freire, P. (1998). *Pedagogy of freedom: Ethics, democracy, and civic courage.* Lanham, MD: Rowman & Littlefield.

Fullbright, J. W. (1969). *The arrogance of power.* New York: Random House.

Gablik, S. (1991). *The reenchantment of art.* New York: Thames & Hudson.

Gadamer, H-G. (1975). *Truth and method.* New York: Crossroads. (Original work published 1960)

Gadamer, H-G. (1976). *Philosophical hermeneutics* (D. E. Linge, Ed. and Trans.). Berkeley: University of California Press.

Gaines, E. J. (1972). *The autobiography of Miss Jane Pittman.* New York: Bantam.

Gandhi, L. (1998). *Postcolonial theory: A critical introduction.* New York: Columbia University Press.

Gay, G. (1994). *At the essence of learning: Multicultural education.* West Lafayette, IN: Kappa Delta Pi.

Gelbspan, R. (1995). *The heat is on: The climate crisis: The cover-up: The prescription.* Reading, MA: Perseus.

Gershman, H. S. (1974). *The Surrealist revolution in France.* Ann Arbor: University of Michigan Press.

Gershon, D., & Straub, G. (1989). *Empowerment: The art of creating your life as you want it.* New York: Dell.

Gilligan, C. (1982). *In a different voice.* Cambridge, MA: Harvard University Press.

Gilmour, J. C. (1990). *Fire on the earth: Anselm Kiefer and the postmodern world.* Philadelphia: Temple University Press.

Giroux, H. A. (1988). *Schooling and the struggle of public life: Critical pedagogy in the modern age.* Minneapolis: University of Minnesota Press.

Giroux, H. A. (1992). *Border crossings: Cultural workers and the politics of education.* New York: Routledge.

Glassgold, P. (2001). *Anarchy: An anthology of Emma Goldman's Mother Earth.* Washington, DC: Counterpoint.

Gleick, J. (1987). *Chaos: Making a new science.* New York: Penguin.

Gleick, J. (1999). *Faster: The acceleration of just about everything.* New York: Pantheon.

Glendinning, C. (1995). Recovery from western civilization. In G. Sessions (Ed.), *Deep ecology in the twenty-first century: Readings on the philosophy and practice of the new environmentalism* (pp. 37–40). Boston: Shambhala.

Goodlad, J. I., Soder, R., & Sirotnik, K. A. (Eds.). (1990). *The moral dimensions of teaching.* San Francisco: Jossey Bass.

Greene, M. (1995). *Releasing the imagination.* New York: Teachers College Press.

Greene, M. (2001). *Variations on a blue guitar: The Lincoln Center Institute lectures on aesthetic education.* New York: Teachers College Press.

Griffin, D. R. (1988). *The reenchantment of science: Postmodern proposals.* Albany: State University of New York Press.

Grumet, M. R. (1988). *Bitter milk: Women and teaching*. Amherst: University of Massachusetts Press.

Guerin, D. (Ed.). (1998). *No gods, no masters: An anthology of anarchism* (P. Sharkey, Trans.). San Francisco: AK Press

Guthrie, W. (1998). *This land is your land.* (Original work published 1956)

Gutierrez, G. (1973). *A theology of liberation: History, politics, and salvation* (Sis. C. Inda & J. Eagleson, Trans.). Maryknoll, NY: Orbis Books.

Hahn, T. N. (1995). *Living Buddha, living Christ.* New York: Riverhead.

Halstead, T. (2002, January 8). Rich school, poor school. *New York Times,* p. A23.

Harris, C. (1999, March 31). Reader provides verses about gays. *The Battalion, 105*(119), 11A.

Harwell, R. (Ed.). (1976). *Margaret Mitchell's* Gone with the Wind *letters: 1936–1949.* New York: Macmillan.

Harwit, M. (1996). *An exhibit denied: Lobbying the history of the* Enola Gay. New York: Springer-Verlag.

Hebert, B. (2002, February 11). The fatal flaws. *New York Times,* p. A29.

Hegel, G. W. F. (1977). *Phenomenology of spirit.* (T. M. Knox, Trans.) New York: Harper Torch Books.

Helminiak, D. A. (2000). *What the Bible really says about homosexuality* (7th ed.). San Francisco: Alamo Square Press.

Henderson, J. G., & Hawthorne, R. D. (1995). *Transformative curriculum leadership.* New York: Macmillan.

Higgins, C., & Wilson-Baptist, K. (2001). Accidental tourist: Curriculum lost in public spaces. In J. Sears & K. Sloan (Eds.), *Democratic curriculum theory and practice: Retrieving public spaces* (pp. 191–203). New York: Education International Press.

Hillis, V. (Ed.). (1999). *The lure of the transcendent: Collected essays by Dwayne E. Huebner.* (William F. Pinar, Coll. and Intro.). Mahwah, NJ: Lawrence Erlbaum.

Hillman, J., & Ventura, M. (1992). *We've had a hundred years of psychotherapy and the world's getting worse.* New York: HarperCollins.

hooks, b. (1993). Altars of sacrifice: Remembering Basquiat. *Art in America, 11*(3), 67–75.

hooks, b. (1994). *Teaching to transgress: Education as the practice of freedom.* New York: Routledge.

Hopps, W. (Ed.). (1996). *Keinholtz: A retrospective.* New York: Distributed Art Publishers in association with the Whitney Museum of Art.

Howard, R. J. (1982). *Three faces of hermeneutics.* Berkeley: University of California Press.

Huebner, D. E. (1991). *Educational activity and prophetic criticism.* New Haven, CT: Yale University Divinity School.

Hudson CEE Explorer. (1996, June-July). Hudson school board rejects AP history text. *CEE Newsletter 3*(2), 1–4.

Hudson Portfolio. (1996). Unpublished curriculum materials. Hudson, Ohio.

Hughes, L. (1973). The negro speaks of rivers. In R. Ellmann & R. O'Clair (Eds.), *The Norton anthology of modern poetry* (pp. 634–635), New York: W. W. Norton

Jackson, P., Boostrom, R. B., & Hansen, D. T. (1993). *Moral life in schools.* New York: Holt, Reinhart, & Winston.

Jardine, D. W. (1992). Reflections on education, hermeneutics, and ambiguity: Hermeneutics a restoring of life to its original difficulty. In W. F. Pinar & W. M. Reynolds (Eds.), *Un-*

derstanding curriculum as phenomenological and deconstructed texts (pp. 116–130). New York: Longman.

Jensen, R. (2000). *Writing dissent: Taking radical ideas from the margin to the mainstream.* New York: Peter Lang.

Jung, C. G. (1962). *Memories, dreams, reflections* (A. Jaffe, Ed.; C. Winston & R. Winston, Trans.). New York: Random House.

Jung, C. G. (1977). Synchronicity: As a causal connecting principle. In *Collected Works* (Vol. 8, R. F. C. Hull, Trans.). Princeton, NJ: Princeton University Press.

Kandinsky, W. (1977). *Concerning the spiritual in art* (M. T. H. Sadler, Trans.). New York: Dover.

Kick, R. (Ed.). (2001). *You are being lied to: The disinformation guide to media distortion, historical whitewashes, and cultural myths.* New York: The Disinformation Company.

Kincheloe, J. L., & Pinar, W. F. (Eds.). (1991). *Curriculum as social psychoanalysis: The significance of place.* Albany: State University of New York Press.

Kincheloe, J. L., Slattery, P., & Steinberg, S. R. (2000). *Contextualizing teaching: Introduction to education and education foundations.* New York: Addison Wesley Longman.

Kirylo, J. (2001). Liberation theology. *Journal of Research on Christian Education, 10*(1), 53–86.

Koch, D. (1991). *Dewey's lectures on ethics: 1900–1901.* Carbondale: Southern Illinois University Press.

Kohl, H. (1998). Some reflections on teaching for social justice. In W. Ayers, J. A. Hunt, & T. Quinn (Eds.), *Teaching for social justice: A democracy and education reader.* New York: Teachers College Press.

Korty, J. (Producer). (1973). *The autobiography of Miss Jane Pittman* [Motion picture]. Los Angeles: Prism Entertainment.

Kozol, J. (1967). *Death at an early age.* Boston: Houghton Mifflin.

Kozol, J. (1991). *Savage inequalities: Children in America's schools.* New York: Crown.

Kozol, J. (1995). *Amazing grace.* New York: Crown.

Krugman, P. (2001a, December 4). A defining issue. *New York Times,* p. A23.

Krugman, P. (2001b, December 11). Laissez not fair. *New York Times,* p. A27.

Krugman, P. (2002, January 29). The great divide. *New York Times,* p. A27.

Kumashiro, K. (2003). *Queer theory and education.* New York: Educators International Press.

Kung, H. (1988). *Theology for the third millennium: An ecumenical view.* New York: Doubleday.

Kyung, C. H. (1995). *In arms for the poor* [Motion picture]. New York: Maryknoll World Productions.

Langer, S. (1957). *Problems of art.* New York: Charles Scribner.

Lasch, C. (1984). *The minimal self: Psychic survival in troubled times.* New York: W. W. Norton.

Lather, P., & Smithies, C. (1997). *Troubling the angels: Women living with HIV/AIDS.* Boulder, CO: Westview/HarperCollins.

Lawrence-Lightfoot, S. (1983). *The good high school: Portraits of character and culture.* New York: Basic Books.

Lawrence-Lightfoot, S., & Davis, J. H. (1997). *The art and science of portraiture.* San Francisco: Jossey Bass.

Lee, E. (2001). School textbooks. In R. Kick (Ed.), *You are being lied to: The disinformation guide to media distortion, historical whitewashes, and cultural myths* (pp. 73–78). New York: The Disinformation Company.

Letts, W. J., & Sears, J. T. (Eds.). (1999). *Queering elementary education: Advancing the dialogue about sexuality and schooling.* Lanham, MD: Roman & Littlefield.

Loewen, J. W. (1995). *Lies my teacher told me.* New York: Simon & Schuster.

Loewen, J. W. (2000). *Lies across America.* New York: Simon & Schuster.

Lorde, A. (1984). *Sister outsider: Essays and other speeches.* Freedom, CA: Crossing Press.

Lum, M. (2001, December 21). Rocker: Texas Ranger MLB pitcher known for antigay, racist remarks traded to the Lone Star State. *Texas Triangle, X*(11), p. 2.

Lyman, H., with G. Merzer. (1998). *Mad cowboy: Plain truth from the cattle rancher who won't eat meat.* New York: Scribner.

Macdonald, J. B. (1988). Theory, practice, and the hermeneutic circle. In W. F. Pinar (Ed.), *Contemporary curriculum discourses* (pp. 101–113). Scottsdale, AZ: Gorsuch & Scarisbrick.

Macdonald, J. B. (1995). *Theory as a prayerful act: The collected essays of James B. Macdonald.* New York: Peter Lang.

Macgillivray, I. K. (2002). *Sexual orientation and school policy: A practical guide for teachers, administrators, & community activists.* New York: Educators International Press.

Madeley, J. (1999). *Big business, poor peoples: The impact of transnational corporations on the world's poor.* New York: Zed Books.

Mancuso, D. (Producer). (1991). *Old man river* [Motion picture]. New Orleans: Aquarium of the Americas.

Mander, J. (1995). Leaving the earth: Space colonies, Disney, and EPCOT. In G. Sessions (Ed.), *Deep ecology for the twenty-first century: Readings on the philosophy and practice of the new environmentalism* (pp. 311–320). Boston: Shambhala.

Marcus, E. (1998). *Vegan: The new ethics of eating.* Ithaca, NY: McBooks.

Maurer, D. (1999, March 2). What suffering children need. *Cleveland Plain Dealer,* p. B7.

McBride, J. (1996). *The color of water.* New York: Simon & Schuster.

McElfresh-Spehler, R., & Slattery, P. (1999). Voices of imagination: The artist as prophet in the process of social change. *International Journal of Leadership in Education, 2*(1), 1–12.

McGibbon, B. (1999). *The end of nature.* New York: Anchor.

McGowan, D. (2001). Anatomy of a school shooting. In R. Kick (Ed.), *You are being lied to: The disinformation guide to media distortion, historical whitewashes, and cultural myths* (pp. 124–127). New York: The Disinformation Company.

McLaren, P. (1991). *Life in schools.* New York: Routledge.

McLaren, P. (1994). *Life in schools: An introduction to critical pedagogy in the foundations of education* (2nd ed.). New York: Longman.

McLaren, P. (1997). *Revolutionary multiculturalism: Pedagogy of dissent for the new millennium.* Boulder, CO: Westview Press.

McNamara, R. S., Blight, J. G., & Brigham, R. K. (1999). *Argument without end: In search of answers to the Vietnam strategy.* New York: Public Affairs.

Merchant, C. (1992). *Radical ecology: The search for a livable world.* New York: Routledge.

Merchant, C. (1996). *Earthcare: Women and the environment.* New York: Routledge.

Merton, T. (1965). *Gandhi on non-violence.* New York: New Directions.

Miller, J. (1990). *Creating spaces and finding voices: Teachers collaborating for empowerment.* Albany: State University of New York Press.

Mitchell, M. (1936). *Gone with the wind.* New York: Macmillan.

Mokhiber, R., & Weissman, R. (2001, November 15). Kill, kill, kill. Message posted to *Focus on the Corporation,* archived at corp-focus@venice.essential.org

Monbiot, G. (2001, October 23). America's pipe dream. *The Guardian.* Retrieved February 25, 2002, from http://www.guardian.co.uk/Archive/Article/0,4273,4283019,00.html

Moore, T. (1992). *Care of the soul.* New York: HarperCollins.

Morgan, A. (2002). *My autobiography.* Unpublished paper. Ashland, OH.

Morgan, G. (1997). *Images of organization.* Thousand Oaks, CA: Sage.

Mostern, K. (1994). Decolonization as learning: Practice and pedagogy in Franz Fanon's revolutionary narrative. In P. McLaren & H. Giroux (Eds.), *Between borders: Pedagogy and the politics of cultural studies* (pp. 182–222). New York: Routledge.

Moyers, B. (Executive Director). (2001). *Trade Secrets.* [Motion picture]. New York: Films for the Humanities and Sciences.

Moyers, B. (2002, January 4). *7th annual Harry Middleton lecture.* Austin, TX: LBJ Library and Museum.

Muhammad, K. (1994, March 11). Nation of Islam speaker urges black students to "wake up." *The Vermilion, XC*(ix), *University of Southwestern Louisiana Student Weekly,* pp. 1–2.

Mullen, C. A., & Diamond, P. (Eds.). (1999). *The postmodern educator: Arts-based inquiries and teacher development.* New York: Peter Lang.

Naess, A. (1995a). Arne Naess on deep ecology and ecosophy. In G. Sessions (Ed.), *Deep ecology for the twenty-first century: Readings on the philosophy and practice of the new environmentalism* (pp. 185–259). Boston: Shambhala.

Naess, A. (1995b). Politics and the ecological crisis: An introductory note. In G. Sessions (Ed.), *Deep ecology for the twenty-first century: Readings on the philosophy and practice of the new environmentalism* (pp. 445–453). Boston: Shambala.

Naifeh, S., & G. W. Smith. (1989). *Jackson Pollock: An American saga.* New York: Clarkson N. Potter.

Newman, J. W. (1997). *America's teachers: An introduction to education.* New York: Addison Wesley Longman.

Nieto, S. (1996). *Affirming diversity: The socio-political context of multicultural education.* New York: Longman.

Nietzsche, F. (1958). Thus spake zarathustra. (A. Tille, Trans.) New York: E. P. Dutton.

Nietzsche, F. (1968). *The birth of tragedy.* In W. Kaufman (Ed.), *Basic writings of Nietzsche.* New York: Modern Library.

Noddings, N. (1984). *Caring: A feminine approach to ethics and moral education.* Berkeley: University of California.

Noddings, N. (1992). *The challenge to care in schools: An alternative approach to education.* New York: Teachers College Press.

Noddings, N. (1995). *Philosophy of education.* Boulder, CO: Westview Press.

Oe, K. (1985). *Nip the buds, Shoot the kids.* New York: Grove Press.

Oliver, D. W., & Gershman, K. W. (1989). *Education, modernity, and fractured meaning: Toward a process theory of teaching and learning.* Albany: State University of New York Press.

Orr, D. W. (1992). *Ecological literacy: Education and the transition to a postmodern world.* Albany: State University of New York Press.

Orr, D. W. (2000, January 24). Green building at Oberlin in a new dream house for environmental science. *Chronicle of Higher Education,* p. A14.

Orr, D. W. (2002). *The nature of design: Ecology, culture, and human intention.* London: Oxford University Press.

Oski, F. A. (1996). *Don't drink the milk.* Brushton, NY: Teach Services.

Pagels, E. (1979). *The gnostic Gospels.* New York: Random House.

Pamuk, O. (2001, September 29). Listen to the damned. *The Guardian.* Retrieved November 15, 2001, from http://www.guardian.co.uk/Archive/Article/0,4273,4266864,00.html

Parenti, M. (1996). *Against empire.* San Francisco: City Lights Books.

Parentelli, G. (1996). Latin America's poor women: Inherent guardians of life. In R. R. Ruether (Ed.), *Women healing earth: Third world women on ecology, feminism, and religion* (pp. 29–39). Maryknoll, NY: Orbis.

Parrish, C. (2001, November 20). Offended? Don't let the door hit ya. *Akron Beacon Journal,* p. A12.

Percy, W. (1982). *The message in the bottle: How queer man is, how queer language is, and what one has to do with the other.* New York: Farrar, Straus, & Giroux.

Percy, W. (1987). *The thanatos syndrome.* New York: Farrar, Straus, & Giroux.

Picasso, P. (1971). Conversations. In H. B. Chipps (Ed.), *Theories of modern art: A source book of artists and critics* (p. 268). Berkeley: University of California Press.

Pinar, W. F. (1972). Working from within. *Educational Leadership, 29*(4), 329–331.

Pinar, W. F. (1988). Whole, bright, and deep with understanding: Issues in qualitative research and autobiographical methods. In W. F. Pinar (Ed.), *Contemporary curriculum discourses* (pp. 134–153). Scottsdale, AZ: Gorsuch Scarisbrick.

Pinar, W. F. (1991). *The White Cockatoo:* Images of abstract expressionism in curriculum theory. In G. Willis & W. H. Schubert (Eds.), *Reflections from the heart of educational inquiry* (pp. 244–249). Albany: State University of New York Press.

Pinar, W. F. (1994). *Autobiography, politics and sexuality: Essays in curriculum theory 1972–1992.* New York: Peter Lang.

Pinar, W. F. (Ed.). (1998). *Queer theory in education.* Mahwah, NJ: Lawrence Erlbaum.

Pinar, W. F. (1999). After Christianity. *Educational Researcher, 28*(3), 39–42.

Pinar, W. F., & Grumet, M. R. (1976). *Toward a poor curriculum.* Dubuque, IA: Kendall/Hunt.

Plant, J. (1997). Learning to live with differences: The challenge of ecofeminism community. In K. J. Warren (Ed.), *Ecofeminism: Women, culture, nature* (pp. 120–139). Bloomington: Indiana University Press.

Pluto, T. (2001, September 13). Rage clouds emotion of religion. *Akron Beacon Journal,* p. A7.

Polakow, V. (1993). *Lives on the edge: Single mothers and their children in the other America.* Chicago: University of Chicago Press.

Polakow, V. (2000). *The public assault on America's children: Poverty, violence, and juvenile injustice.* New York: Teachers College Press.

Polcari, S. (1991). *Abstract expressionism and the modern experience.* Melbourne, Australia: University of Cambridge Press.

Posamentier, A. S. (2002, January 2). Madam, I'm 2002—a numerically beautiful year. *New York Times,* p. A25.

Postman, N. (1996). *The end of education.* New York: Vintage Books.

Protesters ultimately want death for homosexuals. (2001, December 28). *Texas Triangle, X,*(12), p. 7.

Purpel, D. E. (1989). *The moral and spiritual crisis in education: A curriculum for justice and compassion in education.* New York: Bergin & Garvey.

Purpel, D. E. (1999). *Moral outrage in education.* New York: Peter Lang.

Quinn, B. (2000). *How Walmart is destroying America (and the world) and what you can do about it.* Berkeley, CA: Ten Speed Press.

Rampton, S., & Stauber, J. (2001). *Trust us, we're experts! How industry manipulates science and gambles with your future.* New York: Putnam.

Rapp, D. (2001a). Better educational leaders or better sources of inspiration? Using the arts and unauthorized histories to refocus our work. *National Forum for Educational Leadership in Schools Journal, 19*(1), 45–54.

Rapp, D. (2001b). Teaching, researching, and resisting in the "new world order." In J. Sears & K. Sloan (Eds.), *Democratic curriculum theory and practice: Retrieving public spaces* (pp. 83–96). New York: Education International Press.

Rapp, D. (2002a). Secrets, lies, and silence: A plea to educational leaders. Accepted for publication by the *International Journal of Leadership in Education.*

Rapp, D. (2002b). Leadership in the spirit of rebellious, oppositional imaginations. *Journal of School Leadership, 12,* 226–245.

Raskin, M. (1996). Ed Keinholtz and the burden of being an American. In W. Hopps (Ed.), *Keinholtz: A retrospective* (pp. 38–43). New York: Distributed Art Publishers in association with the Whitney Museum of Art.

Ravitch, F. (1999). *School prayer and discrimination.* Boston: Northeast University Press.

Remson, J., & Carm, O. (Eds.). (1996, June). Bread for the world in Louisiana, *Bread for the World, 14*(10), 1–7.

Rich, A. (2001). *Arts of the possible: Essays and conversations.* New York: Norton.

Rifkin, J. (1985). *Declaration of a heretic.* Boston: Routledge & Kegan Paul.

Rifkin, J. (1993). *Beyond beef: The rise and fall of the cattle culture.* New York: Dutton.

Robert, M. (1982). *Managing conflict from the inside out.* Austin, TX: Learning Concepts.

Rohn, M. L. (1987). *Visual dynamics in Jackson Pollock's abstractions.* Ann Arbor, MI: UMI Research Press.

Rorty, R. (1979). *Philosophy and the mirror of nature.* Princeton: Princeton University Press.

Rossiter, H. (2002, February 5). Alternative measures to fight terror. *Daily Record,* p. A4.

Rouse, J. (1987). *Knowledge + power: Toward a political philosophy of science.* Ithaca, NY: Cornell University Press.

Ruether, R. R. (1983). Christology and the Latin American liberation theology. In *To change the world: Christology and cultural criticism* (pp. 25–26). New York: Crossroads.

Ruether, R. R. (Ed.). (1996). *Women healing earth: Third World women on ecology, feminism, and religion.* Maryknoll, NY: Orbis Books.

Said, E. W. (1994). Culture and imperialism. New York: Vintage Books.

Said, E. W. (1997). *Covering Islam: How the media and the experts determine how we see the rest of the world.* New York: Vintage Books.

Sarup, M. (1989). *An introductory guide to post-structuralism and post-modernism.* Athens: University of Georgia Press.

Saxer, E. M. (2002, January 9). How is President Bush performing? *Akron Beacon Journal,* p. A9.

Scheurich, J. J. (2002). *Anti-racist scholarship: An advocacy.* Albany: State University of New York Press.

Schnabel, J. (Director), Brant, P., & Allan, J. (Producers). (1997). *Basquiat* [Motion picture]. Burbank, CA: Miramax.

Schneider, A. (1999, December 10). To many adjunct professors, academic freedom is a myth. *Chronicle of Higher Education, XLVI(16),* A18–A19.

Schubert, W. H. (1992). On mentorship: Examples from J. Harlan Shores and others through lenses provided by James B. Macdonald. *JCT: An Interdisciplinary Journal of Curriculum Studies, 9*(3), 47–70.

Scroggs, R. (1983). *The New Testament and homosexuality: Contextual background for contemporary debate.* Philadelphia: Fortress Press.

Sears, J. T. (Ed.). (1992). *Sexuality and the curriculum: The politics and practices of sexuality education.* New York: Teachers College Press.

Segundo, J. L. (1973). *A theology for artisans of a new humanity,* 1973–1975 (J. Drury, Trans.). Maryknoll, NY: Orbis Books.

Sehested, K. (2001, September 20). In the valley of the shadow: Reflections on the trauma of 11 September 2001. Retrieved November 21, 2001, from http://www.bpfna.org/shadow.html

Sessions, G. (Ed.). (1995). *Deep ecology for the twenty-first century.* Boston: Shambhala.

Shaull, R. (1990). Foreword. *Pedagogy of the oppressed,* by P. Freire. New York: Continuum.

Shimp, T. R. (2001, December 7). Indians deserve our respect. *Akron Beacon Journal,* p. A12.

Silin, J. (1995). *Sex, death, and the education of children: Our passion for ignorance in the age of AIDS.* New York: Teachers College Press.

Sinclair, U. (1906). *The jungle.* New York: Doubleday.

Sinclair, U. (1948). *The flivver king.* London: T. Werner Laurie.

Slattery, P. (1995). *Curriculum development in the postmodern era.* New York: Garland.

Slattery, P. (2001). The educational researcher as artist working within. *Qualitative Inquiry, 7*(3), 370–395.

Slattery, P., & Daigle, K. (1994). Curriculum as a place of turmoil: Deconstructing the source of anguish in Ernest Gaines's Pointe Coupee and Walker Percy's Feliciana. *Curriculum Inquiry, 24*(4), 437–461.

Slattery, P., & McElfresh, R. (2001). Image-ination as a catalyst for critical consciousness and social change: The photography of Sebastiao Salgado. *Journal of Critical Inquiry into Curriculum and Instruction, 3*(3), 46–50.

Smith, D. G. (1991). Hermeneutic inquiry: The hermeneutic imagination and the pedagogic text. In E. Short (Ed.), *Forms of curriculum inquiry* (pp. 187–209). Albany: State University of New York Press.

Sobrino, J. (1985). *Spirituality of liberation: Toward political holiness.* Maryknoll, NY: Orbis Books.

Soulforce. (2000). *There is a wideness in God's mercy: Interview with Rev. Lewis Smedes on Romans 1.* [Motion picture]. Introduction by Mel White. Laguna Beach, CA: Soulforce Productions. Available: www.soulforce.org

Spehler-McElfresh, R., & Slattery, P. (1999). Voices of imagination: The artist as prophet in the process of social change. *International Journal of Leadership in Education, 2*(1), 1–12.

Spretnak, C. (1997). Radical nonduality in ecofeminism philosophy. In K. J. Warren (Ed.), *Ecofeminism: Women, culture, nature* (pp. 425–436). Bloomington: Indiana University Press.

Spring, J. H. (1998). *Education and the rise of the global economy.* Mahwah, NJ: Lawrence Erlbaum.

Stauber, J. C., and Rampton, S. (1995). *Toxic sludge is good for you: Lies, damn lies, and the public relations industry.* Monroe, ME: Common Courage Press.

Stepaniak, J. (1998). *The vegan sourcebook* (2nd ed.). Los Angeles: Lowell House.

Storr, A. (1973). *C. G. Jung.* New York: Viking Press.

Strike, K. A., & Soltis, J. F. (1992). *The ethics of teaching* (2nd ed.). New York: Teachers College Press.

Sullivan, A. (2001, October 7). This *is* a religious war. *News York Times Magazine,* pp. 44–47.

Takeaction. (2001, December 6). Take action for change. Retrieved December 19, 2001: http://www.workingforchange.com/activism/index.cfm

Taylor, D. (1997). Women of color, environmental justice, and ecofeminism. In K. Warren (Ed.), *Ecofeminism: Women, culture, nature* (pp. 39–91). Bloomington: Indiana University Press.

Teilhard de Chardin, P. (1959). *The phenomenon of man.* New York: Harper.

Teitel, M., & Wilson, K. (1999). *Genetically engineered foods: Changing the nature of nature: What you need to know to protect yourself, your family, and your planet.* Rochester, VT: Park Street Press.

This year was the 2nd hottest, confirming a trend U.N. says. (2001, December 19). *New York Times,* p. A5.

Thornburg, M. (2001, October 31). What's wrong with waving flag in face? *Akron Beacon Journal,* p. A15.

Tom, A. (1984). *Teaching as a moral craft.* New York: Longman.

Torassa, U. (1997, March 2). Is the child yours? DNA testing uncovers surprising numbers of dads who aren't the father. *Cleveland Plain Dealer,* p. 1A.

Troyat, H. (1967). *Tolstoy.* New York: Penguin.

Usher, R., & Edwards, R. (1994). *Postmodernism and education.* New York: Routledge.

Valenzuela, A. (1999). *Subtractive schooling: US–Mexican youth and the politics of caring.* Albany: State University of New York Press.

Viruru, R. (1998). *Exploring Indian constructions of the education of young children: A case study.* Unpublished doctoral dissertation, Texas A&M University.

Wald, K. D. (1987). *Religion and politics in the United States.* New York: St. Martin's Press.

Walkerdine, V. (1997). *Daddy's girl: Young girls and popular culture.* Cambridge, MA: Harvard University Press.

Wang, H. (1997). Curriculum as polyphonic authoring: A pedagogy through the "loophole." *JCT: Journal of Curriculum Theorizing, 13*(4), 20–24.

Warren, K. J. (1997). Taking empirical data seriously: An ecofeminism philosophical perspective. In K. J. Warren (Ed.), *Ecofeminism: Women, culture, nature* (pp. 3–20). Bloomington: Indiana University Press.

Weaver, J., Slattery, P., & Daspit, T. (1998). Museums and memory: Toward a critical understanding of the politics of space and time. *Journal of Curriculum Theorizing, 14*(4), 18–26.

West, C. (1993). *Prophetic thought in postmodern times.* Monroe, ME: Common Courage Press.

Whitehead, A. N. (1929). *Aims of education.* New York: Free Press/Macmillan.

Williams, G. H. (1995). *Life on the color line.* New York: Penguin.

Woolf, V. (1929). *A room of one's own.* New York: Harcourt, Brace.

Wright, R. (1940). *Native son.* New York: Harper & Row.

Young, R. (1990). *A critical theory of education: Habermas and our children's future.* New York: Teachers College Press.

Zepezaver, M., & Naiman, A. (1996). *Take the rich off welfare.* Monroe, ME: Common Courage Press.

Zezima, M. (2001). Saving private power. In R. Kick (Ed.), *You are being lied to: The disinformation guide to media distortion, historical whitewashes, and cultural myths* (pp. 219–228). New York: The Disinformation Company.

Zinn, H. (1995). *A people's history of the United States: 1492–present.* New York: Harper-Perennial.

Zinn, H. (1997). *The Zinn reader: Writings on disobedience and democracy.* New York: Seven Stories.

Zwick, J. (Ed.). (1992). *Mark Twain's weapons of satire: Anti-imperialist writings on the Philippine-American War.* Syracuse: Syracuse University Press.

NAME INDEX

SUBJECT INDEX